Truth Matters

Contemporary Psychoanalytic Studies

VOLUME 22

The titles published in this series are listed at *brill.com/cps*

Truth Matters

Theory and Practice in Psychoanalysis

By

Shlomit Yadlin-Gadot

BRILL
RODOPI

LEIDEN | BOSTON

Cover illustration: Photo by Oriane Slupowski.

Library of Congress Cataloging-in-Publication Data

Names: Yadlin-Gadot, Shlomit.
Title: Truth matters : theory and practice in psychoanalysis / by Shlomit Yadlin-Gadot.
Description: Leiden ; Boston : Brill, [2016] | Series: Contemporary psychoanalytic studies ; 22 | Includes bibliographical references and index.
Identifiers: LCCN 2016001511 (print) | LCCN 2016010314 (ebook) | ISBN 9789004301061 (hardback : alk. paper) | ISBN 9789004314993 (E-book)
Subjects: LCSH: Psychoanalysis. | Truth. | Psychotherapy. | Psychoanalysts.
Classification: LCC BF173 .Y24 2016 (print) | LCC BF173 (ebook) | DDC 150.19/5--dc23
LC record available at http://lccn.loc.gov/2016001511

Typeface for the Latin, Greek, and Cyrillic scripts: "Brill". See and download: brill.com/brill-typeface.

ISSN 1571-4977
ISBN 978-90-04-30106-1 (hardback)
ISBN 978-90-04-31499-3 (e-book)

This book is printed on acid-free paper and produced in a sustainable manner.

Printed by Printforce, the Netherlands

Contents

Acknowledgements

I am greatly indebted to many, without whom this book would never have been written.

I wish to thank Professor Uri Hadar, my mentor and first teacher. He initiated me into the world of thought and taught me to appreciate my own. He also taught me how to write. His voice walks me through my thoughts.

I thank Dr Dorit Lemberger and Professor Avi Sagi of the Program for Hermeneutics and Cultural Studies in Bar-Ilan University. This book developed from ideas conceived when writing my doctoral dissertation under their supervision. Special thanks to Professor Sagi for his vision in creating the program where my research was conducted.

I am grateful to Dr Aner Govrin, who accompanied me throughout my research, offering friendship, endless support and good advice. I was fortunate to have him around.

I thank my parents, family and friends for sustaining and supporting me in the vicissitudes of writing, thinking, entering dead ends and finding my way out. I am grateful to Orly Hasson-Katz, Dr Shoulamit Milch-Reich, Chagit Gedasi, Hagar Nachum, Na'ama Bushansky, Dr Merav Roth, Carine Zaroni and Dr Tsiky Cohen for years of friendship and for the generosity with which they lent me their minds and their patience. And, in the parents category, thanks also to Michal Tepper.

My gratitude to my husband, Yotam, and children, Yonatan, Yali and Shay, is without measure. Their love, humor, generosity and trust light my life.

Introduction

This book is concerned with truth. Truth is a traditional age-old topic in philosophy, reflecting the major part it played throughout the history of the human subject. Wars have been fought trying to enforce different truths, gods have been created to articulate them, and particular lives have been formed and reformed in their light. It seems that what we know of truth in a definite manner is that it carries with it weight and sanctity that appertain to its function as a directive, a value or a point of reference.

And yet, it does not seem clear that we know what it *is* or how it gains such force in our lives. Truth has never been defined in a consensual manner, has never revealed itself in a way that is universally accepted. Still, we remain feeling guided or driven by it; we persist in searching for it. It continues to cast its shadow on the content, form and process of our thoughts and experience. The force of truth as experience sets it apart from other abstract philosophical themes. Truth traverses philosophical theory; it is inseparable from the subject's life and, as such, should be an object of inquiry in the psychological and psychoanalytic field.

The complications of dealings with truth are innumerable, first and foremost because it functions on many levels, and the interconnections between them are unclear. We may sometimes *feel* something is true, *knowing* it is not. We may sometimes know something is true, and yet find it *truly* unacceptable to us. We sometimes find that our truth does not cohere with the truth held dear by our social environment. We may also be puzzled as to what these truths have to do with the formal definitions taught in philosophy classes.

This book undertakes a psychological inquiry of truth, relating to each other the experiential, philosophic and psychoanalytic accounts of it and showing them to be rooted in a distinct, common circumstance. The philosophic, psychoanalytic and experienced truths, I will show, are jointly determined by basic psychological needs of the human subject. The thinking of the historical subject expressed in philosophical writings mirrors the workings of the mind of all or any particular subject.

In the present book, psychoanalysis is the point of departure and the end station of my inquiry, engaging in its course philosophic, semiotic and phenomenological analyses. The main thesis presented here is that truth is not just an abstract construct, external to the subject, but also, and perhaps more importantly, an inherent group of distinct and definable organizing principles of the psyche. This formulation, I contend, explains the multiplicity of truths in philosophy and psychoanalysis and enables the understanding of the logic

 | DOI 10.1163/9789004314993_002

that gave rise to the different truth paradigms in both fields. By the same token, my notion of truth as it relates to basic human needs explains the obstinate refusal of man to relinquish his hold of truth, even after the postmodern turn which, on the face of it, has given truth a mortal blow.

My thesis on truth has consequences and implications for both psychoanalytic theory and psychoanalytic practice. After explaining in detail the theoretical consequences, I will show, by means of clinical vignettes, how these seemingly complex abstract issues are negotiated intuitively by psychoanalysts in their daily clinical work, and how the principles of this intuitive work may be formulated and elaborated so as to enrich the available guidelines for clinical technique.

From its earliest days, psychoanalysis has maintained a complex relationship with the concept of truth, a relationship characterized by frequent vicissitudes. I will briefly survey here the main truth paradigms that have informed psychoanalytic thinking. Psychoanalysis was born into one truth, the scientific or the Correspondent theory of truth. At the meta-theoretical level, this truth was there to anchor psychoanalysis's standing as a science and to supply a rationale for clinical psychotherapy. Freud aspired to discover and bring to light a genuine reality – a personal history that was traumatically experienced and then repressed. However, very soon there was no option other than to acknowledge that Freud's hopes were unsubstantiated; that psychoanalysis did not meet the criteria set by science and had to settle for being regarded as a myth, a narrative, or an effective therapeutic instrument. In other words, the discipline had to base itself on either Coherent or Pragmatic truth, rather than on the truth of Correspondence to reality. There are those who saw this transition as a decline in psychoanalysis's standing. Others saw the potency of these developments in the clinic, creating a diversity of guidelines for achieving mental therapy.

The reliance on more relative conceptions of truth – Coherent and Pragmatic, alongside the Correspondent conception – can already be seen in the writings of Freud himself, by his adoption of a more modest position *vis a vis* the historical truth value of psychoanalytic work. In his article 'Constructions in Analysis' (1937), Freud argued that "an assured conviction of the truth of the construction…achieves the same therapeutic result as a recaptured memory" (SE 23:265). Here Freud relates to two versions of truth: Coherent truth as expressed in the construction achieved in the course of therapy and which the patient accepts as truth; and Pragmatic truth as revealed by the construction's therapeutic effects. These truths informed the clinical thinking and practice of such key theoreticians as Roy Schafer and Donald Spence (Schafer 1980; Spence 1982).

In psychoanalytic theories of personality, the Ideal truth appears as a structure which contains a formative force. The individual assesses, judges, and guides himself in relation to and in line with ideals which don't necessarily have an objective existence, but are experienced as being discrete, fixed, and possessing motivational and directive value (Kohut 1985). The structure of the Freudian ego-ideal demonstrates the workings of the Ideal truth, wherein an internalized ideal motivates the individual, interprets his world and guides processes of character formation. In clinical theory, the Ideal truth informs therapeutic methodology and objectives, especially in the manner in which transference is seen as facilitating personality development and growth.

Subjective truth was introduced into psychoanalysis with Winnicott's transition of psychoanalytic focus from knowledge to experience and his definition of the 'true self' and its authentic existence (Winnicott 1960). Heinz Kohut legitimized and then reinforced the status of subjectivity as an accepted truth at the metapsychological level and as a methodological principle in the clinic. These thinkers did not deny the existence of an external reality and its truths, but questioned their relative importance in psychic life when compared to subjective inner realities and truths (Kohut 1984).

The Intersubjective truth was the last to be acknowledged as a metapsychology and a therapeutic methodology. Intersubjective truth is embedded in the basic premise of intersubjective epistemology: A person attains his sense of certainty about objective reality through the agency of an 'other'. According to this approach, the reality and truth that psychoanalysis achieves are mutually constructed through the organization of experience within an intersubjective field of reference (Stolorow, Orange and Atwood 2001a).

From the brief review above, one can see how each psychoanalytic school based itself on a different truth in the formulation of its metapsychology, its therapeutic objectives, its methodology and in its perception of self, all of which developed along parallel lines: The Freudian objective self (the Ego) gave way to Kohut's and Winnicott's dreamy, ruminative self. This self, in turn, led to the narrative self, described by Schafer and to Spence's pragmatic self, as well as to Mitchell's and Hoffman's (Mitchell 1991; Hoffman 1991) intersubjective self. Freud's one truth splintered into a gamut of truths: Subjective, Intersubjective, Coherent and Pragmatic truths (pursued respectively by Kohut, Winnicott, Orange and Hoffman, Schafer and Stern). As a result, psychoanalysis was split into schools with varying conceptions of truth and self. Every school within the discipline adhered to different definitions and accordingly formulated its understandings. The crystallization into various schools was accompanied by antagonism, rejectionist critiques and difficulties in mounting real dialogue among them (Summers 2008).

Postmodern thought went even further with its conceptions of truth and self, and may be seen as bringing to the extreme the reliance on intersubjective and subjective truths, increasing the perceived importance of language, particularity and contextuality. For postmodern thinkers, generalizations and categorizations are a form of symbolic violence that the thinking subject imposes on the objectives of his thought. Accordingly, postmodernism does not perceive the self as coherent and unitary, but rather as multiple and decentered, an overarching structure of multiple organizations and perspectives, fluid and contextually determined (Mitchell 1991), as well as in a dialectical relation with an illusory sense of coherence and continuity (Bromberg 1998).

Personal identity in this conception arises from an ongoing dialogue between aspects, qualities and self-states. Contemporary thinkers usually assume the plurality of self-states, sometimes construed as temporary responses, valid only to the situations in which they arise (Rowan 2010). Truth met a similar fate of fluidity and contextualization. Bromberg claims that truth is "*a phenomenon that serves to support the subjective need of each state to feel legitimate in itself...*" (Bromberg 2009, 350). From this formulation, a therapeutic goal is derived: "[Treatment] *allows the state-dependent experience of any given truth to give up some of its sovereignty to a more flexible self-other experience*" (ibid.).

While these perceptions of self and truth express liberal, pluralistic thinking that challenges dogmatism and authoritarianism, they suffer three significant flaws: Firstly, they do not lend themselves to generalized theoretical formulation of psychoanalytic principles and ideas. Consequently, they do not contribute to the systematic formulation of clinical technique. Secondly, they fail to address the certainty and relative constancy ordinarily present in first-person perspective and experience. When most people refer to themselves as 'I', they experience intimate familiarity and continuity, not accounted for by the postmodern formulations. Thirdly, despite the contemporary theoretic deconstruction of truth, differing truths are naturally and unfailingly present outside and inside the clinic. People come for treatment believing their distress will ease when they find out who they 'truly' are. They often feel the world doesn't know or appreciate the true self that is known intimately by them; others feel that they do not live up to the truths they hold dear, and others yet feel that only other people enable them to experience truth, while without those people they feel lost and false to themselves. Patients and therapists constantly use the concept of truth and its derivatives.

To further complicate the matter, different therapists will offer different directives and objectives in joining their patient's efforts, resulting in different methodologies. Some will offer the unearthing of an historical-factual truth and will work with free associations, focusing on memories and dreams; others will orient themselves towards helping their patient embroider a narrative truth; others will set out to discover Subjective truth, using empathy and mirroring to create safety conditions for its emergence. Therapists oriented toward Intersubjective truth will lend themselves openly to the co-construction of truth with their patient. In different ways, therapy is often experienced as a journey of analyst and patient that traverses the world of the patient, motivated by a deep yearning for truth. This yearning for truth has not abated, despite its theoretical debilitation.

Perhaps the most interesting phenomenon is the resilience of truth. Philosophical thinking has posed logical, epistemological and ethical debates challenging the validity of the concept. And yet, we refuse to renounce it, we hang on to it on the basis of our gut feeling and of our clinical experiencing. The present book sets out to explain this resilience in a psychological framework. It offers a new conceptualization of truth and self without regressing to the single truth of modernism and without relinquishing the demand for articulate definitions.

Truth is no longer conceived of as existing 'out there' in the world, but rather as constituted by our epistemic and symbolic construals of the world, construals motivated by the demands of the psyche. This does not lead to relativism or infinite regression. On the contrary, it demands the understanding and formulation of the universal ways in which truth is created, identifying the determinants of its constitution, the way it is tied up with needs, developmental challenges and the organization of the psyche.

This account of truth begins with the Kantian assumption that we live in a reality which our consciousness constructs. The mind-independent external reality around us is an incomprehensible one. We can know it only in a mediated fashion. We mold and remold our realities in light and by means of different organizational principles, thus creating for ourselves Archimedean points of stability and certainty. Without these constructions, we are unable to comprehend realities or locate ourselves within them. The demand for certainty titles these points of stability as truths.

Throughout history, the persistent demand for it, more than any empirical support, has driven the construction of truth. Originally, when truth was 'One', it was divinely ordained, absolute, and supplied the world and mankind with order and meaning. With the 'death of God' and the crumbling of His order, the human subject remained directionless and constantly threatened by the possible disintegration of his own and his world's identity. The Enlightenment's belief in human wisdom- in man's ability to think and create order, meaningfulness, and morality by relying on intelligence and rationality- offered humankind an alternative anchorage. Thus, the concept of scientific truth was born. The transition from a divine truth to a scientific one was suffused with the hope that the latter would succeed in stepping into the shoes of its predecessor. However, very quickly, almost as soon as it was offered as a replacement for the divine truth, cracks and fissures appeared in the newly discovered scientific truth, which is the purest form of the Correspondent theory of truth. An array of counter arguments, ranging from logic to ethics, was mounted against it.

And yet, man's quest for truth and his devotion to it continued unabated. Truth was not abandoned. Instead it became the recipient of additional definitions and meanings, reflecting the emotional and cognitive demand for an anchorage in truth and certainty. This persistence, in the face of numerous contradictions and contraindications, is the embodiment of the crucial need for stability, certainty, coherence and common constancies which man does not outgrow. The truth that has been formulated as a logical, analytical, or existential concept may now be recognized as a way man has of organizing his world, as reflecting the psyche and the workings of the mind, rather than the objectives of our thought. When truth is conceived as an abstraction of a psychological need, it is naturally drawn into the field of psychological inquiry, and investigated as part and parcel of the subject's emotional-cognitive makeup.

In this book I identify six paradigmatic notions of truth that frequent Western philosophic, linguistic and psychoanalytic theory: Truth as correspondence to reality, truth as a coherent comprehensive system, truth as a derivative of intersubjective agreement, truth as an ideal, truth as defined by pragmatic consequences of beliefs, and Subjective-Existential truth that expresses a subject's experience of his particular authenticity. For clarity, I denote the six paradigms with capital letters (Ideal, Correspondent, etc.). These will be shown to satisfy the psyche's need for stability and certainty across critical dimensions of the subject's life.

The Correspondent conception of truth, introduced into Western thought by Aristotle, checks the compatibility between a subject's belief and what he perceives as realistic facts. The Coherent conception of truth, anchored in Spinoza's thinking, sees truth value as dependent on a belief's compatibility with a whole system of beliefs. Here, a belief is true *to the extent* that it is in accord with other beliefs. The Intersubjective conception of truth, as in Husserl's concept of transcendental intersubjectivity, regards objectivity as established by interpersonal agreement, sometimes explicit, often implicit. The Pragmatic conception of truth as developed, for example, by William James, defines a true statement as one that, in a future experience of the subject, achieves the results he expected and hoped for. The Subjective-Existential conceptions of truth, seeds of which can be found in the work of Kierkegaard, perceives truth as highly personal, embodying the subject's experienced authenticity. The Ideal conception of truth, usually grounded in religious or rationalistic epistemologies, determines truth values by the compatibility between particular perceptions and beliefs and their corresponding eternal decrees or forms.

These truths will be discussed as organizing principles of the mind that enable the human subject to order his world. Each truth is the nodal point of a symbolic paradigm which organizes perception, emotion, and thought: It selects data and organizes disparate elements, while determining orders of preference and enforcing certain rules of combination. Every organization of this kind produces a distinct image of reality, together with a definable experienced selfhood which resides within it and directs itself in line with its truth. In the words of philosopher and psychoanalyst Gemma Corradi Fiumara:

> ...speaking of reality...we are not referring to the world in itself...but rather to the sort of reality which the individual laboriously carves out... as a construct negotiated within the limits of what may be thought and done within his symbolic horizon.... Before we decide to inhabit a specific epistemology...we may have gone through several epistemological migrations.
>
> FIUMARA 1992, 8

My basic contention is that we do not decide in which epistemology to dwell. Rather, our basic psychological needs determine our multiple existences within several epistemologically defined realities. The complex of epistemic assumption, characteristic self-state, image of reality and its experienced truth form together a *truth axis*. Each of the axes functions in accord with one of the psyche's essential needs. In the order in which I present here the various truth conceptions, these needs comprise, respectively, the need to manage factual reality (Correspondent truth), the need to lend internal coherence to perceptions of self and world (Coherent truth), the need to construct a shared interpersonal reality (Intersubjective truth), the need to maintain loyalty to one's authenticity (Subjective-Existential truth), the need to promote goals and to uphold guiding ideals (Pragmatic and Ideal truths). These needs give rise to the created truths axes, maintaining their relevance, explaining their potency as constituting, organizing principles of psychic spaces.

Each truth axis functioning as an organizing principle produces a distinct image of reality: Correspondent truth creates a 'factual' reality enabling us to negotiate the mind-independent reality around us; Coherent truth produces for us a cohesive and consistent reality at the level of both personal identity and perceived externality; Ideal truth embodies a reality to which we aspire and believe in; Pragmatic truth creates a reality that resonates our objectives and interests; Subjective-Existential truth produces a person's subjective-authentic image of reality; finally, Intersubjective truth creates the reality as shared by us and those around us.

Within each image of reality resides a definable self-state, embodied in a unique perceptual-emotional-cognitive stratum. Thus, the experience of familiarity and intimacy with the self, originating in the Subjective-Existential axis, differs completely from the objectified self of the Correspondent axis, considered in the third person when reflected upon by the subject. The Intersubjective self offers yet another experience, always set against a singular or a plural other, the latter being sometimes a comfortable 'we', at other times a threatening 'them'. A different state of self is induced when the subject experiences himself in his ideal form or, alternatively, when given completely to realizing his interests.

Through the lived experience of the varying axes of truth, a different *encounter* with the world is created; the vulnerable Subjective-Existential self of inner truths, to which experiences of shame, exposure and fear of annihilation are linked, differs from the matter of fact, realistic self of the Correspondent axis. The self of the Intersubjective axis is the one supported by social agreement or lost in it. This self may experience anxieties of alienation and lack of belongingness. The self that scrutinizes itself against its Ideals and senses either guilt or satisfaction is once again a self that differs from the Pragmatic one, which aims to calculate and understand the ways reality would benefit the self.

In the final analysis, every truth axis has a unique grammar, different rules and priorities determining the possible combinations between elements of experience and thought. Thus, in the Coherent theory, elements are ordered and checked for truth value not by correspondence to reality, but by inner consistency. The Subjective-Existential axis, on the other hand, is not subject to rules of logic. It not only allows for paradoxes, but also establishes itself through the tensions within them. The present is dominant in the Subjective-Existential axis, negligible in the Ideal axis, and is but a step towards the future in the Pragmatic axis of truth. Sense data is pertinent in the Correspondent axis, irrelevant for the Ideal axis, and provides a base for common signification in the Intersubjective axis.

I suggest that in the mental space of every person, in different forms and ratios, all six truth axes are present. These axes sometimes overlap, but are often incompatible with each other, generating tensions within the psyche. In every person, one axis is usually more dominant than other axes and has different relations with the others. The self is defined as the experience arising from the succession of definable axial self-states and the configuration formed through their interrelations.

The unique configuration of truth axes in the mind of any person reflects a specific emotional history which encouraged the development of certain axes and curbed or suppressed the development of others. Every axis – by virtue of its very existence and the extent of its dominance over other axes – is an outcome of complex interaction and engagement between an inborn disposition and the way it shaped a specific developmental history. As I will show in detail, the fact that axes of truth are anchored in profound emotional needs and are established by surmounting developmental crises explains their capacity to function as structural and organizing principles in the psyche. This is so not only in relation to perception and thought, but also with respect to the emotional and experiential dimension as a whole. The successes and failings of a developmental-emotional history are marked by the symbolic-experiential ways in which a person organizes and structures his world.

An important conclusion of this conceptualization is that one of the key therapeutic objectives of the psychoanalytic process is the articulation and understanding of the movement between the different truth axes. The therapeutic undertaking is regarded as a detailing, a depiction and an understanding of the various specific truths. It locates tensions between the various truths and the way they have been allocated their conscious, unconscious or dissociated positioning in the psyche. The specific terms of the truth axes provide a methodology for creating potential spaces and instruct the formation of therapeutic interventions that elaborate these intra and inter-axis spaces.

In my formulations, potential spaces are the product of heteroglossia, namely, the recognition of different mental languages in the psyche and the possibility given them to co-exist, while negotiating with and validating each other. Thus, the condition for facilitating the development of a potential space is the conscious avoidance of rendering exclusive a single, axis-related grammar or collapsing exclusively into its particular directives. In a process of ongoing self-analysis, an analyst may identify the languages of truth governing his thought processes, as well as his responses to them. Thus, he becomes aware of the preferences which he sets in making decisions among possible interpretations. The analyst accepts the challenge of honoring and acknowledging languages that are not necessarily natural to him, familiarizing himself with their various dialects, allowing their complex discourse entry to his consciousness.

By doing so, the analyst becomes able to guide a patient to undertake a similar investigation of his own mind, to create a dialogue between the distinct and different truths in a way that makes possible the construction of transitional spaces. This dialogue involves the articulation and portrayal of each truth axis, noting the singularity of what may be said only by means of its particular grammar. Through open dialogue among the axes, the multidimensionality of any statement is revealed, as are the needs, anxieties and hopes related to it. At its best, the dialogue between languages of truth holds the potential of unravelling the dynamics of dissociation, denial and repressive authoritarianism. It sets in motion the *encounter with and the recognition of the other*. This 'other' holds positionings of the self that are different from its usual constructions.

The book's first chapter offers a modern philosophical inquiry into the human quest for truth. American and Continental philosophic perspectives are presented, describing the manner in which man aspires to construct a comprehensible universe in place of inchoate experience. This is predicated upon the notion of truth and the certainty that it affords. The gap between the conceptualization of truth as absolute and its conception as a theory formulated out of a *yearning* for certainty defines the chasm between metaphysical truth and the postmodern era, bereft of truth. Despite the postmodern ethos, the contemporary subject still continues his search for the certainty and regularity that allow him stable definitions of himself and his world. With this search at the background, the rationale for bringing the analysis of truth into psychological and psychoanalytical theory is formulated.

The chapter ends with Freud as a case in study, illustrating the human need for truth and certainty. What is shown in this analysis is the way Freud's positive perception of technological progress is heavily imbued with the needs and tendencies that constituted the religious truth he vehemently rejected. Despite criticizing the absolute truth of god as an infantile wish, Freud immediately replaces it with a scientific truth, endowed with the idealized attributes of religion.

The second chapter identifies six paradigmatic notions of truth in Western philosophy. Each of these truth notions reflects a discrete and definable epistemology that coheres with the work of a major thinker. The truth notions relate to the works of Plato, Aristotle, Spinoza, Husserl, Kierkegaard and James. They will be presented in retrospect as given intertextually, showing how each conception evolved in relation to the critique of former definitions.

The shift from the philosophical to the psychological plane reconceptualizes truth as a nodal point of a symbolic paradigm, as the abstraction of a dynamic principle that gives rise to viable constructions of the subject's experience of his world. The different notions of truth are presented in their organizational function and the concept of 'truth axis' is presented and defined. The axes are described as embodied in distinct cognitive, experiential, and emotional modes that comprise different images of reality. In each person's psyche, these six principles of organization function simultaneously. Each axis is shown to be predicated upon a vital relation between the subject and his world that provides for a basic human need.

The third chapter discusses the use the analyst makes of theories from two essential fields of knowledge- semiotic and psychoanalytic. These theories are ordinarily applied in the analytic encounter in a semi-automatic and semi-conscious fashion that enables the analyst to understand, decipher and decode his patient's speech. Analyzing theories in these two fields I will show how they reflect the different truth organizations specified in Chapter 2. Each truth as expressed in psychoanalytic or semiotic theory enhances the identification, definition and understanding of particular mental phenomena. Each articulates different meanings and modes of understanding. Through analysis of the hermeneutic extension of truth theories, I will explain the work often done by clinicians in the most intuitive way.

The therapist's conscious observation of a particular object of analysis is always directed through the prism of a certain epistemology and its derivative truth – be it Realistic, Pragmatic or Intersubjective but, in tandem, he also intuitively considers possible meanings arising from the prisms of other epistemic perspectives. He processes these meanings consciously and subconsciously and assesses compatibilities, overlaps, conflicts or tensions among them. In that sense, the different semiotic and psychoanalytic theories create a heterogeneous arc which, rather than being in competition with one another, parallel the epistemic multiplicity of the mind.

The fourth chapter describes the interrelations among truth axes, basic psychic needs and developmental processes. Each of the axes is rooted and functions in accord with one of the psyche's essential needs: the need to manage factual reality, the need to lend internal coherence to perceptions of self and world, the need to construct a shared interpersonal reality, the need to maintain loyalty to one's authenticity, the need to promote goals and the need to uphold guiding ideals.

The chapter explores the ways truth axes are constituted in the psyche, and follows the particular processes of emotional achievement and development that are required for their establishment and brand their logic in the psyche. These needs and developmental processes give rise to the truth axes, maintain their relevance and explain their potency as organizing principles of psychic experience. Each axis can be constructively or pathologically inclined but, across this spectrum, its logic is the one embodied in the related epistemology.

The fifth chapter discusses the concept of self, alongside processes of repression and dissociation, in relation to the truth axes as organizational principles of the psyche. Self-states are understood as appearing within and across the different axes in the form of axis-specific experiential modes. The self as a whole emerges from these discrete and definable states and the interactions they create. The various states of the self are not viewed as sporadic, infinite or situational, which is the accepted position of many relational and post-modern writers (Bromberg 2009, Mitchell 1991, Rowan 2010). Rather, they are conceived of as being rooted in a limited number of modalities that can be formulated and defined. The unconscious- as process and content- consists of those truth axes that are partly or wholly inhibited or foreclosed due to innate tendencies and environmental influences.

The chapter then demonstrates how clinicians can implement this model in their work. Therapeutic work comprises of detailing, depicting and understanding the various specific truths that inform specific clinical situations, as well as the tensions among them. This includes identifying the conscious and dissociated positioning within the psyche of the various truth axes. Their developmental history is investigated in order to depict the full itinerary of their evolution. The intra-psychic conflicts that arouse tension and distress are conceptualized in terms of difficulty in experiential organization within a certain axis or, alternatively, in terms of difficulties in reconciling between different axes and their derivatives. Still other difficulties may be borne of the suppression and exclusion of axes as process or product. These restrict both the life experience of the subject and his ability to mentalize. The uncovering, articulation and instigation of movement between the different truth axes is, in effect, a methodology for creating potential spaces.

The clinical demonstrations in the sixth chapter (Taken from the work of Irwin Yalom, Donald Winnicott, Neville Symington, Christopher Bollas, Uri Hadar and the author's) will show the implementation of methodological and theoretical concepts developed throughout the book. By means of the clinical material, the truth axes will be identified as functioning on three levels: immediate sensory experience, encounter with the world and characteristic grammars.

The vignettes illustrate the threefold way that truth axes work with clinical material. Apart from viewing the truth axes as they structure the patient's experience and images of reality, the analyst monitors the differential emotional reactions *to the truth axes themselves* of both the patient and himself. These reactions include the extent of empathy, identification or antipathy aroused by some materials related to one axis, in contrast to other materials, related to another axis. The analyst tries to examine the way his semi-conscious axial preferences contribute to the shaping of the transference. The positioning of therapist and patient on differing truth axes may explain some kinds of analytic impasse or analytic resistance. Rationale and examples of diagnostics and intervention will be presented, showing how one truth axis may dominate content, while a different one governs analytic relations, etc.

In the last chapter of the book, the movement between axes is examined as it occurs within the paradigmatic processes of translation, dialogue and dialectic influences. The process of translation involves the replacement of one grammar by another. Dialectic refers to processes in which competing grammars create, preserve, and negate each other in a dynamic, ever-changing relationship. Moving toward integrations that are never complete, the different syntactic poles gradually acquire characteristics of what was at first conceived as their 'other'. Dialogue is construed as an exchange in which the singularities are retained and space is constituted through the negotiation of differences.

The chapter explores the vicissitudes of meaning, analytic stance and relations in each of these paradigmatic processes, focusing on the implications for enhancing and developing creativity, agency and the experience of self. This hermeneutic inquiry culminates in a shift from the epistemological to the ethical, where the prioritizing of truth axes becomes, in effect, an ideological action, often not articulated and therefore not accounted for in the psychoanalytic clinic.

CHAPTER 1

The Desire for Truth, Its Crisis and Mental Life

Truth has been the subject of philosophical debate since time immemorial and has been at the center of epistemological and metaphysical quest since the dawn of human history. Is truth something that exists out there in the world? Is it an objective of human engagement with the world or rather an adjective of it? How may we get to know it? Various answers have been offered to these and other related questions, some of them cohered and some were contradictory. One fact remains clear: These questions continue to be constantly asked.

In this chapter, I describe the crisis of truth in 20th century philosophy and ascribe its survival as a pivotal concept of philosophy to the deep psychological needs that it fulfills. I will begin by presenting the key concepts necessary for this discussion and the briefest account of the historical context in which it takes place. I shall then present a philosophical tradition associated in modernity with Nietzsche, in which philosophers put their minds to explaining the intractability of metaphysics and the attraction of absolute truth. I shall illustrate the enormous need for certainty as described by these philosophers, bringing forth their contention that truth and the quest for it persist because man needs it for the structuring and the positioning of his mind, his psyche, his soul. For both the particular and the historical subject, there is no substitute for truth and the certainty it provides. The need for the truth is its progenitor. This analysis supplies the rationale for drawing truth as a nodal concept into psychological and psychoanalytic theory.

The Discussion of Truth: Concepts and Context

The discussion of truth must begin with a brief and schematic definition of a few closely related concepts that heavily influence its understanding, namely: Metaphysics, epistemology and ontology.

Metaphysics formulates claims as to what exists. Traditionally defined, metaphysics is the science of 'being as such' or of 'the first causes of things' or of 'things that do not change'.[1] These terms imply the existence of a mind-independent

---

1 Aristotle's definition of metaphysics is articulated thus: "There is a science which investigates being as being and the attributes which belong to this in virtue of its own nature. Now this is

 | DOI 10.1163/9789004314993_003

order of being, an order that may nevertheless be grasped by the mind. Thus, for example, the prime figures of Greek philosophy, Aristotle and Plato, both believed in the existence of unchanging, mind independent orders: Plato in his theory of ideal forms and Aristotle in his theory of substances. 'Ideal forms' and 'Substances' are, in that sense, the building blocks of the orders that Plato and Aristotle suggested. Plato's kind of philosophy is now called 'Objective Idealism', where reality is made of eternal, ideal forms that may be rendered accessible to the mind. Aristotle's kind of philosophy is now called 'Metaphysical Realism' or 'Realistic Epistemology', one that assumes that the physical world of substance can be directly and accurately perceived by our senses.

Whereas metaphysics studies what exists, *epistemology* studies how we get to know the things that exist. Etymologically, the Greek origins of 'epistemology' are the words *episteme* and *logos*, meaning 'knowledge' and 'account'. Defined narrowly, epistemology is the study of knowledge and justified belief (Hetherington 2012) and it is concerned with such questions as: What are the necessary and sufficient conditions of knowledge? What are its sources? What is its structure, and what are its limits? What do we know of the ways a knower *knows?*

An important aspect of the above definition relates to the term 'justified belief', an expression that points to the possibly fallible and definitely hermeneutic character of most of our knowledge. Of course, the term means, first and foremost, a skeptical assessment of ourselves as knowers. But what is the nature of the skeptical assessment that is implicit in justified belief? Does it mean that there is no definite reality to be known? Or, does it mean that such a reality exists but we can never know it because of the limits of our minds? It is also possible that we cannot know reality because of the inherent incompatibility between our minds and the external world, an incompatibility that will never allow us an accurate grasp of reality.

The first of these issues- 'is there a reality to be known?'- suggests already the important differentiation between epistemology and metaphysics. Generally speaking, epistemologies are defined by basic assumptions regarding the

not the same as any of the so-called special sciences; for none of these others treats universally of being as being. They cut off a part of being and investigate the attribute of this part; this is what the mathematical sciences for instance do. Now since we are seeking the first principles and the highest causes, clearly there must be some thing to which these belong in virtue of its own nature. If then those who sought the elements of existing things were seeking these same principles, it is necessary that the elements must be elements of being not by accident but just because it is being. Therefore it is of being as being that we also must grasp the first causes" (Aristotle Metaphysics, 4:1 Accessed 23.7. 2015, http://classics.mit.edu/Aristotle/metaphysics.4.iv.html).

'knower', the 'known' and the possible relations between them. By and large, in the past, the reigning epistemologies assumed as self-evident the existence of a mind-independent order of eternal, unchanging essences. Epistemology was therefore occupied with the question of *how* we get to know them. Contemporary thought, however, views the positing of such an order as a metaphysical assumption in itself, an assumption that requires proof.

The concept of *ontology* is the summation of what we know within the framework of a specific epistemology. Ontology is thus a description or inventory of the basic kinds of entities that are supposed to exist according to a particular theoretic framework, as well as the possible relations among them (Simons 1987). In a world of multiple epistemologies, ontology and truth become immanent to epistemology.

The above definitions place us in a precarious position with regard to the subject of truth, because they imply that truth is established by recourse to a more thoroughgoing metaphysics or epistemology. Explaining the nature of truth involves the application of principles that originate in some larger system, with truth inheriting significant presuppositions of this larger system. Different epistemologies imply different definitions of truth. Truth varies across the various epistemologies from the absolute certainty of realism to the lesser certainty of 'justified belief'.

Having briefly defined these concepts and their interrelations, I will place them now, again very briefly, in their historical context as pertains to the discussion of truth. The pertinence of the question of truth and the tension aroused by the different answers to it is already evident in ancient Greek philosophy. Thus, for example, Plato's theory of eternal forms clashed with Protagoras's notion of "man being the measure of all things",[2] a notion that leaves everything open to interpretation and contradicts the possibility of a single truth. The eternal nature and objectivity of Plato's 'idea' was pitted against the dangers of subjectivism, relativism and the loss of the meaning of 'truth'. Since then and to this very day, philosophy continues in its attempt to define truth, much of which hinges on the distinction between objective and subjective knowledge.

Immanuel Kant and Georg Wilhelm Friedrich Hegel, two giants of modern philosophy, challenged this age-old distinction between the objective and the subjective. Kant did so in his detailed analysis of the 'categories of understanding', namely, the subjective factors that are inevitably a part of every seemingly objective conceptualization. In Hegel's view, every thought has to

---

2 As quoted in Plato's 'Theaetetus', Accessed 23.7.2015, http://classics.mit.edu/Plato/theatu.html.

be understood in the context of its historical development. This 'historicization' of reason effectively incorporates within it an element of subjectivity at any given moment in time.

Stating in abstract form the revolution that Kant and Hegel effected in philosophy, we may say that they brought to the fore the analysis of epistemology, while implicitly defining metaphysics as a science that cannot be operationally defined or rigorously pursued. For Hegel, all phenomenal elements are given in processes of transformation, including truth. For Kant, we will never grasp reality in itself, and therefore cannot characterize it in a valid way. We can only give account of our modes of knowing it. Both Kant and Hegel outlined our limitations as knowers and therefore emphasized our restricted ability to make metaphysical assertions.

In the early 20th century, philosophy underwent a major shift towards *multiple* epistemologies due to the '*linguistic turn*', which posited that all knowledge is predicated upon the structure of the language in which it is formulated (Fultner 2003). This further challenged our ability to define objective reality, since access to reality was viewed as biased by linguistic and conceptual schemes. Language changes from place to place and from one period to another. To the extent that reality is determined by language, it too must inevitably change. Thus, the linguistic turn undermined confidence in the singularity and permanence of knowledge, leading to epistemological and cultural relativism.

Different philosophical routes led Analytic and Continental philosophy from metaphysics to a philosophy of (linguistic) signification. The outcome of these diverse philosophical endeavors led to a remarkably similar conclusion, namely, that meaning is prior to fact. We recognize facts within the constraints of the meanings that we can formulate. And yet, surprisingly, the linguistic turn didn't end in a stoic relinquishing of 'objectivity' and 'truth'. Even in the face of the wide range of epistemological, logical and ethical arguments, the quest for truth continued, defining and redefining its status and method, taking into account its problematic nature and criticizing earlier arguments. Indeed, latter day thinkers, for whom the linguistic turn was pivotal, also continued to debate the concept of truth and show its complex nature in novel ways.

The vital continuance of the search for truth begs the question of its intractability. What drives this search? What are its origins? *The history of philosophical thought suggests that the answer to this question is clearly of a psychological nature*: Human beings have a need for certainty, security, control and the elimination of doubt. Subversively, this implies that *truth is founded not on facts, but rather on a psychological need.* If until now the search for truth involved three orders- reality, propositions, and the constraints of human consciousness- we now add a fourth order: that of the psychological needs of the subject-as-thinker, of him who formulates propositions and seeks the truth. Understanding and articulating these orders and the interactions between them becomes a contemporary challenge, not only for philosophy, but for any discipline seeking to understand the human subject and the way he inhabits his world.

Below, I describe the crisis of truth in 20th century philosophy, starting with Nietzsche's critique of metaphysics. His work is the modern origin of the line of thought that led to the disassembling of our naïve belief in metaphysics inasmuch as it aspires to give rise to absolute truth. Undertaking this feat, he and many of the pragmatic philosophers following him, argued that truth persists as an outcome of the subject's organic need for it.

To illustrate the potency of the metaphysical tendency and the gravitational strength of truth, I will show how some critical thinkers, while analyzing truth as our own creation and an outcome of our mental and psychological needs, nonetheless establish new truths and adopt the same patterns of thought they had originally criticized. After showing the centrality of truth in our conscious life, I shall propose a way in which we can regard and retain it as a valuable concept in our understanding of the human mind. I shall reconceptualize truth as a dynamic principal that structures our external, internal and social worlds in ways that afford the experience of permanence and stability.

Nietzsche, Perspectivism and the 'Desire for Truth'

In his analysis of the role of truth in a person's life and, above all, *in making* the inexorable link between truth and life, Nietzsche paved the way for the pragmatic thinkers who followed him. Nietzsche argued that the question 'what is truth?' is one that ascribes to truth an existence as a fact, which is the very issue that we need to investigate. Therefore, we need to ask first: 'why truth?' focusing our attention on the role of truth in our lives. Only after we have answered this second question, Nietzsche argued, and understand the way in which the concept came into being, can we address with any validity the question of its nature.

Nietzsche (2009) argues that, detached from its subjective value in the conduct of life, truth is meaningless. Moreover, the detached search for truth carries the danger of subordinating the relevant, useful and contextual meaning of things to the illusion of objective knowledge. Nietzsche denied the possibility of objectivity, the possibility of knowing a mind-independent reality. Indeed, he claimed, there is no way of setting knowledge of any kind separately from its context, separately from the way in which consciousness construes it. In his words, all knowledge takes place within an 'horizon' of meaning, a specific, contextualized perspective (Nietzsche 2009, cl. 188). This horizon is already incorporated into what we perceive as reality. Thus 'Perspectivism'- a context specific model of knowing – is Nietzsche's proposed alternative to objectivism.

Perspectivism can be seen as a development of Kant's transcendentalism, in which knowledge is shaped by the ways consciousness captures reality, the ways consciousness apprehends what it understands to be real (e.g., the categories of time and space). According to Kant, the ability to investigate reality in a credible and relevant way depends on an understanding of the investigative consciousness – its needs, features and modes of functioning. In contemporary terms, one can see Nietzsche as arguing that we don't have a view 'from nowhere' (Nagel 1986) that could provide us with an objective perspective, with the 'truth'. Every truth is shaped by the psychology that creates and drives the search for it.

Nietzsche's Perspectivism is tied up with his rejection of a universal perspective, a divine point of view. In this sense, his understanding of truth is closely linked to his views on god. In '*The Gay Science*' Nietzsche describes a madman with a burning lantern in his hand, running in broad daylight to the market, incessantly crying out that he is looking for god. He eventually announces his death, declaring himself and his companions as the murderers. "What did we do when we unchained the earth from its sun?" he asks. "Wither are we moving now? Are we not perpetually falling?" (Nietzsche 1974, cl.125) For Nietzsche, the death of god is simultaneously a necessity and a problem. It is the unlinking of earth from the sun, the loss of a center of gravity, of anchorage and direction. The death of god leads to disillusionment, to the bewildered understanding that the ultimate meaning of our lives, previously construed in terms of our connection to god, has been substituted by circumstance and contingency. However, between the existence of a god and the perception of the world as a random chain of events, man had erected an additional barrier – rationality.

Rationality and justified belief were posed as a new basis for knowledge, giving rise to methods of validation involving seemingly mind-independent criteria. We may not have answers from god, but we are able to test the validity of our understandings against reality and thus evaluate their truth value. However, Nietzsche showed that the very idea of a single master perspective is always implicitly theological. Only a divine point of view can surpass human perception and ensure its accuracy. The belief in god and the belief in truth thus converge, both catering to man's need for stability and benign order.

When we ponder truth we are merely looking at a reflection of our needs as they mold our modes of thought.

Nietzsche does not in any way deny the existence of a mind independent reality. In this sense, he is not involved in Cartesian exercises of doubt. He acknowledged ontological realism- a reality that can be known- but insisted on epistemic relativism and strongly criticized what he termed 'the prejudice of philosophy', namely, the assumption that there is one correct way of perceiving and understanding reality (Nietzsche 2009). Nietzsche shows that the issue of truth is never a neutral one. He discusses the different meanings attributed to truth across history and shows that the way they fulfill human needs and express the prejudices of their originators is always prior to their content. In this way, Nietzsche compels his reader to accept that truths are nothing other than:

> A mobile army of metaphors, metonyms, and anthropomorphisms: in short, a sum of human relations which have been poetically and rhetorically intensified, transferred, and embellished and which, after long usage, seem to people to be fixed, canonical, and binding. Truths are illusions which we have forgotten are illusions – they are metaphors that have become worn out and have been drained of sensuous force, coins which have lost their embossing and are now considered as metal and no longer as coins).
>
> NIETZSCHE 1976, cl.1

In Nietzsche's view, when we aim for objectivity we buy ourselves stability, anchorage and direction, but we sacrifice the relevance of our knowledge for local purposes of living.

> ... Such a Will to Truth..., a metaphysician's ambition of the forlorn hope has participated therein: that which, in the end, always prefers a handful of 'certainty' to a whole cartload of beautiful possibilities; there may even be puritanical fanatics of conscience who prefer to put their last trust in a sure nothing, rather than in an uncertain something.
>
> NIETZSCHE 2009, cl.10

By bringing the human need for certainty to the fore, Nietzsche illustrates the human tendency to transform vital and interesting contemporary thought into fossilized and anachronistic truth, in exchange for certainty, security and the absence of doubt. This 'Will to Truth' is characteristic of a more general psychological tendency for self-deception. Man lacks the courage to endure uncertainty, lacks the strength and integrity needed to contain his natural curiosity (ibid. cl.227). Nietzsche's conclusion is that certainty needs are the pivotal factor in the creation of the ideal of an absolute truth. Man needs truth so that the earth will continue to revolve around its axis in a way that will not surprise him and will not throw his life off balance. Truth enables the illusion of eternal knowledge.

Thinkers on both sides of the Atlantic have been influenced by Nietzsche's view that the role of truth is to provide anchorage for man's mind and consciousness. In the liberal and democratic atmosphere that prevailed in the United States, a pragmatic view developed, which posited that the concern of truth was to advance the welfare of the individual. Thinkers such as Charles Sanders Peirce, William James, John Dewey and Richard Rorty saw truth as a means to an end of improving humanity's lot.

On the other side of the ocean, the human yearning for truth was analyzed by Martin Heidegger and, in his wake, by Jacques Derrida and Emmanuel Levinas. In contrast to the pragmatic-humanistic debate in the US, the continental angle on truth was strongly influenced by the horrors of the war in Europe during the 1940's: it linked the discussion of truth to the origins of xenophobia and the strife for dominance and authority. Heidegger saw the creation of an absolute truth as reflecting man's need to control the world in general and death in particular. Levinas and Derrida, who saw Heidegger as imploding into the same metaphysical stance he had tried to dismantle, discussed truth from an ethical perspective, understanding the pure and eternal as what man seeks and positions as a guarantor of his integrity and identity.

Through Derrida's critique of Heidegger, I will show how thinkers who criticized naïve notions of truth and explained the psychology that led to those notions, themselves fell prey to the seductive attraction of truth by formulating new definitions in place of those discarded. Clearly, the gravitational force of truth is of such magnitude that awareness of the motivations that underlie its pursuit does not stop one from acting upon their directives. It seems that man's psychological makeup cannot sustain the absence of truth.

Analysis of the Absolute in American Pragmatic Philosophy

The pragmatic American philosopher Charles Sanders Pierce, like Nietzsche, saw a close connection between truth and the needs of the subject. Pierce's starting point was to incorporate into the definition of truth the *motives* driving the search for it. In Pierce's view, the search for truth can be regarded as impartial in only a very trivial sense because it is, in fact, aimed at substantiating a belief. As a result, the 'truthfulness' of truth is of minor import. Pierce noted that:

> ...the sole object of inquiry is the settlement of opinion. We may fancy that this is not enough for us, and that we seek, not merely an opinion, but a true opinion. But put this fancy to the test, and it proves groundless; for as soon as a firm belief is reached we are entirely satisfied, whether the belief be true or false. ... The most that can be maintained is that we seek for a belief that we shall think to be true. But we think each one of our beliefs to be true, and, indeed, it is mere tautology to say so.
>
> PEIRCE 1877, 5

Yet another pragmatic philosopher, John Dewey, was aware of what he termed 'the need of the human mind for absolute truths', and cited the self-defeating statement of his realist contemporary adversary Chesterton that: "Pragmatism is a matter of human needs, and one of the first of human needs is to be something more than a pragmatist" (Chesterton 2005, 5). But Dewey believed that such needs were subject to developmental processes and that one could therefore expect them to transform and change. According to Dewey, everything needs to be considered in an historical context, as we can see most clearly in the history of metaphysical and religious thought. Dewey suggested that ideas and ideological movements that served at first as tools of intellectual and social liberation (Greek metaphysics, Christianity, the bourgeois manifesto, the Hegelian system) later ossified and became instruments of suppression.

Linking knowledge, life and the needs of the subject in an inextricable manner, Dewey claimed that it is not possible to distinguish between the search for truth in and of itself and the search for ways of improving man's life within a set of given social conditions (Dewey 1960). Therefore, Dewey reasoned, all the binary distinctions made in philosophical thought such as mind/body, objective/subjective, theory/practice, etc. were, at the time, of benefit to humanity. This applied especially, in Dewey's view, to the distinction between subject and object, a distinction on which the Correspondent theory of truth is predicated. When formulated, these distinctions were instrumental in improving social conditions. But, over time, they stopped being useful and crystalized into dogma that hindered progress. Humankind's ability to develop, Dewey argued, requires their abandonment and the development of new formulations. He believed that, just as Christianity had overcome the need to prove correspondence between biblical text and a reality, so too, civilization as a whole, would be able to free itself from the need to believe in an absolute truth.

Richard Rorty continued the tradition of his pragmatic predecessors. He too described how deep seated emotional needs are gratified by the Western rationalist tradition, precisely as they were previously gratified by the belief in a super-human, divine judgment. Rorty cites Dostoyevsky's reference to these needs, in saying that if god doesn't exist, everything is permitted. Western rationalist tradition stepped in as a secular version of Western monotheism, fulfilling similar functions. The truth, like god, Rorty opined, supplies order, direction and moral justification (Rorty 1988).

Rorty shared Dewey's hope and belief that humanity would mature and outgrow its cravings for eternal certainties. Like a child growing out of its need for parental care and the belief in the omnipotence and goodness of its parents, so perhaps humanity may be able to forgo both its need to believe in a divinity preoccupied with its welfare *and* its covenant with the non-human power known as the 'Intrinsic Nature of Reality' (Rorty 1998, 82). This 'Intrinsic Nature' is the extension of Aristotle's substances, and assuming it is effectively reinstating metaphysics and its associated one absolute truth.

Rorty argues that there are many alternative ways of talking about our experience without in any way getting closer to things as they really are. In this situation, he suggests, strictly referential speech, which presumes realistic truth, is a form of oppression and man is better off using language that is better attuned to social context. "Instead of asking: 'are there truths out there that we shall never discover?' we would ask: 'Are there ways of talking and acting that we have not yet explored?'" (Rorty 1998, 6). Rorty suggests here that we should not talk naively (and presumptuously) about how truthful or accurate our theories are. Instead, we should try to establish what kind of theory is best suited to enhance well-being and moral progress in human living in terms of its intellectual underpinning. Rorty believes that by doing this, we would better promote the original aspiration for truth, namely, promote the hope for productive and meaningful lives. In fact, Rorty says, insisting on truth and objectivity specifically endangers the development of a humanistic liberal vision:

> I see rhetorical flourishes designed to make practitioners feel they are being true to something big and strong: the Intrinsic Nature of Reality. On my view, the comfort derived from this feeling is, at this stage in the maturation of Western humanity, as unnecessary and as potentially dangerous as the comfort derived from the conviction that one is obeying the Will of God.
>
> RORTY 1998, 82

When we discuss the 'real nature' of the world, says Rorty, we are liable to stumble and attribute 'real' features of superiority and inferiority also to different classes and kinds of man. Here Rorty implicitly ties up truth with violence or, in Derrida's choice of terms, explicates the tie between violence and metaphysics (see below).

The Continental Analysis of Truth

Heidegger's aletheia: On the other side of the Atlantic, Martin Heidegger was also preoccupied with the psychological roots of the quest for truth and with the overturning of Western metaphysics that gives rise to absolute and eternal truth. In his work he distinguished between what was accepted as truth in traditional Western thought and the notion of 'aletheia' – the ancient Greek predecessor for the concept of truth. Heidegger interprets the Greek term for truth, aletheia, as having the etymological sense of 'dis-closing', 'un-covering', 'dis-covering', 'revealing', that is: "The *being true* (truth) of the statement must be understood as *discovering*" (Heidegger 1996, 201\219). Truth is what allows an entity to 'be seen' in its uncoveredness.

For Heidegger, truth as aletheia is a happening, a "how of discoveredness" (ibid.), an originary event. It always involves a movement out of concealment, through which the authentic 'being' of entities is revealed. The meaning of "authentic 'being' of entities" is best understood by contrast to a tacit anticipation of an ontological character or, in other words, what may be revealed of entities when we do not impose our pre-existing knowledge upon them. Truth is a transitory state, a state of transition. It runs contrary to persistence and permanence.

For Heidegger, the interpretation of truth as 'correctness', as fixed and eternal, disconnects truth from human life, from being. Moreover, a truth that we receive ready-made from others, a truth that is quoted or remembered, lacks the original power of revelation and becomes stilted. It then congeals into an everyday sense which lacks the quality of originary urgency, lacks the power to stimulate. What has been pointed out and repeated becomes re-veiled in a way that eventually forms a common consensus. This kind of public knowledge, which appears in Heidegger's concept of 'publicity' (Offentlichkeit), represents the inauthentic kind of awareness typical of 'das Man', typical of the 'they'. Adopting this kind of knowledge is a symptom of Dasein's inevitable 'falling prey', when man's daily living is mostly inauthentic (Heidegger 1996, 204\222).

Alongside the temporal element, Heidegger stressed the necessary involvement of Dasein in the becoming of aletheia. Truth discloses itself only within the realm of intention. This intention is an act of opening by which Dasein becomes receptive and hospitable to the being that will face his own. The act of opening, an act that holds the essence of Dasein's humanity, establishes a clearing for a disclosure, one that may appear or have the potential to appear.

Since Dasein is the source of intelligibility, truth as un-concealing is possible only because there is Dasein. What follows is that, without Dasein, there would be no truth. Entities require Dasein in order to be intelligible at all: "Truth in the most primordial sense is the disclosedness of Dasein to which belongs the discoveredness of innerwordly beings" (ibid. 205\223). But Dasein must be oriented in a certain way towards other beings so that aletheia may occur.

In what are known as the 'Parmenides lectures', delivered between 1942–43, Heidegger discusses the 'gaze' in its originary form and in its modern guise. The former holds within it what is required for the appearance of aletheia, while the latter is an expression of man's relentless drive to control his surroundings. In the course of this discussion, Heidegger claims that, in its original state, the gaze doesn't at all belong to the individual, but to 'being' as it appears in the spaciousness of aletheia. In this area of gazes, man has to be willing *to encounter the experience* of being. In other words, he offers his gaze as a clearing for the disclosing of the essence of what it is that he is encountering and what he himself *is* and may be. This encounter is described as the advent of self on both sides of the gaze, as it brings being to its essence, and man to his own essence. The encountering gaze is characterized by its passivity and absence of reflexivity, its qualities of inclusion and acceptance. This, from Heidegger's point of view, is the human gaze in its appropriate and original guise.

By contrast to Heidegger's authentic gaze stands another gaze, the modern, metaphysical gaze of the subject observing an object. Here, the subject fixes his gaze upon the object, but in fact sees nothing other than himself. His gaze becomes an active act of a sovereign consciousness. This imperial gaze flattens the differential dynamics of being into a territory that is being classified and colonized. Whilst throughout human history, in its encounter with the world, the gaze has always been both active and passive, in modernity its responsiveness and openness have faded and become subordinated to its active, controlling and objectifying element.

This belligerence of modernity is tied up for Heidegger with the fear of death. Since Dasein is a condition of intelligibility, entrenched in its historicity and finitude, all knowledge is likewise transitory, "subject to the changes of day and night" (Heidegger 1996 379\413). But Dasein is never at ease with its temporality, its finitude. It is always striving for permanence, for lastingness, for an illusion of empowerment in the face of the inevitability of death and his smallness in the face of death.

By reducing his world to permanence and solidity, Dasein tries to establish a realm of eternal truth and knowledge, thus placing human rationality as the answer to death's challenge. And yet, "the fact that there are eternal truths will not be adequately proven until it is successfully demonstrated that Dasein has been and will be for all eternity" (ibid. 208\227). This pretense is the blind and fear-driven negation of both mortality and the historic nature of the subject's existence. Human thought cannot detach itself from its own historicity, and therefore can never achieve the abstract and permanent knowledge idealized in Western culture.

The Persistence of Metaphysics in Heidegger's Thought: On the face of it, Heidegger objected strongly to the entrenchment of insights and ideas and to posing them as truth. Moreover, he saw this tendency as rooted in the denial of time and finitude, a form of non-authenticity. It would be expected that after the linguistic turn, with its now famous statement that "language is the house of Being" (Heidegger 1993, 239), Heidegger's position with regard to the metaphysical anchoring of truth would be that of unconditional opposition. With his new emphasis on language and its ability to disclose being, Heidegger could be expected to replace the notion of universal and absolute truth by the notion of truth-eventuating-in-language. Yet, this was not exactly how Heidegger's position developed. As Derrida shows, Heidegger effectively gave in to the binary opposition that structured the kind of metaphysics he vehemently criticized.

Heidegger situated Being within language, a move which should have prevented any possibility of establishing its pure presence. On the other hand, Derrida shows, Heidegger often construes this same Being as a *transcendental signified*, irreducible to the order of signification as such. Thus, Derrida says: "... it must be remembered that, for Heidegger, the sense of being is never simply and rigorously a signified" (Derrida 1976, 22). Being for Heidegger, contends Derrida, is never just a matter of meaning; its presence is always of a different order than that of words or sentences, "strangely privileged as the virtue of disclosure and dissimulation" (ibid. 23).

Another form of metaphysical regression is clearly seen in '*Letter on Humanism*', where Heidegger again seemingly distances himself from metaphysical distinctions, but simultaneously falls back into traditional logocentric formulations:

> In written form, thinking easily loses its flexibility" and "... But, in writing, it is difficult, above all, to retain the multidimensionality of the realm peculiar to thinking. The rigor of thinking, in contrast to that of the sciences, does not consist merely in an artificial, that is, technical-theoretical exactness of concepts. It lies in the fact that saying remains purely in the element of the truth...and lets the simplicity of its manifold dimensions rule.
>
> HEIDEGGER 1993, 241

Derrida points to an additional metaphysical tendency in Heidegger's writings, the one expressed in his positing of a binary opposition between the authentic and the inauthentic. This reinstatement of purity and its other is for Derrida, again, a reinstatement of the metaphysical stance. Moreover, as Pimentel (2009) discusses in detail, Heidegger's graded classification of authenticity is tied up with social organization and politics. In this, Heidegger follows the footsteps of Plato's hierarchical ranking of discourse types, where rational discourse is closely related to the ideal state. For Plato, the inner essence of the state is tied up with the discourse of being and rationality, while its externality comprises of the lesser discourses – sophistry, poetry and democracy. In his critique of metaphysics, modernity and technology Heidegger tried to reunite with pre-metaphysical man, the one free of the constraints (and falseness) of metaphysical thinking. But by doing so, Heidegger creates a new ideal, an ideal rooted in ancient Greek thinking, which must be unearthed and held as a model for both personal and social life.

Fatefully, Heidegger did not leave this issue in an abstract form, but proceeded to link the German man with the ancient Greek ideal. The German people have a special place because of the "special inner kinship between the German language and the language of the Greeks and their thought". (Heidegger 1981, 62). Similarly, and in a way that brought him fatefully close to the Nazi party, Heidegger saw traditional German rural life as realizing values and meanings that may counter the insidious effects of contemporary technology. All in all, while struggling against metaphysics and the modern culture reflecting it, Heidegger set up categories that answered for the same hierarchical logic.

Levinas, Derrida and Comments on Metaphysics: Levinas and Derrida continued Heidegger's project of dismantling metaphysics at the very point in which they perceived him as floundering, having witnessed the terrible ideological and political implications of this failure. Both theorized in the wake of the catastrophic failure of rationalism during the Second World War. In different ways, both saw the horrific violence effected in that war as rooted in metaphysics and attempted to develop an ethical philosophy that steered clear of the violent ramification of traditional philosophic thought. For both, the conclusion was that of strong objection to the gravitational force of binary metaphysics and the manner in which it created absolute truths and structured Western thought and language along categorical lines.

In the view of both Derrida and Levinas, the violence inherent in Western metaphysics originates in the principles of identity and totality underlying Greek philosophy. These principles give rise to rapacious violence directed at any and all who fall into the category of otherness and impurity. The Greek ideal is of a world of light and of unity, a world of uniformity and absence of difference (Derrida 1981, 102). In this world, man knows what is 'true' and what is 'false' and is assured in his distinctions between 'good' and 'evil'. Moreover, Greek knowledge enables the identification of *who* is good and *who* is evil. The 'good' is that which defines self and self-identity, whereas the 'bad' is otherness as personified in the stranger. As such, the unfamiliar constantly represents a threat to one's self and contaminates it. Its exclusion and removal become a vital necessity. In this way, Greek philosophy brings together the true and the ethical, aspiring to identity and similarity, thus giving rise to xenophobia and compromising the right of the 'other' to exist.

Derrida and Levinas, along different routes, attempt to invalidate the initial premise of pure presence – the primary assumption of absolute truth. Levinas focuses on the impossibility of defining the self and its existence independently of an 'other'. Derrida, in his exploration of logocentrism, discusses the signifier as being the feared other of signification and challenges the distinction of these orders.

Levinas placed at the center of his investigation the inability of the self to appear in pure form. Heidegger, in his basic assumption of 'being-in-the-world' and in his emphasis on Dasein's immersion in 'care', seemingly overcame the object-subject divide he so strongly objected to. And yet, in many of his writings, he seems reluctant to rid Dasein of its originary status, one that is prior to its being-with another. For example he states clearly:

> Only because Dasein can expressly choose itself on the basis of its selfhood can it be committed to others. And only because, in being toward itself as such, Dasein can understand anything like a 'self' and, furthermore, attend to a thou-self at all. Only because Dasein, constituted by the for-the-sake-of, exists in selfhood, only for this reason, is anything like human community possible. The phenomenon of authentic self-choice highlights, in the most radical way, the metaphysical selfhood of Dasein, and this means transcendence as transcending ones' own being, transcending being as being-with others, and transcending beings in the sense of nature and items of use....
>
> HEIDEGGER 1992A, 190

Levinas, by contrast, refutes this *a priori* assumption of existence and presents the other as a condition necessary for and prior to subjective selfhood.[3] In order to constitute the subjectivity of the subject, the other is needed, an other

3 For a detailed analysis of the metaphysical elements in Heidegger's Dasein see also Gordon 2001.

that cannot be a part of that subject. He must be transcendent, external to the subject and infinitely different in his otherness.

For Levinas, there is neither thought nor meaning prior to the encounter with the other. Sensation is the mode of experience prior to it, and is characterized by enjoyment and pleasure. In contradistinction to Heidegger, who assumes that we live in a world of objects and understand them by means of care and usage, Levinas sees these objects as something that the self wants to digest and that serves as its nourishment. The self wants to assimilate all into itself:

> Nourishment, as a means of invigoration, *is the transmutation of the other into the same*, which is the essence of enjoyment; an energy that is other, recognized as other,recognized…as sustaining the very act that is directed upon it becomes, in enjoyment, my own energy, my strength, me.
>
> LEVINAS 1969, 111

Enjoyment comprises the self's existence, its thoughtless, happy, egoistic plane of living. The ethical moment is the one in which the self encounters something it wishes to enjoy and to incorporate, but it finds that this 'thing' cannot be subjugated. This thing is the other as presented by his face. The other is unknown and cannot be known. In that sense, he refuses to be digested and assimilated into the self: "The face speaks… He at each instant undoes the form he presents" (Levinas 1969, 66); "The face is present in its refusal to be contained" (ibid. 194), "The face resists possession, resists my powers" (ibid. 197).

For Levinas, human knowledge is based to a large extent on the portrayal of otherness through resemblance to ourselves, projecting upon it the framework of our conceptual categories. This involves, according to Levinas, a violent act of imposing our subjectivity upon the other. As the other cannot be *known*, he is experienced as a force that opposes and negates me. In that sense, the other has powers over me that originate in his externality, in his unwillingness to submit to my categories of thought. What we have here is a dual influence of our inability to know the other: On one hand, it is experienced as a threat. On the other hand, it secures the other's autonomy, his freedom from the tyranny of the subject. Yet, the subject imposes his knowledge every time he expresses himself, because self expression is always through self categories. Escaping the subject's knowledge also implies escaping self expression, which wields both a power and a demand:

> The being that expresses itself imposes itself, but does so precisely by appealing to me with its destitution and nudity- its hunger- *without my*

> *being able to be deaf to that appeal.* Thus, in expression, the being that imposes itself does not limit but promotes my freedom, by arousing my goodness.... The face opens the primordial discourse whose first word is obligation, which no 'interiority' permits avoiding... The will is free to assume this responsibility in whatever sense it likes; *it is not free to refuse this responsibility itself; it is not free to ignore the meaningful world into which the face of the Other has introduced it.*
>
> LEVINAS 1969, 200–201, 218–219

The self in itself, for Levinas, is not human before its ethical experience of responsibility as a reaction to the unknown other. Tto be (hu)man is to be transcendent in that precise sense of facing the other. The basic functions of life such as eating, enjoying and playing – these do not possess the transcendence that they have in Heidegger's approach. They are normally 'in-différent' and they become 'non-in-différent' only in the face of difference (from the other). This play of words emphasizes the fact that *subjectivity and significance can only be achieved by recourse to the face of the other, through the reaction of responsibility to the other*: "non-indifference, is responsibility" (Levinas 1981, 139). Responsibility is "the essential, primary and fundamental mode of subjectivity...the very node of the subjective is knotted in ethics understood as responsibility" (Levinas 1985, 95).

This ethical moment of responsibility is when the self acquires its transcendence. It is also the moment when the world is endowed with meaning, because "the face brings the first signification" (Levinas 1969, 207); the face is the "source from which all meaning appears" (ibid. 297). "Meaning is the face of the Other, and all recourse to words takes place already within the primordial face to face of language" (ibid. 206). "The face, preeminently expression, formulates the first word: the signifier arising at the thrust of his sign, as eyes that look at you" (ibid. 178).

The self, therefore, cannot be constituted as subjectivity in and of itself. Subjectivity is predicated upon the encounter with the other. This encounter and the responsibility it gives rise to is the origin of all meaning. This does not imply that, in being a subject, one is reduced to the other, rather on the contrary. Because the otherness of the other may never be known or appropriated, self, other, meaning and signification are inextricably bound together in a way that defies any possibility of pureness of self.

Like Levinas, Derrida also analyzes the human yearning for the absolute and the way in which it has structured Western philosophy. Derrida argues that the absolute enters philosophy through the most basic notion of logic, namely, the notion of identity, which does not allow for contradictions and strives for consistency and rationality. He coined the term Logocentrism in order to discuss the principle of identity, showing that it implicates the whole logic of complementarity, where two 'pure' opposites serve as components of any given whole. For every identity, one of these opposites predicates 'self', while the other predicates 'other'. Each category in the binary opposition is defined jointly with the other category, like 'day' is with 'night', 'good' is with 'bad', etc.

Derrida draws our attention to the fact that the polar opposites of Western metaphysics are never perceived as independent and equal entities. They are value-imbued and hierarchically ordered, giving one term temporal and qualitative priority over the second. In general, these hierarchical oppositions privilege unity, identity, immediacy, and spatial *presentness* over distance, difference, and deferment (Johnson 1981). Derrida steers clear of simply reversing this value system. Rather, he attempts to show that the very possibility of opposing two terms is an illusion. Identity, in and of itself, is challenged, and taken to be 'always already' infiltrated and contaminated by its other, its alleged opposite. At the heart of Derrida's deconstruction lies the obliteration of the hierarchical differentiation of signifier and signified, but it does not begin and end at that. It extends to the deconstruction of all dyads informing metaphysics: good/evil, true/false, essence/appearance, inside/outside, etc. (Derrida 1981, 103).

Searching after the roots of Logocentrism, Derrida turns to Plato and examines the logic of the difference between speech- which seemingly encapsulates presence- and its other, the written word, encapsulating absence. Derrida claims that this fundamental distinction is at the root of all binary oppositions that comprise the logic of metaphysics, with its crucial distinction between the true and the false.

In his '*Plato's Pharmacy*' (Derrida 1981), Derrida describes Plato's conception of speech (logos) as living presence. The spoken word expresses the delicate movements of the soul and adapts to the circumstances of the speaker and the effect he wishes to arouse in his interlocutor. By contrast, the permanent form of writing is incapable of such attunement and flexibility. Moreover, the written word, argued Plato, in its pretense to permanence, may cause the subject to 'forget' his intention and lose sight of what he wanted to say. His memory, the locus of his soul, may become lax and dull, having handed over his thoughts for safekeeping to the seeming permanence and immutability of the written word. Writing causes memory to slumber. It dims the vitality of the soul; it violates its memory and knowledge. Derrida then points to an internal paradox in Plato's thinking:

> Memory is finite by nature. Plato recognizes this in attributing life to it. As in the case of all living organisms, he assigns it, as we have seen, certain limits. A limitless memory would in any event be not memory but infinite self-presence. Memory always therefore already needs signs in order to recall the non-present, with which it is necessarily in relation. The movement of dialectics bears witness to this. Memory is thus contaminated by its first substitute: hypomnesis. But what Plato dreams of is a memory with no sign. That is, with no supplement. A mnesis with no hypomneisis.
>
> DERRIDA 1981, 111

The unwritten memory, mnesis, is allegedly pure interiority, clean of the written hypomnesis. Such purity, says Derrida, can only be a dream, a wish for purity, the dream-wish of metaphysics. Speech, as much as writing, is already necessarily structured by difference and distance. In that manner, presence is itself a mode of signification, and the transcendent signified is always already infused with the signifier. The purity of presence, ascribed so confidently to the signified, is forever contaminated heretofore by the signifier cleaving its core.

In its deconstruction of the identity principle that underlies Western metaphysics, Derrida's work promotes an alternative logic: the logic of difference and supplement. This logic is derived from the coincidence of meanings in the French verb: *differer*, which means both 'to differ' and 'to defer', and *supplement* which means both 'an addition' and 'a substitute'. In the framework of this logic, as soon as there is meaning, there is difference. The neatness of the metaphysical binary oppositions is undermined. Indeed, each of the elements is no longer even identical to itself, as difference inhabits the very core of what appears to be immediate and present. As Pimentel (2009) phrases it, the Derridean specter involves a painful awakening from the ancient dream of pure presence, which is philosophy's age-old ideal.

As I explain above, both Derrida and Levinas undermine the fundamental belief in the unity and purity of presence – the bedrock of Western philosophy as it grew out of ancient Greek thought. The Derridean gesture of splitting presence by means of the sign is reiterated in Levinas's work by the inexorable splitting of the self by the other. Purity of presence receives here a lethal blow. This immediately renders impossible a whole range of hierarchical distinctions that emerge from diverse binary oppositions. The result of recognizing this is far reaching as far as Derrida and Levinas are concerned. *It removes from philosophy the core of metaphysical violence that inheres in the logic of binary purities.* For both thinkers, purity of presence can only be bought at the price of that presence eliminating its 'other'. This involves violence and persecution.

Removing the practical instantiation of the hierarchical distinctions that leads to demonizing the other and fearing him may pave the way to the restitution of tolerance and diversity. But again, the humanistic strain undermines the possibility of truth.

An Interim Summary

In my short review so far I focused on philosophers who criticized the naïve, metaphysical approach to truth and showed the inherent contradictions of this approach. They went on to suggest more psychological reasons for the relentless pursuit of truth: Truth offers anchor and direction, a promise of order, identity and purity, and distances man from his fears of the chaotic, the transitory and the alien. To be able to understand the process and consequence of the search for truth, it is necessary to understand the nature of the needs that drive it. This may then allow us to distinguish between the drive for truth on the one hand and the results of the search on the other hand. Clearly, the extraordinary thing here lies in the dialogue between content and structure in the pursuit of truth. The content may change; the structure is intractable.

Nietzsche, in trying to expose and overcome the yearning for the absolute, turned the Platonic distinction between idea and matter upside down.[4] Heidegger recognized Nietzsche's revolutionary overturning of Platonic thought, but criticized him for staying within the constraints of its logic. Nietzsche managed to destabilize the traditional standing of the abstract and eternal, but placed in its stead the sensuous as an ideal and a valued way of life. Sensual life led Nietzsche to posit what for Heidegger seemed to be a new presence, no less essential and foundational than its predecessors – the Will for Power. Where life exists so does the Will for Power and sometimes the world in and of itself is described as such (Nietzsche 2009, cl.36). In this sense, Heidegger argued, the contents of metaphysics might have changed, but the binary hierarchical structure remained intact.[5]

Heidegger changed the Nietzschean–Platonic concept of presence by replacing it with temporality, a dynamic concept based on an essential movement of coming into being. Instead of the binary opposition of object and subject, Heidegger introduced his concepts of Dasein and being-in-the-world, concepts that capture the human condition of man inherently indecipherable

4 For a detailed review of Nietzsche's discussion of Western metaphysics see Haar (1996).

5 A discussion of Heidegger's intellectual relationship to Nietzsche may be found in Bambach (2003) and Storey (2015).

from the world he cares for. However, as Derrida and Levinas showed, he too imploded into binary logic, promoting an ideal that is associated with truth and truth-in-living that is external to modes of signification and may be interpreted as free of otherness. He too remained a captive of the metaphysical dream of purity.

In Pimentel's view: "We are witnessing a narrative of reversion: Every generation attempts to deviate from two thousand years of metaphysics and the generation that follows exposes the way in which the deviation of its predecessor simply managed to trap it once again in its basic structures" (Pimentel 2009, 249). This raises the question of whether it is at all possible to avoid the metaphysical formulations of truth building.

The American analytic philosopher Donald Davidson answers this question in the negative. In his view, the concept of truth is a necessary condition of language and of thought:

> Sentences are understood only on condition that one has the concept of objective truth. This goes also for the various propositional attitudes sentences are used to express. It is possible to have a belief only if one knows that beliefs may be true or false.... Without a grasp of the concept of truth, not only language, but thought itself, is impossible. Truth is important, then, not because it is especially valuable or useful...but because without the idea of truth we would not be thinking creatures, nor would we understand what it is for someone else to be a thinking creature.
>
> DAVIDSON 1997, 72

The concept of truth, then, is basic in the sense that other concepts cannot exist without it. This is because the logical form of all concepts- the propositional form- already implies the possibility of truth. If a certain entity is part of a language, then it being 'true' or 'false' is part of its meaning in that language. Davidson relates to the truth as an analytic concept in the Kantian sense of being primary and axiomatic. As such, it may not be defined in every instance, but still be essential for the classification and association of other concepts. Moreover, as Davidson sees it, we cannot think or speak in a comprehensible manner, without truth lending thought and language their basic structure and their possibility of holding and conveying meaning.

Whether approached from the angle of psychology in terms of anxieties and needs or from the analytic angle of specifying the basic conditions of human thought, truth returns again and again as an irremovable, subject-defining notion. It may do so by allowing the subject to experience certainty and coherence or by ensuring his ongoing integrity and identity in the face of another, or it may enable the subject to structure his thought and diverse semantic fields. Whether we intend it or not, our thought and our psyche demand the anchoring of truth in order to function in what otherwise might become unbearable or meaningless. In the next section I will present the way in which even Freud, with his self-analysis and heightened awareness, demonstrates for us the gravitational psychic forces that determine and re-determine truth.

From Divine to Scientific Truth and Beyond: Freud as Case in Study

Divine truth provided sense, meaning and direction to Man. Established religion had found ways in which to instill its truth into the life and thinking of the subject, thus creating a coherent lacing of truth, man and society. With the death of god and the disintegration of his order, the subject was threatened with the disintegration of his identity and his world. The Enlightenment offered anchorage and meaningful order predicated on man's intelligence and capacity for rational thought. Thus, the concept of scientific truth came into being.

The transition from the divine to the scientific truth was suffused with the hope that the latter would succeed in stepping into the shoes of the former. From the psychological perspective, Freud discussed this paradigmatic transition in his article 'The Question of a Weltanschauung'. In this article, Freud posed religious belief as the consequence of man's succumbing to his desire for a regulating, compassionate higher power that would rectify injustice and hardship, and guarantee beneficent and eternal truths. In Freud's view this yearning for answers characterizes both man's and mankind's infantilism.

> Religion is an attempt to master the sensory world in which we are situated by means of the wishful world which we have developed within us as a result of biological and psychological necessities. But religion cannot achieve this. Its doctrines bear the imprint of the times in which they arose, the ignorant times of the childhood of humanity. Its consolations deserve no trust. Experience teaches us that the world is no nursery... [Religion] appears not as a permanent acquisition but as a counterpart to the neurosis which individual civilized men have to go through in their passage from childhood to maturity.
>
> SE 22:167

In this vein, the man who clings to his belief in god and who is not affected by rational considerations reconstructs a phenomenon often witnessed in analysis: "If a usually sensible patient rejects some particular suggestion on specially foolish grounds, this logical weakness is evidence of the existence of a specially strong motive for the denial- a motive which can only be of an affective nature, an emotional tie" (ibid. 169).

In support of this emotional denial, religion banned critical thinking and Freud depicts the possibilities that adopting science may hold:

> Our best hope for the future is that intellect- the scientific spirit, reason- may in process of time establish a dictatorship in the mental life of man. The nature of reason is a guarantee that afterwards it will not fail to give man's emotional impulses and what is determined by them the position they deserve. But the common compulsion exercised by such a dominance of reason will prove to be the strongest uniting bond among men and lead the way to further unions.
>
> IBID. 170

The interesting aspect here is in Freud's chosen vocabulary and heightened hopes regarding the scientific 'spirit', which he endows with qualities resembling those of religion. Freud foregoes god but does not take up the step that Nietzsche held as a necessary consequence of it, namely, abrogating the unique and absolute authority of truth. He admits that science does not supply the comprehensive scope that religion did, but science's truth, even if it is partial and fragmented, is the 'real' truth. That is the source of its comfort and superiority.

In a detailed analysis, Brunner (2007) shows how Freud, in his opposition to the religious worldview and his desire to objectify nature, is a typical representative of the enlightenment, who strives to replace illusion with instrumental knowledge. This includes relinquishing romantic concepts of affinity with nature and recognizing the fundamental gap that separates man from it, a gap reflected in the inherent tension between the Id and the Superego. From Freud's point of view, renouncing religion is the key to modern civilization, but he persists in linking science and technology to an absolutist epistemology and the crystallization of a new power. The paradox is striking: If man were only ready to forgo illusory omnipotence, he will gain 'real' omnipotence, that is, control over nature.

Freud's praise of and enthusiasm with technology stand out against the background of his characteristic sober pessimism:

> Long ago...[Man] formed an ideal conception of omnipotence and omniscience which he embodied in his gods.... Today...he has almost become

> a god himself… Man has, as it were, become a kind of prosthetic God [*Prothesengott*]. When he puts on all his auxiliary organs he is truly magnificent; but those organs have not grown on to him and they still give him much trouble at times. Future ages will bring with them new and probably unimaginable great advances in this field of civilization and will increase man's likeness to God even more.
>
> SE 21:92–93

Jose Brunner finds highly surprising Freud's shortsighted passion for technology and robust defense of it in the face of any actual or potential critique. Even more surprising, in Brunner's view, is that someone like Freud, who so vehemently set out to undermine religious belief, should present a technology as a prosthetic god, a god like entity, without perceiving the illusory implications of this simile. Freud, who has exposed magic and religion as lackeys of infantile desires, presents technology as a force equivalent to religion and does so without overt notice to the religious tone tinting his enthusiasm. His customary warnings against omnipotence disappear when describing the wondrous qualities of technology (Brunner 2007, 74).

Brunner is in fact saying that Freud's approach to technology and science resembles an immature man's approach to god. Freud idealizes technology and seems unaware of the dangers of both technology and science. In science, Freud saw knowledge that was not only 'real' but also necessarily munificent, like the power of the lost god. Brunner's analysis of Freud's transition from divine truth- which he so adamantly opposed- to science as a new divinity reveals his irrepressible enchantment with illusion, omnipotence and the truth.

What are we to make of this circular motion? This rejection of one truth and the crowning of another in its stead? The clear answer is to be found in everything that has been thus far said. *Man needs truth. He needs truth not only as an anchor in the face of his fears but also as an Archimedean point for his thoughts.* Without truth's anchor of stability and certainty – in any of its guises or definitions – man is unable to safely perceive and articulate his world.

The assumption I have presented in this chapter and exemplified by the analysis of Freud's and Heidegger's unwitting loyalty to some versions of truth and metaphysics is that *truth and the psychology of the subject are inseparable.* Truth is not external to the subject; it always implicates him; it is always associated with his needs. The need for truth is truth's progenitor. Recognized as part and parcel of the psychology of the subject, it is drawn into the psychoanalytic field of inquiry; investigating truth is effectively investigating the subject's needs and their ramifications.

Truth has received various definitions in philosophic Western thought, six of which I will present in the next chapter. I will show how, despite the major weaknesses in each of its definitions, truth retained its vitality in motivating philosophical investigation, reflecting the human need in order and stability across different dimensions of living. Presenting six philosophic paradigms of truth, I will analyze and elaborate the link between the philosophic and the psychological. I will show how each notion of truth is relevant and indispensable to the subject's life, addressing a basic need within it. The abstract philosophic notions of truth will be shown to reflect the workings and the organization of any particular psyche.

CHAPTER 2

Notions of Truth in Philosophy

What I propose to do in this chapter is to describe the main notions of truth that have featured in Western philosophy since its beginnings in ancient Greece. Four of these notions appear most frequently in contemporary theory, both philosophical and psychoanalytic. These are the Correspondent, Coherent, Intersubjective and Pragmatic notions of truth (Hanly 1990; 2001; Kunne 2003; Lynch 2001). To these I add one classical notion, the Ideal truth, presented already by Plato. This truth is often considered obsolete outside religious context, but I will illuminate its enduring relevance in psychoanalytic theory and practice. I add also the Subjective-Existential truth, which like Intersubjective truth, is often associated with the postmodern critique of truth.

The rationale for adding Subjective-Existential truth to my paradigmatic notion of truths is twofold. Firstly, by being associated with postmodernism, it is often considered as radically contemporary and nihilistic to the point of lacking use-value. Presenting its historical-philosophical roots in continental philosophy, I will re-examine its validity and enduring relevance. Secondly, this truth appears in explicit and implicit ways in psychoanalytic theory and practice, reflecting its immense influence on psychic life. It is therefore important to establish its ties and relations with the other accepted notions of truth.

First I present each notion of truth in the context of its relevant epistemology. After this, I will move from the philosophical to the psychological realm, investigating the mental correlates of these truths and their mode of function *within our psychic, experienced lives*. I will show how each truth creates a point of certainty in the subject's life and addresses a basic dimension of living and a profound human need.

Six Notions of Truth

Examination of the history of ideas allows the identification of six paradigmatic notions of truths that frequent philosophical, linguistic and clinical theory: Ideal, Correspondent, Coherent, Intersubjective, Subjective-Existential and Pragmatic truths. Each of these reflects a discrete and definable epistemology that is associated with the work of a number of thinkers. For simplicity, I associate my truth notions with, respectively, the works of Plato, Aristotle, Baruch Spinoza, Edmund Husserl, Soren Kierkegaard and William James.

 | DOI 10.1163/9789004314993_004

In developing my perspective, I will examine the manner in which, throughout history, those who investigated truth fell within one of the above paradigms.

The Ideal and the Correspondent truths are absolute in the sense that their definitions presume and incorporate an order of reality that is independent of consciousness or human history. The four other notions entail an essential softening of the truth (Hempel 1935\1994) in the sense that they involve particularity, historicity and contextuality. I will present them in an intertextual manner, showing how each notion involves a critique of former definitions. I do not do this only for style or clarity, but rather in order to bring to the fore the interrelations between the various notions and the neglected or problematic aspects that prevent each notion from being conclusive.

The Ideal notion of truth: Plato developed his ideas in the context of two different schools of thought with whom he engaged throughout his dialogues: Pythagorean and Sophist philosophy. The former was actually a religion, based on the belief that mathematical formulas, which are essentially concepts or ideas, accurately describe the true or essential nature of all things. The sophists were a heterogeneous school, but I will bring Protagoras here as their representative because he held views which were in direct opposition to Plato's. A key text attributed to him is 'Truth', which opens with the sentence: "Man is the measure of all things, of the things that are that they are and of the things that are not that they are not".[1] This is interpreted as a claim of the relativity of the truth of all judgments to the experience or belief of the individual making the judgment. In other words, the way things really are is, in fact, the way they seem to an individual. This logic is the one governing *subjective epistemology*, an epistemology that understands reality and truth as constituted by the subject's perceptions and beliefs.

Plato's theory of forms may be seen as an extension of Pythagorean thinking and as debating the relativistic stance of the sophists. Originating in Plato's work, the Ideal notion of truth posits that truth values stem from the compatibility or lack thereof between an ideal form and its empirically perceived particular cases. According to Plato, all true ideas or forms originate from The Good or The Form of the Good.[2] This form is superior to all others, indeed it is

1 Plato Theaetetus, accessed 23.7.2015, http://classics.mit.edu/Plato/theatu.html.

2 At Republic VI 508E-9a, the Form of the Good is distinguished from all other objects of knowledge: "Now, that which imparts truth to the known and the power of knowing to the knower is what I would have you term the idea of good, and this you will deem to be the cause of science, and of truth in so far as the latter becomes the subject of knowledge; beautiful too, as are both truth and knowledge, you will be right in esteeming this other nature as more beautiful than either; and, as in the previous instance, light and sight may be truly said

their progenitor. It is posited as a single metaphysical agent that gives rise to all that is true, good and beautiful – including mathematical and factual truths and virtues like justice, honor, and generosity, all of which have their own independent existence.

A form is the ideal essence of something, a transcendent entity that is perfect, immutable, and indivisible. The things of our everyday world are imperfect copies of the forms; they are multiple, but the forms themselves are one. The forms are a priori; they precede experience and transcend it. They are eternal, irrefutable, and permanent as opposed to what is merely a changing copy or likeness of the former. This notion may be embedded in a religious belief system or, alternatively, in an *objective idealistic epistemology*. Despite the differences between them, the common denominator of both versions is the existence of an immaterial external system that is independent of the perceiving subject.

Plato sees our knowledge as divided between that which we gain through our senses, and that which we know intellectually. In Plato's hierarchy, sensible knowledge is faulty and a mere shadow or representation of true knowledge, which can only be cognized by mental measures and in the form of knowledge. Only the latter may be accepted as an intelligible mental process that may give access to the realm of ideas. This image of knowledge is brought forth in Plato's Allegory of the Cave.[3] What we see in the physical world, compared to true, intelligible knowledge, is like shadows cast by fire on the wall of the cave, compared to the reality of the objects outside the cave that cast these shadows. But even this reality is a mere shadow of the sun itself (The Form of The Good).

The system of ideal forms is effectively innate knowledge, because it precedes any personal experience or individual existence. Its truth may be recollected, uncovered or accessed only through a laborious rational process and, even then, only approximated and never fully achieved.[4] Plato describes the process leading to the reflective knowing and understanding of the ideas, but even without knowing them, our mere ability to think and speak depends on these forms. The linguistic terms we use acquire their meaning by naming these forms that the objects we perceive represent.

---

to be like the sun, and yet not to be the sun, so in this other sphere, science and truth may be deemed to be like the good, but not the good; the good has a place of honour yet higher". Plato book VI of the Republic, accessed 23.7.2015. source http://classics.mit.edu/Plato/republic.7.vi.html.

3 Plato Book VII of The Republic, accessed 23.7.2015, http://classics.mit.edu/Plato/republic.8.vii.html.

4 Plato Book VI of The Republic, accessed 23.7.2015, http://classics.mit.edu/Plato/republic.7.vii.html.

The Correspondent theory of truth: Aristotle grew up under the influence of Plato's world view, but eventually developed his own independent philosophy and turned Plato's principles of a divine order upside down. Aristotle objected to the idea that reality could only exist on a transcendental level and replaced Plato's concept of eternal ideas with his own universal categories, construed as attributes which the mind can grasp through the senses. These attributes, Aristotle argued, do not exist independently, but are always and necessarily tied up to 'substance', which is the primary kind of being. Everything that exists is substance-based and objects are made of different kinds of substances. This suggests a model of the natural world consisting of individual, separate substances that share certain attributes and that may be apprehended in a fairly accurate way by the senses. Aristotle's conception of the world held great appeal in comparison to Plato's abstract approach, in that it placed truth within closer reach of man's common sense and understanding.

The Correspondent notion of truth maintains that truth values are established by compatibility, correspondence, conformity or agreement between a proposition and an external mind-independent reality. It is anchored in a *realistic epistemology* which maintains that the world has an existence that is not reliant on the consciousness of the subject, but which the subject is able to perceive and know.

Aristotle defined truth as follows: "To say of what is that it is not, or of what is not that it is, is false, while to say of what is that it is, and of what is not that it is not, is true".[5] This definition can be translated into modern philosophic terminology according to the following familiar formula: the truth of a sentence exists in its conformity with reality. Aristotle refers to the 'underlying things' which grant sentences their truth values, and argues that they are facts or logically constructed situations which exist in the world. And indeed, the definition of the noun 'truth' in the English Oxford Dictionary is: 'Conformity with fact; agreement with reality'.

The Correspondent notion of truth is perhaps the most intuitive and widespread notion of truth. According to this approach, an argument (statement, sentence, belief) is true to the extent that it complies with a fact or a situation. This approach was represented by Russell and Moore in the early 1900's (Russell 1994; Moore 1993) and by Wittgenstein's Tractatus Logico-Philosophicus (Wittgenstein 2010) [hereinafter referred to as the 'Tractatus']. In the Tractatus, Wittgenstein explains the idea of correspondence by recourse to the pictorial

5 Aristotle *Metaphysics* IV part 7, accessed 23.7.2015, http://classics.mit.edu/Aristotle/metaphysics.4.iv.html.

mode of representation. "We make to ourselves pictures of facts… The picture agrees with reality or not; it is right or wrong, true or false… In the agreement or disagreement of its sense with reality, its truth or falsity consists. In order to discover whether the picture is true or false we must compare it with reality" (Wittgenstein 2010, cl. 2.1–2.223).

Alas, the verification of truth is problematic in all representational forms, be it in pictures or in propositions, in sentences or in beliefs (as truth-bearers). If truth is defined by correspondence, agreement or conformity to a reality, the elements of this reality must be identified, be they facts, events or objects and examined against truth-bearers. And this identification procedure causes problems: How do we define a fact? What must we assume in order to know that we may, by mental means, represent reality-as-it-is? How do we recognize it in its purity? How do we put aside our preconceptions of it? And once we manage to define a fact in its pure form, independent of the workings of our mind, how do we choose among the related representations the one against which we perform the verification process? And supposing we manage to work through these problems, how can we compare two things that are essentially different from each other such as a fact and a proposition? How do we compare an internal entity in our head with an external entity whose nature we presume to know? These questions have never been adequately resolved, forcing us to set aside the aspiration for pure objectivity; an aspiration that made the Ideal notion of truth so attractive and that, for a moment, the Correspondent theory of truth seemed to salvage.

However, the loss of certainty and mastery that resulted from the decline of objective, Correspondent theories did not end the quest for truth: Rather, it brought truth closer to the human subject. Here post-modern sensibilities meet another ancient ally, St. Thomas Aquinas, who was very much aware of the limitations of knowledge, and suggested soberly that 'Truth is the equation of thought and thing'.[6]

This definition begs once again the question of how to relate mind and object, and how to understand the consequences of this relation. Lund (2002) notes that, in defining truth as the correlation between the object and its *mental form*, we necessarily fall into relativism, because truth is defined in relation to the subject of knowledge. If truth depends on the connection between the mind and the object and if the mind is the judge of this connection, it follows that there may be as many truths as there are minds. This would immediately place us back in the realm of subjective epistemology and its hopeless relativity.

6 *St. Thomas Aquinas Summa Theologiae*, Of Truth Article 1. accessed 23.7.2015, (http://www.sacred-texts.com/chr/aquinas/summa/sum019.htm).

Aquinas solved this problem by defining the divine intellect as the receptacle of the one truth that unifies between reality and belief. Stated abstractly, he incorporated an objective ideal element so as to ensure the validity of his definition of Correspondence.

Those who did not rely on divine intellect attempted to bypass the problem of the knowing subject by defining correspondence through the practices of validation and refutation of beliefs (Popper 1969). A standard positivist view may take the validation principle even further and equate truth with the possibility of its validation.

However, even in this construal, truth cannot be fully objective because its discovery remains constrained by our ability to identify and verify and these, in turn, are constrained by our epistemic situation. Popper recognized that even in scientific procedures of validation and refutation we bear the mark of subjectivity: "Observation is always selective. It needs a chosen object, a definite task, an interest, a point of view, a problem. And its description presupposes a descriptive language, with property words; it presupposes similarity and classification which, in its turn, presupposes interests, points of view, and problems" (Popper 1969, 155). Even the most rigorous validation procedures do not fully circumvent the subjective mind.

The Coherent theory of truth: The Coherent theory of truth is associated with idealism. There are many forms of idealism, but they all stress that what we know of reality is derived from entities like ideas, thoughts and perceptions. Plato articulated the anti-materialistic essence of idealism when he presented matter as deriving from ideas and inferior to them. He viewed sense-experience as unreliable truth material, contending that the only basis for true knowledge is consciousness, because we can never be sure that matter or anything in the outside world really exists. Thus, the only real things are mental entities.

A brand of idealism termed 'absolute idealism' posits a single creative principle that is absolute, unconditional and gives rise to the unity of the world. In itself, it is abstract, unknown and prior to all other principles that must conform to it in different ways. At times, this principle has been posited to be god, but it could also be posited as the essence of the human spirit or some other abstract principle that can be ascribed as the source of all experiential phenomena. From this point of view, what appears as disconnected phenomena represents a temporary failure of understanding.

Spinoza is often considered to be a major influence on the German idealists who followed him (Hegel, Schelling, Fichte) and may be thought of as a classical representative of absolute idealism. Faced with the plurality of the world, Spinoza reasons his way to the positing of a unifying principle which he identifies as God.[7] God is the one entity, the only genuine cause. From God, infinitely many things flow in infinitely many different ways. But everything coheres with its common core: "Nothing in the universe is contingent, but all things are conditioned to exist and operate in a particular manner by the necessity of the divine nature" (Spinoza 1989, I prop. xxix).

Since all that happens radiates from the common core, everything hangs together as part of a coherent whole. This applies to both things and ideas: "The order and connection of ideas is the same as the order and connection of things" (Spinoza 1989, II prop. vii). Naturally, for Spinoza the understanding of god as the embodiment of the principle of infinite substance lies at the heart of human knowledge: "Intellect, in function (actu) finite, or in function infinite, must comprehend the attributes of God and the modifications of God, and nothing else" (Spinoza 1989, I prop. xxx).

The human mind is capable of three distinct kinds of knowledge: The first kind is *opinion*, as derived from vague sensory experience or from the signification of words in memory or imagination. This kind of knowledge relies on unstable experience and ought to be discarded. The second kind, *reason*, sets out from simple, transparent ideas and, by analyzing their causal or logical relations, derives higher order ideas, affording the understanding of more general causes. The third kind is *intuition*. Here, the mind deduces the structure of reality from the very essence or the idea of God. This is the highest form of knowledge and the ultimate guarantor of truth (Spinoza 1989, II Prop. xl). The acquisition of knowledge, then, begins with discarding the testimony of the senses (opinion). From there, it proceeds by reason to analyze ideas of any existing thing, reasoning back to its eternal source or divine essence. From this knowledge of the divine essence, all else might be intuited.

The sum up of Spinoza's logic is that the mind can only access its own contents, so truth resides in identifying its own unifying principle. This is the

---

7 His reasoning is given thus: In Book I of the '*Ethics*', Spinoza defines substance as 'that which is in itself', independently of other existences, but also as 'conceived through itself', namely, as graspable by consciousness (Spinoza 1989, I def. iii). As he sees it, causal interaction is impossible between two substances that do not have anything in common (ibid. prop. iii), so if two substances do not share a common essence, then they cannot affect each other. Each is the cause of its own existence and, since it cannot be influenced by anything outside itself, must also be absolute and infinite. Finite individuals interacting with each other cannot be substances. They can be nothing other than modifications of a self-caused, infinite substance (ibid. prop. v–viii). This infinite substance is God. Moreover, God has infinitely many attributes that are themselves infinite and do not accept limits of any kind (ibid. prop xi). Infinite substance then, according to Spinoza, must be indivisible, eternal, and unitary. Since everything else is wholly contained in the infinite substance, there can be only one entity of this kind.

Coherent notion of truth, where the truth value of a proposition derives from its relation to other propositions and the extent to which it coheres with other propositions. Coherence, then, is ultimately a measure of consistency within a whole system of propositions. While the Correspondent approach bestows a truth value that is either positive or negative, the Coherent approach leads to 'proportionate' values. A belief is true *to the extent* to which it is consistent with other beliefs.

The Coherent epistemological approach solves many of the problems that remained unresolved in the Correspondent approaches. Since it positions itself wholly within the mind, this theory does not demand separating fact from belief. In the Coherent logic, all facts are beliefs regarding facts and the truth value of any belief is determined only in relation to other beliefs. We do not exit our mind, only seek coherence within it. And coherence may originate in various kinds of connections between propositions, the prime kinds being those of causality, implication and consistency. A system of beliefs is coherent to the extent that the relations among its various propositions satisfy one of these prime kinds.

The problems of the Coherent truth are similar to those of absolute idealism. Coherent systems may be constructed, but how may we know their relation to the life we live or their relevance thereof? This question stated in the abstract, concerns the metaphysical question of how spirit externalizes itself and how the concepts it generates can represent anything true about nature. James opposed idealism on grounds of its indifference to particularity and diversity, as well as its distance from lived experience. A moral element is also implied by this criticism, in the sense that absolute idealism imposes a lawfulness that is completely predetermined and leaves the subject without free will.

Moore's rebellion against absolutism found expression in his defense of common sense against the radically counter-intuitive conclusions of absolutism. Wittgenstein expressed this sensibility with the dictum: "Back to the rough ground!" (Wittgenstein 1999, cl.107).

For Wittgenstein, stepping back onto firm ground involved relinquishing ideal entities, as well as ideal infallible knowledge of reality and the illusion that we are able to verify beliefs, thus transforming them into firm truths. When loosening our hold of absolute truth, we must accept the equation: 'I know = I am familiar with it as a certainty'. We must accept that "we just can't investigate everything, and for that reason we are forced to rest content with assumption" (Wittgenstein 1977, cl. 272, 343). Wittgenstein the logician redirects us into the fabric of our lives: "My life consists in my being content to accept many things" (ibid. cl.344). These 'many things' include our habits, patterns of behavior and modes of thought, namely, the various networks of rules within which we live. From the pinnacles of ideals and metaphysical realism we move into the subjective and the intersubjective, into the world of habit, thought and feeling.

The Intersubjective theory of truth: Following Spinoza, German idealism bifurcated in two directions. The first, as illustrated by Hegel, continued to develop the notion of the absolute and grasp it as a central building block. The second, as illustrated by Berkeley, came to be called Subjective idealism. The objective idealist begins his investigation of truth with the problem of *a priori* knowledge and concludes it with the idea that there is one single explanation of the world: The Spirit or the Absolute. By contrast, the subjective idealist places his emphasis on the perceiving and thinking subject.

Berkeley, like Spinoza, postulates God as the source and anchorage for all permanence, but he emphasizes that no idea may exist without the particular mind that perceives it. Therefore, if some reflective agency (ultimately God) does not perceive something, then it doesn't exist. Or, in Berkeley's famous quote: "Their ESSE is PERCIPI, nor is it possible they should have any existence out of the minds or thinking things which perceive them" (Berkeley 2002, Principles, 1:3). Whereas in absolute idealism there is 'intuition' as source of absolute knowledge – through which the sublime may be known by its orders and essence – Berkeley does not think we may know God or anything equivalent to God. We may only know ourselves:

> For all the notion I have of God is obtained by reflecting on my own soul, heightening its powers, and removing its imperfections... My own mind and my own ideas I have an immediate knowledge of; and by the help of these, do mediately apprehend the possibility of the existence of other spirits and ideas. Further, from my own being, and from the dependency I find in myself and my ideas, I do by an act of reason necessarily infer the existence of a God, and of all created things in the mind of God.
>
> BERKELEY 2002, Dialogues: III

For Berkeley then, the point remains that we are dependent, almost exclusively, on our own particular mind. Phenomenology – studying as it does the structures of conscious experience from the subjective or first person point of view – may be seen as a methodological expression of Berkeley's epistemology. Here, the first-person perspective is considered to be the proper foundation of all knowledge and the only means by which we may acquire truth. Phenomenology preserved the transcendental function of subjectivity, but Husserl's version, which I present here, advocated departure from abstract metaphysical speculation and a return to contact with concrete living experience. Despite its return to the 'real' world, the emphasis of phenomenology on examining *only* the structures of consciousness still presents a challenge to third-person attempts to explain consciousness in terms of natural science.

I will present here the Intersubjective approach to truth by means of this prism in order to show the interrelation between the subjective and intersubjective as they intersect in epistemological definitions. Husserl declared that phenomenology was an egocentric philosophy, saying "transcendental subjectivity is the universe of possible sense" (Husserl 1999, cl. 41). For him, there is only one road to knowledge, that of radical and rigorous self-investigation. His latter movement into intersubjectivity may be seen as a precursor of a dominant trait in the philosophy of the 20th century, the movement from an isolated, self-aware ego onto the language of community.

Husserl coined the term 'intentionality' to express the idea that the subject's consciousness is always directed at something – an object of consciousness that is external to it. Intentionality, he thought, must always be held in mind when we come to investigate the nature of its objects. The nature of the object is, in fact, the manner in which it appears to a given consciousness and this must be the focus of all philosophical inquiry. This phenomenological investigation requires the establishment of a mental state that differs from the day to day consciousness, one that has prepared itself for the revelation of the object. Husserl calls this state of consciousness the 'epoche': Here, all previous knowledge is put into brackets in order to allow the inquiring subject to transcend the contingent and to grasp the essential properties of an object. The epoche creates a new area of consciousness – the transcendental cogito – where all knowledge is phenomenologically verified.

Bracketing the whole natural world, including ourselves, allows us to meticulously examine the particular in order to extract the essence of the objects and the principles of the transcendental function (Husserl 1983, 1:33–49). The problem with this technique is that it leaves the perceived world, potentially, as nothing but an eidetic creation of the cogito, namely, as remaining possibly in the realm of mental ideas. Despite the ongoing tension between subject and object in Husserl's thought and in spite of the central role of observation, Husserl's theory remains open to criticism on grounds of methodological solipsism and claims that it is exposed to the danger of creating detached subjective worlds that cannot explain the harmony that exists between the perceived worlds of different subjects.

To counter the above kind of criticism, Husserl turns to intersubjectivity, where subjective individual cogitos intersect in order to create objective world views and even objective realities. According to Husserl, we perceive the other through a physical, bodily-based, empathic process which places us amidst other subjects who experience and cognize just like us. In the empathic process, the other is not perceived as a figure of our consciousness or as an eidetic version of ourselves, but rather as a separate entity of distinct existence, transcendent to the self. Through the presence of foreign subjectivity, the world achieves its true transcendence, its objective reality, thus extricating itself from being a product of the self's consciousness alone. In this way, Husserl's phenomenological investigation of intersubjectivity is an analysis of the creation of transcendental reality rather than an examination of sociality or interpersonal relations.

According to Dan Zahavi (2003), Husserl contends that meaning may be formed only by means of an other, as are the categories of transcendence, objectivity and reality. Only after knowing the existence of a perceiving other, can I know that objects may not be reduced to being merely my intentional correlates, as they are also experienced by others. This intersubjective experiencability of the object underwrites its transcendence to objectivity. That is why the other is so vital. If the other were not other enough, if he were himself only an intentional variation of the subject, he would not possess this power of validation.

The transcending powers of intersubjectivity act not only at the level of cognizance, but already at the level of perception, in establishing the object as a set of features. Here, individual differences mark the passing, contingent features of the object, while similarities mark its essential features. The object has many possible appearances that may not be actualized by a single subject who is restricted to a single perspective. This creates a plurality of the object that may be apprehended only by a plurality of subjects. Therefore, only the intersubjective perception of the object ensures its true cognizance and is capable of validating individual statements about the object:

> Thus, everything objective that stands before me in experience and primarily in perception has an apperceptive horizon of possible experience, own and foreign. Ontologically speaking, every appearance that I have is from the very beginning a part of an open endless, but not explicitly realized totality of possible appearances of the same, and the subjectivity belonging to this appearance is open intersubjectivity.
>
> HUA XIV/289; SEE ALSO HUA IX/294, XV/497, quoted by ZAHAVI 2005, 239

The formation of the object's objectivity, then, is always intersubjective. Moreover, intersubjective-transcendental sociality is the source of all real knowledge, of truth as a mode of being: "Here we have the only transcendence that is really worth its name, and anything else that is also called transcendent, such as the objective world, depends upon the transcendence of a foreign subjectivity" (ibid.). The primary acknowledgement of the other and the creation of the intersubjective space are initially filtered through the subjective. Later, intersubjectivity acquires a transcendental role and knowledge is attained by the constant movement between subjective and intersubjective perspectives.

William James proposed that a methodology of radical empiricism establishes the same logic of connection between the transcendental, the objective and the intersubjective:

> If your objects do not coalesce with my objects, if they be not identically where mine are, they must be proved to be positively somewhere else… Practically, then, our minds meet in a world of objects which they share in common, which would still be there, if one or several of the minds were destroyed…. On the principles which I am defending, a 'mind' or 'personal consciousness' is the name for a series of experiences run together by certain definite transitions, and an objective reality is a series of similar experiences knit by different transitions.
>
> JAMES 2010, 79–80

A modern representative of the Intersubjective theory of truth is Richard Rorty. Whereas James and Husserl remain faithful to the experiencing of the object and its attributes, Rorty sees this fidelity as often unnecessary, especially outside the realm of natural sciences. In the world of humanities and social ideas, Rorty argues, the term 'intersubjectivity' could be replaced by 'objectivity', implying that no other objectivity is real. Rorty refers here to Dewey who, unlike Husserl's transcendental perspective, regards intersubjectivity as a set of investigative practices. For Dewey, objectivity is only the intersubjective agreement achieved by an open and free discussion between holders of all possible different opinions and hypotheses. Such a discussion allows us to examine our justifications for construing things one way and not the other. Rorty identifies between 'idealized rational acceptability' and 'acceptability to us at our best', because acceptability for him is not a matter of reason as such, but rather a matter of social agreement. He claims that there is a connection between intersubjectivity and ethnocentrism, which presents man and his wellbeing as the Archimedean point of all reference (Rorty 1998). The 'true' according to Rorty is not defined only in relation to a common ontology, but by reference to the future, to the best that exists in us as humans. Transcendence is rooted in our ability to look beyond our current practices towards the development of better future practices. In other words, Rorty supports examining the present in relation to the future, exclusive of claims for the eternal.

Such examination is always in the context of community and common consent, that is, connectable to a particular social reality. In Rorty's Intersubjective truth we find already a clear strain of pragmatism.

The Intersubjective theory of truth redeemed man from the dangers of solipsism implicated in Coherent truth and subjective epistemology, but it underlined others, that return again to the individual subject and his experiences: In what way do Intersubjective truths take the individual into account? How do they influence his interests? What are their practical implications as they are translated to the terms of a particular personal perspective? How do they maintain their practical link to the private life of the individual? To his emotions? And how does truth relate to other dimensions that are critical to human life such as time and development? The Pragmatic and Subjective-Existential theories of truth, which I will now present, addressed these neglected dimensions of experience.

The Pragmatic theory of truth: As a radical empiricist, James aimed for formulations derived solely from direct experience, with minimal conceptual filtering of sense data (James 2010). In other words, he objected to formulating experience in fixed and distinct units which, he felt, necessarily deny the significance of the *connections* among these units as delivered by experience itself. This theory of connections is central to James's approach. Connections are essential for perceiving the ever moving stream of consciousness which continuously fluctuates between the identified and conceptualized units, even if our speech is too dull to 'nail down' and describe the transitions. James's throbbing awareness of movement necessarily introduces the element of time into his theory of truth.

According to the Pragmatic theory, truth is what the future proves to be true. Both Peirce and James, who are the main representatives of the Pragmatic theory, agree on this point. James's truth is process based. Its validation is always situated in the future and tomorrow, today's truth may be no more than an opinion (James 2004). An idea becomes true by the occurrence of events:

> Day follows day, and its contents are simply added. The new contents themselves are not true, they simply COME and ARE. Truth is what we say about them .... That new idea...makes itself true, gets itself classed as true, by the way it works.... New truths thus are resultants of new experiences and of old truths combined and mutually modifying one another.
>
> JAMES 2004, 77

Charles Sanders Peirce advocates what came to be called 'pragmaticism', a philosophical viewpoint that is related to pragmatism, in which truth is viewed as an endlessly ongoing process. In Peircean thought, truth and meaning (semiosis) are inseparable, both between themselves and in relation to their objects of reference. The semiotic process moves through a chain of interpretants. An interpretant is a sign that interprets a sign that appeared before it and determines the one that will follow it. The interpretant contains the understanding we had reached of a former sign or sign-object relation. It effectively offers a 'translation' of the original sign, allowing us a more complex understanding of the sign's object. The appearance of the interpretant defines it as a sign in itself, thereby giving rise, immediately, to another interpretant. Each interpretant relays additional information regarding the object of inquiry and, in that way, the interpretative chain leads towards an evolving truth. Thus, the semiotic process moves backward in relation to the object that triggered it while, at the same time, moving forward in relation to the interpretant.

If any sign must generate an interpretant in order to be a sign, and any sign is itself the interpretant of an earlier sign, then clearly, with regard to any given instance of signification, there are infinite signs preceding it, as well as infinite signs proceeding from it. 'The dynamic object', as Peirce terms it, generates a chain of signs that, in turn, allows an understanding of the object by assimilating it into our system of signs. Peirce calls 'the immediate object' that which we presume to be real throughout the course of our inquiry. The immediate object is an informationally incomplete version of the dynamic object, a version that is generated at some interim stage in a chain of signs. Semiosis is an act of knowing by an infinite regression, with each interpretant passing on the 'torch of truth' (Peirce 1958, 339).

By presuming truth to be an unending series of interpretations, Peirce takes an epistemological position that is fallible and anti-foundational. In his theory, truth is always an evolutionary process and can never be fully realized. For him, the only important element of scientific thinking is to apply the scientific method. He held this method to be essentially public and reproducible, as well as self-correcting in the following sense: Peirce believed that no matter where different researchers began their research, if they followed the scientific method, their results would eventually converge toward the same outcome. This ideal point of convergence is what Peirce refers to as 'truth', and 'reality' is the eventual product of what we deem as truth. Outside the transcendental ideal realm, "…the nature of the belief, …(can only be) the result of investigation carried sufficiently far; and if, after the extinction of our race, another should arise with faculties and disposition for investigation, that true opinion must be the one which they would ultimately come to" (Peirce 1878, 4).

Peirce continues to offer a psychological theory of truth – "at every given moment, our truth will translate into a habit: …What a thing means is simply what habits it involves...Consider what effects...we conceive the object of our conception to have. Then, our conception of these effects is the whole of our conception of the object" (Peirce 1878, 3).

Like Peirce, James defined the subjective conditions of belief and a particular methodology as constituting what we know of truth. In the context of scientific ideas, both theoreticians agreed that truth is intersubjectively constituted. They believed that true ideas lead to the continuity, stability and development of human discourse. They viewed as indicative of falsehood such features as eccentricity, isolation or futile thinking and found much relevance in the public consideration of belief. Still, they also ascribed truth value to beliefs that concern the individual. James, for example, is willing to grant truth value to an individual belief if it leads the believer to experience life differently.

When there is no valid reason to choose between arguments that contradict each other, there is truth value in choosing to believe in the argument that seems to lead to the more satisfying result (James 2004). Clearly then, James's theory of truth concerns the usefulness and practicality of an idea *in the context of the particular believer's life*. Truth theory is thus personalized: A true phrase is a phrase that reflects a desire on one hand and leads to achieving the desired results on the other. A false phrase is a phrase that will not lead to the desired results. When examining the truth value of a phrase we must ask: 'what difference will the truth of this phrase bring to my life?'

Pragmatic truth, like pragmatic epistemology, avoids abstract philosophical formulations. It lays concrete criteria for the determination of truth; criteria which have actual implications on the lives of actual people. The Subjective-Existential theory of truth continues this line of thought and moves away from intersubjective definitions in order to attempt to define the unique authentic truth that guides the life of any given person.

The Subjective-Existential theory of truth: "Existence is prior to essence" (Sartre 1956, 12). This is one of the best-known phrases coined by Jean-Paul Sartre, who was the leading post-war philosopher in continental Europe. The phrase means that the actual existence of the individual takes precedence over any a priori essence or meaning and is the primary core of any truth whose subject is human. This idea is at the root of the Existential theory of truth, which takes further the line of thought laid out by James when he argued that truth is established by personal life, out of our involvement in life and through the actions we take. But this theory adds a complex argument regarding the role of the 'other' and the role of reflection, responsibility and authenticity in the subject's formation of his own truth. I will present this theory, as I did others, by showing its interrelations with the previously presented theories.

Dale Cannon (1996) protests the fact that the Existential theory of truth does not appear in introductory literature on philosophies of truth and argues for the pertinence of this theory, initially formulated by Soren Kierkegaard and later elaborated by Heidegger, Jaspers and Marcel. In his dissertation,[8] Kierkegaard presented Socrates's sceptical character and the decree he bequeathed: 'know thyself'.

According to Elleray's interpretation (2007), Kierkegaard first distinguished between the theories of Plato and Socrates. While Plato based his thinking on the Theory of Forms – of which our experiences are no more than particular examples – Socrates was an ironic sceptic who forced us to look into ourselves and our existence when making decisions (Elleray 2007, 1). When one understands this, one cannot avoid responsibility for truth. One cannot escape to absolutist standards of objectivity. The Socratic formulation of the 'know thyself' dictum brings forth a new conceptualization of selfhood. The individual is grasped as essentially linked to truth and *he must know himself before he can know anything else*. This approach positions both knowledge and truth in the person himself. In order to access them, one must address experience, as reflective thought does not suffice. In 'Philosophical Fragments' Kierkegaard (1985), through the mouth of Climacus, declares his intention to transcend Socrates's reflectiveness: it does not suffice.

In order to describe the manner in which the subject reaches truth, Kierkegaard/Climacus uses the concept of the 'moment' as opposed to the Socratic concept of 'remembrance'. The 'moment' is the transitional instance from disbelief to belief, from false to true. It is the moment of subjective truth in the sense of free choice that searches not for justification in an external objective standard, but for developing an individual way of life. 'Moment' allows Kierkegaard to think of the individual as an actual subject on an active journey to the truth, a journey that involves the transformation of his being. Kierkegaard thinks of truth not as an object of knowledge but as an actual living, a human practice. This is the manner in which he takes the Socratic notion of truth one step further. The truth one lives by is subjective and it realizes a person's life and the way he chooses to live it. It is necessarily particular and subjective.[9]

As shown in the Intersubjective theory of truth, the notion of the 'other' circumvents the danger of subjective solipsism and allows the establishment of transcendence and objectivity. But this same other, in the Existential

8 "The Concept of Irony with Continual Reference to Socrates" (Kierkegaard 1841/1989).

9 As detailed in Chapter 1, Heidegger's 'aletheia' incorporates the elements of subjectivity, temporality and realization that Kierkegaard introduced as crucial in the definition of truth.

approach, is a constant threat to the freedom, authenticity and truth of the individual. For Heidegger authentic truth is always in danger of being subjugated by the common sense of the 'they' (Heidegger 1996). For Sartre this subjugation is effected by the objectifying gaze of the other, whereby the subject gazed upon experiences himself as an object and suffers from a loss of singularity and freedom (Sartre 1956).

The other creates a world that competes with my world and intersubjectivity leads to the loss of subjectivity. This encounter may be the only way in which I can become conscious of *my* world, but it poses its possibilities and truths as something I must now struggle for. So, even intersubjectivity cannot bring us peace, we must emerge from it and continue our search after our individual world and truth.

The Existential theory seeks relative freedom from the gaze of the other and its abstraction in a universal truth. Socrates, Plato, Kant and Husserl, all focused on the universal, unified subject and the ethical concepts of truth and good for all. The closer one gets to truth and moral integrity, the more similar one becomes to others who are at the same stage of advancement. Kierkegaard responded to this line of thought by maintaining that each subject must find both personal truth and integrity and an individual way to achieve it. His followers emphasized the inevitable and ongoing tensions between the self and its truths and the validating and nullifying other.

Combined Models and Influences

So far I have presented the various truth notions in their 'pure' form, in order to show how each notion is embedded in a broader epistemological context that determines its logic. The Paradigmatic notions of truth reflect paradigmatic world views and modes of being. The religious person who exists in a transcendental world leads a life different from the life led by a person who exists in the exclusive kingdom of his own five senses. A person searching for inner mental coherence is different from a person who searches for consensus among his peers. The existential person will often find himself in conflict with his interpersonal environment, while he tries to extract, explain and clarify his truths. In each of these worlds, truth is an Archimedean point, a focal point around which the experience of the self can crystallize at any given moment.

However, it seems that no person lives according to one particular, pure world view. It is more likely to presume that, while a person wanders between his religious world and his practical world, while his day includes Subjective-Existential and Intersubjective experiences, as his dreams unravel the coherence he managed to embroider into his day, to that extent, these worlds exist for him simultaneously. Every person entertains different modes of being that represent these perspectives; in fact, all of them, in one way or another. Seen this way, the different philosophical views act as simplified abstractions of the diverse modalities of actual existence. Each attempts to sketch one of these experiential worlds in its deepest purity.

A glance at additional definitions of truth will shed some light on the manner in which they combine a number of pure versions and take epistemological elements of different theories into account. By demonstrating these mixed models, I will show that, although each truth theory assumes one central link as determining definitive truth value (such as the link between fact and belief, or the link between different beliefs), it usually is unable to deny additional connections which are emphasized in other theories and necessarily exist in the philosophic horizon and discourse of the theory at hand, even if they do not stand at the forefront of it.

I will show how crucial elements of one theory 'infiltrate' another. Then I will go on to argue that the lack of ability to stick with one pure epistemology and rely on a single criterion for deriving truth values proves that, at any given moment and in most contexts of the subject's conscious horizon, there are numerous relevant truth criteria. But to fully realize a person's mental potential, it is not enough to logically accept the simultaneous existence of the various truth theories. We must understand that the multiplicity of truth reflects a deep existential tenet of mental life: The subject exists in a number of different epistemologies and lives according to the various truths they give rise to.

An example of combinatory influences upon truth definitions can be found in the Semantic theories of truth. These theories attempt to mediate between Intersubjective components, as they are expressed in language, and intuitions that comply with the Correspondent theory of truth. They offer an a priori definition of truth as inherently connected to language and seek linguistic agreements to enable a clear and intuitive definition of truth. In his formative paper 'The Semantic Concept of Truth' (Tarski 1994) Alfred Tarski derives truth values from specific syntactic forms. This radically relativizes truth, because a sentence may be true in one language and false or meaningless in another language.

By deriving truth from syntactic structures, Tarski distances himself from any metaphysical commitment. For him, truth in a logical sense may hold only to sentences that are part of a language and only within this language. In fact, the picture is even more complicated. For Tarski, sentences can only be determined for truth by recourse to two languages, one that contains the target sentence, called object language (L), and one that contains the whole of the first language and its truth definitions, called metalanguage (M). In this model, every definition of truth is given in what later came to be called 'a T structure'. For example, the sentence 'snow is white' is true if and only if snow is white.

Here, the sentence 'snow is white' appears with quotation marks on the left side of an equivalence structure, but not on the right side of it. The left side holds a formal object ('the phrase') that is isolated in the structure by comas, the way names often are, while the right side holds its meaning, its connection with external reality (the phrase). The general form of truth appears in this relation of equivalence as a logical, abstract definition, where the formal part (FP) is given in an object language L, while the informal part (IP) is given in M. The reduced form of this principle is (T) FP is true if and only if IP

The truth definitions of L are given in M, which circumvents the antimonies and paradoxes of semantically-closed languages (languages that contain their own truth criteria). Here, the conditions for correct reference do not imply correspondence to facts, but rather adherence to the way in which the language defines its objects. The semantic system of the language already includes the particular properties of those objects that are part of the language. Sentences have to cohere with these properties in order to achieve truth value.

Tarski has naturally been accused of circularity, reducing truth to the status of adequate use of linguistic semantics. Indeed, he was one of the progenitors of what was later termed 'Deflationary' theories of truth.[10] Yet, in trying to

10 Stated in great simplification, Deflationary theories may be defined as theories that treat the truth predicate as having only a logical or grammatical function, rather than as ascribing a property or relation to a truth bearer, as in Correspondent, Pragmatic and Coherent notions of truth. Among these deflationary theories are the Redundancy, Disquotation, Preformative and Minimalist notions of truth. Ramsey (1927), associated with the *Redundancy* theory proposed, that the predicate *true* makes no substantive contribution to what is asserted in a statement. For example: "'it is true that Caesar was murdered' means no more than that Caesar was murdered" (Ramsey 1927 157); meaning that 'It is true that…' is redundant. Closely related is the notion of *Disquotationism*. Addressing the T structure, disquotationalists will claim that the ascription of truth just cancels the quotation marks. It is enough to utter a sentence, the truth predicate is superfluous. The usefulness of the truth predicate is to be found in such contexts such as generalization. For example, when asserting "John believes everything that Mary says is true", we are spared the explication and validation of all of Mary's statements in infinite conjunction. The convenient expression of such generalization is precisely the role of the truth predicate in language. Another deflationary theory, describes how the addition of 'true' to a sentence that relates to a sentence that had appeared formerly, makes the latter a *'prosentence'*. A prosentence is a device to reference a word or words uttered previously in a conversation, just as pronouns are devices to reference names uttered previously in a conversation. Strawson (1950) sees such a prosentence as having also a *performative* role. In asserting

overcome the conceptual hardships of the Correspondence theory, he exposed the intimate tie between truth and language. Although he originally addressed formal languages in his formulations, Tarski effectively showed that it is impossible to separate the knowledge of a language from knowledge of the world. Since here truth is immanent to a given language, it is determined by intersubjective rules and habits.

Just as Tarski's Semantic theory echoes the Correspondent theory of truth, and Husserl's transcendental Intersubjective theory does not exclude subjectivity as a source of truth, pronounced empiricists like Willard Quine and Karl Popper utilize subjective and intersubjective components in order to distance themselves from naïve realism and the quest for the absolute. As an empiricist, Quine addresses truth from a scientific research perspective, but he also examines it in a linguistic context. Only when we are positioned in the framework of an existing theory can we look back and determine if a spoken sentence is true. Determining the truth of a sentence depends on the logic of a specific theory in conjunction with its language-specific properties (Quine 1960). In this sense, truth is immanent to our theory of the world, and its existence is always relative to a language. Therefore, like Tarski, Quine argues that the definition of truth values may change from one language to another (Quine 1960, 76; 1995, 16).

Popper's commitment to the theory of Correspondence places him in the realist school of thought. But following Kant, Popper opposes the positivist stance, where basic statements (present tense observational sentences with sensory objects) 'report' sensations that are passively perceived by a processing mechanism. Popper recognizes that these sentences are descriptions of what has been seen, as construed by the viewer and in relation to a defined theoretical framework. Thus Popper, like Peirce, emphasizes the universal possibility of making an error, a possibility deeply rooted in human thinking. The brain works in a crowded theoretical framework, both on the cognitive level and on the interpretive level. For this reason, a basic sentence is not a

that *p* is true, we not only assert that *p*, we also perform the "speech act" of signaling our agreement or approbation of a previously uttered assertion or confirm some commonly held belief or imply that what we are asserting is likely to be accepted by others in the same context. Horwich's theory of truth (1990) known as the *Minimalist theory*, takes the primary truth-bearing entities to be propositions, rather than sentences. According to this view, truth is indeed a property of propositions (or sentences, as the case may be) but it is so minimal and anomalous a property that it cannot be said to provide us with any useful information about or insight into the nature of truth. It is fundamentally nothing more than a sort of metalinguistic property. The minimalist thesis asserts that the conjunction of all of the instances of the T-structure provide us with the most we will ever have as a definition of the property of truth.

sealed statement but an open assumption: It has a causal relationship of some sort with experience, but it is not defined and set according to it. Moreover, the sentence cannot be validated or refuted by experience only. Thus, he says, "Basic statements are not justifiable by our immediate experiences, but are... accepted by an act, a free decision" (Popper 1959, 109). This argument obfuscates the clarity of Popper's theory of refutation. A piece of data used to refute a theory must first be accepted as valid and relevant data. This is a 'free' and an arbitrary act.[11] Popper travels the dialectic territory ranging between convention (Intersubjective theory of truth) and the realistic approach to truth (Correspondent).

The human 'gaze' and the kind of descriptions that originate in gaze are inextricably saturated by theory. This is how a seemingly surprising common denominator emerges between Popper and Heidegger's Dasein approach. Popper refers to the knowledge-laden background needed for forming a sentence. Heidegger calls this background ontology. Human understanding is formed at every moment by intersecting the ongoing state of mind with the background ontology. Such intersections are called 'Dasein' and form the basic human condition. One must first understand the nature of Dasein in order to learn how to interpret reality: People, objects and concepts. Dasein as a being-in-the-world discovers entities and discloses them by means of his gaze.[12] Therefore, all theoretic statements are secondary to the basic manner in which Dasein relates to the world: "In accordance with the essential kind of being appropriate to Dasein, all truth is relative to the being of Dasein" (Heidegger 1996, 208/227).

Rather than subsisting as a transcendental quality, Heidegger asserts that Dasein produces the truth of its world through the way that it exists in its world. Not only does Dasein establish the truth of entities through this process of uncovering, Dasein discloses the truth of its own existence through the manner in which it approaches its lived in world. Dasein understands itself in terms of its projected possibilities. Similarly, in apprehending reality, it projects previous understandings at specified topics. The world can be evaluated and described in many ways that are not necessarily consistent with each other and choices are made, says Heidegger, by finding out which ontological approach explains the creation of a particular point of view in a particular state of mind.

11 This line of thinking is the one elaborated and developed by Kuhn (1962\1996) who revealed the sociological substrata of scientific discovery.

12 "In that Dasein essentially is its disclosedness and as disclosed, discloses and discovers" (Heidegger 1996, 203/221).

Davidson, like Heidegger, rejects the object-subject divide and offers a theory of truth in which equal weight is given to the empiric, the semantic and the interpersonal elements as they join in a communicative event. Davidson (2001), like Quine (1960) subordinates truth to language; taking an additional step, he goes on to link it to a particular time and speaker. Seeing truth as originating in the connection between sentences, speakers and transitory states of affairs, he connects it with two other basic terms: meaning and belief. The assumption here is that most of our beliefs are correct in the sense that they hold some value of truth.[13] Davidson poses this as an analytic truth and a fact regarding the manner in which we use language.

Here Davidson presents the logic of his argument: The mere possibility of correct understanding of speech, beliefs, wishes and intentions, together with the wide array of personal references, implies that most beliefs are true in their appropriate context. The ability to formulate a meaningful statement already entails the assumption of its truth and "what ultimately ties language to the world is that the conditions that typically cause us to hold sentences true *constitute* the truth conditions and hence, the meanings, of our sentences" (Davidson 1996, 275). To wit, the very meaningfulness of sentences already presumes their truth in relation to the belief that is associated with them. What we believe to be true determines the implied meaning of our speech and so, indirectly, the truth value of our sentence. At this point Davidson comes full circle to where he began when relating truth to time and speaker. Truth is bound up with language, where any particular utterance is governed by a speaker who holds particular beliefs. These are embedded in a particular, temporary state of affairs.

Davidson's theory offers a prominent contemporary example of a truth theory that is tightly woven into a broader outlook. His theory of truth is valid only in a world that is experienced directly by a subject, without the mediation of sensory information, representation or linguistic articulation. In this world, the subject-object divide is collapsed and language does not carry a representational function. Thought is created and formulated, at the very basis, in the communal realm of interpersonal communication that takes place in a shared material world. As long as the dialogue between us and our surroundings endures, thought continues to evolve. This is the triangular Davidsonian situation: Two creatures who are communicating about a common world constitute themselves as thinkers in the context of their shared empiric reality. The ultimate source of objectivity is, according to Davidson, intersubjectivity situated

13 "...belief is in its nature veridical" (Davidson 2001,146).

in such a reality.[14] The triangle Davidson refers to exists in the actuality of a given context. Yet, it implicates an interpretation, a meaning that is assigned post hoc. The need for interpretation intertwines truth and meaning in an inextricable manner.

A consequence of posing the Davidsonian triangle as a condition of thought is that it is not possible to assign epistemic priority to the self's beliefs or the other's beliefs. In a similar way, since truth is crucially dependent upon linguistic formulation, one cannot assign epistemic priority to the external world. The three sides of the Davidsonian triangle are of equal epistemic import and therefore no logical or other boundaries can be drawn among objective, subjective and intersubjective knowledge. This is an ambitious declaration that transcends scepticism of the senses on the one hand and of other minds on the other (Davidson 2001, 87, 219).

Truth and Reality in Epistemological Framework

As can be seen from the discussion above, there are different approaches to the question of how our perceived reality is created. The simplest answer may be that of metaphysical and epistemological realism: We see the world the way it 'is'. We are equipped to do so. Facts and situations are independent of sentences and statements. Their independence allows the former to be compared to the latter and form the basis for Correspondent truth. But this situation changes once we understand that there is no perceivable fact that is not already permeated by our linguistic reality. Elements of language and thought are woven so deeply into facts and situations, that the possibility of setting them apart and comparing between them is non-existent. Davidson recognizes this and assumes that all we know of truth and reality is constituted in the intersubjective context of linguistic communication. In contradistinction, the advocates of Coherence see truth as created by the consistent and harmonious interrelations among our beliefs. Existentialists do not acknowledge any essence prior to existence and therefore see truth as constituted through direct experience of being. As noted earlier, objective idealists see our world as faintly mirroring ideal forms that we may approach by rational means. Different

14 "The possibility of thought as well as communication depends…on the fact that two or more creatures are responding, more or less simultaneously, to input from a shared world, and from each other… It is this triangular nexus of causal relations involving the reactions of two creatures to each other and to shared stimuli in the world that supplies the conditions necessary for the concept of truth to have application" (Davidson 2001, 83).

epistemologies give rise to different realities. *Experienced reality is the embodiment of an ontology that is tied up with an epistemology on the outer side and with truth on the inner side, as a point of certainty.*

In discussing the Correspondent theory of truth, Rorty (1998) distinguishes between two assumptions that are crucially different from each other: The assumption that the world exists 'out there' and the assumption that the truth exists independently of the cognizing minds. The first assumption states that the world is not a creation of our minds. It is similar to the claim that most elements in space and time are the effect of phenomena that are not human; especially, they are not states of mind. Rorty has no trouble with the first assumption. Yet, to claim that the truth is independent of the cognizing mind means that sentences, propositions and beliefs are not an essential part of the concept of truth and that is untenable for him (ibid). The world is a given, but descriptions of the world are not. In so far as the word 'knowledge' has any meaning, the world is knowable; but it is interpretable otherwise, it has no one meaning behind it, but countless meanings. Here we come full circle to Nietzche's Perspectivism.

Nietzsche's Perspectivism can be seen as a development of Kant's transcendentalism, in which knowledge is shaped by the ways consciousness captures reality. According to Kant, it is vital always to distinguish between the distinct realms of phenomena and noumena. Phenomena are the appearances that constitute our *experience*; noumena are the things that are presumed to constitute *reality*. All of our judgments apply only to the phenomenal realm, not the noumenal. It is only at this level, with respect to what we can experience, that we are justified in imposing the structure of our concepts onto the objects of knowledge. Since the thing in itself (*das ding an sich*) would, by definition, be entirely independent of our experience, we are utterly ignorant of the noumenal realm.

> What we have meant to say is that all our intuition is nothing but the representation of appearance; that the things which we intuit are not in themselves what we intuit them as being, nor their relations so constituted in themselves as they appear to us, and that if the subject, or even only the subjective constitution of the senses in general, be removed, the whole constitution and all the relations of objects in space and time, nay space and time themselves, would vanish. As appearances, they cannot exist in themselves, but only in us. What objects may be in themselves, and apart from all this receptivity of our sensibility, remains completely unknown to us. We know nothing but our mode of perceiving them – a mode which is peculiar to us, and not necessarily shared in by every being, though, certainly, by every human being. ... Even if we could bring

> our intuition to the highest degree of clearness, we should not thereby come any nearer to the constitution of objects in themselves. We should still know only our mode of intuition, that is, our sensibility. … What the objects may be in themselves would never become known to us even through the most enlightened knowledge of that which is alone given us, namely, their appearance.
>
> KANT 2013

According to Kant, then, the rational human faculties lead us to the very boundaries of what can be known. Beyond those boundaries, our faculties are useless. Within them, we explore not only the phenomena, but what Kant termed our 'subjective constitution', through which we can study the different ways in which our consciousness brings reality to us.

Whereas Kant addressed the way consciousness structures phenomena, James gave an analogous account of the way consciousness structures experience and, thereby, subjectivity. As he saw it, experience is a never ending flow of images, sensations, thoughts and words (James 2013). This influx consists of singular moments that do not resemble one another. A person moves in this stream and tries to orient himself by generating meaning within it. In James's line of thought, a distinct unit of meaning can never be fully grasped, because its delineation is always an artefact and its significance is inherently tied up with the direction and connectivity in thought and experience. Even when a distinct image is displayed on the screen of our consciousness, its meaning is determined by its surrounding periphery (James 2013, 1:271). Similarly, meanings of words cannot always be directly examined or introspectively analysed. They can only be sensed as mental chaperons of a word, directing our thought towards additional images, words and actions. Language provides us with tools to create order and fulcrums within the stream of experience. However, there is no symbolic function, not even in the complexity of language, which can fully grasp and express experience in its entirety.

Experience is always broader than its representation; its transcribeable elements are no more than crumbs from the rich meal of experience (ibid. 276). Few as they may be, without these crumbs we have nothing, no 'islands' in the stream, no memory material. The symbolic role of consciousness is in identifying or constructing forms that distinguish themselves from the stream of consciousness and have the stability that allows their transcription. We will not find the full meaning 'in' any of the orders we create. Parts of it will be found in them and other parts will be found beyond them, in the logic of the connectivity between them. James's description provides us with a pragmatic and subjectively oriented version of the Kantian insight.

According to the theory I am about to present, *truth axes* are organizational principles that provide us with different viable construals of reality. They extract the forms from the background magma of reality. They create the Jamesian islands in the stream, and present us with abstractions and formal definitions of our modes of consciousness, of the automatic activity of subjective constitution. The activity of our consciousness is not detached from our emotions and needs and its forms provide answers to our deep need for certainty, security and direction. This need is expressed in relation to a number of different dimensions: The physical world, the realm of values, personal goals, social milieu, existential sensibilities and integrity of self. The need for certainty has as many manifestations as notions of truth.

From Truth Notions to Truth Axes

The different paradigmatic truths that I describe here are nodal points of certainty in the symbolic paradigms that organize our world and give rise to our images of reality. In order to understand them as such, one must put aside a number of common assumptions about truth. First, one must give up the idea that truth is one and absolute. Second, one must keep in mind that truth is inextricably tied up with the subject and determined by his needs. Third, truth is not static; it is not a specific point of reference regarding a particular fact or statement. Instead, it is a dynamic product of a long and gradual process of ordering. Fourth, different notions of truth do not invalidate each other. Each notion relies, in one way or another, on the way that another notion captures a different aspect of reality.

As happens in other subject-relevant domains, the individual subject recapitulates the path of the historic subject. The abstract notions of truth reflect the particular subject's search for stability and constancy according to which he can anchor his understanding of himself and of his world. This particular subject seems to know something about each and all of these abstract truths though he may not know their articulation. He has an inner knowledge of them, an intuitive grasp of their meanings.

The interface between subject and world is a complex one, mediated by the subject's needs. And here I return to Nietzsche's quote, underlining his reference to the interpretative role of human needs and their potential tyranny: "It is our needs that interpret the world; our drives and their 'For' and 'Against'. Every drive is a kind of lust to rule; each one has its perspective that it would like to compel all the other drives to accept as a norm" (Nietzsche 1968, cl.481).

This point, whereby the world is construed in accordance with our needs, is a nodal one. We create the realities we need. But as we have *various* needs and various images of the world, we form realities in accordance with them. Every reality gives rise to its own organic truth. Thus, we remain with different realities and different truths. In addition, every need has a 'lust to rule'; it craves exclusivity. Man tends to succumb to the promise of an unshifting image of reality, the comfort of a single truth. Nevertheless, all needs continue with their 'interpretations' of the world, creating images of reality and truth that do not necessarily overlap or cohere.

Each image of reality captures a possible, yet incomplete, aspect of experience. Its organic truth serves as a point of certainty within it. In each reality resides a characteristic self-state that is guided, directed and motivated by its truth. The complex of epistemic assumption, characteristic self-state, image of reality and its experienced truth form together a truth axis. In that sense, a truth axis is a multi-dimensional mental domain. The truth axes, their products and their motivational forces exist on all levels of mental activity, from basic experiences of sensation and emotion, to ground level representations (memory, imagination, etc.) and then to outlooks on life, both intuitive and formulated (e.g., in language). They give rise to the subject's interpretations of the world, as well as to his experience of himself.

Truth Axes and Psychological Needs

To wit, truth axes organize the world in certain paradigmatic ways that are meant to provide for several basic human needs. *Each organizational principle provides for a deep emotional need which motivates its formulation.* These needs unify each axis in a particular logic and motivate its development. Let me briefly sketch these needs.

At the root of the *Correspondent axis* is the need to be in touch with external reality so as to enhance the chances of survival, through explaining, responding to and anticipating events that influence the exchanges between man and the mind-independent world around him.

At the root of the *Coherent axis* of truth is the need for compatibility and harmony among a person's beliefs, expectations, and behavioral tendencies. Coherence allows the smooth transition among the various activities that the subject is engaged with, as well as among different fields of knowledge and different experiences. This, in turn, allows the individual to create a sense of identity, continuity and regularity across time.

Man's need for perfection and completeness, for that which bestows guidance, meaning, and validity to daily life and allows overcoming the repulsive, the abhorred and the arbitrary, is at the root of the *Ideal axis* of truth. Ideal truths give man a sense of the eternal, of harmony and beauty on the macro level, serving as both directives and sources of motivation.

The *Subjective-Existential axis* arises in the subject's need to be loyal to *himself*, to be positioned at center stage as a criterion for planning his life and determining meaning without subordinating himself to a universal concept of subject or truth. This axis of truth also embodies acutely bodily sensitivity and experience.

The organization of experience in terms of future benefit is the basis for the *Pragmatic axis* of truth. This axis addresses the need to feel effective in one's ability to achieve one's goals in the world. It embodies active agency and overcomes the experience of helplessness and inevitability. It differentiates between forward and backward in a person's life and allows a sense of progress or regress as time goes by.

At the root of the *Intersubjective axis* of truth is the profound need for a connection with those around us and a shared reality with them. At the center of this axis resides the representation of the psychoanalytic object and the ability of the subject to cohere with the inner dynamics of this representation. But the axis also generalizes the need for a singular object to the gratifying experience of belonging and cohering with a whole social field.

On the whole, the basic need is the one that drives the creation of the truth axis and maintains its relevance throughout the subject's life. These pairings of needs with truth conceptions is summarized in Diagram 1.

Each of the above needs is satisfied by *a vital link* between the experiencing subject and an aspect of his inner or outer world. Thus, the need to negotiate external reality is addressed by the link between the belief of the subject and

Truth Axes and Corresponding Needs

Truth Axis	Basic Psychological Needs
• Correspondent	• Need to handle factual reality
• Coherent	• Need for internal coherence in perception of self and world
• Intersubjective	• Need for shared interpersonal reality
• Subjective-Existential	• Need for living authentically
• Pragmatic	• Need to promote goals and interests.
• Ideal	• Need for guiding ideals.

DIAGRAM 1 *Truth axes and corresponding needs*

what he perceives as realistic facts. Coherence is negotiated by the link between the subject's various beliefs and tendencies. The need for attachment and commonality with others is, of course, provided for by the link with others. The need for authentic existence is ensured by means of the subject's link to what he perceives as his true self. The aspiration for perfection is realized by examining the correspondence a subject finds between beliefs or tendencies he has and what he perceives as his ideal. The need to enhance future benefit is provided for by the subject's ability to associate between belief or action and their future implications. These same links are the ones from which truth values are derived in the various truth notions.

Each truth axis organizes the subject's world in a way that best accommodates the constitution and the preservation of a particular link between the subject and an aspect of his inner or outer world. On the whole, the basic need that is provided for by any particular link is the one that drives the creation of the truth axis and maintains its vitality and relevance throughout the subject's life. These links are not innately given, but rather involve the surmounting of developmental challenges and crises, as I will describe in detail in Chapter 4.

Truth Axes and Realities

Each truth axis yields a viable potential construction of the stream of consciousness and experience. As it organizes raw elements of experience in different ways, each gives rise to a distinct image of reality. The question of reality becomes a question of understanding the mutual relations between the different elements of a particular organization and the transitions among them. The various truth axes co-exist in consciousness as prisms through which various realities are construed, each giving rise to a different experience of self and world.

The Correspondent truth axis creates a 'factual' reality enabling us to negotiate the mind-independent reality around us. In this reality we rely heavily on sense information, observe and try to master the realistic constraints in which we live our lives. The Coherent truth axis produces for us a cohesive and consistent reality at the level of both personal identity and perceived externality. This axis often functions to relegate facts and tendencies that do not cohere with one's core beliefs about self and world. The Ideal truth axis embodies a reality to which we aspire and in which we believe. It exists within us and at times outside of us. We move toward its realization in many things we do and find guidance within it. The Pragmatic truth axis creates a reality that resonates our objectives and interests. Here, we may plan and decide in ways that determine what may best enhance our well-being. We exist within it as active, initiating agents. The Subjective-Existential truth axis produces a person's subjective-authentic image of reality, containing his private, often hidden truths; finally, the Intersubjective truth axis creates the reality we share with those around us. The realities corresponding to the various axes are shown schematically in Diagram 2.

The six organizing axes exist in the psychic space of every person in different forms and degrees of dominance. Each person may have one or two dominant axes, whose relation to other axes may vary considerably. One person may be more responsive to ideals, while another responds to the people around him and allows them to determine his aspirations, fears and wishes. This person will probably experience a sense of belonging and creativity when he is part of an establishment, while another person will only experience self-worth when he is guided predominantly by his inner truths. Every organizing axis can have constructive or pathological expressions but, in both cases, the underlying logic of truth will be apparent. Of course, a person does not always respond to events with the same logic of truth. Different contexts arousing different needs may activate one or another of the axes at particular times.

Loosely phrased, the epistemological assumptions of the subject are a part of his procedural unconscious in the sense that they rule the processes that give rise to his construals of the world. While the subject is rarely aware of the process that gives rise to his experienced reality, he is aware, often acutely, of

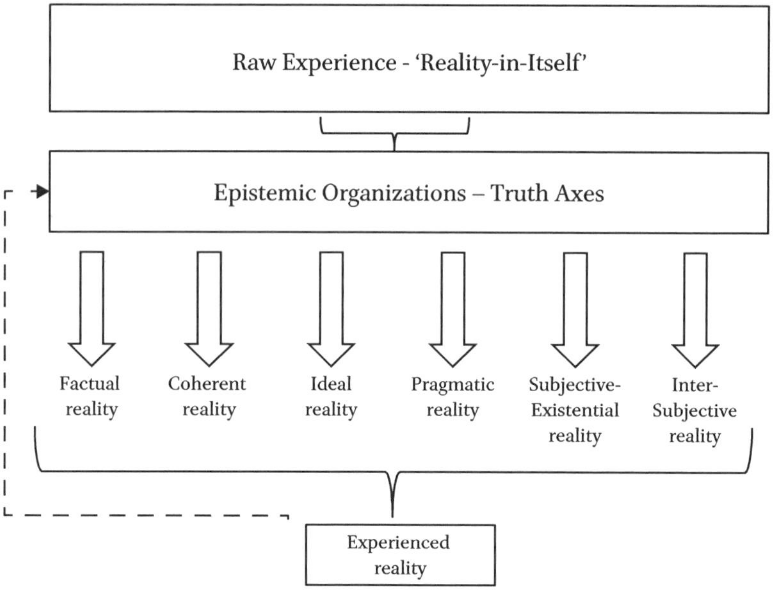

DIAGRAM 2 *Truth axes and corresponding realities*

the truths within this reality. These truths, alongside the validity attributed to them, indicate the differential dominance of the various axial organizations his psyche employs.

All in all, we have different levels of abstraction at which truth axes are here discussed. The *metaphysical* level refers to the needs of the human subject as expressed along different dimensions of his life. The *epistemological* level seeks to lay out the different general modes by which we organize, construe and conceptualize our world in line with these needs. The *ontological* level, which is based on the epistemological level, creates a platform for the detailed myriad content that fills these epistemic outlooks. *Experientially*, the subject lives in a *reality* which is an embodiment of a particular ontology, and in which certain *truths* are valid. The truth is the potently experienced point of gravity in each image of reality. The various epistemic approaches yield corresponding ontologies, which are in effect, the 'parallel worlds' in which the subject resides. Truth and reality here are effectively the experiential counterpart of the ontology formed within each epistemology.

Usually, one lives according to directives of various different truth axes simultaneously. This multiplicity, its richness and complexity, is revealed in the human experience of the world. All that we experience in the world is transcribed in our psyche in several discrete registers. Anything we experience is, in that sense, a *multiple happening*. We experience any event as a factual happening, as an intersubjective and subjective event, as a pragmatic occurrence and so on. The same event may arouse in us different emotions in different registers of reality, granting happiness in one register and arousing anxiety in another. Life, as we experience it, eclipses any one register, and is perpetually given in multiple significations.

In the next chapter I analyze psychoanalytic theories with the objective of illustrating how each theory designates certain truths as its object of inquiry. For each theory, I describe its locus in the psyche, starting with the definition of the need and continuing through associated desires and dreads, to its specific view of pathology and health. I show that the various psychoanalytic theories form a theoretical arc that reflects the epistemic multiplicity of the mind. I then analyze semiotic theories as well, showing them to be categorized and predicated upon the same notions of truth. This analysis brings out a remarkable fact, namely, that all disciplines that address the constitution and development of the subject give rise to epistemic multiplicity. *Epistemic multiplicity emerges as a dominant and universal characteristic of subjectivity.*

CHAPTER 3

Truth, Meaning and the Psychoanalytic Encounter

The former chapters have underlined the all-pervasive need for truth and the way it is both structured and expressed across our realities as we know them. In the present chapter I will review the issue of truth as it relates to psychoanalytic theory and practice. Under different terminological guises, the discussion of truth and epistemology abounds in psychoanalytic literature. It would be a near impossible feat to cover this discussion in its entirety and do justice to the many thinkers who have enriched it with their contributions. Nevertheless, I will try to bring something of this discussion here, albeit in brief and partial manner, with three main objectives in mind that structure my discussion and serve as a rationale for selecting the thinkers presented.

The first objective is to show how the various truth notions gleaned from philosophy express themselves in psychoanalytic theory. I will review these truth perspectives as they function on two levels. The level of meta psychology will investigate various epistemologies that have been offered as appropriate frameworks for psychoanalytic thought. The level of experienced truths will be investigated as formulated in psychoanalytic theories and encountered in clinical work. As I will show throughout my inquiry, these differentiated levels of epistemic assumption and experienced truths are closely interrelated. This interrelation will be shown to influence clinical methodology and objectives. My review will employ an historical perspective, presenting the epistemological shift that has been effected in the past few decades in psychoanalytic thought and its impact on our attitudes towards various truths.

The second objective of this chapter is to illustrate how the same epistemic multiplicity found in psychoanalytic theories is mirrored in semiotic theories of meaning. Semiotic theories are pertinent to the psychoanalytic encounter because they account for the way we attribute meaning to speech. In the analytic encounter the analyst ordinarily applies in a semi-automatic and semi-conscious fashion both psychoanalytic and semiotic theories. These enable him to understand, decipher and re-present his patient's speech. The various approaches in both psychoanalysis and semiotics will be presented as articulating the different categories of truth notions, namely: Correspondent, Coherent, Intersubjective, Ideal, Pragmatic and Subjective-Existential. Thus, each approach illuminates and captures a dimension of human experiencing and communication that complements the dimensions captured by others. This illustration brings forward my central claim about the study of the human subject, namely, its epistemic multiplicity.

 | DOI 10.1163/9789004314993_005

I will then proceed to show how the application of a given theory – psychoanalytic or semiotic – involves an epistemic 'choice' that bears immediate consequences for clinical work and entail practices that are often implicit and not consciously chosen. Each semiotic and psychoanalytic theory, due to the epistemological assumptions informing it, upholds a different image of the subject and the world he lives in. So actually, while seemingly 'only' understanding speech, we are necessarily recruiting a whole world view within which this speech is contextualized and given its signification. Listening to a patient, we already assume the reality he is referring to, be it an inner, outer, ideal or intersubjective one. We also determine, quickly and intuitively, always in a fallible manner, if our patient is telling us of family myths that are accepted as truths, or if the reality he is presenting us with is imbued by his subjective intuitions or pragmatic dealings.

After presenting the manner in which epistemic multiplicity displays in semiotic and psychoanalytic theory, I will present the traditional psychoanalytic debate that seeks to find the 'correct' epistemology for psychoanalysis. Following this, I will approach the third objective of this chapter by presenting an alternative to the traditional debate. The alternative I offer accepts epistemic multiplicity as an inherent characteristic of the human psyche. Moreover, it seeks to investigate its sources and ramifications, as applies to psychoanalysis, both theory and practice.

Truth and Psychoanalysis

From its earliest days, psychoanalysis has maintained a complex relationship with the concept of truth. This was examined by scientists and philosophers, alongside psychoanalysts who deliberated, again and again, how it served as their object of inquiry. Whose truth was at stake in clinical practice? The patient's, the analyst's or perhaps the truth of psychoanalytic theory? What was the role of objective reality in this respect and what was its relation to subjective experience?

Psychoanalysis, as Freud understood its essence and evolution, was borne of empiric, scientific methods. At the meta-theoretical level, the Correspondent theory of truth was there to anchor psychoanalysis's standing as a science and to supply a rationale for clinical psychotherapy. After Freud, truth paradigms in psychoanalysis were often presented as divided between modern and postmodern theories (Hanly, 2006) but, in fact, many of them could not be captured solely by the modern-postmodern divide. In the following sections, I show how different truths made their explicit and reasoned appearance in psychoanalysis- Subjective-Existential, Intersubjective, Coherent, Pragmatic and Ideal truths – and how they contributed to the epistemological shift that has eventuated thereof. The different approaches were developed after Freud, but I will show how their origins could be found in Freud's writings as well, despite his staunch commitment to scientific truth.

Realistic Epistemologies: Freud, Klein, Winnicott and Kohut: Even after Freud, some of the prime psychoanalytic thinkers- like Klein, Winnicott and Kohut- promoted realistic epistemologies insofar as they all constructed their theories around the basic differentiation between internal and external reality. That being said, I will present their radically different perspectives (within this epistemology) in a way that illuminates metapsychological shifts and emphasizes different sensibilities regarding the nature of truth. I will show how their work prepared the ground for the epistemological shift in psychoanalysis from the realistic to the idealistic.

Freud, loyal to the Correspondent notion of truth, often compared his analytic work to archeologic excavations, basing his claim for scientificity on the idea that analysis treated remnants of a real history that had eventuated and were later forgotten and repressed.[1] Freud pointed out that the two processes, psychoanalysis and archaeology, were very similar, although the analyst worked in better conditions than the archaeologist, because the latter often needed to work with partially or wholly ruined objects, while the former dealt with undamaged objects that were still well preserved, albeit, under various guises. Indeed, "it depends only upon analytic technique whether we shall succeed in bringing what is concealed completely to light" (SE 23:258).

According to this approach, for interpretation to be effective, it must cohere with what has 'really happened' to the patient, and only a correct interpretation could lead to insight, which in turn could cure neurosis. Freud underlined this issue on several occasions. He recommended psychoanalysis not "as a method of treatment but on account of the truths it contains" and he remarked "that the relationship between analyst and patient is based on a love of truth, that is, on the acknowledgement of reality, and that it precludes any kind of sham or deception" (SE 23: 247). Eissler (1965, 1971) described Freud's complete work as based on a sole value of the discrimination between true and untrue.

---

1 One of the early expressions of this appeared in his early 'Fragment of an Analysis' in 1905: "In face of the incompleteness of my analytic results, I had no choice but to follow the example of those discoverers whose good fortune it is to bring to the light of day after their long burial the priceless though mutilated relics of antiquity. I have restored what is missing…but, like a conscientious archaeologist, I have not omitted to mention in each case where the authentic parts end and my constructions begin" (SE 7:11).

In *The Question of a Weltanschauung* (1933), upholding Aristotle's concept of truth, Freud leaves no doubt as to which path psychoanalysis should follow: "Scientific thinking" he states, "is concerned carefully to avoid individual factors and affective influences;...Its endeavour is to arrive at correspondence with reality – that is to say, with what exists outside us and independently of us... This correspondence with the real external world we call 'truth'" (SE 22:169). In this lecture he also repudiates 'the anarchist theory' which, according to him, argues that it is entirely a matter of indifference what opinions we adopt, since the criterion for truth-correspondence with the external world- is absent in the analytic method. Freud criticizes such a view on the ground that "it breaks down with its first step into practical life" (ibid. 175).

In 1897 Freud abandoned the seduction theory and the assumption that neurosis was rooted in a concrete incident that had occurred in external reality, i.e., a sexual trauma experienced by the patients during their childhood. By doing so, Freud surrendered his purely positivist stance and his assumption that actual incidents in external reality were the cause of mental disorders. From this point on, the seduction stories told by his patients were no longer construed as concrete events, but as the creations of the patients' inner reality, namely, as fantasies arising in the context of conflicted sexuality.

The sexual content of the story remained the same, but its locus of eventuation changed: from the outer to the inner world, from material reality to psychic reality. This was the first time Freud acknowledged the fact that pathogenic events can be internal, subjective and a figment of fantasy. Here began Freud's dual loyalty to the Correspondent truth, on the one hand, and to the recognition of the centrality of experiential and Subjective truth, on the other.

Following the distinction that Freud had already drawn between thought-reality and external reality in his *Project for a Scientific Psychology* (SE 1: 373), the term 'psychical reality' first appeared in *The Interpretation of Dreams*, where it was contrasted with material reality: "If we look at unconscious wishes", Freud wrote, "reduced to their most fundamental and truest shape, we shall have to conclude...that psychical reality is a particular form of existence not to be confused with material reality" (SE 5: 620). It is important to note that, for Freud, the concept of psychical reality is indicative of the real existence of ideas that have become unconscious and that have thereby acquired a 'reality value' in the sense that they refer to real events, irrespective of whether or not real events were reflected in them.

What we clearly find here is a differentiation between the two levels on which these truths are functioning – the meta-theoretical and the theoretical. On the theoretical level, as part of the content of his developing theory and corresponding to the two truths he encountered in the clinic, Freud describes insights that cohere with the Subjective-Existential and the Correspondent truths. The former is located in psychic reality and the latter in material reality, of which psychic reality is a part. The fact that these two truths may be differentiated by an *observer/analyst*, though not necessarily by the *experiencer*, indicates that we are still safely anchored in a realistic epistemology.

The wonderful interplay between the two truths and their hopeless disconnection as they appear before the analyst can be found in Freud's description of melancholic self-perception:

> It would be equally fruitless from a scientific and a therapeutic point of view to contradict a patient who brings these accusations against his ego. He must surely be right in some way and be describing something that is as it seems to him to be. Indeed, we must at once confirm some of his statements without reservation. ... Nor is it difficult to see that there is no correspondence, so far as we can judge, between the degree of self-abasement and its real justification. A good, capable, conscientious woman will speak no better of herself after she develops melancholia than one who is in fact worthless; ...The essential thing, therefore, is not whether the melancholic's distressing self-denigration is correct, in the sense that his self-criticism agrees with the opinion of other people. The point must rather be that he is giving a correct description of his psychological situation. He has lost his self-respect and he must have good reason for this. It is true that we are then faced with a contradiction that presents a problem which is hard to solve.
>
> SE 14:246–247

Freud realizes here that the Subjective-Existential and the Correspondent truths do not cohere. Indeed, this discord for him is the hallmark of neurosis. One truth is based on correspondence to psychic reality and the other on correspondence to external reality. In this way, the melancholic's self- description is true not because of its correspondence to external reality, but because it is consistent with an inner reality (Govrin 2004, 52). On the metapsychologic level, we remain in the realm of objective correspondence, because the *analyst* remains able to differentiate between the external and the internal even when his patient cannot. What is common to both truths (Correspondent and Subjective-Existential in the form they take in the Realistic-Correspondent meta-theory) *is that they are found or revealed; they are neither constructed nor co-constructed.*

Freud recognizes both Correspondent and Subjective-Existential truths, but poses a clear demand to tease them apart: "...our perceptions are subjectively conditioned and must not be regarded as identical with what is perceived" (SE 14:171). He concedes that individual factors have an influence on what we perceive yet, scientific thinking "is concerned carefully to avoid individual factors and affective influences; it examines more strictly the trustworthiness of the sense-perceptions on which it bases its conclusions" (SE 22:170).

Some researchers still entertain the hope that the Correspondent and the Subjective-Existential truths may overlap and merge to form a monistic reality for mental life, even if this monism is not *fully* achieved. In Arlow's words:

> This, I think, is the proper understanding of the concept of psychic reality. It is not a fantasy that is taken for the real truth, for an actual event, but the recollection of a psychic event with its mixture of fact and fantasy. During analytic work, it becomes the responsibility of the therapist to undo the defensive distortions which have been imposed upon the material offered as memory and to recognise in the patient's productions a kernel of what really happened. This is not the same as the 'objective reality', which can be observed by outsiders and validated consensually.
>
> ARLOW 1996, 662

This echoes what Freud writes of screen memories (SE 3: 301) and his hope regarding various constructions that occur in therapy. For Freud, any individual construction is "a conjecture which awaits examination, confirmation or rejection" during the psychoanalytic process (SE 23: 265). He believes that it is possible to establish the laws which psychoanalytic processes obey and follow, as well as their "mutual relations and interdependences unbroken over long stretches" (SE 23:158). These laws may not grant immediate, direct access to the object of inquiry, but Freud is hopeful that with additional "intellectual scaffolding...we look forward to their being modified, corrected and more precisely determined as further experience is accumulated and sifted" (ibid. 159). The hope implicitly voiced is that, with the perfection of investigative methods, the truths of correspondence and subjectivity will coalesce.

The construal of external and psychic realities and their inter relations is brought forth in the Freudian, and later in the Kleinian and Winnicottian, conceptions of development. In all, the infant, in the very beginning of his life, requires insulation from external reality. For Freud, early psychological development involves moving from an initial solipsistic world of wish fulfilment to a frustrating external (yet sustaining) reality. The separateness of the two has always been a cornerstone of the Freudian theory, accompanied by the transformation of an early 'pleasure-ego' into a 'reality-ego' (Freud 1911). Yet, in 'Instincts and their Vicissitudes' (1915) he argues that there is, in fact, a still earlier *original* 'reality-ego'. This original 'reality-ego', instead of proceeding directly into the *final* 'reality-ego', is replaced, under the dominating influence of the pleasure principle, by a 'pleasure-ego'. As Strachey explains, in Freud's thought about the development of the original reality ego, the auto erotic libidinal instincts encourage diversion towards a 'pleasure-ego', while the *non*-auto erotic libidinal instincts and the self-preservative instincts encourage a direct transition to the final, adult 'reality-ego'. This latter development occurs when survival needs dominate early growth. Only close and prolonged parental care of the helpless infant facilitates the primary state of narcissism and, with it, the development of the 'pleasure-ego' (SE 14:134).

Whereas Freud posited an early recognition of external reality that was later lost and had to be won again, Klein (1930) assumed that the early reality of the infant is wholly phantasmatic, wholly internal. As she describes it, the infant's first objects are structured as part of his innate drives and create partial bodily images (Klein 1932). These phylogenetically determined preconceptions develop through such mechanisms as splitting, projection, introjections and identification. These eventually allow internal and external worlds to become differentiated by experiences of love and hate between the subject and his objects, part and whole.

Freud's concepts of neurosis and psychosis retained the signature of non-compliance with reality's demands. Similarly, Klein's concept of 'position' implied the ability to move *in* and *out* of depressive reality-testing. It was Winnicott who first treated as an entity the realm *between* the inner and the outer, speaking of the 'place where we live' (Winnicott 1971), where internality and externality interact and lose their separateness.

Young (1994) points out that, holding in mind the Kleinian theory, Winnicott faces a philosophical issue: "For Kleinians, psychoanalysis is solely about internal objects. The very idea of something that is partly internal, partly external, or of a zone of third world between the internal and the external, is to them a sloppy thinking". This may be said of Freud as well. In Freudian and Kleinian thought, we have frequent 'crossings' of the boundary between the internal and the external. These crossings mediate our development and experience continuously; we project from the inside out and we introject from the outside inwards. Sometimes we engage complicated manoeuvres such as projective identification, when an external agency is used in order to process our internal issues. And yet, the process that Klein presents as projective identification allows us to know "what comes from whom" (Hanly and Hanly 2001, 527). Indeed, in classic psychoanalytic thinking, analysts are expected to know the locus of particular events and be able to determine the external or internal nature of their patients' productions. If they get confused, it is a lapse that must be overcome. The demand for this sort of knowledge is an uncompromising one. Even with regard to such complicated events as transference and countertransference, their external-internal nature must be grasped by the analyst (Hanly 1990). As observers-analysts, we have the responsibility and presumably the ability to be accurate in this regard and overcome constraints imposed by our personality, language, historical context, ideology, and so on.

Winnicott introduces into psychoanalytic thinking a third area of intermediateness and presents it as the main interest of clinical psychoanalysis. In this area- the potential or transitional space- Winnicott collapses the subject-object divide that is inherent in the notion of Correspondence. In addition to the psychic and external realities the subject inhabits (corresponding to the experiential areas of 'relating' and 'usage'), Winnicott introduces a "third part of the life of a human being, a part that we cannot ignore, an intermediate area of experiencing, to which inner reality and external life both contribute. It is an area which is not challenged, because no claim is made on its behalf except that it shall exist as a resting-place for the individual engaged in the perpetual human task of keeping inner and outer reality separate yet interrelated" (Winnicott 1951, 230).

It is important that the newly proposed component of mental life has volume; *it is an area, a space*. It is not in the realm of sharp boundary-maintenance referred to as reality-testing. It is "illusion, that which is allowed to the infant and which in adult life is inherent in art and religion" (ibid. 230). Winnicott describes the way in which "infants and children and adults take external reality in, as clothing for their dreams, and they project themselves into external objects and people and enrich external reality by their imaginative perceptions" (Winnicott 1989, 57). But he means something more than the inner world, involving also external reality and the commerce between them: "...we really do find a third area, an area of living which corresponds to the infant's transitional phenomena and which actually derives from them. In so far as the infant has not achieved transitional phenomena I think the acceptance of symbols is deficient, and the cultural life is poverty-stricken" (ibid.). Winnicott's concept of *psyche-soma* echoes the subject-object collapse in the potential space. Whereas in binary ontology the psyche and soma fall into the respective categories of inner and outer, for Winnicott this division is a distortion, similar to the one eventuating in a dominant false self that takes over space and functions from the true self (Winnicott 1949).

Winnicott here is doing more than acknowledging psychic life and Subjective-Existential truth, he is challenging the possibility of their delineation in different areas of human life, and in this sense he is effecting an epistemological shift, *but only within this third area of experience* (the transitional space). Outside of it, we may still make clear the differentiation of inner and outer, psychic and external reality. But as this third area is the critical one in the psychological life of the subject, in exploring it we move away from the classical pre-existent truths and form a new understanding of knowledge as a process of becoming. An immediate consequence is a change in the position of the analyst as the one who knows, which seriously shifts his source of authority.

In his understanding of what comprises knowledge and truth in clinical work, Winnicott scoffs at the idea that some objective truth should be available to the therapist. In his view, "the significant moment [in therapy] is that at which the child surprises himself or herself. It is not the moment of my clever interpretation that is significant" (Winnicott 1971, 50). Whereas for Freud interpretation involves the analyst's gift of truth to the patient, Winnicott states: "I have always felt that an important function of the interpretation is the establishment of the limits of the analyst's understanding". Indeed, the analytic act distances itself from the surgeon's and takes on a resemblance to the act of a midwife: "Interpretation, at its best, is delivered by the analysands, not the analyst. At its worst, interpretation outside the ripeness of the material is indoctrination and produces compliance" (Winnicott 1960, 149).

And yet, despite relinquishing, as a clinician, the analytic authority that had accompanied the positivistic psychoanalytic stance, Winnicott as a theoretician does not commit to a particular epistemology. He realizes that different stances are required in dealing with different phenomena. In observing mother-child interactions, in diagnosing mental pathology, in excavating historical truths- in all of these, Winnicott thinks and behaves according to a realistic epistemology. Only in regard to the transitional space he promotes a non-realistic epistemology, where an intersubjectively created realm of subjective experiencing allows for truths to be created, woven and interwoven in different ways.

With regard to the external-psychic divide, when it appears in his thought, Winnicott seems to lean towards the Subjective-Existential truths, as is perhaps most obvious in his discussion of the true and false selves: He attributes the adjective 'true' to the subjective mode of being: "In particular, what I divide into a True and a False Self with Freud's division of the self into a part that is central and powered by the instincts (or by what Freud called sexuality, pregenital and genital), and a part that is turned outwards and is related to the world" (Winnicott 1960, 140). False is formed by concessions to the outer world. True originates in the body and inhabits the inner mental space.

In this conception, the traditional dualism of world and self is maintained. *Values*, on the other hand, *begin a movement of reversal,* because the inner 'true' is valued more highly than ever before. Freud wanted Ego where there was Id. Winnicott, endowing the Id with the respected adjective of 'true', offers it vindication. In this way, Winnicott's chaperoning of Subjective-Existential truth and the transitional realm he created, in which the inner-external divide is collapsed, might well have played a part in the gradual acceptance and legitimation in psychoanalytic theories of Subjective-Existential and Intersubjective truths, as well as later epistemologies.

Another great thinker busy with the tensions of Subjective-Existential and Correspondent truths is Heinz Kohut. Kohut's discussion of these truths is closely bound up with his analytic and methodological technique. In his book 'How does Analysis Cure?', Kohut (1984) argues against guiding the patient's focus to his original trauma, questioning both the possibility and the therapeutic value of such an endeavour. Govrin (2004) points out that Kohut and Freud both believed that, during therapy, it might be impossible to accurately recall primal traumatic incidents. But whereas Freud may accept that it is sometimes simply impossible, Kohut does not attribute much therapeutic importance to the retrieval and articulation of traumatic events. As he sees it, the developing self withdraws from frustrating experiences and creates compensatory structures in order to overcome narcissistic injuries. In transference relations, the analyst will not encounter the original form of the self, but the compensatory forms that evolved following the trauma. These forms are the important ones to access and to work with in order to effect change.

Not only does Kohut deny the primal relevance of the objective truth in the past, in the present as well, he prioritizes the patient's subjective needs over the principle of reality. The patient/child's conceptions distort reality from the outset, simply by virtue of being driven by needs. The role of the analyst/parent is not to detach consciousness from its originary needs, but rather to strengthen the subjectivity of the patient/child in the face of reality (Kohut 1971). Kohut explicitly claims that the self-psychologist does not confront the patient with objective reality, which is allegedly 'truer' than inner reality. Instead, he validates the patient's concept of reality even if it conflicts with the reality that the therapist is familiar with (Kohut 1984). The core area of psychoanalytic metapsychology occupies, for Kohut, an imaginary position inside the psychic organization of the individual, the position of an observer with whose insights the analyst vicariously identifies through the process of empathy.

And yet, the point that remains valid in Kohut's thought, as in the thought of his predecessors, is that inner and outer realities may be delineated by the analyst. The analyst may believe, may strive even, to fortify the patient's subjectivity and its truths, but he does this without losing his clear hold on the differentiation of psychical and material realities.[2]

The Epistemological Shift: Bion, Spence, Schafer and Relational Theory: Freud, Klein, Winnicott, Kohut and indeed Bion himself, in his early writings, assumed that truth and reality (both external and internal) may be differentiated and known in different degrees. This knowledge has been ascribed to different agencies, both conscious and unconscious, sometimes those of the analyst and sometimes those of the analysand. The thinkers I will discuss here represent the move towards idealistic epistemology inasmuch as they challenge the internal-external divide, upon which realistic epistemology is predicated.

Ideal epistemology is divided into the objective and the subjective.[3] Pragmatic, subjective and intersubjective epistemologies belong to the latter general category; intersubjective epistemology grants intersubjectivity (as culture, language or group consensus) a transcendental function that is prior to subjectivity; subjective epistemology reverses this order, as in Husserl's early phenomenology, and pragmatic epistemology grasps existing situations in their entirety as constituting and influencing both the subjective and the intersubjective, with future

---

2 I am presenting here my analysis of Kohut's epistemology. Others, such as Gedo, situate him in a phenomenological-subjective epistemology, stating that: "Kohut (1977; 1978; 1984) and his followers (e.g., Goldberg 1978) have founded a school of psychoanalytic thought conforming to the principle that our theories should be as near to personal experience as possible. As a result, the propositions of self-psychology deal only with issues that can be articulated in the language of subjectivity" (Gedo 1997, 782). Fosshage also perceives Kohut as updating psychoanalytic epistemology by means of the method of observation he introduced into the clinic. "Kohut (1982) recognized "the relativity of our perceptions of reality", "the framework of ordering concepts that shape our observations and explanations" (ibid. 400), and that "the field that is observed, of necessity, includes the observer" (Kohut 1984, 41). ...Deeming the patient's subjectivity the principal focus of the analytic endeavor, Kohut (1959; 1982) delineated how our method of observation relies on empathy and vicarious introspection, what he called the "empathic mode of observation", and designated it the method by which the field of psychoanalysis itself is defined (Kohut 1977, 302)". (Fosshage 2011, 140). Thus, when all is filtered through the analyst's subjective processing, epistemology transforms into the subjective-phenomenal.

3 As formerly detailed, the historical roots of objective idealism are usually ascribed to Plato, while subjective idealism is usually ascribed to the work and thought of Baruch Spinoza (1632–1677) and Bishop Berkeley (1685–1753). Whereas Plato, an objective idealist, proposed ideal forms as essences that underlie reality and act as a directive for those rational processes that may appropriate them, Berkeley, a subjective idealist, argued that we can never step outside of the realm of the mental to reach the truly external, be it material or spiritual. Therefore, mental events are the only possible objects of cognition. All propositional knowledge relates to this reality and all that is outside of it is unknowable.

consequence functioning as a determining factor in present situations. Each of the thinkers I present will be shown to have adopted one of these epistemologies as a framework for his theorizing.

A prominent psychoanalyst who delved deeply into issues of thought, knowledge and truth is Wilford Bion. His ideas on the subject are dense and complex and the following brief review will not do them justice. I will, though, describe them here in a way that illustrates how his important psychoanalytic formulation of truth plays a part in the evolution of psychoanalytic epistemology from the realistic to the idealistic.

Bion begins his late theory of knowledge with the basic axiomatic premise that psychic reality and truth *cannot be known*. This point of departure is reminiscent of Kant's incomprehensible reality – the noumena – and in a like manner defines an unsurpassable gap between reality and what we know of it. As reality itself cannot be known, we exit realism and move necessarily into the realm of the tentative, exploring the ways we construe what we may know.

Most of what may be understood of Bion's conception of truth is formulated by two key signifiers that he introduces: 'K', 'O' and the interrelation among their diverse presentations. O is an opaque psychoanalytic concept, often associated with the domains of mysticism and faith (see for example Eigen 1981; Grotstein 2001; White 2011). I will approach it here from a philosophic-epistemological perspective. Bion defines O as truth, while K signifies knowledge. In philosophy, the usual epistemological methods regard truth as the aim of knowledge. The latter is in a predictable relation to truth and moves towards it in a syntagmatic, asymptotic trajectory. Bion, by contrast, draws complex relations between the two. He defines O and its relations with K in the following way: "I shall use the sign O to denote that which is the ultimate reality, represented by terms such as absolute truth, the godhead, the infinite, the thing-in- itself. O does not fall in the domain of knowledge or learning save incidentally; O can 'become', but it cannot be 'known'" (Bion 1970, 25).

As we can see, for Bion there is no convergence between knowledge and the particular truth that is signified by O. Knowledge (K) *may* have claims on truth, but we cannot formulate in any simple and systematic manner the way in which it can approximate the particular kind of truth that O represents. The reason for this is that K is basically sense-based, while O is of an essentially different nature: "The scientific approach, associated with a background of sense impressions…in so far as it is associated with the ultimate reality of the personality, O, …is baseless" (Bion 1970, 87). Therefore, the psychoanalytic and the scientific truths (and realities) are fundamentally different from each other: "The realities with which psycho-analysis deals, for example: fear, panic, love, anxiety, passion, have no sensuous background, though there is a sensuous background (respiratory rate, pain, touch, etc.) that is often identified with them and then treated, supposedly scientifically. What *is* required is...a science that is not restricted by its genesis in knowledge and sensuous background. It must be a science of at-one-ment" (Bion 1970, 88).

Only by means of 'at-one-ment' may O be touched upon and approached. At-one-ment is a way of being or becoming which is not only different from knowledge, but is indeed, at times, obstructed by it. This is emphasized by Bion's celebrated recommendation, that analysts should make "a positive act of refraining from memory and desire" (Bion 1970, 30). Inasmuch as both memories and desires are, by definition, sense-based, they can only hinder the contact with the realm of the unknown and unknowability.[4] Although K obstructs O, O "is incommunicable save through K activity" (Bion 1970, 29). Therefore, one may ask what state of mind is welcome if desires and memories are not. "A term that would express approximately what I need to express is 'faith' – faith that there is an ultimate reality and truth – the unknown, unknowable, 'formless infinite' " (Bion 1970, 29–30). The act of faith leads the analyst *to become* O:

> In so far as the analyst becomes O he is able to know the events that are evolutions of O... Restating this in terms of psycho-analytic experience, the psycho-analyst can know what the patient says, does, and appears to be, but cannot know the O of which the patient is an evolution: he can only 'be' it. He knows phenomena by virtue of his senses but, since his concern is with O, events must be regarded as possessing either the defects of irrelevancies obstructing, or the merits of pointers initiating, the process of 'becoming' O.
>
> BION 1970, 26

Whether he does so or not (become O) cannot depend on rules for O, or O → K, but only on his ability to be at one with O (ibid. 31).

4 "Memory is a part of K...But memory depends on the senses. It is limited by the limitations of the senses and their subordination to the pleasure-pain principle; memories are therefore fallacious and memory has the defects of its origin in functions of possessiveness and evacuation" (Bion 1970, 29). As K, the objects in the memory of the analyst obstruct at-one-ment; "He is concerned with these objects in his analysand because he is concerned with the working of the analysand's mind" (Bion 1970, 31). But they are not objects of inquiry in and of themselves, rather as vehicles and reflections of O (in a way that phenomenon may serve as vehicle of noumenon, or a particular instance may serve as a partial reflection of a platonic Form). The "analysand will express his awareness of O in people and things by formulations representing the intersection of evolutions of O with the evolution of his awareness" (ibid.).

Bion's Ultimate Truth seems at times to echo Kant's 'Thing-in-itself', as given by its incomprehensibility and the impossibility of its perceptual grasp. But Kant's reality maintains a fixed distance from consciousness. One cannot over-reach or change the structured limitations of consciousness. In contradistinction, the objective ideal reality of Plato's eternal forms allows knowledge to approximate them or reach differential distances from them.[5] Irrespective of knowledge and the knower, and in a way that is unaffected by human perception, Bion attributes a special, elevated status to his realm of O:

> The truth, or true thought, does not require a thinker- he is not logically necessary... Nobody need think the true thought: it awaits the advent of the thinker who achieves significance through the true thought. The lie and its thinker are inseparable. The thinker is of no consequence to the truth, but the truth is logically necessary to the thinker. His significance depends on whether or not he will entertain the thought, but the thoughts remains unaltered... If entertained, they are conducive to mental health; if not, they initiate disturbance... True thought requires neither formulation nor thinker.
>
> BION, 1970, 102

And yet, what *does* change is the accessibility of O, and to this Bion refers when discussing evolutions and transformations of O. Bion states that O is essentially: "...darkness and formlessness but it enters the domain K when it has evolved to a point where it can be known through knowledge gained by experience, and formulated in terms derived from sensuous experience" (Bion 1970, 25). He states that psychoanalytic events are conducive to transformations both in O and in K, but "Their value therapeutically is greater if they are conducive to transformations in O; less if conducive to transformations in K" (Bion 1970, 25). Despite O's epistemological priority and its dimension of being an originary 'cause', Bion states that O may also be an object of causation, and as such be subject to transformations: " 'Causation', as a dimension of O, has the characteristics of all other dimensions of O that are subjected to the various processes of transformation and inspected at various stages in the process" (Bion 1965, 151).

5 Bion at times draws an analogy between O and Plato's forms: "The Platonic theory of Forms and the Christian dogma of the Incarnation imply absolute essence which I wish to postulate as a universal quality of phenomena such as 'panic', 'anxiety', 'fear', 'love'. In brief, I use O to represent this central feature of every situation that the psycho-analyst has to meet. With this he must be at one; with the evolution of this he must identify so that he can formulate it in an interpretation"(Bion 1970, 88; See also Bion 1965, 151).

In a manner that brings forward the intersubjective context that accentuates its element of process and evolution, Bion describes in the following passage an eventuation of O as a shared, Heidegger-like happening:

> The interpretation is an actual event in an evolution of O that is common to analyst and analysand…the practising analyst must wait for the analytic session to 'evolve'. He must wait not for…an actual event, but for an evolution to take place so that O becomes manifest in K through the emergence of actual events. Similarly, the reader must disregard what I say until the O of the experience of reading has evolved to a point where the actual events of reading issue in his interpretation of the experiences. Too great a regard for what I have written obstructs the process I represent by the terms 'he becomes the O that is common to himself and myself'.
>
> BION 1970, 26–7

O here is clearly an ultimate truth, a truth pertaining to pure essence of emotion and experience, unencumbered by any prior premise or restraint. But its *evolution* is *influenced by the knower and by the authentic contact and experiences he creates with others.* The knowledge of this truth (in affinity to Heidegger's althaea) must never become detached from its novelty in every present moment and interaction. In its saturated, transparent forms, knowledge might very well prove useless and obstructive of truth. True thinking, even if it tends to repeat accepted truths within a subject's corpus of knowledge, must be able to break out of their comforting hold, despite the fear of the unknown (Bion 1965, 158).

Bion's true knowledge carries a paradox: On one hand, truth is abstract and of a different order from the knowing process. On the other hand, it must have a particular form, attainable by the senses, as well as the senses of others: "In the K Activity…namely in knowing, I have to be conscious of my emotional experience and able to abstract from it a statement that will represent this experience adequately… The criterion for the statement must be its value in facilitating testing by more than one sense or by the senses of more than one person" (Bion 1962, 49–50). But the paradox may be resolved if we understand that, for Bion, mental health and human growth involve oscillation between states of O and K.

O is reality at its most incomprehensible, absolute truth, beyond human capacity to know or understand emotionally. Near-O states involve risking the loss of both meaning and the continuity of consciousness. Being O means entering an encapsulated mode of being and, consequently, losing hold of one's self in the experiencing of O and the likely transformation that this may initiate. 'Becoming O' gives rise to psychic change, because the subject is forced to use knowledge (K) in order to bind the inchoate experience: "The process of binding is a part of the procedure by which something is 'won from the void and formless infinite'; it is K and must be distinguished from the process by which O is 'become' " (Bion 1965, 151). Knowledge can be understood as successful containment of one's unique experience of becoming O, with containment signifying a process of transformation that preserves the continuity of self. The transformations engendered by becoming O affect, in turn, the experience of O itself and gives it a new form.

Bion's ideas about mental development are not easy to understand, but his epistemological assumptions are even harder. Taken in bits, his formulations may be viewed as 'stepping stones' in the river of psychoanalytic thought, which marked the gradual transition from the realistic to the contingent. In order to bring this out, I summarize below the prime markers of this transition in Bion's theory:

1. There is a realm- O, which is understood to 'be' a truth, rather than a realm that contains truths to be known. In itself, it can never be known. It is prior to every other mental event and impacts all personified experience, similar to the manner in which arithmetic impacts geometry (Bion 1965, 150).
2. The only guideline to approaching O is abandoning K, and the experience of O will be the criterion of its validity, i.e., the truth of O is an absolute and ultimate form of *experience and being*. The method and criterion of its appropriation are completely subjective and experiential. The need of its communicability and its integration into other realms of experience 'pulls' it back into the realm of the comprehensible.
3. In Bion's theorizing, all knowledge is achieved by means of the transformation of the unbearable element (beta) into the bearable and thinkable element (alpha), mediated by a 'container' in *an intersubjective event*. This means that everything known is always imbued by subjectivity and coloured by an intersubjective event. As Bion puts it: "...the situation represented by these abstract terms xKy is identical with xLy or xHy" (Bion 1962, 47), i.e., all knowledge is created in the context of intersubjectivity.

To sum up, Bion's premises may be the beginnings of what was later clearly formulated as a subjective epistemology for psychoanalysis. Its basic tenets may be formulated in general terms that are clearly derived from Bion's formulations: The only relevant truth and reality for psychoanalysis is lived experience (O in Bion's case); accessing any knowledge involves an intersubjective event; finally, all knowledge is necessarily infused with subjectivity and validated by it.

From a different direction, and by reference to Coherent and Pragmatic truths, Spence and Schafer did their part in effecting the epistemic shift in psychoanalysis. As with many contemporary ideas, both referenced Freud in the development of their thinking. Alongside Correspondent and Subjective truths, Freud discussed Coherent and Pragmatic truths that in later years were elaborated as both technique and epistemological assumptions.

Let me examine again Freud's statement that "an assured conviction of the truth of the construction...achieves the same therapeutic result as a recaptured memory" (SE 23:265). Freud engages here two notions of truth: the Coherent truth, appertaining to the fit between a newly formed construction and earlier conceptions held by the patient ('assured conviction'); and the Pragmatic truth, in which the construction is examined according to its therapeutic consequences ('the same therapeutic results'). Freud forms here a new equation between the practical implications of a belief and its presumed objective truth-value.

Spence extended the purview of the Pragmatic approach in psychoanalysis by claiming that practitioners no longer feel they are interested only in a general science of deciphering the unconscious message. The individual subject stands at the center of the psychoanalytic world and, as such, his wellbeing forms the criteria for truth. The elements that will constitute this truth are the changing elements in this particular subject's present: The state of his transference, the compatibility among different parts of his conversation, the quality of articulation and, sometimes, aspects of discourse that contribute to persuasion (Spence 1982). Persuasive discourse is markedly different from remembering in the truth notions that support it: While the latter assumes a realistic epistemology, the former engages a pragmatic epistemology, alongside measures of coherence and aesthetics. The aim here is like that of good theatre: The suspension of disbelief. What is provided is not a historical, but rather a narrative truth.[6]

---

6 Spence gives here a detailed definition of what he terms narrative truth and of its constitution: "To the extent that a narrative is persuasive and compelling, it acquires features of what might be called narrative truth. Goodness of fit seems particularly significant in bringing about this change. A particular clinical event – an association, for example, or a partly-recovered memory – may seem to clarify the unfolding account of the patient's life history so precisely that both patient and analyst come to the conclusion that it must be true...under these conditions, narrative fit is usually taken to be conclusive, and if a piece of the past

This narrative truth becomes a truth in analysis insofar as it effects for the patient (and the analyst) the outcomes desired of analysis. Spence provides a lucid description of the way Pragmatic truths are formed in analysis:

> If it is true that many interpretations function as pragmatic statements, it becomes clear that whatever truth value they possess lies more in the future than the past. By making an interpretation, the analyst hopes to make the patient aware of a new view of his life; if the interpretation is accepted, then it may bring about a reformulation of certain fixed conceptions, allowing the patient to see them more accurately and respond more perceptively; as a result, he will behave differently and experience his world in a rather different manner. To the extent that it brings about a successful experience of this kind, the interpretation becomes true; yet as we have seen, its truth value could not necessarily be predicted from its initial utterance, nor could it necessarily be validated by reference to the past.
>
> SPENCE 1983, 467

Spence describes narrative (Coherent) and Pragmatic truths, but he does not think that they replace, or indeed *should* replace, the search for historic (Correspondent) truth. Indeed, he believes that every clinician should create in every analysis a broad data base that will be transcribed and analysed, in order to discover the contradictions we accept, alongside the microstructures that are nested within the larger patient-analyst conversation. Such methodology of analysis may uncover the biases and the wrongs done to historical truth. Spence acknowledged that analytic discourse can create the desired outcome when the patient, empowered by the transference, has sufficient faith in the analyst to adopt the creative qualities of interpretation, the truth that is created when providing coherence and congruence among events separated in space and time. But he does not find this to be ideal practice. Indeed he warns that "the discipline of...the methodologies of unpacking and microstructure analysis...may be our only defense against the perils of narrative persuasion." (Spence 1983, 480).

---

completes the unfinished clinical picture in just the right way...then it acquires its own truth value and no further checking is necessary. Many of Freud's constructions seem to have followed this path. What was originally hypothetical and problematic, possessing no known truth value, turns out to bring together pieces of the patient's life story which, up to that point, had seemed disconnected and even contradictory. The construction that began as a contribution to the coherence of the narrative...gradually comes to acquire truth value in its own right and is assumed to satisfy the criteria of accuracy.... As soon as that step is taken, the construction becomes a reconstruction – a piece of the past that is taken to be as real as the name of the patient's father or the date of his birth" (Spence 1982, 181).

Spence may be seen as acknowledging the power of Coherent and Pragmatic truth, but he objects to the acceptance of subjective and intersubjective epistemologies that grant them a status equal to the truth of Correspondence. On the contrary, he advocates a return to the bedrock of realistic epistemology, to the truth of Correspondence. In contradistinction, Schafer, basing his theory on these same Coherent and Pragmatic truths, advocates an epistemological shift, demoting Correspondent truth from the privileged status Spence granted it. As he understands it, the perception of 'one' reality and truth is an illusion: "We have only versions of the true and the real. Narratively unmediated, definitive access to the truth cannot be demonstrated. In this respect, therefore, there can be no absolute foundation on which any observer or thinker stands; each must choose his/her narrative version" (Schafer 1992, xv).

The basic assumption of what came to be called the 'Narrative Approach' is that people construct stories of their lives in order to better understand them. This telling and retelling of stories is understood as a part of human nature. Every person creates many stories about himself, his environment and his relations with others. These narratives are constructed over the years based on experiences with, and feedback from, the environment. They are highly significant in the sense that they effectively become sources of one's emotions, choices and behaviours.

As Schafer sees it, the analyst relies also on versions of truth operationalized in his or her commitment to various storylines of development. The psychoanalytic 'stories' of the Oedipal conflict, separation/individuation or narcissistic fragmentation cannot comfortably be taken to have a definite reality outside that of a narrative version. From this viewpoint, theoretical formulations that were accepted as descriptions corresponding to reality are given the status of master narratives. The analyst's detailed interpretative efforts may then be regarded as story lines that are manifestations of these master narratives. The narrative rendered is always provisional, ready to admit other potential retellings:

> …the point being made and defended here is that any concept of knowledge must imply its verbal formulation and its communicability. These implications necessarily open up an examination of how the knowledge is being told to oneself and to others, within which tradition, with which set of aims, to which audience, and much else besides. This point of view does not deny truth. There is plenty of truth. It is just that truth comes in different versions. It always has. In this regard, the entire matter may be formulated as one of giving up denials.
>
> SCHAFER 1996, 250

Two epistemological shifts are here effected. Firstly, we part from the realm of realism, the realm of biographical, Correspondent truth. Secondly, we relinquish monistic epistemologies in favour of the possibility of parallel, potentially incongruent truths. Thus, pragmatic, subjective and intersubjective epistemologies accept that several truths may be pertinent to a particular subject, when mental materials are contextualized in different areas and phases of a person's life. This means that psychic realities do not lend themselves to unitary formulation. Particular truths will be created within particular constellations.

The narrative approach leans heavily on Coherent truth. Yet, in the psychoanalytic context, it carries also a significant element of intersubjectivity inasmuch as the analyst, even only in the role of supplying the context and the legitimation of the telling, plays a role in the constitution of the patient's narrative. Acknowledging the analyst's influence in the evolving truth, we situate ourselves in a form of subjective epistemology called 'constructivism'.

Constructivist approaches in psychoanalysis contend that human behaviour is not determined by reality, which cannot be known and therefore cannot be posited as existing in relations of causality, but by the constructions of human beings. Gill differentiates between 'radical' and 'ordinary' constructivism (Gill 1994, 764). Whereas the former assumes an unknowable external reality, the latter holds that we *can* know something of reality, but only as mediated by our own beings. The same holds true for Donnel Stern's understanding of constructivism. He assumes the existence of objective material facts leading to 'unformulated experiences', from which individuals then construct their realities (Stern 1983, 71). Hoffman (1991) acknowledges material facts that are constructed in different ways by different individuals, but denies the factual existence of social realities. Quoting Mitchell, he says: "All social realities are 'sandcastles' (Mitchell 1988, 195), jeopardized by awareness of mortality" (Hoffman 1991, 95).

Gill states explicitly that "the criterion of validity of a particular view of reality is not correspondence with an unknowable reality as such but only of comprehensiveness and consistency" (Gill 1994, 764). This however, pragmatically speaking, does not mean that all constructions are valid as truths. When constructions fail because they are not compatible with reality- for example, if the actions that they imply do not attain the desired aims- then they need to be revised in a manner that addresses *reality*. In this way, "the only aspect of the 'real' world that actually enters into the realm of experience is its constraints" (Glasersfeld 1984, 24) and, by inference, "the 'real' world manifests itself exclusively there where our constructions break down" (ibid. 39). In this way, it may be that we form negative knowledge about reality (for example in the sense of Popper's theory of refutation) and retain vestiges of realism in constructivism.

Closely related to the narrative approach is the hermeneutic approach, deriving from Gadamer's understanding of the humanities (Gadamer 1976). This approach does not 'explain' facts by causes, but rather seeks to understand their meaning. Ricoeur promoted the idea that psychoanalysis is a science of interpretation rather than a science of observation, more comparable to history than to psychology (Ricoeur 1970, 345).

In the traditional hermeneutic approach, the object of inquiry possesses a truth in-itself, one that may be approached by the hospitability of a non-objectifying dialogue. For Gadamer, this involves an openness that is radically undogmatic, welcoming everything which wants to be understood. This means that there are certain *givens* that await the interpreter, givens that must be listened to and understood within their historical horizon. We truthfully understand the other only when we accept the fact that this other makes a truth claim upon our very being. This posits a truth value that is prior to intersubjective engagement. For Gadamer, this is never the truth of science, it is the truth of understanding. But the process of understanding is anchored in something external to it, possessing horizons and meanings of its own (Gadamer 2004).

As Bouchard sees it, psychoanalytic understanding as hermeneutics takes place in the medium of language. Not a language that is transparent in the representational sense, but a language that functions as a 'set of perspectives' (Schafer 1992), put to the use of uncovering, translating and constructing hidden, obscure and incoherent truths of the unconscious mind. Language here is not understood as creating the object of (psychic) reality, but rather as disclosing it in particular ways that are determined by the question that we address to reality. In this way, the reality of the unconscious is relative to the 'hermeneutic constellation' (Ricoeur 1970, 437) that reveals its meaning. The hermeneutic constellation is formed, in Bouchard's opinion,

> by the patient's free associations and the analyst's suspended yet attentive listening, including the transference and countertransference situation and the various effective metapsychologies at work. These are understood as semi-formal generalizations, serving as both useful and necessarily limiting traditions, a priori assumptions in our listening, attempts to provide coherent frameworks to the observations derived from the previous application of the psychoanalytic method... I might say that the hermeneutic approach is the methodological condition of the possibility of the realism of the unconscious.
>
> BOUCHARD 1995, 536

Given as hermeneutic activity, the truths of psychoanalysis remain temporal and ever-evolving, deeply entrenched in the emotional and linguistic context of both participants. Appelbaum downplays the realistic element of hermeneutics, and places larger emphasis on its intersubjective element. He claims that psychoanalysis is in no need of a foundation, scientific or otherwise. Foundationalism is about truth, about what is known. Hermeneutics is about interpretation, about the generation of meaning, of understanding as an experience, where truth values are irrelevant. In the case of analysis, the very possibility of alternate meanings is, in and of itself, therapeutic:

> Hermeneutics…understands the analysand in the analytic situation as engaging in the intersubjective and interpersonal search for meaning… The analysand and the analyst are co-authoring the ongoing text of the analysis. The relation of the analyst and the analysand with regard to the writing of the analytic text is one of co-authorship rather than that of editor to writer. The analyst is not the editor correcting and having his or her suggestions accepted by the writer.
>
> APPELBAUM 2011, 11

In this approach, psychoanalysis dwells in a domain of multiple truths because its methods address possibilities rather than necessities and does not adhere to limitations imposed by scientific or other theoretical models. In the hermeneutic approach, truth is unveiled through interpreting and reinterpreting of psychic objects. The outcome of one round of interpretation is always given to transformation in the next round of interpretation, due to either changing perspective or the consideration of additional materials. Similarly, in clinical practice, the analysand and the analyst engage in a dialogue that interprets and reinterprets the analysand's unconscious – the existing psychic object. Here, the status of the analysand's material is not considered as facts or memory as such, but already includes an element of interpretation of both life events and earlier events that have occurred in the course of analysis and outside of it.

Appelbaum here draws the hermeneutic closer to a pure intersubjective epistemology wherein objective reality, stability and truth are constituted through agreement with the other. According to Stolorow and colleagues (Stolorow et al. 2001), an infant, from the very start, validates his experiences of reality not empirically (by means of trial and error), but by comparing his experiences with those of his significant others. Donna Orange (1992) maintains that, in therapy, as in development, truth and meaning emerge from conversation between and among people with different points of view, which are not always consistent with each other. People come from different histories, backgrounds and traditions; they have different assumptions, personalities and previous experiences. Two or more subjective systems are always involved in establishing truth.

In this context, the analyst does not 'know better' than the patient what corresponds with outer reality and what does not. Each participant in the conversation has his own perspective of a fragment or aspect of reality. There are many possible perspectives. Since we cannot escape the limits of our personal perspective, our truth is inevitably partial, but conversation can help us broaden our vision. This 'perspectival realism' acknowledges that the only reality accessible by psychoanalysis is the subjective/intersubjective organization of experience (Orange 1992; 1998). Meaning and truth are determined by joint effort in what is already a common reality.

Orange has invested considerable effort in articulating an epistemology for intersubjective psychoanalytic theory. Her theorizing reflects an immense effort to integrate epistemologies. She criticizes radical constructivism and does not waive realism easily:

> One of us (Orange 1995) has argued extensively that experience is both given and made, and that a perspectival realism is epistemologically and practically superior to both relativism and objectivism in any of their forms. To tar intersubjectivity theory with the constructivist brush, one must avoid defining terms and making distinctions.
>
> ORANGE ET AL. 1998, 570

But this vestige of realism is, in her terms, a 'moderate one' in which "the real is an emergent, self-correcting process only partly accessible via personal subjectivity but increasingly understandable in communitarian dialogue" (Orange 1995, 62). At times, as in the quote just given, she seems to grant subjectivity a transcendental priority, with intersubjectivity carrying an elaborative and clarifying function. At other times, she seems to prioritize intersubjectivity, as when identifying her approach with Wittgenstein's intersubjective epistemology as expressed in the linguistic turn:

> So I claim his support for my claim that there is reality, but that perspective and culture limit my knowing of it, that it is meaningful only within systems, and that conversation is required for its meanings to emerge. The process of making sense- a process including, in his terms, both saying and showing- together with whatever we find, I call understanding.
>
> ORANGE 2003, 484

Orange's epistemology may be seen as an admirable effort to combine elements of epistemology, while her 'mixed-model' aspires to encompass the wide range of psychoanalytic phenomena that cannot be articulated or understood by means of only one particular epistemic perspective.

As can be seen here, proponents of different truths in psychoanalysis continue to grapple with the difficulties of epistemology, and yet, a clear transition may be identified and articulated. In the last decades of psychoanalytic thinking, the epistemological focus has shifted from reconstruction to construction, from object to subject, from realism and objective idealism to subjective idealism, from a Correspondent concept of truth to an Intersubjective one. Psychoanalytic truth in contemporary thought is often understood as constructed by interpretations; its criteria are often those of 'usefulness', namely, the extent to which interpretations may improve the patient's conditions, be they conditions of growth, or of intersubjective recognition, either by the patient or of him.

The Relating of Truth and Epistemology in Psychoanalytic theory: As I clarified throughout the above discussion, epistemology and truth are not one and the same, but they are inter related. *Each epistemology has a notion of truth that it naturally gives rise to.* Thus, realistic epistemology is the natural home of Correspondent truth. Objective idealism may retain the possibility of pure objective truth, but recognizes that the road leading to it is imbued with experiential subjectivity and intersubjectivity and limited by inherent constraints of consciousness. Thus, the Bionion O of psychic experience carries inherent truth value, but can only be known vicariously, in subjective and intersubjective contexts of experiencing. Subjective epistemology, as in phenomenological thought, grants subjectivity a transcendental function and therefore Subjective-Existential truths are the most valid here. In Intersubjective epistemology, intersubjectivity (as expressed in truth, culture or language) is a precondition for subjectivity and precedes it logically and epistemologically. Therefore, Subjective truths will always be coloured by the intersubjective and, in a way, subordinated to it.

Each epistemology, alongside its primary version of truth, *also accommodates the other truths, but it values them differently*. For example, Coherent truth is a pivotal and valid possibility in idealist epistemologies, but it will be considered, at most, a narrative within a realistic perspective. In the same manner, the experience of Correspondent truth for a subjective epistemologist is, of course, an illusion. This has important implications for psychoanalysis. As mentioned above, the Subjective truths of the analysand have been given recognition from the early days of Freud, as I illustrated by reference to *'Mourning and Melancholia'* (SE 14:237–259). But these Subjective truths were regarded by Freud as neurotic symptoms and mental health was asymptotic to the one objective truth. By contrast, Kohut and Winnicott acknowledged Correspondent truth but *valued* Subjective-Existential truth as expressing the core essence of being human and as being the vehicle of therapeutic effect and progress. Spence acknowledged Pragmatic truth but warned of its destructive effect on clinical methodology and objectives. Epistemologies may *recognize* various truths, but they favour the truth that is primary to them. *In the context of psychoanalysis, this valuing of truths is reflected in the definition of therapeutic objectives and methodologies.*

As the value and status of the analysand's Subjective truths are defined differently across different theories, so are the Subjective-Existential truths of the analyst. These were understood by Freud as counter-transferential responses that obstruct the analyst's ability to maintain his neutral, analytic stance. Following Freud, attitudes changed gradually and counter-transference became a prime vehicle for insight and interpretation. Ogden, for example, wrote of many experiences in which these Subjective-Existential truths evolve in the analyst's reverie and form an essential part of the movement of understanding. Reverie is a particular, ruminative state of mind, in which the analyst draws on his own musings, feelings and fantasies in order to understand what is going on, from moment to moment, in the mind of the patient. He then communicates his insights back to the patient in a way that is attuned to the thematic context (Ogden 1994a).

Hanly also recognizes this kind of process: "There is a subjective, personal component in our responses to patients" but, in his opinion, it is one that can and should be drawn into the service of reality testing about the patient's psychic life through recognition of the transference and the associations that reveal it. "A passionate engagement by the analyst in analytic work with the analysand need not deprive the analyst of a measure of objectivity, defined as gaining access to the psychic life of the patient as he or she is experiencing it, and as not crucially distorting it in its construction by the analyst" (Hanly 2001, 518).

Benjamin expresses the need to approach the patient with the analyst's subjective responses and act upon them in different therapeutic ways, but she writes at a time when this principle has already received diverse formulations: "Thus even an emphasis on the analyst's subjectivity can have very different consequences, some emphasizing the analyst's contribution through interaction, others through emotional introspection and identification; some emphasizing containment, others mixing it up with the patient" (Benjamin 1997, 793).[7]

---

7 "To simply cast the opposition in terms of those who believe the analyst participates in the relationship and those who strive for analytic objectivity leaves out the equally crucial differences among those who believe in using one's subjectivity. For example, we can delineate a difference between the self psychological use of subjectivity to resonate and create empathic

Clearly, for Hanly and Benjamin the usefulness of Subjective-Existential truths is beyond doubt, but it always leaves open various possible interventions that are qualitatively different from each other and do not grant Subjective-Existential truth immediate priority.

Another way that psychoanalytic theories incorporate different truths (and determine their value and function in psychic life) is by means of their embodiment in psychic structures. In Freudian theory, for example, intersubjective truth appears as constitutive of the superego because, as a personality structure, the superego embodies socialization. Its agents are parental, alongside social conventions. Intersubjective truths that are internalized as personality structures are often depicted as being in conflict with other truths, embodied in different structures: Subjective-Existential, for example, as in Freud's Id or Winnicott's True self. Freud advocates the supremacy of Correspondence as expressed in reality testing. Winnicott, of course, believing in the True self and its spontaneous, body-based creativity, might find the reign of Correspondence restrictive, rendering emotional life poorer.

A similar picture can be observed regarding Ideal truths. In certain psychoanalytic theories of personality, the Ideal truth appears as a psychic structure such as Freud's ideal ego. In *On Narcissism: an Introduction*, Freud (1914) introduces the idea of 'ideal ego' as a construct through which the ego can evaluate its own efforts. Its origins are mostly narcissistic:

> This ideal ego is now the target of the self-love which was enjoyed in childhood by the actual ego. The subject's narcissism makes its appearance displaced on to this new ideal ego, which, like the infantile ego, finds itself possessed of every perfection that is of value. As always where the libido is concerned, man has here again shown himself incapable of giving up a satisfaction he had once enjoyed. He is not willing to forgo the narcissistic perfection of his childhood; and when, as he grows up, he is disturbed by the admonitions of others and by the awakening of his own critical judgement, so that he can no longer retain that perfection, he seeks to recover it in the new form of an ego ideal. What he projects

participation, the Kleinian use of subjectivity to receive projective identification and the relational-conflict use of subjectivity to analyze a co-created, relationship of mutual influence. Mitchell (1993) usefully suggested that these opposing views could be complementary insofar as 'thinking about the analyst's participation serves as a corrective for those…who believe that they, in fact, know what the patient needs' whereas in reverse, theories that track the patient's 'subjective experience can provide a useful corrective…where there is a tendency to drift into a preoccupation with the analyst's participation'" (Benjamin 1997, 794).

> before him as his ideal is the substitute for the lost narcissism of his childhood in which he was his own ideal.[8]
>
> SE 14:93

The ideal is central in Heinz Kohut's theory, where it appears in various forms: As a necessary condition for healthy object relations, as an internalized figure which represents the ideal and as a structural pole of the self that embodies the content and the motivational force of ideals and aspirations. The ideal guides the subject and directs his actions, as well as influences his construal of his world. The individual assesses, judges, and directs himself in relation to and in line with ideals which don't necessarily *have* an objective existence, but are experienced as though they do; they are perceived as being discrete, fixed, and possessing motivational and directive value (Kohut 1985).

Most psychoanalysts would agree that ideals are often regarded as truths by their patients. However, differences abound regarding their therapeutic use by analysts. Kohut believes a life bereft of Ideal truth is barren. Without ideals "the healthy capacity for enthusiasm will be lost- the enthusiasm for goals and ideals which people with a firm self can experience vis-à-vis the admired great who are their guide and example or with regard to the idealized goals that they pursue". Moreover, "The ideal-hungry feels the persistence of the structural defect and, as a consequence of this awareness, he begins to look for- and, of course, he inevitably finds- some realistic defects in his God. The search for new idealizable selfobjects is then continued, always with the hope that the next great figure to whom the ideal-hungry attaches himself will not disappoint him" (Kohut 1978, 420).

These ideas translate into methodology, where analysis offers a renewed possibility of development by means of idealizing relations with the analyst.[9] Kleinians, on the other hand, find fault in the acceptance of ideals as truth, suggesting the influence of splitting that acts as a defence in the face of aggression. Benjamin criticizes the willingness of analysts to pose as ideal selfobjects for

8 In 'Group Psychology and the Analysis of the Ego' (1921) Freud again relates to the ego ideal as a configuration that is distinct from the ego and which enables the understanding of diverse phenomena in which the other is perceived as superior. This explains submission to hypnosis and to leadership, infatuation and admiration, etc. when, according to Freud, the subject projects his ideal ego upon another person. Nunberg (1955) differentiates the superego from the ideal ego by saying that the subject complies with the latter out of love, whereas with the former he complies with fear. The ideal ego, he continues, is modelled on beloved persons, while the superego is modelled on feared ones.

9 The possibility of mitigating a persecutory superego through identification with the analyst as a benign, tolerant, auxiliary superego function was stressed early on by Strachey (1934).

their patients. As she sees it, the analyst who poses *an* ideal or *as* an ideal might seriously compromises the inquiry of the patient's experiences of lack, weakness and damage, both in analysis and outside of it (Benjamin 1994a).

Similar considerations apply to the analytic use of the Coherent-narrative truth. Whereas for Schafer Coherent truth is a condition of communication and knowability and, beyond that, often supplies the analysand with a solid structure for formulating and enhancing his identity, Levenson (1988) and Laplanche (2008) speak of narrative structures as defensive by definition, translating into congealed ego language the inchoate mental richness of the unconscious. For Laplanche, the act of liberating thought from these defensive forms is that of 'de-translation', where coherence should be relinquished in favor of more powerful formulations. He views de-translation as the properly analytic vector, contrasted with the reconstructive, synthetic, defensive one (Laplanche 2008).

What is clear from these short illustrations is that analysts from different psychoanalytic schools acknowledge the different truths that influence mental life generally and analysis particularly. But they ascribe their value differently, often as dictated by their epistemological convictions, and interpret differently the processes that are set in motion when pursuing a particular truth. From the vantage point of the Ideal truth, Pragmatic truth may seem inferior. The reverse may hold as well, when Ideal truths are understood as defence against action, freedom and personal responsibility.

The discussions I presented above do not culminate with conclusions or agreement; indeed, they often seem to be running in parallel lines. As Hanly aptly stated, issues of epistemology and truth are no less controversial in philosophy than they are in psychoanalysis (Hanly 1995, 901). What they do bring forward very clearly is the *existence* of multiple truths, as well as of multiple epistemologies. The former appertain to personal experience and the latter to meta-theoretical assumptions that lead to the values ascribed to the different notions of truth.

Truth and Semiotics

Semiotic theories are theories of sign and signification. What semiotic theoreticians try to do is to explain how meanings are formed, to explain the way in which systems of signs, like language, function so as to afford understanding and allow communication. As I will now proceed to show, semiotic theories, like the psychoanalytic ones, fall into the same categories as philosophical truth notions, namely: Correspondent, Coherent, Pragmatic, Subjective-Existential,

Intersubjective and Ideal. Before beginning a detailed theoretical analysis of how epistemological assumptions carry their hermeneutic function, I will illustrate the diverse, truth-related meanings that an utterance may generate.

Imagine hearing a neighbour cry out loud: "there is a witch on the second floor!" On hearing this sentence, the hearer immediately scans a number of alternative meanings that may be attributed to this statement. Put differently, the hearer debates in what reality he may search for the signified of this statement. In the realm of objectivity, knowing witches to exist, the hearer might wonder about her personal characteristics: Is she a big witch or a small one? Is she well-meaning or wicked? These characteristics will be derived either from previous meetings with witches (along the Correspondent axis) or in relation to a fixed, abstract mental (Ideal) representation of a witch in the hearer's mind. In the realm of Subjective-Existential truth, he might be having an immediate recollection of a clairvoyant moment he once had with a woman he just happened to pass by. Witch would then mean some extraordinary, medium-like abilities. Of course, he could just as well visualise his mean and offensive flatmate, creating a meaning that touches upon the nasty. Speaker and hearer may be living in a common culture in which a witch is intersubjectively understood to be a woman who tempts men sexually. The Pragmatic meaning of the utterance might be 'run for your life!', if the hearer ascribes to witches extraordinary destructive powers. Coherent meaning would lead our hearer to think of other extra-human beings such as the devil, god or spirits and their relations with humans.

My point here is that no meaning can be generated at all without the context of a given epistemology. Meaning as such requires a frame of reference that always defines a reality, a possibility that may be construed as real. These epistemological frameworks are not articulated or conscious, but they manifest in our images of reality in our experienced truths, in every understanding that we form. The construal of realities and significations by means of these epistemologies are the automatic processes our mind effects in order to ensure that we move within comprehensible worlds.

Showing, as I do below, that semiotic theories fall into the same categories as truth conceptions underlines two observations. The first concerns the overarching influence that epistemological assumptions carry into all dimensions of symbolic action – hermeneutic in addition to psychological. We see the hermeneutic effects of these assumptions on psychoanalysis, both at the level of theory, and at the level of clinical interpretation. The latter, of course, concerns primarily meanings that are articulated in speech. *In the context of communication in general, and the therapeutic encounter in particular, the question of truth becomes also a question of meaning.*

The second observation is that, with the addition of semiotics to the disciplines that are structured by epistemological assumptions, we effectively theorize about what it means to be a subject. I discuss this issue more expansively in the next chapters, but I wish to formulate this implication in a generalized form: The multiplicity of truth conceptions is a design feature of subjectivity. Put differently, the subject is constituted by multiple epistemic organizations.

I begin with presenting the paradigmatic, truth-inspired division in semiotics and briefly illustrate how psychoanalytic ideas relate to the semiotic formulations. My logic here is simple: Interpretation (in analysis) assumes a theory of meaning. This idea brings about a continuity in psychoanalysis between metatheory and the theory of interpretation. Both give rise to the truth-inspired categories. I continue by presenting the traditional psychoanalytic debate among epistemic perspectives and conclude with my own model by analyzing multiplicity as a basic characteristic of the human mind. It reflects not only in meta psychology, but also in clinical psychoanalysis and in developmental theory.

The referential-realistic theories of meaning reside, of course, in a realistic epistemology. Sharing the basic premises of the *Correspondent notion of truth*, they assume a recognizable and stable differentiation of inner and external realities. They assume that linguistic expression tells us something about the world. In that sense, linguistic expression is derivative of the actual situation to which it refers. Here, the initial meaning of expression is its reference, be it an object, a term, an idea or a complex system of related events.[10] The reference is always external to the linguistic expression itself.

In his formative essay *On Sense and Reference* (Frege, 1952), Frege reproduces in the realm of signification the age old philosophical distinction between external and internal objects, between the physical and the mental. The *reference* of a linguistic expression, according to Frege, is the external object that the expression refers to. We can name the external object and create the class of equivalence between names and meanings in the form of dictionary-like definitions. Frege illustrates this with his celebrated formula: the evening star = Venus. The *sense* of the expression is the internal concept that allows the reference to carry meaning for a cognizing subject. It is what

10 This definition is similar to that defined by Aristotle in 'On Interpretation': words symbolize concepts and concepts symbolize things. It is also equivalent to what Jakobson (1960) termed the 'referential function' of language: intentionality towards the referent and orientation towards the context – the thing or person discussed. A common conclusion in this line of referential semantics is that the truth conditions of a sentence are in actual fact the sense of the sentence, as argued by Gottlob Frege.

the speaker understands when processing the linguistic expression and therefore the basis for linguistic communication. *The linguistic expression points to its reference and presents its sense.*

Sense, like reference, has an objective existence which is independent of the particular speaker. As a representational entity, Frege positions sense in between reference on the one hand and the *subjective image*, on the other hand. To clarify this, Frege presents another one of his celebrated illustrations, that of observing the moon through a telescope. The act of observation can be analysed as if it is a linguistic expression.

> I compare the moon itself to its reference: it is the object of the observation, mediated by the real image projected by the object glass in the interior of the telescope, and by the retinal image of the observer. The former I compare to sense, the latter is like the idea or experience....[as] each one would have his own retinal image .
>
> FREGE 1952, 59

The sense is of abstract objective quality. It is conventionally linked to the *linguistic expression,* as opposed to *the speaker*. Sense is differentiated from reference on the one hand and from image on the other, the image being the idea that exists in the subject's mind, in a private and varied manner. Thus, the signifier refers to a three layered signified, comprising of a reference, a sense and an image.

It is easy to see how Freud attributed referential-realistic meanings to his analysands' speech. He believed there was an object in reality – an event of sexual seduction or elements thereof – which referentially dictated the meaning of the signifier (the hysterical symptom). Later on, when Freud abandoned the theory of seduction, he dealt more with the dimension of sense than with the dimension of reference. This dimension of sense continued to carry a fixed and abstract meaning, the content of which was forbidden passion and seduction – but it was already situated in the psyche and contained the mental grammar embedded in it.

As opposed to the referential meaning created by phenomena in the outside world, the *mentalistic-ideal definition of meaning* derives from the association of words with mental representations. In this view, like in the *Ideal notion of truth,* what renders language meaningful is its participation in the structured field of 'forms' that are mentally, but not sensually, accessible. Stable principles and forms (representations) are posited as the a priori basis of thought. In this manner, the word 'cat' receives its meaning from a (possibly innate) representation in our minds and not from a realistic existent object which is independent of our consciousness. This, of course, is reminiscent of the way Plato believed that language acquires meaning through its participation in, and expression of, ideal forms. The mentalistic approach to language does not relate to the world or to language at face value. A sentence is not perceived as an independent object in the world, but as a combinatorial structure in the mind of the speaker. This structure can be shared with other speakers by use of visual or acoustic signs.

Like in idealism generally, the potential danger of the mentalistic approach to meaning concerns the dangers of solipsism. Stated differently, the mentalistic approach needs to account for the communicational function of language. Two philosophers from the mentalistic school of thought offered two different accounts: Fodor (1975) did so by assuming a mechanism that connects between mental concept and physical world by causal relations, thus incorporating a realistic element in his idealistic epistemology.[11]

Jackendoff (1992) took a radical stand by renouncing the connection between words and things in the world and relating only to the linkage between words and *conceptual structures*, which form the subjective component of perception and thought. Here, the investigation of language is an investigation into the mind of a *person* who speaks and understands the language. For Jackendoff, meaning is based on the association of signifier with image in Frege's sense of an internal, subjective entity. However, in order to account for communication, Jackendoff assumed an implicit agreement between speaker and listener, whereby they share the conceptual structures of the speaker.

In psychoanalysis, Kohut and Winnicott effected the move towards Jackendoff's kind of meaning, where spoken words are tied up with images in the mind of the analysand. They downplayed both the importance of the reality that is external to the subject and of a pre-existing abstract objective sense. Instead, they placed center-stage the patient's subjective experience alongside the meanings and truths pertinent and particular to him.

The linguistic turn shifted theories of signification from realistic and ideal epistemologies further into the intersubjective realm. It recognized that the referential intuition of a stable and permanent meaning was inadequate and

11 Fodor (1975) supposes an innate language of thought often referred to as 'mentalese'. By doing so he approximates the classic rationalist tradition. According to his theory, the basic building blocks of mentalese exist from birth and are actualized in neural patterns of activity. Sentences in mentalese become representations by cognitive-causal relations, similar to the causal relation between the moon and its reflection in a lake. Thus the thought 'here is a cat' is activated in the brain when a cat is present and perceived. The concept 'cat' means cat because it is consistent with all cats and only with cats. According to Fodor, causal relations which stand at the base of the meaning of mental representations are determined by the laws of the natural world.

offered intersubjective agreement in its stead. Here, *intersubjectivity salvaged the notion of meaning* just *like it salvaged the notion of objectivity in the realm of truth*. What was lost as an absolute was regained as a relative.

The linguistic turn reversed the order of precedence between nature and culture, as it did, indeed, between language and thought. Whereas in classic philosophy nature precedes culture and thought precedes language, after the linguistic turn it was culture that determined the portrayal of nature and language that constrained the structure of thought. From this vantage point, language, saturated with cultural values and structured by them, is the vehicle of every particular thought and therefore carries a constitutive function in relation to it. This is why it is not possible to fully express in one language the meanings of an idea formulated in another language. Taken to its extreme, this approach sees language as mediating perceptual processes as well, thus situating speakers of different languages in different realities (Boas 1964; Sapir 1964).

Classic semantic approaches retained the association between signifier (a unit of signification like a letter, a road sign or a word) and signified (an object, a concept or a subjective image). By contrast, theories characteristic of the linguistic turn relinquish the traditional role of the signified and implement in its stead social constructs and contracts. Thus, for example, in *Philosophical Investigations* (1999), Wittgenstein sees the meaning of every sign as determined only in the framework of a language game, together with the life forms and the intersubjective contracts that define it.[12] Wittgenstein's linguistic turn added two essentially intersubjective dimensions to the field of semiotics and the philosophy of language: The dimension of contractual social agreement and the dimension of language usage as a rule-ordered activity specific to particular communities of speakers.

Language is anchored in social context and rules. The implementation of these rules grants words their meaning. Words lose their meaning when they are detached from the field they belong in. This emphasizes the fact that a

12 In the transition from the Tractatus to Philosophical Investigations, Wittgenstein ceased to believe in the correspondence between the logical structure of sentences and actual situations in the world. Moreover, he began to oppose the idea that words receive their meaning by representing something that is exterior to language and independent of it. Wittgenstein did not deny the existence of the physical world or the fact that words refer to objects, but he did not accept this fact as supplying a satisfactory explanation for the meaning of words :"When we say: 'Every word in language signifies something' we have so far said nothing whatever;" (Wiitgenstein 1999, cl. 13). When discussing objects in the world, we are acting in the framework of a 'word game' that reflects our point of view and life style, as reflected in the game's grammar. This grammar constitutes the meaning of the words participating in it.

word does not stand alone, isolated, it always depends on a context, not only of the sentence it is in, but also of the form of life it is surrounded by:[13] "Here the term 'language-game' is meant to bring forward and accentuate the fact that the speaking of language is part of an activity, or of a form of life" (Wittgenstein 1999, cl. 23). Speech is not founded on a fixed set of abstract rules (like logical relations). It is a social behaviour, a rule-governed social activity that is embedded in other activities. As such, it changes and can evolve in any number of ways according to the type of activity it is combined with and the way of life it is rooted in.

This approach is implemented in the context of psychoanalysis in various ways. Consider, for example, Paula Heimann's (1952) landmark question concerning psychoanalytic practice. Whenever the patient speaks, she says, one must ask: 'who is the speaker?'. The accepted assumption has always been that the speaker is a subject, the patient, who has created a therapeutic alliance with the therapist and is reporting his inner psychic states. But Heimann understood that, at any moment, the patient could be expressing the concerns or distresses of one of his significant others like his mother or father. This could manifest in the kind of voice that the patient adopted, both physically and thematically. Here, signification arises from the unfolding of agency in speech and the awareness that this agency may shift from one's own self to some other introjected agency. Of course, the whole meaning of a sentence may change in accordance with the agental voice. Moreover and inseparable from the question of agency, at all times, each agental voice functions in a particular language game that critically influences meaning. From an intersubjective viewpoint, the analysand's speech introduces different agencies from his psyche. These interact across different language games and create separable domains of signification.

In *structural-coherent theories of signification* meaning is independent of social context and constructed wholly within the order the signifier. Every element of every semiotic system is grasped in relation to other elements in the same system. This logic is the one that dominates the constitution of *Coherent truth*. In this framework, semiotic entities are never monadic, but rather events

13 As implied above and according to some interpretations, in clauses 244–271 of Philosophical Investigations Wittgenstein (1999) denies the possibility of a private language. At the same time, and in compliance with the existing tension among all theoreticians between the objective and the subjective, the public and the private, some find it possible to interpret Wittgenstein in a way that enables the existence of private language within the boundaries of his intersubjective theory. See: Kripke (1982), Baker (1998), Mulhall (2007) and Stern (2011).

that occur in relation to other entities, with meaning arising from the differences between them. The linguistic 'thing' – the signifier – does not signify in isolation, it lacks an intrinsic identity. Every signifier is differentiated from the others, but remains dependent upon them by relations of metaphor and metonymy such, that a change in one signifier necessarily leads to changes in the related signifiers (De Saussure, 1986).[14]

The principles of signification in the structural approach inform Lacan's theorizing, where the subject is constituted through the other and therefore is cleaved in his core. This characteristic bears a direct affinity to the manner in which signifiers acquire their meanings in the semiotic-structural approach. For Lacan, language and culture impose their pre-existing forms and structures upon a developing subjectivity, determining its potential lines of development. The evolving self first identifies its unity by mirroring, by being reflected in and as an other. This identification contains an irremovable falseness, a bias towards completeness that is not in the subject in the first place. The subject is always trapped in this sort of 'misrecognition', incorporating an element of the alien other in his very core. Alienation re-appears at the symbolic level through the properties of language: They too impose their own logic upon the subjectivity of the subject.

According to Lacan, what often motivates people to seek analysis is their inability to accept the inherent internal splitting of their psyche and their closely related dependence upon others, their repeated frustration with getting free of otherness. In the course of therapy, the analysand "ends up by recognizing that this being (himself) has never been more than an imaginary construct and that this construct disappoints all his certainties" (Lacan 1977, 42). From within this recognition of lack and its consequent frustration, the subject tries to recreate himself as a singular being. But "in this labour which he undertakes to reconstruct *for another*, he rediscovers the fundamental alienation that made him construct it *like another*, and which has always been destined it to be taken from him by another" (ibid. original italics). In other words, the subject is never fully whole and present, never a pure signified.

14 Structuralistic implementations include the capacity of the signifier and signified to switch their positions. While in traditional theory, the order of the signified determines the meaning of the signifier, Barthes (2001) shows how a signifier becomes a signified itself within a chain and hierarchy of significations. Bourdieu (2011) shows how signifiers determine the signified, namely, how representations define the social order existing outside of them and organize it accordingly. A sign may represent reality or conceal it, conceal the lack of a signified and even create a signified in its image. These dynamics strengthen the creative potential of language and emphasize the relative and dynamic nature of meaning.

Since he can only be a subject as a language user, through the act of speaking, he always depends on signifiers, which immediately insert otherness at the heart of his subjectivity. The gap between subject and other, between signifier and signified, 'always already' entails the split nature of the subject.

What then takes place in therapy? As professionals of the symbolic function, analysts investigate the patient's discourse. Dreams, slips of the tongue, symptoms – all these are perceived discourses that articulate the analysand's alienated desire, unknown even to himself. The symbolic means of therapy are such that "the art of the analyst must be to suspend the subject's certainties" (ibid. 43), which are expressive of nothing but imaginary constructions. In the place of these imaginary certainties, the subject, by means of symbolic discourse, decomposes and then recomposes his truth. Truth is defined by Lacan in a very complex way: "I might as well be categorical. In psychoanalytic anamnesis, it is not a question of reality, but of truth, because the effect of full speech is to reorder past contingencies by conferring upon them the sense of necessities to come, such as they are constituted by the little freedom through which the subject makes them present" (ibid. 48). The "assumption of his history by the subject" in a way that incorporates his desire "constitutes the emergence of truth in the real" (ibid. 48–49).

This same act of appropriating history by means of discourse is the essential act of subjecthood: " 'That he sustains as subject' means that language allows him to regard himself as the scene-shifter, or even the director of the entire imaginary capture of which he would otherwise be nothing more than the living marionette" (ibid. 272). Lacan ascribes the creative function of speech to this precedence of the Word in the constitution of subjectivity. As a result, the subject does what he can to recreate the Word in his vision of himself, instead of the reverse: "the Word...we live in its creation, but it is the action of our spirit that continues this creation by constantly renewing it" (ibid. 61). And yet, this is forever done "in the intersubjective continuity of discourse" (ibid. 49). Thus, the locus of the struggle of the subject to extract parts of himself from the reign of intersubjectivity is plunged in spiral form deeper and deeper into his soul.

The workings of a structural principle of signification can be easily traced in the analytic discourse. When an analysand reorders past contingencies, he isn't ordering factual events or exposing a hidden history. Everything he is dealing with is within the purview of the signifier, a symbolic entity that is not directly related to his life events. In this symbolic order, the patient positions himself as the author of the history of his desire. His reorganization of the signifiers allows the subject to put himself more fully behind them and, through this, subjectify his whole being. This is the therapeutic goal according to the early Lacan. What takes place in therapy is 'directing'; the subject reorders signifiers so as to place himself at their epicentre, to be the first person of his biographical stories. We can see that the critical significance of the organizing of signifiers is to identify their *organizer*. This is apparent both in the definition of the Lacanian unconscious ('the discourse of the other') and in his formulation of the goals of psychoanalysis ('where it was, there shall I be').

Roman Jakobson, one of the most influential structural linguists, described the stable relation between linguistic structures and the speech-related functions they serve. The meaning of a statement, he said, is the sum of what is effected by its utterance. This idea is at the center of the *functionalist-pragmatic* theory of signification. Its logic is identical to the logic that functions in *Pragmatic truth*, when the validity of a belief is investigated in the context of its consequences.

The basic constituents of Jakobson's (1960) communicational model are the sender, the receiver and the message. In order for the message to function, it requires a distinct context that is similarly perceived by the sender and the receiver. The message itself requires a code that is also, at least partially, common to sender and receiver. Finally, successful communication requires contact – an actual and psychological channel between sender and receiver which enables them to form and maintain communication. When the necessary conditions are satisfied, communication fulfils a number of *functions*. The *referential* function transmits information and corresponds to the shared reality between sender and receiver. The *emotive* function relates to the sender and expresses his attitude regarding the topic he is communicating about. The *conative* function transmits intentions regarding the receiver, as in imperative forms. The *phatic* function is regulatory of communication itself and serves to start, maintain and end the communicative activity. The *metalingual* function decodes the message linguistically, but always involves general knowledge about the code, which is not contained in the message per se. Finally, the *poetic* function focuses on the message as an object, with its own form and aesthetics. The structural principle in Jakobson's thinking is expressed in the fact that meaning is formed out of the relations between the different basic elements of a message (and their associated functions). Every element receives its meaning in relation to other elements and arises from their interrelations. It is no coincidence that Roman Jakobson had attended Lacan's seminars for a number of years.

Jakobson's model may help us understand how speech and interpretation work in the psychoanalytic situation. Consider, for example, a patient who notices that her therapist has had her hair cut and asks "where do you have your hair cut?" The therapist will usually hear beyond the referential function of inquiring about hairdressers. She may examine the *emotive* tone of the statement: is there anxiety regarding the change of hairdo? Is there anger?

Consideration of the *phatic* function may lead to examining whether the patient is trying to open a channel that subverts the formality of analysis and is instead much more mutual and so on.

Loewenstein recognized Jakobson's potential contribution to the analysis of communication in the psychoanalytic setting. He indicates the manner in which understanding the *conative* function of language may help us to manage enactment in transference (Loewenstein 1956). Ogden states that: "it is essential for the analyst to use language that aspires to a particular form of evocative, sometimes maddening, almost always disturbing, vagueness" (Ogden 1997, 10). Here Ogden is actually referring to the *poetic* function of language, one that cultivates the ambiguity of language and so enables the creation and enrichment of nuance.

The discussion of the functions of language effects a shift from formal and logical semantics towards pragmatics, namely, the way in which the performative context influences meaning and changes it. In his book *'How to do Things with Words'* (Austin 1973), John Austin contends that the meaning of sentences, statements and words is not found only, or even mostly, in their literal interpretation but rather in their influence on the actions and thoughts of those present and participating in the event of communication. Alongside statements that may be assigned truth values (constative utterances), stand the performative utterance, which has an actual effect on the world, but no truth value. For example, when a teacher says "it's break time", he is effectively ending the lesson. Here, the utterance causes an effect on something that is outside of the purview of conversing.

As earlier mentioned, psychanalytic thought has long ago recognized that language 'acts' beyond its referential function and literal content. Although it has not been expressed in linguistic terms, an investigation of this sort treats language as a speech act and observes the intent driving it, alongside the influence it generates (the illocutionary and the perlocutionary dimensions respectively, see Austin 1973, 101–103). Ogden draws close to these ideas in saying that: "Similarly, it is through effects created in language in an analytic setting that meanings/feelings are created and conveyed that lie beyond what is being said" (Ogden 1997, 16). He suggests that the performative dimension of speech lies at the heart of the Kleinian idea that transference is a global feature of the analytic intercourse. Here, like in Jakobson's model, the generation of meaning is relocated from a person's internality to his shared interaction with others. Pragmatic meaning, like Pragmatic truth, is analysed and understood as the effects that speech generates.

The performative function of speech requires collaboration among various participants in the speaking event, which emphasizes the social and pragmatic dimension of meaning. But, according to Ivan Fonagy (2001), there is an additional dimension of meaning that is essentially personal. This additional dimension is more allusive and, in order to be grasped requires the suspension of automatic or literal understanding of meaning. I refer to this dimension as the *Subjective-Existential meaning* of speech.

The literal meaning of a word reflects the communicational history of the language community. By contrast, the personal dimension of meaning arises in the *feel* of the word, its emotional valence and the kind of episodic associations that it arouses in the language user. Such personal connotative meaning is gradually formed as a word is learned, used and gets linked to an array of personal experiences. Often, the feel of a word entails a physical sensation. Thus, for example, the Subjective-Existential meaning of the word 'school' entails different experiences for different people according to their specific educational experiences. The statement 'it was like going to school' may imply an enriching learning experience for one person, while for another it could be associated with bothersome duties.

For Merleau-Ponty, the Subjective-Existential dimension of meaning arises from the expressive connection to a bodily 'gesture'. The word, the utterance, breaks through a primordial silence and causes a physical vibration through the body, creating a sensual experience commensurate with the communicative intention. This kind of meaning belongs to an active 'speaking language', as opposed to a passive 'spoken language'. The latter is 'institutionalized', with ready-made meanings that arouse only 'second-order thoughts' and "demand from us no real effort of expression and...from our hearers no effort of comprehension" (Merleau-Ponty 1958, 213–214). The former, on the other hand, acts "beneath the chatter of words"; it is "a gesture, and its meaning, a world" (ibid. 214). The speaking language expresses the emotional essence of our encounter with the world and establishes new meanings in a manner analogous to how intentional movement grants meaning to an object-like organ.

Davidson's familiar contributions to the philosophy of language revolve around the relation he formed between truth and meaning, and the particularization that this relation underwent by means of the formerly described Davidsonian triangle that relates two speakers, their spoken (true) beliefs and their shared empirical world. In 'A Nice Derangement of Epitaphs' (1986), Davidson takes another step in the direction of particularity and idiolect, when he contests the importance usually assigned to conventional meanings in the understanding of conversation. Davidson distinguishes between the literal and the personal dimensions of meaning. Whereas most semioticians describe understanding as predicated on common language and accepted literal meanings, Davidson ascribes understanding to a common *world*. That being given,

Davidson argues for another crucial element without which understanding cannot evolve; this element is the *determination of the hearer to understand the speaker's intent* in the context of their shared world.

For Davidson, convention-based accounts of language fail to capture the role of meaning in communication. The essential meaning in conversation is not the literal, but what Davidson terms the *first meanings* (Davidson 1986). First meanings are understood by means of ad hoc theories that the hearer devises. These are highly contextualized and pertain only to a particular time and a particular speaker. They capture the momentary intention of the speaker and may not be valid in the next moment or for a different speaker using the same utterances. Only in the intersection of the *literal* and the *first* meanings can full, specific understanding be achieved. In this way, Davidson prioritizes the position of idiolect and personal meaning in language.

On the whole and as shown above, epistemic assumptions always underlie semiotic theories and define the different contexts in which the listener searches for meaning. The semiotic, like the psychoanalytic field, reveals the epistemic multiplicity of the human psyche and mind. In communication, my theory allows us to infer the different possible meanings that arise in any particular communicative event.

Clinical Implications of Epistemic Choice

As I said at the beginning of this chapter, psychoanalytic and semiotic theories enable the analyst to understand his patient's speech. In the analytic encounter, he ordinarily applies them in a semi-automatic and semi-conscious fashion. What I have shown so far is that theories in these two disciplines fall roughly into the same categories as truth theories, namely: Correspondent, Coherent, Intersubjective, Ideal, Pragmatic and Subjective-Existential. I will now argue that these truth categories are not limited to abstract, theoretical constructions. Rather, they bear immediate implications for clinical action and entail practices that are often taken up by analysts without awareness or explicit decision.

Firstly, the different semiotic-psychoanalytic theories *view differently the nature of the signified in the analysand's speech and ascribe it to different origins.* That signified may be sought in external or internal reality, may arise from pragmatic considerations or be understood in relation to social contracts. It may, for example, comprise a small number of foretold significations. This is the case of classic psychoanalysis, where the signified tends to fall into a small number of abstract universals such as the *Oedipal complex, castration anxiety* or the *primal scene.*[15] Alternatively, the signified may be ascribed to the relations among signifiers and vary according to the structural features of speech and the agental voices adopted by the patient (Lacan 1977; Schafer 1992).

Secondly, since the epistemic assumptions indicate the domain wherein the analytic investigation is conducted, they determine some central aspects of the *therapeutic methodology*. When we rely on ontological assumptions and the concept of truth is positivistic, the existence of an independent reality is implicit in every understanding we have. The question then becomes '*how* do we *reveal* this independent, historic past?' In his early days, adhering to positivistic causality, Freud concentrated on retrieving the repressed reality of his patients. This led him to induce in the patient regressed mental states and produce free associations aimed at overcoming the repression of memories.

Winnicott and Kohut shifted the psychoanalytic focus from the objective reality that must be exposed and retrieved from repression to a reality that is created subjectively and constitutes a subjective world. The methodology used in order to investigate *this* reality is different from Freud's. The nurturing of subjectivity implied the provision of empathy, emotional containment and holding. These were expected to create the conditions for accessing fragile, intimate and hidden truths.

Bion posited a reality and a truth that can't be accessed through the content of thought or through observation. This led to a methodology that, befitting ideal epistemologies, directed the analyst to withhold his memory and desire so as to avoid all sensual discourse. In contradistinction, for the intersubjective approach that sees intersubjectivity as holding transcendental functions, it is "dialogue… that lies at the heart and essence of analytical practice and creates the emerging reality of the analytic dyad" (Stolorow, Orange and Atwood 2001, 47).

Epistemology thus dictates methodology, and methodology reflects the different therapeutic objectives. Freud aspires to reality testing. Bion finds growth inextricably bound to the unique experiencing of the realm of truth (O). Winnicott nurtures subjectivity and Kohut equates the fortification of the self with the constitution of its ideals. Many intersubjectively oriented therapists

---

15 It is interesting to note that Freud always searched for the personal history that expressed these abstract universals in psychic life. This mirrors his relation to myths as well, where he saw an element of historicity that validates them in a Correspondent manner. Jung, for example, was interested almost purely in psychic reality. Thus, in myths meanings are archetypal, when the collective unconscious speaks to the ego (Jung 1970, 1969). Jung grounded the idea of archetypes in ancient experiences of humankind that were genetically reproduced, innately registered and removed from historic context (Jung, 1969). This marks Jungian analysis as situated in an epistemology of objective idealism.

will posit the recognition of the other's subjectivity and the ability to co-construct meanings and realities as a hallmark of psychic health.

Finally, and closely related to methodology, is the way epistemic assumptions define the *professional authority of the analyst*. Where a realistic or ideal objective epistemology is assumed, the therapist is authoritative and omniscient. His theoretical knowledge supplies him with valid a priori knowledge regarding the patient and his unconscious, together with a methodology to uncover it. This knowledge is privileged relative to the knowledge that the patient has of himself. By contrast, in the subjective epistemology, the patient is assumed to master his own truths and have priority in accessing and expressing them. In the intersubjective epistemology, the therapist acts as a co-writer and re-writer of the patient's history, alongside the patient himself, but without prioritizing the patient's insights. These general observations illustrate the manner in which epistemological assumptions define the psychoanalytic objective, its technique, its conception of authority, and its portrayal of the therapeutic relations.

Epistemic Choice vs. Epistemic Multiplicity

In the traditional psychoanalytic discussions of epistemology, each school takes a position that attests to the 'correctness' of a particular epistemology, by contrast to other schools. It explains its advantages as a framework for psychoanalysis, while arguing that other epistemological approaches are erroneous in one way or another and may even endanger psychoanalytic practice. The discussions among various schools are often accompanied by antagonism, rejectionist critiques and difficulties in mounting real dialogue among them (Summers 2008). A review of these detailed discussions and mutual criticisms may be found in Cavell (1983; 1998). Here, I will only bring a few points that highlight the issues addressed in these discussions and underline the discussants belief that a choice should be made regarding the appropriate epistemology for psychoanalysis. I will then propose an alternative approach that accepts the epistemic multiplicity of the psyche as a point of departure and explicates the kind of investigation that such a vantage point calls for.

Hannah Segal, a contemporary advocate of realism and Correspondent truth, argues that the therapist's role is to uncover the one truth of the intrapsychic world and make it accessible for the patient. She believes that the "shared ground of psychoanalytic concern" consists of "attaining and furthering the truth regarding psychic reality" and that the psychoanalytic endeavour is "to bring about change through the search for truth" (Segal 2006, 287–288). Segal is of the opinion that "psychoanalysis shares the world-view of science, which has as its aim to see life 'as it is' and that what is peculiar to psychoanalysis is that in its scientific endeavour, in its steady pursuit of truth, it is in itself restorative" (ibid. 290).

Segal criticizes psychoanalytic schools that purport to achieve change not by seeking truth but by focusing on the unique influence of the therapist, namely, the support, advice or sympathy he provides. In Segal's words,

> ...the Middle Group, which changed its name to the Independents...and later in the United States, Kohut...went against the psychoanalytic effort to bring about change through the search for truth. For when the analyst actively takes upon himself the parental role, he invites the patient to live in a lie. This in turn promotes concrete functioning rather than symbolization and psychic growth.
>
> IBID. 288

Segal maintains the positivist conception of objectivity as a corner stone of the clinical method and demands of analysts to distinguish between their own contribution to clinical events and the contribution of their patient. The therapist is required to be objective and dedicated to the impersonal passion to know the lives of others. This stance will be in ongoing tension and conflict with the therapist's subjectivity, and must be won and re-won by him. Acting otherwise inhibits the patient's potential of growth.

This conception of psychoanalysis has been criticized from many directions in many discussions, of which I will only mention a few major points. Firstly, Freud is accused of leaving as heritage a *distorted image of man*, "a mechanical, genetic, pessimistic viewpoint of man as the victim of his sexual drives" (Van Bark 1955, 4; see also Brottman 2009; Chessick 2003). This self is by definition reified:

> A consequence for psychoanalysis of assuming the scientific model would be that the subject of psychoanalysis would become, as it does in science, a reified object... If psychoanalysis is to have any objective reality it cannot have it on the same terms as science that is by relating to an object that is a given. Psychoanalysis for its part does not relate to individuals as objects nor does it necessarily consider what is present as 'given' nor as something to be acted upon, measured, predicted or explained.
>
> APPELBAUM 2011, 3

This image of the subject is complemented by the *surgical notion of the analyst* (Blum 1981; Balsam 2008; Carveth 1984). The analyst of positivistic psychoanalysis is posited by its opponents as an omniscient authority in the analytic relationship. Stolorow et al. (2001) express this powerfully:

> Only an analyst, who possesses esoteric knowledge of the universal contents of this unconscious realm, can lead the way down into the patient's private hell, and thus back out into relief... Or, in a Freudian metaphor for the detached expert, the patient needs a psychological surgeon who skilfully penetrates and rearranges the unconscious insides of the patient. The Freudian concept of the unconscious, with contents dictated by theoretical doctrine and already 'known' by the analyst prior to any collaborative exploration, is responsible for many of the authoritarian features of traditmional analysis. With privileged knowledge of the unconscious, the analyst is readily viewed as a *Besserwisser* or 'know-it-all'.
>
> STOLOROW ET AL. 2001, 44

Benjamin (1997) objects to the positivistic stance because she rejects the idea of the analyst as 'the one who knows' in favour of viewing the analyst as 'the one who knows *me*'. Here, the image of the analyst is of one who empathically understands, who is emotionally with me, embracing the maternal ideal of holding or mirroring, by contrast to the phallic image of the penetrating knower (Benjamin 1994, 545). Aron (1996), Mitchell (1997) and Hoffman (1991) criticize the positivistic conception of the therapist's objectivity, arguing that it grants excessive authority to the therapist's opinion, while denying the patient's role in articulating therapeutic insights. Implied is also the denial of the patient's unique particularity by the omniscient analyst.

Benjamin contends that, although Freud often presented himself as a staunch positivist, his writings are rather "a mixed or ambiguous discourse, which at times describes conflicts of force subject to an energetics and at times describes relations of meaning subject to a hermeneutics" (Benjamin 1991, 525). She cites Habermas as pointing out that it was Freud's own scientistic self-misunderstanding that gave rise to later misunderstandings of psychoanalysis as a hard science: "It was a misunderstanding insofar as it was only through the hermeneutic deciphering of dream texts, the penetration of illusion through the interpretation of symbolic connections, that Freud arrived at the 'mechanical' notions of defence and symptom" (ibid.). Benjamin argues that the strong ambition of classical psychoanalysis to *explain* mental processes, rather than merely *understand* them, effectively confuses explanation with interpretation. Furthermore, she argues, the psychoanalytic technique of establishing truth has little to do with scientific evidence, based as it is on the patient's subjective validation of the analyst's statements, be it through recollection, association or explicit agreement.

This last point of criticism regarding the positivistic stance is *methodological*, claiming that psychoanalytic truths do not qualify as scientific, because they can be validated only through subjective criteria. Addressing this issue Collins (2011), for example, both sticks to and deviates from realistic epistemology. Like Segal, she views the reconstruction of the patient's past as a therapeutic goal. Reconstruction, by definition, implies a realistic epistemology, because only an external, independent reality can, strictly speaking, be reconstructed. On the other hand, Collins states that the validation of the reconstructed reality is through the emotional, authentic and immediate experience of the patient.[16] Moreover, these subjective experiences are examined against the broader observations and clinical materials collected in the analytic process. Here, authenticity and coherence become measures for the evaluation of the historical truth and therefore do not qualify as Correspondent truth.

Ricoeur, also from a methodological point of view, points out that the notion of psychoanalysis as an empirical science- like biology or physics, is not really tenable. Reviewing Freud's metapsychology he explains: "As soon as the economics is separated from its rhetorical manifestations, the metapsychology no longer systematizes what occurs in the analytic dialogue; it engenders a fanciful demonology, if not an absurd hydraulics" (Ricoeur 1970, 371). Beginning with the psychoanalytic dialogue- the discourse between the analyst and the patient in the consulting room- Ricoeur looks at the phenomenological aspects and points out that 'causality' in psychoanalysis is more like the study of history than the study of physics. For a case is not really capable of being wholly observed as a standardized set of clinical data that can be checked by a number of 'objective' observers (ibid. 374). Investigating the validity of a set of interpretations is more like investigating the connection between historical events than conducting a scientific experiment.

Additional criticism may resort to classical issues in epistemology, *arguing that there is a fundamental fault with the very differentiation between the objective and the subjective.* What is contested here is not the positivistic image of analyst, patient, analytic relations or authority, neither is it the method of

16 "In authenticity, the analyst searches for genuineness and trustworthiness of an historical account within the context of the transference/counter-transference relationship. The analyst's observations are anchored in the present, and his/her thoughts about the past originate in the context of a contemporary relationship with the patient. In that way 'authenticity' in reconstruction denotes a genuineness of origin that is both sourced from and is faithful to a unique and current stage of an analytic encounter" (Collins 2011, 1393).

verification, but rather the very possibility of epistemological realism. Classical theory ascribes to the analyst an objectivity that contemporary theory cannot accept. Here, the differentiation between inner and outer is not considered valid or possible, so the subjectivity of mental processes is assumed across the board for both patient and analyst.

In subjective epistemology, clinical materials are understood to be the co-creation of patient and analyst and there is no epistemologically valid way of differentiating between the two sources. Renik (1998), for example, contends that we must acknowledge the therapist's irreducible subjectivity and recognize the impossibility of bypassing it. Renik summarizes his position by saying that "unlike an essentialist conception of truth as an a priori thing-in-itself, waiting to be discovered, the conception of truth that informs my analytic activity is pragmatic. Thus, from my point of view, analytic work consists of constructing new meanings rather than revealing old, sequestered ones". He adds: "Obviously, implied here is an evolution in the concept of unconscious, beyond Freud's original notion of a domain of pre-existing, unavailable contents." (Renik 1998, 493).

In intersubjective epistemology, the observer and the observed, the analyst and the analysand, are inextricably involved with each other, to the extent of determining their reality mutually and reciprocally. Hence, in analysis the patient's associations and transferences do not necessarily convey who and what the patient is, but rather who and what the patient is *in relation to the analyst* (Stolorow and Atwood 1997). Different versions of the psychoanalytic understanding of reality have developed under the heading of subjectivist and intersubjectivist approaches, the common factor among them being the disbelief in the existence of one, well circumscribed objective reality. Here, the task of the analytic dialogue shifts from a classical concern with interpreting reality of any kind to an interest in the process by which analyst and patient create and shape an impact on the other through the play of mutual influences.

The subjective and intersubjective approaches engendered fierce epistemological arguments. Friedman, for example, reprimands what he refers to as "a philosophical and literary campaign against what incorrectly is labelled positivism or, more accurately, essentialism" (Friedman 1999, 402). He discusses the contemporary idea "that science no longer believes in objective reality and that therefore psychic reality is the only possible reality" (ibid. 403). According to Friedman, scepticism is vital, as it draws attention to the dependence of meaning on context. That said, claims Friedman, radicalizing the significance of context to the extent of cancelling the existence of reality and meaning is a kind of intellectual laziness:

> unlike the old, debating nominalism, which was willing to do battle, what the new nominalism has learned from two millennia of inconclusive thinking about the problem is never again to take thinking seriously. And with that unseriousness (quite different from the spirit of the hardworking and dedicated positivists, empiricists, Wittgensteinians, and logical pragmatists), the ground is now prepared for a teasing, bantering postmodernism.
>
> FRIEDMAN 1999, 411

Like Friedman, Bell (2009) also harshly criticizes the tendency towards radical relativism and pluralistic epistemology. Acknowledging psychoanalysis's primary concern with inner experience, he argues that:

> It is important to disentangle a commitment to recognizing the importance of the subjective, a deep involvement with it, from the doctrine of Subjectivism, which claims that subjectivity is all there is in the world (in other words, Idealism). In fact, recognizing the importance of subjectivity is part of an attempt to be more objective, whilst labouring under difficult conditions. There is, thus, no necessary connection between deep involvement with human subjectivity and subjectivism as a philosophical position.
>
> BELL 2009, 335

In a psychoanalytic interpretation of the pluralistic approach, Bell suggests that Freud viewed human limitations as essential failings reflecting structural incompleteness, rather then as curable illnesses. The postmodern ethos makes an omnipotent attempt to challenge the negative constitution of knowledge by promoting unrealistic pluralisms that will not force man to accept limitations. For Bell, the limitations inherent in the "distinctions between objective and subjective, inner and outer…and our struggle with these apparent polarities is constitutive of our humanity" (Bell 2009, 344–345).

Bell contends that the core characteristics of psychoanalysis necessarily place it in the framework of realistic-modernism, since it is committed to profound explanations, differentiation between reality and phantasy and causal relations between biography and personality. He claims that the weak epistemology of pragmatics leaves no place for psychoanalysis as a body of knowledge, separate from its effectiveness in assisting patients. In other words, if one relates to psychoanalysis only as a practical science, measured only according to effectiveness, it loses its broader relevance. Mills sees this withdrawal from realism as a move that compromises the status of psychoanalysis as a legitimate human science by rejecting the realistic aspects of objectivity, interpretation and truth (Mills 2015). He adds that a

> further danger of embracing a 'relativistic science' is that psychoanalysis really has nothing to offer over other disciplines, which may negate the value of psychoanalysis to begin with (e.g., empirical academic psychology), let alone patients themselves, whose own opinions may or may not carry any more weight than the analysts whom they seek out for expert professional help.
>
> MILLS 2005, 167

Mills raises another point that lies at the heart of the conflict between subjectivism and critical realism: The autonomy of the subject-patient. He shows that transcendental intersubjectivity of the kind adopted by Relational theory implies that:

> ...notions of freedom, liberation, individuality, personal independence, authenticity, and reflective deliberate choice that comprise the essential activities of personal agency are altogether disassembled. What all this boils down to is the dissolution of the autonomous, rational subject. In other words, the self is anesthetized.
>
> MILLS 2005, 165

For Seligman (2003), "the analyst and patient are co-constructing a relationship in which neither of them can be seen as distinct from the other" (Seligman 2003, 484–485) but this, argues Hanly (2009), runs counter to the notion of the patient as agent, as 'owner' of his life, as an individual with boundaries and meaning. Mills claims that "...the social-linguistic platform...deplete(s) the notion of individuation, autonomy, choice, freedom, and teleological (hence purposeful) action because we are constituted, hence caused, by extrinsic forces that determine who we are" (Mills 2005, 169).

Hanly underlines the same point in terms of autonomy and resilience of the self. He states that at the heart of psychoanalysis lies the

> question of being. ... Is the patient the bearer of his or her own life, an individual life that is intelligible in its own right, knowable in itself and existing independently of our experiences of it and our ideas about it?... As I see it, the autonomous independence of the patient's being is evident in his turning inward, instead of persisting in his grandiose demands

> upon me, in his own search for the strength to do for himself what I could not do for him.
>
> HANLY 2009, 372

According to Hanly, subjective epistemology 'infiltrated' psychoanalysis through its concern with transference and counter transference and specifically through the broad definition of counter transference accepted today, which infers the patient's reality from the therapist's responses and feelings. Clinical attentiveness and interest in transference and counter transference have gradually turned into interactionism and intersubjective epistemology, with their typical blurring of the epistemological distinction between object and subject. These perspectives first shift the analytic focus to the 'here and now' and then take things further in viewing the past as a particular perspective of the present. For them, the past is always re-written by the present. Hanly acknowledges the ability of psychoanalysis to provide new and coherent narrative, but argues that it is wrong to seriously dismiss the history of a person's life. Discussing the meta psychology of clinical interventions, Hanly calls for the combining of different truths – Pragmatic, Coherent and Correspondent. He prioritizes Correspondent truth because it offers sufficient and necessary criteria for the assessment of other theories (Hanly, 2009).

Bromberg presents the opposite pole on the epistemological axis and similarly bases his criticism on underlying psychological needs. 'Truth' and 'objective reality', as he sees them, exist solely as "anchoring points to relieve the fear of drowning" (Bromberg 2009, 359) in the inchoate clinical process. In the absence of these docking points, one must find an alternative source of safety which will allow the therapist to be with the patient without putting at risk the personality structures they have both formed for themselves. This safety is essential as a jumping board for achievements that may or may not be reached. Bromberg believes that the mistaken illusion of truth may be relinquished and the needed source of personal safety can be found in the non-authoritative human connection. Accordingly, in his opinion, "truth…*is state-dependent and subjective"* (ibid. 350).

Mills (2005) states that construing truth thus may confuse patients. Moreover, at times, it may be downright dangerous and irresponsible on part of the therapist to dismiss Correspondence in the face of Subjective truth. Masson (1984) polemically reasserted the importance of factual reality and went much further than previous critiques, claiming that the concept of psychic reality itself served to abuse patients by doubting their actual experiences.

From Epistemic Resolution to Epistemic Multiplicity

The intransigence of the above debate and the inevitability of its open-endedness seem to suggest that psychoanalysis requires, and may be on the verge of, a new paradigm shift. Before presenting my view here, I wish to differentiate it from the paradigm shift effected by intersubjective and relational approaches. The latter's main effect, in my mind, has been the relinquishing of realism and the introduction of an alternative epistemology. Thus, relational theorists show us the constitution, logic and workings of the intersubjective epistemology that they have adopted, noting its singular characteristics, such as heavy reliance on language and the positing of permeable personal boundaries.

The view that I wish to develop here does not propose to choose between epistemologies, but rather to create the theoretical space for multiple epistemologies and the practical space for multiple truths. These are recognized as inherent features of our psychic function. Nietzsche is probably the first to ground truth in a psychological reality and explain it as a phenomenon that arises from the human need for certainty. Following this line of thought, I suggest we continue to *understand the way different kinds of truths arise as a response to different basic needs and the part they play in the construal of our realities.* This is not a postmodern or relativistic statement, rather an epistemological one that calls for the articulation and definition of these truths and proposes a comprehensive investigation of their function in psychic space, as well as in psychoanalytic theory and practice.

As Mills stated: "If psychoanalysis is to achieve some form of consiliatory paradigm, it must be willing to attempt to explain its activities on multiple plains of discourse with sound methodological coherence". He continues that this sort of paradigm must find a way to explain and integrate "methodologies and modes of discourse that have legitimacy within their own frames of reference and perspective purposes" (Mills 2011, 244). I would add here that an additional challenge of this paradigm is to articulate the patterns and the logic that function in the interrelation of these discourses.

There is a line of work in psychoanalysis that may be identified as accepting the phenomenon of multiple epistemologies. Here, the plurality of epistemologies is grasped as an integral characteristic of mental life. The different images of reality that manifest themselves through the various epistemologies are seen as inherent to the interpretative construction of the world. Thus, no single structure renders other structures redundant, but rather relies on the way in which the other perspectives 'capture' different aspects of mental life.

Schafer articulates the inevitable paradox of psychoanalysis: "On the one hand is the fiction of the analyst standing outside of the field of observation.

This fiction is necessary for presenting a rounded and balanced theory of mind and of the analytic process and the changes it can induce". Here stands realistic epistemology and the analyst as able to achieve Correspondent truth. This same analyst instils Coherent and Pragmatic truth to the materials presented by the patient alongside the 'dynamic explanations' of theory (these stable dynamics and structures may be understood as psychoanalytic theory's Ideal truths): "This is the observer who speaks confidently of change in psychic energy, rationality, autonomous functions, stable structures, and so on, and who then organizes all these variables into a picture of the whole mind…and who is consistently concerned with the analysand's welfare". He continues that the analyst must *also* come to terms with the "inevitable recognition and acceptance of perspectivism as the only epistemological stance that makes sense, accompanied by a rejection of positivistic argument" (Schafer 1995, 228).

Actually, what Schafer is here saying is that the analyst must embrace all these truths within his analytic stance. He summarizes thus his position:

> Confronting this paradox, one must, I believe, come to the following conclusion: no one approach can do a complete clinical and theoretical approach all by itself. It is in the nature of each and every systematic approach that it sets limits on what is available to it. Each approach equips us with instruments of thought that bring both light and darkness to its subject matter. Its epistemological and methodological grounding can never be of the sort that precludes alternatives or skepticism.
>
> IBID. 228–229

Rosegrant (2010) brings forward the same epistemic multiplicity as it expresses itself in the three psychoanalytic views of reality: factual, psychic and co-constructed. Rosegrant shows that in the history of psychoanalytic thought, these realities, at the meta psychological and clinical levels, are often in conflict with one another. He demonstrates the way in which psychoanalytic theory and practice gave rise to different versions of reality, each with its own selected phenomena ('facts') and typical, recurring meanings. None of these versions proved more adequate for understanding mental life, which brought Rosegrant to the conclusion that these versions of reality represent different ways of disambiguating psychological information. Instead of a decisive resolution as to what is the 'right' way to perceive reality, Rosegrant suggests that the human condition demands continuous differentiation and integration of every one of the versions of reality.

Schermer (2011) offers a similar insight in his discussion of psychoanalytic interpretation. As Schermer construes it, four interpretative perspectives co-exist in the psychoanalytic context: The first is the Freudian-Aristotelian perspective, which interprets so as to uncover predetermined structures and meanings (realistic approach). The second strives for subjective truth, where interpretations aim to remove objectifications in general and those of ego functioning in particular (subjective approach). The third perspective, which he calls dialogic-existential, sees interpretation as an ongoing relational process. The fourth perspective understands interpretation as creating a transformative presence in both the therapist and the patient. The last two approaches to interpretation are embedded in an inter subjective epistemology. Schermer claims that these four perspectives are not mutually exclusive. Rather, they all influence the therapist's 'free-floating' attention and partake in the mutuality of the psychoanalytic dialogue.

Viewed as co-existent, the various theories of truth and meaning have clear practical implications, which I now wish to spell out only in general terms (I discuss practical implications in some detail in Chapter 6). Generally speaking, the clinical application of *multiple epistemologies* leads to some basic questions: *How* does a person order, understand and negotiate this multiplicity? What is involved in becoming aware of it? How do we figure out the inter relations of multiple epistemologies and formulate their relevance to a person's life and well-being? In the next section, I wish to clarify the relation of epistemology, truth and reality as they manifest in clinical phenomena.

Truths and Reality in Clinical Discourse

The work of the analyst involves, not always consciously, attention to the various kinds of truth and their corresponding images of reality. While listening, the analyst automatically considers various possible interpretations of the analysand's speech: He examines what the patient is referring to in the world around him; at the same time, he scrutinizes the internal coherence of what is being said in relation to the speaker and in relation to what is understood to be his inner world. The therapist compares this inner world with the world as he experiences it and understands what he is being told according to the relevant social contexts. He hears the various elements of the evolving narrative and understands the verbal message in terms of his own subjective response to it. He also, at the same time, forms hypotheses regarding the intentional origins of the message. These rapid, complex, unconscious processes reflect the multifaceted features of the human mind as implied by the different notions of truth.

Every issue in a person's life appears differently in different images of reality. The image portrays certain qualities in one experienced reality and different qualities in another, but all of these qualities are represented simultaneously.

Let me illustrate this with a short, schematic but plausible clinical issue. Consider a patient who raises money issues with his therapist, requesting a discount in fees. In doing so, the patient evokes diverse and non-overlapping representations of money that relate to diverse realities: There is the matter of the actual money which either is or is not in the patient's bank account and which will need to be transferred to the therapist's bank account. This is the factual aspect of the money that is represented on the Correspondent axis. Next, there is the representation of money in its value laden image. This representation is on the Ideal axis, and it would probably inform us about the patient's attitude towards money in general. He may consider it as a necessary evil, a desired goal to be pursued and so forth. The representation on the Subjective-Existential axis would consist of personal experiences and meanings which the patient accumulated in relation to money and which for him create its personal valence. The representation of money on the Intersubjective axis includes its image in culture, both in close circles and on community level. On the Coherent axis, we would find the representation of money as it is related to other elements that are part of the patient's larger narratives: The money as it functions in securing love, trust, adequate nutrition etc. Finally there is the money's significance on the Pragmatic axis as derived from the localized interaction between the therapist and the patient at a particular moment, formed and shaped by specific needs and wishes and in relation to the relevant interests of both parties. Pragmatic considerations determine what impact is rendered by the patient making the request, as well as the impact of the therapist rejecting or accepting the request.

The different representations of money are not in competition. They are in fact complementary, reflecting various organizations of experience, that is, differing realities in which the psyche dwells. Often, the experience and directive derived from one organizational principle are not compatible with those stemming from others. A person sometimes perceives reality as external to him and at other times as embedded within him. Sometimes his reality is coloured and shaped by ideals and at other times by his own particular interests. At still other times, reality may be none other than the image agreed upon between the subject and those around him.

The truths that correspond to these realities in both their function as reference points and as methods of organization are naturally and unfailingly present outside and inside the clinic. Patients and therapists constantly use the concept of truth and its derivatives. Thus, we can imagine a patient saying: "I felt that something real was happening to me in therapy", which expresses a Subjective-Existential experience. Similarly, in saying "There is nothing I can do about it…it's the truth", the patient expresses a sense of externality and discontent in relation to considerations along the Correspondent axis. Occasionally, a patient may pit one truth against another, as in "Perhaps it's right, but it's not my experience, to me it doesn't ring true". Here, a Correspondent truth is set against a Subjective-Existential truth. To further demonstrate the scope of possibilities here, consider a patient saying "That's true, but so what?" Here the patient agrees that the therapist's description of some situation or other corresponds to reality, but for him the statement doesn't offer a way forward, has no Pragmatic truth value. "I'm sorry to say that it's entirely correct but it's completely wrong to claim that that's how I want to be". What is the patient upset about in this utterance? I suggest that the patient's Ideal truth in this instance comes injured from an attack by the Correspondent truth. "From their point of view that's the way it is and that's the truth, but as far as I'm concerned, it's a betrayal of my principles". The conflict between Intersubjective and Ideal truths is here obvious. Such statements, whose basis may be Intersubjective, Correspondent or Ideal, negotiate among themselves and express different positionings of the self. In each of them, the speaking subject aligns himself with one truth or another, this alignment effectively defining his self-position.

In analysis, we can help our patients understand and articulate the different realities they inhabit. It may well be that, while doing so, we will discover the tensions and the difficulties that arise from the different intersections, tensions, contradictions and incompatibilities among these realities. We grant legitimacy to the various truths, admitting that life is too complex to be accounted for by one reality alone. We avoid re-traumatization of our patients who, in the past, may have had their Subjective-Existential truths banned, their actual experiences ignored, their Pragmatic truths dismissed on moral grounds, their Ideal truths scoffed at, and so on. We learn the Intersubjective truths that shaped our patients' sensibilities and probably co-construct with them some new ones. We may allow patients to know, acknowledge and articulate the multi-dimensionality of their living and its discontents.

As this chapter has shown at some length, any thought or theory about the human subject is situated in a definable epistemology. This reflects the fact that the subject himself is continuously processing his world through the same epistemologies, expressed as organizational principles in his psyche, giving rise to various truths and images of reality. In a like manner, we can see how different psychoanalytic theories have stressed, focused and positioned as pivotal a particular truth in the framework of a particular epistemology. Looked at from this perspective, we may see particular theories as bringing into focus one of these realities and articulating its particular phenomena and dynamics. Thus, rather than being in competition, each theory may be understood as reflecting a characteristic truth or epistemic organization of the psyche. Their multiplicity reflects the epistemic multiplicity of the mind.

In the next chapter, drawing on philosophical and psychoanalytic theories, I will examine the constitution of the various truth axes from a developmental point of view. Developmental achievements and failures brand the logic of the various axes in the mind, determining the subject's future construals of himself and of his world. Through developmental considerations we can understand how a particular axis has acquired a particular saliency in the psychic economy of the subject. In that sense here, like in other models, developmental considerations hold the key to understanding personality.

CHAPTER 4

The Philosophic-Psychoanalytic Interface: Truth Axes and Psychic Development

Truth, then, reflects the subject's way of organizing his world. Each truth axis yields a particular image of reality, with a particular notion of truth serving as its Archimedean point of certainty. As I described in detail in Chapter 2, *the overarching need for truth is expressed across several dimensions of the subject's life. Each truth axis creates an image of reality and a truth within it that ensure the provision of a deep emotional need which motivated its formation*. Reiterating briefly, the needs I refer to are the need to negotiate external reality, to form coherent knowledge, to maintain attachment and share a common reality, to retain authenticity in a world that is often alienating, to transcend partiality and insufficiency and to insure and enhance future personal interest.

As formerly explained, each of the above needs is satisfied by *a vital link* between the subject and an aspect of his inner or outer world. Thus, the need to negotiate external reality is addressed by the link between the subject and what he perceives as realistic facts external to him. Coherence is negotiated by the link between the subject's various beliefs and tendencies. The need for attachment and commonality with others is, of course, established by the link with others. The need for authentic existence is ensured by means of the subject's link to what he perceives as his true self. The aspiration for perfection is realized by examining the correspondence a subject finds between beliefs or tendencies he has and what he perceives as his ideal. The need to enhance future benefit is provided for by the subject's ability to associate between belief or action and their future implications. These same links are the ones from which truth values are derived in the various truth notions.

Each truth axis organizes the subject's world in a way that best accommodates the constitution and the preservation of a particular link between the subject and an aspect of his inner or outer world. On the whole, the basic need that is provided for by any particular link is the one that drives the creation of the truth axis and maintains its vitality and relevance throughout the subject's life. These links are not innately given, but rather involve the surmounting of developmental challenges and crises. These challenges can be observed not only at the level of personal development, but also in the history of ideas, in both philosophy and psychoanalysis.

 | DOI 10.1163/9789004314993_006

Every axis – by virtue of its very existence and the extent of its dominance over other axes – is an outcome of complex interactions between an inborn disposition and its surrounding environment as they shape a specific developmental history. Developmental processes, in turn, leave their traces on the workings of each axis. In this way, the successes and failings of a developmental-emotional history are marked by the symbolic-experiential way in which a person organizes and structures his world.

The potency of truth axes in understanding individuals and guiding therapy comes in no mean way from the ability to describe the kind of challenges and crises through which each axis has developed. Let me now examine each axis from the vantage points of needs, development and challenges.

The Constitution of Truth Axes in the Psyche

Constitution of the Correspondent axis: In order for an individual to be able to make good judgments about correspondence to reality, he has to establish a distinction between his representations of inner and outer reality, as well as be able to compare them and determine differences and similarities between them. This may sound simple yet, from Plato's time and to this very day, philosophy deliberated the extent to which it is possible to either separate or compare inner from outer.

All through antiquity, the differentiation between wakeful and dream products was recognized as epistemologically useful, but ontologically suspect. When the lines of demarcation were probed deeply enough, they tended to wobble, if not to disappear. This probably underlay the tendency of creative thinking, across times, to tantalize the mind with the thought that dreams are real and that the 'real' world is a dream (Miller 1994). Descartes begins his meditations by pointing out how difficult it may be to differentiate dream from reality, and how aware we must be of the ease of confusing the two. The images produced during wakefulness and those produced by dreams may be similar in a way that completely obscures the mental states from which they arise. Hume held the differentiation of perception and dream as a point of departure in skeptical philosophies, tracing it back to Socrates and Heraclitus.

The first comprehensive psychological outline of the way in which the internal world is structured and delineated from external world was offered by Freud. He depicted the relation between internal and external as a line of conflict, permeated with tension and given to perpetual construction and destruction. The ability to distinguish between these two worlds is a defining characteristic of the healthy personality, one that is often compromised in the context of neurosis and psychosis. Freud developed his conception of inner and outer worlds on the basis of scientific-biologic assumptions regarding man and his development, both individual and as species.

For Freud, mental life is driven by instinct, "a concept on the frontier between the mental and the somatic…the psychical representative of the stimuli originating from within the organism and reaching the mind, as a measure of the demand made upon the mind for work in consequence of its connection with the body" (SE 14:121). The first two groups of primal instincts were identified as the ego or self-preservative instincts and the sexual or object related instincts. The former promoted the survival of the individual, while the latter promoted the survival of the species. Both were assumed to answer to the pleasure principle, aimed at reducing pain and tension and increasing satisfaction and pleasure. On the basis of these distinctions, Freud had to figure out how the psychic apparatus may brave dangers, tackle challenges and overcome obstacles in order to survive and thrive in the particular world in which it is situated.

The problem is that the ego has no wish to recognize reality. Although born with the ability to do so, "…the original 'reality-ego', which Freud endowed with the ability to distinguish internal and external…changes into a purified 'pleasure-ego', which places the characteristic of pleasure above all others. For the pleasure-ego the external world…feels…hostile…the ego-subject coincides with pleasure, and the external world with unpleasure (with what was earlier indifference)" (SE 14:135). The pleasure ego has no wish to engage with this hostile reality and will do so only when the pleasure driven hallucination fails to procure satisfaction of its needs:

> It was only the non-occurrence of the expected satisfaction, the disappointment experienced, that led to the abandonment of this attempt at satisfaction by means of hallucination. Instead, the psychical apparatus had to decide to form a conception of the real circumstances in the external world and to endeavor to make a real alteration in them. A new principle of mental functioning was thus introduced; what counted for the mind was no longer the agreeable but rather the real, even if it happened to be disagreeable. This constitution of the reality principle proved to be a momentous step.
>
> SE 12:218

With the appearance of the reality principle, the psychic apparatus develops various functions – attention, reasoning, memory – that enable it to replace crude motor discharge with intentional action aimed at transforming reality.

Energy no longer flows freely among ideas, but is tied up with objectives, thus begetting the beginnings of thought. By mastering these functions, the Ego mediates between the psyche and reality. The thinking ego is located between the demands of the Id and the action that aims to satisfy these demands. Appraising the ongoing situation in the light of past experiences, the Ego calculates the implication of the desired act and decides if to allow it or inhibit it. At times, when desire itself is deemed dangerous, the Ego might repress it, along with the act it may inspire. The Id is subjugated to the Ego and they conflict in their struggle for the control of both perception and action. Only if the Ego gains the upper hand, the principle of reality effects an appropriate differentiation between internal and external.

By nature, the Id hates reality and its representation in the Ego and the Superego. The conflicts among the three agencies continue throughout life:

> the id, will not allow itself to be dictated to by reality. Both neurosis and psychosis are thus the expression of a rebellion on the part of the id against the external world, of its unwillingness – or, if one prefers, its incapacity – to adapt itself to the exigencies of reality (SE 19:184). In neurosis the relation to reality is compromised by means of denials, repressions and distortions. In psychosis another 'autocratic' step is taken by the creation of a new reality which no longer raises the same objections as the old one that has been given up. "and there can be no doubt of two facts – that this new world is constructed in accordance with the id's wishful impulses, and that the motive of this dissociation from the external world is some very serious frustration by reality…which seems intolerable…delusion is…like a patch over the place where originally a rent had appeared in the ego's relation to the external world."
>
> SE 19:150

For Freud then, the encounter with reality is inherently traumatic and reality testing is not a simple ability. To perceive facts and represent them as external to psychic reality is a developmental achievement that is necessary for the constitution of a correspondent truth axis. It arises from biologically determined processes and it is aimed, first and foremost, to enable man as a biological creature and, later, as a social one, to survive and thrive in the world.

Constitution of the Coherent Axis: The establishment of a coherent axis of truth requires the ability to connect between thoughts. In philosophy, Hegel's theorizing may be seen as articulating the ideal of coherent thought and the process of its evolution. For Hegel, philosophical statements can be attributed values of truth only within their dynamic, systemic context. The understanding of any statement requires the understanding of the system to which it belongs in its entirety. Without this systemic understanding, a statement can only be an empty abstraction, whereas within it, it becomes a coherent summary of the rules comprising the system (Yovel 2005, 65).

For Hegel, a concept cannot acquire a truth value through its correspondence to reality for the simple reason that no differentiations exist between concept and reality. Indeed, the source of the concept is not in our consciousness. Rather, the concept operates in the reality that is the subject of our knowledge. It is continuously challenged, opposed and decomposed while new concepts evolve, integrating the historical experience of former contradictions. This, in Hegel's theory, is how the spirit, the 'Geist', always needs its 'other' in order to develop, the other being the real phenomenon, the contingent, empirical existence.

The spirit must become other from itself in order to return to itself on a higher level as a realized or objectified entity. This 'phenomenology', as Hegel called it, constitutes dialectics as a science, but carries an additional function, a subjective didactic one, aimed at delivering the subject from his individual consciousness to the philosophical realm of truth. The passage from one position to the other is effected by this dialectical process in which oppositional forces propel individual consciousness to transcend its own contingency and reach a form of stable generality.

The self-conscious spirit is described by Hegel as occupying an unexamined life of complaisance and plenitude. "Expelled from this paradise by the power of reflection and universal thought (Enlightenment), the spirit is thrown into a world of abstraction, cut off from concrete life, suffering an acute sense of loss of reality" (Yovel 2005, 75, 77). This rupture produces an acute sense of deprivation, sorrow and alienation, which will be overcome by the same force that caused it: Rational thought will proceed into reason until it produces a reconciliation that integrates the formerly separate elements of concept and reality, of the individual and the abstract human spirit. Identity is formed when the subjective consciousness unifies its images according to rational patterns.

Gradually, the subject understands that his patterns of consciousness are those that make up the unity of the objective world within which his consciousness exists. In this way, the particular subject learns that reality is not contingent, alien and external to himself, but that all its elements, as well as the regularities of their interconnections, reside also within himself. For Hegel, the self's individuality is constituted through its relation with the absolute. This relation presupposes the complex mediation of rational concepts, social practices and a long historical evolution (ibid. 81). Evidently, subject, reason and history are here realized in the same process.

The substance of reality, then, is not qualitatively different from the substances that constitute the subject. Consciousness bridges the gap between itself and reality by discovering and refining the concepts of which it is built. Thereafter, consciousness enters a dialectic that decomposes these concepts and builds them anew. In this way, the subject travels from his subjective consciousness to abstract concepts that transcend his original identity as he becomes identified with a coherent world that is no longer experienced as alien to himself.

Wilfred Bion saw the ability to think as the greatest achievement of the human psyche and as a marker of health. Like Hegel, Bion thinks reality is built in a way that allows it an integral association with the subject. Unlike Freud, who posited a clear delineation between inner and outer realities, Bion posited a subject who is equipped with innate preconceptions to perceive a certain version of reality. This reality, however, already contains thoughts that are waiting for a subject, a thinker (Bion, 1970). For Bion, the realm of thought is comprised of 'no-things' waiting to become thoughts, and of permanent patterns waiting to be noticed (Bion 1965, 105). In this way, Bion too draws a bridge between mind and matter, de-alienating them and bringing them together in a coherent unity.

Man's ability to experience the contingencies of reality and pattern them in his thought is the process around which Bion's whole theory revolves. The 'alpha function' is the cornerstone of this process. It is conceived by Bion as a hypothetical mechanism capable of transforming sense data into "dream thoughts and unconscious waking-thinking" (Bion 1962, 6). When this function is not operative, sense impressions and emotions remain in their original state, which Bion describes as beta elements. The alpha function digests reality, transforms it into something that can be thought, and creates the links within this thought. Bion's 'grid' depicts the transformation of sensory impression into a scientific, deductive system in a process that may be understood by reference to Hegel's dialectics, where the rise to higher orders occurs through a process that transforms the subjective into an 'objective' abstraction.

In the grid, the movement from stage to stage is effected by the contact between unsaturated parts of the concept and reality. This again echoes Hegel's dialectics of collapse, where concepts undergo a process of contradiction, decomposition and reconstruction. The development of thought is represented in the grid by cycles of saturation: preconceptions get saturated through intercourse with reality and transform into conceptions which, in turn, produce more preconceptions and so forth. And yet, the contact between mind and matter and their association by means of linking are not self-evident. Indeed, they require a highly particular intersubjective process, together with the evolving ability to tolerate psychic pain.

The 'link' is a key concept in Bion's cognitive and personality theory, as well as his explanation of what enables movement between positions. Whereas Freudian and Kleinian theory anchor themselves in content, Bion concentrates on links among objects, sense impressions and thoughts. The possibility and the quality of these links will determine the development, structure and health of the personality. The link operates on many levels, combining preconceptions into conceptions, as well as associating between conceptions, building and articulating hypotheses and connecting hypotheses to each other. Even prior to these relatively higher mental processes, the link is the primary connection between the baby and the breast and, through it, the mother. This primal emotional link enables all future links.

Bion's unknown ultimate reality is transformed into an object of thought by means of these links and their combinations. Reality may either be represented coherently, in a depressive fashion that integrates loved and hated aspects or, in a fragmentary, persecutory fashion, which keeps apart positive and negative feelings. These possible modes of representation form two contrasting points on a continuum. One side comprises of meaningful combinations, forming a coherent, thinkable world, while the other side consists of things-in-themselves, lacking significance and integration. The ability to think is what enables the transition from a formless, chaotic state (the Kleinian paranoid-schizoid position) to a state in which coherent understanding may be formed (the Kleinian depressive position).

In this way, psychosis is related to linking, indeed defined as the result of attacks on linking (Bion 1954). The psychotic part of the personality is that part that leaves the world fragmented. These fragments are highly charged with drive and emotion. In a psychotic line of development, inner reality is experienced as unbearable and is therefore attacked, split and fragmented into small objects that are projected from within the psyche and become bizarre objects that replace thought (Bion 1954, 116–118). In psychosis, all links are attacked and all linking functions are damaged, including verbal and imagistic thought (Bion 1959).

The non-psychotic part of the personality has to manage the encounter with an integrative representation of psychic reality, including abhorred or hated parts. This involves the pain of relinquishing purely good objects and the willingness to integrate negative feelings. On the coherent side, thoughts are formed as a result of linking between a preconception and *negative realization*, crudely defined as the lack of a real object that is compatible with the preconception.

Developmentally, the critical determinant defining the direction of development is the *container* that encounters frustration of lack as manifested in persecutory bad objects. The mother-analyst container organizes these unbearable elements and processes them emotionally and thoughtfully by means of a "reverie" (Bion 1962, 36). These contents will then be transformed into digestible elements that may be returned to the child. Inability to make use of the container, be it because of the mother's refusal or because of the projecting child's hatred and jealousy of the container, will lead to the destruction of the link between the baby and the mother, which will inevitably result in obliterating curiosity and the possibility of learning that is dependent on it.

Bion's theory places the etiology of the link as the basic building block of thought, and thus also of the Coherent axis of truth. The ability to construct a coherent structure of thought is a developmental depressive achievement, testimony to survival in the face of anxiety, hatred and jealousy. Its prime ally is *symbolic signification*, a function that enables the child to tolerate the pain and the frustration that are bound up with the perception of reality. At any point, an attack on linking may fragment meaningful combinations into things-in-themselves that may not be thought.

Constitution of the Intersubjective axis: In the Intersubjective axis, truth is consensual. The 'objective' does not exist in itself but rather reflects agreement about facts among persons who partake in a given community. The scale of the consensual group is logically immaterial: Agreement may hold for wide circles such as cultures or societies, as well as for narrow circles such as sects, families or even small, deluded, psychotic groups.

The establishment of an Intersubjective axis of truth demands the presence of another person – a subject – whose existential status and ability to make epistemic decisions is equivalent to one's own. But the existence of other subjects in the self's world is not simple and, according to many philosophical and psychoanalytic viewpoints, is not a primary given in the evolving world of the infant.

Every idealistic philosophy has to deal with giving an account of the way a subject becomes aware of other minds and acquires the belief in their independence of the self. Hegel described the process of recognition between two independent consciousnesses and the inevitable struggle implied therein in his famous allegory of the master and slave (Hegel 1977). There are two accepted interpretations of this allegory. The first describes the drama of master and slave as enacted within one consciousness, describing two conflicting moments that engage in mutual dialectic (similar to the dialectic of consciousness and world described above). The second interprets the allegory as depicting a drama enacted between two distinct agencies. I will focus on the second interpretation so as to illustrate the struggle of giving recognition to the other, an interpretation that inspired in psychoanalysis such thinkers as Lacan and Benjamin.

In the master-slave allegory, self-consciousness is a primarily simple existence of the self for the self, a self-identity created by exclusion of all that is other from itself. In its desire for pure and complete self-existence, self-consciousness moves about in the world, negating all otherness and assimilating it within itself: "It takes its essential nature and absolute object to be Ego" (Hegel 1977, cl.186). This is an endless process that is checked when consciousness encounters another negating consciousness that belongs to a desiring being and which cannot be assimilated by the subject (ibid. cl.175).

Consciousness, in its encounter with another consciousness, demands full and complete recognition of itself, but here arises a paradox. Consciousness does not want to recognize the other, but needs this other in order to receive recognition. The latter places the same demand upon the former. Each demands of the other recognition, while withholding the granting of it to the other. The ensuing dynamics is that of a life and death struggle: "They must enter into this struggle, for they must bring their certainty of themselves, the certainty of being for themselves, to the level of objective truth, and make this a fact, both in the case of the other and in their own case as well. And it is solely by risking life that freedom is obtained" (ibid. cl.187).

At the end of this struggle, the two consciousnesses will be transformed into two unequal beings, with different kinds of rights and duties. The recognized consciousness becomes a master and the recognizing one a slave. The master is the one who had been willing to risk his life, and the slave is the one who had lowered his gaze in his desire to live, in his failure to endanger his life in the world of things. The master now owns his being by virtue of the slave's recognition, and he also owns the being of the slave. Sending the slave out to labor in the world, the master becomes idle, does nothing and receives all satisfaction of his needs and enjoyment.

Alas, this position carries little satisfaction for the master. The master is recognized by someone whom he does not recognize and recognition from one side is not sufficient. His objective existence is not confirmed by another self-conscious being and can never be realized by recognition granted by a slave or a thing.[1] This is when the inevitable is recognized by consciousness: Only recognition from that which is itself recognized may offer the truly confirmatory recognition desired and needed: "Each is the mediating term to the other, through which each mediates and unites itself with itself; and each is to itself and to the other an immediate self-existing reality which, at the same time,

1 Indeed, Hegel claims that it is the slave, through his labor and the curbing of his desire, who continues to evolve, transcending his consciousness as he shapes the world in his image (ibid. cl. 190, 192, 196).

exists for itself only through this mediation. They recognize themselves as mutually recognizing one another" (ibid. cl.184).

In Freudian metapsychology, like in idealistic philosophies, the point of departure in theory is the monadic subject (the Id-based bodily Ego in Freud's terminology). This monadic entity begins its life in an oceanic state of narcissism, creating contact with the other as a means of satisfying the demand of instinct. The process of recognizing an autonomous other, that is *not* a product of the ego's defensive measures, is part and parcel of the ego's recognition of reality. But it seems that this other remains heavily imbued with his coloring as object of the subject's drive. In contradistinction, the drama of recognizing an other as a differentiated and autonomous subjective agency and as *uniquely different* is central in theoreticians such as Lacan, Winnicott and Benjamin.

Benjamin deals with the recognition of a distinct subject by direct reference to the Hegelian dialectic. She describes primal infantile subjectivity as the narcissistic omnipotent wish for exclusivity and control of the environment, and sees Freud's pleasure-ego as echoing Hegel's consciousness in its demand to assimilate within it all that is good and to negate all else. Hegel's life and death struggle is mirrored in the psychological state of an omnipotent self, dependent upon an other, yet unwilling to acknowledge his differentiated existence and to relinquish the self's ability to control him.

Benjamin delineates two distinct categories of relationship with the other: The first is the relation to the other as object, the second is the relation to him as subject. In the first type of relationship, the other's subjectivity is not recognized and he is treated as a provider, at times a mere derivative of the subject's needs and desire. In Benjamin's view, relating to the other as object curtails the subject's ability to achieve a full and satisfying experience of his own subjectivity. The full realization of subjectivity may be achieved only by means of an other, and only after that other has been understood to be an autonomous center of subjectivity and agency. Recognizing the subjectivity of the other is an ongoing process that needs to be attained and re-attained throughout a subject's life. It is a process that may at any time collapse into the autocaratic wish to control the other, objectify him and subjugate him to my needs (Benjamin 1990; 2000).

In explicating this developmental process, Benjamin draws on Winnicott's theory and the transition he described between 'relating to' and 'using' the object. In the mode of *relating*, the object is comprised of projections and the subject believes it is under his control. In the mode of using, the object is differentiated from the subject, having his own agency and unique, 'real' attributes. In an optimal facilitating environment, the mother is able to maintain for her baby the illusion that he omnipotently creates the object that satisfies his needs. This illusion is supported by a mother who, through her primary maternal preoccupation, can identify her child's needs and be accurate in timing her response to his needs. This illusion of omnipotence in creating the satisfying object (or: allowing the baby the mode of relating) is, according to Winnicott, essential to the development of mature and healthy self-esteem.

As the baby develops and the mother 'recovers' her subjectivity, she gradually stops 'bringing the world to her child' and allows him growing degrees of frustration. Through this experience the baby gradually becomes aware of his mother as a separate being and as one who exists outside his realm of control. The drama evolving here is the one Winnicott describes in 'The Use of the Object' (1971). This interpersonal drama involves the infant-subject's destruction of the object, perceived at first as being in his control. The object who will survive the subject's hatred and rage will now be of real significance, loved and 'used'. This will involve the experience of its subjectivity and constancy. With the recognition of mother as subject, the infant's subjectivity is realized.

When mutual recognition fails, when the intersubjective field does not survive destructiveness, the main mode of relations remains that of 'relating', both internally and in relation to external others. Benjamin stresses that, even when mutual recognition is achieved, on another plane the subject's desire and need to control his objects continues to exist. As Benjamin sees it, the Winnicottian passage from relating to using should not be understood as a one-time event, but rather as an ongoing tension between the negation and the recognition of another's subjectivity.

Lacan adds to Benjamin's description of the challenge of recognizing the other by addressing the inherent frustration a subject experiences as he realizes that his own subjectivity is given and formulated by an 'other'. The other is therefore always both the object of the subject's desire and his means of seeking himself. Yet, the other remains elusive, indecipherable and tantalizing. More than anything else, he mirrors to the subject his own inherent lack, the way in which he is always divided, unattainable to himself. The moment in which the subject becomes aware of how wholly dependent he is upon another in defining his own desire is the moment in which the phantasy of the death of the analyst is borne, the analyst signifying for the analysand his inherent dependence on otherness. Lacan too employs the Hegelian master slave metaphor in order to illuminate the dependence of the subject on the other (Lacan 1977, 100). The slave can kill the master, but that will necessarily bring on his own demise as well.

Whereas Lacan deals with the subject's inner representations of the other and Benjamin deals with the 'real' contact between subjects, they entertain a basic assumption: The struggle for recognition involves the primary position of negating the other. The drive of the subject to destroy the other may only be resolved through mutual recognition given to, and received from, this other. For Lacan, before the stage of mutuality there is a phase in which the subject tries to extricate himself from the imaginary order, where he is wholly encapsulated in a dynamic of projection and internalization of an other, totally trapped in his gaze. Slowly and laboriously, the subject makes use of the small freedoms he has towards owning and signifying the history of his desire. This process of owning and strengthening his subjectivity may help free the subject from his past experiences of being controlled by an other and allow him to come to terms with the other's existence. This intersubjective achievement is not straightforwardly articulated in Lacan's writing, but may be inferred from it (Hadar 2001, 54).

Constitution of the Subjective-Existential axis: A Subjective-Existential axis of truth is contingent on the complex process which makes possible the existence and genesis of a 'true', identified and experienced self. Only in relation to such a self, which serves as point of reference for the axis as a whole, can Subjective-Existential truths be formed and maintained.

The tensions and struggles described as inevitable in the process of recognizing the other assume the existence of an innate, stable and potent Subjective-Existential self that is constitutionally biased towards self-assertion. In existential philosophy, the stability and resilience of such a self is not taken for granted. Rather, it is conceived of as an ongoing process of realization, involving endless recreation in the face of otherness.

In Heideggerian language, Dasein exists always in implicit understandings, in practical involvement with the world and in the structure of care for others: "The world of Dasein is a *with-world*. Being in it is being-with-others" (Heidegger 1996, 112/119). This understanding discloses possibilities and possible significations of things in the world, amongst them the possibilities of Dasein itself. In its involvement with the world, Dasein exists as the projection of its future possibilities. This existential state of viewing itself in terms of its possibilities is Dasein's authentic mode of being (ibid. 135/144).

The state of being-in-the-world includes others and the understanding of others. This understanding is not the outcome of rational knowledge but, rather, a mode of being and living primordially given and intertwined irrevocably with the existence of others. Despite the fact that others are primary in Dasein's world, the danger for Dasein lies in their possible influence upon him. The authentic self-knowledge and the authentic mode of being-with-others may be compromised by Dasein's occupation and preoccupation with others. This preoccupation, "falling prey to the world", undermines Dasein's authentic possibilities and drives it to superficial satisfactions with external substitutes (ibid. 164/176).

This danger of inauthenticity is described by Heidegger through the use of the terms 'they' (or 'Das Man') and 'distantiality'. 'They' is the socially constituted set of norms that we necessarily belong to. It lacks Dasein's particularity and cannot address its unique situation. Distantiality is the particularity and difference that sets us apart from others. The relations between 'they' and 'distantiality' hold the tension of being like others and yet unique. Failing to maintain this tension, Dasein may fall back on the common sense of 'they'. In this state of being, Dasein does not choose and decide to act one way or another. Rather, he accords himself passively with others. This frees him from responsibility and choice, and allows him an easy, albeit insignificant, existence. In this state, everyone is 'das man', and no one is himself. In order to exist, Dasein needs to differentiate itself: "If Dasein is to be brought back from this lostness of failing to hear itself…it must first be able to find itself as something that has failed to hear itself and continues to do so in listening to the 'they'" (ibid. 261/271).

The point Heidegger is making is a complex one. His self is not the Cartesian enclosed self. It is immersed primordially in the world of others, who constitute an inherent part of this self's being. Also, everyday existence necessarily implies a life within sociality, but Heidegger does not allow this sociality to eclipse or subjugate the existential possibility of reflection and self-contemplation. The particular 'I' must be present in order to replace the anonymous 'one'. Das man (in the sense of 'throwness' into a particular cultural and historical situation) may limit the scope of the existing possibilities but, in order to be authentic, Dasein projects itself toward a variety of possible futures, thus avoiding any dictatorship of facticity and of otherness. Losing distantiality, losing oneself in 'they', is inauthentic existence.

Winnicott's true and false selves define a similar tension that exists between a spontaneous, creative and authentic way of being, and a state of being that is guided by reactivity to the others. For Winnicott, the true self is the innate potential of the subject, the core of his being which, given an appropriate accommodation to the environment, may develop and express itself freely. This environment is given in the good-enough-mother's care for her child, in her ability to enable his experience of 'going-on-being'.

The experience of going-on-being is for Winnicott the prerequisite for the true self. This existential platform is, in effect, the infant's spontaneous and self-generated activity, as opposed to an existence that is a reactive to another. The mother enables her infant this ongoing state of spontaneity by creating an environment free from external impingement and internal demands (which are at first also experienced as external). Perpetual impingement arouses extreme anxiety and results in what the infant experiences as an existential threat of annihilation (Winnicott 1956).

The infant's experience of himself develops through the mirroring that his mother's face offers him. When a mother fails to mirror her child, his creative abilities are stunted, because his spontaneous gestures have gone unnoticed. When a mother's face does not resonate the infant's spontaneity, but rather remains fixed, or expresses only her own being, conforming reactivity will be fixated in the psyche, replacing the possibility of an enriching dialogue. The child becomes dependent on the maternal gesture, and his potential authentic creativity gradually becomes atrophied (Winnicott 1967).

Both psychoanalytic and philosophical thought acknowledge that the constitution and maintenance of authenticity is an enduring challenge, especially in the face of norms and social demands for conformity. Only its attainment and the care given to it enable the existence of Subjective-Existential truth for which it serves as a criterion of correspondence.

Constitution of the Ideal axis: In order to establish an Ideal axis of truth, a person needs to have experienced a relationship that allows positive mirroring and idealization. This relationship is gradually internalized and assimilated as a part of the personality. The subject's drive to form principles and ideals may be seen, at least in part, as an evolutionary result of his biologically determined and existentially experienced need for a grand plan.[2] Erich Fromm contended that we all desire a 'Frame of Orientation', a road map or consistent philosophy by which can we find our way in the world without losing our mind (Fromm 1968, 69). It is not enough for this frame to be useful; man wants it also to be *meaningful*. This often arouses man's longing for an entity larger than himself, to whom he may dedicate himself: An idea, a goal, an order, a man or a god.

In 'The Will to Believe', William James (2009) investigated the human need to articulate ideals and to believe in them in order to transcend the flaws of the world as we know it. A world devoid of an ideal entity or order may arouse fear and disgust, indeed may plunge one into despair (James 2009, 41–42). In this vein, James suggests that pessimism is a religious malaise that may be cured by belief in an invisible spiritual and benign order, where the meaning is revealed of all that has previously seemed contingent and perverse. In the face of helplessness, lack of meaning and despair that are tied up with the arbitrariness of the world, the ideal is 'a sort of faith':

> It is a fact of human nature that men can live and die by the help of a sort of faith that goes without a single dogma or definition. The bare assurance that this natural order is not ultimate but a mere sign or vision, the

2 Herrick investigated the biological neuro-developmental basis of the human need for ideals and values, and deemed them as possessing evolutional value in their ability to enrich human life (Herrick 1956).

> external staging of a many-storied universe, in which spiritual forces have the last word and are eternal, – this bare assurance is...enough to make life seem worth living... Destroy this inner assurance...and all the light and radiance of existence is extinguished...the suicidal mood will then set in.
>
> JAMES 2009, 57

In personality theory, we do not encounter perfect objective forms, but we find ideals that fulfill the former's function in psychic life. These ideals are, for the subject who holds them, a perfect shape, often experienced as having an independent objective existence. The subject judges and directs himself in accord with them, and they serve as his motivation and inspiration (Kohut 1985). In some psychoanalytic theories, the ideals are expressed in personality structures, as in Freud's 'ideal ego' or Kohut's 'pole of idealization'. These always appear as developmental achievements, results of successful relations with others.

The ideal plays a central role in Kohut's theory of personality and development. For Kohut, the basic element of the psychic mechanism is the self. The weak infantile self depends on the mature personality functions of others in order to achieve an experience of unity, constancy and resilience. These others, called 'self objects', lend the child their mature personality functions, which will later be internalized in the child's psyche. Two relational patterns with the self object are the basic determinants of the child's personality structure and future development. In the first, the child exhibits his evolving abilities and receives recognition of them. This dynamic brings the child to an experience of omnipotence and grandiosity, which will later transform into healthy self-esteem. In the second dynamic, the child creates an idealized image of at least one of his parental figures with whom he feels identified and merged. This dynamic will be expressed in a personality that is guided by strong values and principles. These manifest in the ability of the subject to set meaningful goals and live according to ideals in a way that empowers his experience of self. From these relational patterns, the two poles of the nuclear self will evolve – the pole of ambition and the pole of ideals (Kohut 1978).

For Kohut, ideals sometimes hold a motivating force that is more intense then the drive to survive. Indeed, he defines courage as man's ability to strive and dare not to betray his ideals, even in the face of death. Analyzing the dynamics that motivated self-scarifying heroes in history, Kohut describes the way the tragic man's narcissistic ideal acquires the dimensions of eternity and universality. Despite the collapse of his physical and mental capacities (like Oedipus) and despite his actual death (Hamlet), the tragic man emerges from his travails as victor, because his nuclear self remains intact and its mastery cannot be further challenged. This immortal legacy of truth and ideals becomes, through myth and tradition, part of mankind's most precious assets (Kohut, 1985). With his death, the hero becomes immortal, while his ideals acquire the quality of eternity that Plato conferred as a given upon his Ideas and Forms.

Kohut, like Freud, stresses the motivating force of the ideal, its structural positioning in the psyche and the way it holds a guiding and directing function throughout life, indicating the way the subject perceives the world and makes his behavioral choices. Like the other axes of truth, it is clear that the Ideal axis is an achievement, not a given, it necessitates certain conditions without which it cannot develop. It comes into being as an answer to a basic human need and its logic is branded in the psyche through the developmental history with which it is associated.

Constitution of the Pragmatic axis: A pragmatic axis of truth necessitates a flexible conscience that allows a person to behave in accordance with principles of self-benefit. These benefits should become apparent in a future the subject anticipates. In order for this axis to exist, it is essential to have had the experience of influencing reality, together with functional flexibility and the ability to deal with vagueness. These allow the subject to act in the world without relying on established knowledge. He should be able to withstand the situation in which his truths are validated only retrospectively.

As formerly detailed, truth for James is the correspondence between the actual consequences of a certain belief and the anticipated consequences of that same belief, especially in their capacity to enhance the subject's objectives. In that sense, each subject may hold his own truth according to his tastes, needs and values. This characteristic of truth is in line with James's conception of Humanism, which he understands as a particular emotional state of mind that implies: "a real change of heart, a break with absolutistic hopes" (James 2010, 248).

This state of mind depends on two developmental achievements: The ability to relinquish the absolute and accept the relative and the belief in one's power to shape reality. In psychoanalytic terms, the former involves the Kleinian depressive positioning, allowing the ability to compromise and to withstand imperfection without losing a benevolent optimism. The latter involves a sense of self efficacy of the kind that Erik Erikson called the 'virtue of competence'.

Like Freud, Erikson assumes that a crisis occurs at each stage of development. For Erikson (1963; 1968), these crises are of a psychosocial nature because they involve psychological needs of the individual as they interact with the demands and decrees of society. According to his theory, successful completion of each stage results in the acquisition of a basic virtue, a characteristic strength which the ego can use to resolve subsequent crises. Failure to successfully complete a stage can result in reduced ability to master further stages, thus impeding the development of a smoothly functioning personality and a healthy sense of self. These stages, however, may be resolved successfully at a later time.

Erikson described the fourth psychosocial crisis as the one in which industry (competence) contrasts with inferiority. This stage occurs in the latency period, roughly parallel to the first years of elementary school. In this period, children learn to independently carry out tasks and manage their daily living on their own. The child demonstrates to society his evolving skills and competencies and begins to develop a sense of pride in his accomplishments. If children are encouraged and reinforced in their initiative, they feel industrious and develop confidence in their ability to achieve goals. For the child to feel competent and trust his own abilities, initiative must be encouraged and not restricted by parents and teachers.

Interim Summary

In summing up the significance of developmental challenges and their effects on the psyche, I want to emphasize a few points.

Firstly, every truth axis as a principle of psychic organization originates in a basic need. This need drives the constitution of a linkage between the subject and an aspect of his inner or his outer world, a linkage that is necessary for the need's provision. This preliminary linkage is then enriched with associated experiences and develops into a mental apparatus and a whole mode of experience. Further development of such an apparatus as manifested in typical organizational patterns of cognition and emotion is predicated upon the motivation to nurture and maintain the core linkage.

Secondly, aligning with the overarching need for certainty, guidance and structure, each perspective gravitates around its particular truth, a truth that is predicated upon the basic linkage that provides the need driving the axis. Every truth axis gives rise to its own truth. The binding force of these truths, as experienced by the subject, leads to their repeated use and enactment.

Thus for example, the basic need of significant others drives the association of the subject with his human surroundings. This linkage will give rise to the construal of a reality that the subject may share with others. Within it, the Intersubjective truth is the binding point of certainty. Adhering to this truth reinforces the bind between subject and others and enriches their shared reality. Similarly, the need one has for ideals drives relations of idealization and the constitution of ideals by their means. These ideals give rise to an ideal reality that, in turn, dictates its own Ideal truths that enrich and strengthen it, and so on. Schematically expressed the sequence looks like this:

Basic Need→Linkage of subject to aspect of his world→Image of reality that serves to ensure the link→Truth→Motivations for activity that strengthens original linkage.

The provision of needs here is not given in an act of satisfaction, a discharge, a fulfillment of a wish. The provision of each need requires a total epistemic construction, comprising of an image of reality, an experienced truth and a self that constantly negotiate need in a joint dynamic. The potency of the truth axes arise from the needs that drive each perspective and from the particular processes of emotional development that are required for their establishment and that brand their logic in the psyche with the wealth of association accrued in the course of the subject's life.

As I have shown throughout the chapter, the constitution of each linkage involves successfully traversing a developmental challenge. The challenges described are always colored by the subject's inborn constitution as it interacts with his environment. The successes and failures in this development will be inscribed in the patterns according to which the subject construes his life, in the differential dominance of certain axes and their conscious or dissociated positioning in the psyche.

Certain dispositions are prone in certain developmental directions and different environments and cultures meet these tendencies in different ways. In one disposition the innate need for efficacy and achievement may be stronger than the need for attachment or ideals, while in another, the need for authenticity in living eclipses all others. Different cultures employ different modes of socialization in which these needs are differently prioritized. This may be also time related in both subject and culture. When a culture (narrow or wide, family or nation) is in danger it tends to emphasize Ideal and Intersubjective truths, restricting the scope of legitimacy and expression allowed for Subjective-Existential truths. The opposite holds in liberally oriented and unthreatened societies.

Any circumstance in the subject's world, either external or internal, may touch upon and activate a certain association. Thus, a person might be freely and spontaneously engaged in a project that can be validated mostly by his Subjective truths. Then, criticism or feelings of others that are a consequence of his actions may activate either association to his ideals or association to his significant others. The activation of these associations will change the subjects 'take' on his reality, shift his perspective. The image he now sees of reality may be the one derived from his ideals, or the one he shares with significant others. The related truths may not necessarily coincide. It may happen that acting upon one truth related to one need (and its derivative linkage) gives rise to anxiety concerning conflict with another linkage and the frustration of another need.

The different images of reality are the consequence of the subject's change of aspect. When such a change occurs, facts that are denied or discarded in one image of reality may appear in another. Anxieties that do not arise in one perspective may be overbearing in another. Different wishes may come into being and others subdued. Often, when a subject feels he has 'rediscovered' himself or meanings in his life, the experience involves nurturing a formerly neglected linkage, its corresponding image of reality and the possibilities it holds. At times this change of aspect causes confusion, as indeed may occur in epistemological shifts.

As one may see clearly, every philosophic or psychological account of development and self-realization begins with different basic premises regarding the human subject and his relations with his world. These premises give rise to different questions and developmental itineraries. Idealistic philosophies will always take for granted the existence of a delineated mind and will be troubled with answering the questions associated with other minds. Intersubjective epistemologies (or psychologies), on the other hand, will need to address the issue of subjectivity and its delineation and relative autonomy from the intersubjectivity wherein it evolved. Whether beginning with a monadic or an intersubjective conception of the mind, theory needs to address both the issue of subjectivity and the issue of intersubjectivity. Similarly, realistic or subjective epistemologies, both need to give account of what the subject perceives as his external reality and the way it affects his experience and behavior.

My point is that it is not crucial what our point of departure is. I do not try to enforce orders of priority, but simply to acknowledge basic needs and associations that are recurrent in philosophical, psychoanalytic and psychological thought. Each perspective is expressed in philosophical or psychoanalytic thought as an abstract truth or as a discrete epistemology and is here presented as an organizing principle of the psyche.

By taking this theoretical attitude, I hope to create a theoretical space in which we can address the crucial questions about the ways in which truth-seeking shapes the complexities of the psyche. What is complex in its theoretical formulation is surprisingly familiar when encountered in everyday experiencing, as I try to illustrate in the following section in the interplay of different axial realities and their corresponding self-states.

Experiencing Truth Axes

The different truth axes create a multidimensional experience that is given by the various experiences of self. The self's object complements the different states of the self and is expressed across the same dimensions. For example, imagine the familiar situation of a parent and his child returning from a PTA meeting in which problematic things have been said about the child. The parent's mind is probably racing with questions: Who, truly, is this child of mine? What has he to do with the ideal child that I have created in my mind? Who is my child as he is perceived by his teachers? Who is my child as he perceives himself to be? Also, who is the 'objectively perceived' child described in the assessment done last year at that top notch institute? Or: What should I do with this child? Do the images of these different children converge into one figure? And in paraphrase: Will the 'true' child please step forward?

Had the 'true' child stepped forward, regardless of being disappointing or pleasing to the parent, the latter would have experienced the relief of clarity and comprehension. The price of this relief would have been the loss of the complexity and multi-dimensionality in his understanding of the child. This same experience of the child would not have been confusing if, in the first place, all axial productions had not been available in consciousness. For example, the parent might have felt, had his object been determined along the Ideal axis, something like: My child is perfect. Always was, always has been. Any other view of him really merits no attention. Similarly, if Intersubjectively determined, the reaction might have been: That is the truth! How could I have been so blind before? Or, a Coherently determined image of the child might have gone like this: Well, he is not scholastic, but he *is* super athletic and has such a good heart, so maybe it isn't all that important, all in all he's a good kid… and so on.

Of course, this parental drama in face of the object – the multifaceted child – takes place in a subject who himself is a multifaceted parent. How would the Ideal parent react to his child? How would the Pragmatic parent relate to him? And what about the parent who follows intersubjective dictums? How would he react here? For example, suppose that the Intersubjective self of the parent is not critical of the system and does not denounce it. He accepts that his child is lazy and maybe also dull. He might fear terribly that no one will want to play with the child and now it may seem that his fears come true. In a Subjective-Existential self-state, this same parent will be searching for his inner intuitions of the child. He might be thinking: It is true something is wrong with the child, but that is not it. He is not lazy, I need to figure out what it is. I know I'll recognize the truth when I hit on it. The Pragmatic parent will come home, make a few phone calls, find a proper tutor for his child, believing a few private lessons will do the trick. A Coherently determined response might be: Well that makes sense, he is just like his two cousins and four uncles, this has always been a feature of my family. An Ideally determined parent will search his mind to figure out the best way he can deal with this. He may ask himself: Have I been the best parent I could've been to this child? Regardless, I do not believe in Ritalin. Whatever happens I will not give him drugs. I don't believe that should be done, even though the (Correspondent representative) doctor said it should.

Now, as can be seen, different thoughts and sensations accompany the different self-states of the parent: Serenity if he acts in accordance with his Ideal self; anxious groping if he tries to intuit his feeling about the child, that really has nothing much to do with this PTA meeting, but rather with a host of hazy impressions that are difficult to shape and articulate but that he actually feels in his bones. These feelings are of course determined along the Subjective-Existential axis, searching inside, hanging on to no 'givens' from the surroundings. The Pragmatic parent might be feeling very competent and confident ('I've definitely handled situations more complicated than this') or alternatively depressed ('oh my, oh my, I have so much on my plate now that I can't anyway handle, how am I going to fit *this* in now?').

The more perfunctory the parental approach, the smaller the scope of possible reaction. The need to formulate comprehension, thought and action may cause the parent to collapse into a place where he 'looses' the polyphony of his previous stand. The continuum here is between the pole of complexity and possibility and the pole of reduction and simplicity. This complexity may cause the parent to be undecided and distraught for a while, but allows deep and multilayered signification of the situation. This distraught parent is not yet a disappointed parent (because he is not relating to the child only as Ideal), or a parent in denial (because what was said of his child was not congruent and consistent with previous perceptions of him), he is not critical of the system and does not denounce it (out of exclusive loyalty to the authentic developmental processes of his child), neither is he angry and critical of the child (for being 'lazy' according to Intersubjective definitions), etc. He stands at the crossroad of his multi-dimensional experience, with its many different aspects and possible scripts, trying to hold the tensions while structuring his inner understandings of himself, his child and reality.

Two things are illuminated in this short illustration. The first is the multidimensionality of experience as discussed. The second is the automatic way in which these realities are construed. We follow the parent through the different construals of himself and his object, through the various emotions triggered across the different realities. What we do *not* follow or observe is the way these images of self and reality are formed. Their constitution is automatic, and the different modes and processes of construction are unconscious, indeed, they may be thought of as comprising a procedural unconscious of sorts.

The fact that this construction is unconscious carries significant implications for our understanding of the psyche, because it means that we construe meanings in a way of which we are not conscious. Now, it may be that we encounter here something counter-intuitive inasmuch as we are used to thinking of processes of meaning and signification as conscious. This is of course true on many levels. We think about issues, formulate and reformulate them, create meaning in our inner dialogues and in our dialogue with others. But the point here is that meaning is also created by means of organization that is prior to all content.

What exactly does that mean? How can modes of organization determine content? A simple way to illustrate this is by reference to Ideal truth. As formerly explained, an Ideal truth is created by correspondence of an instance or a belief to any ideal. This ideal may be god, an idea, a political leader, a person's own ego. The point is that the *process* by which truth is derived is autonomous of its context and content. Applied in a certain context it may be expressed in religiosity, fascism or narcissism. These three states of mind, though so far apart in content, will have quite a few structural characteristics in common. For example: God\the leader\myself are above all else. What they signify immediately defines in a clear way what is right or wrong, good or bad. A binary structure is imposed on reality; power structures organically evolve, and so on.

Every truth axis, as aforesaid, relies on a basic link which it thereon preserves. It preserves it by means of enforcing certain rules that constitute the reality that accommodates the link and adapts it to its function. Every axis has its own rules, which I will hereon call 'grammar'. The term is borrowed from semiotics and I will explain here in length why I adopt it and how it contributes to our understanding of the psyche.

Truth Axes, Grammar and Its Autonomy

A crucial aspect of the operation of truth axes is their automaticity and encapsulation. Once a truth axis is established, it functions automatically, without requiring an explicit intention and without changing course due to the operation of other axes. There are a number of ways in which autonomy may be understood, one of which is Chomsky's view of grammar in the representation of linguistic knowledge (Chomsky 1965). Grammar is commonly defined as a linguistic subsystem that provides rules for the grouping of words into phrases and sentences. Now, the claim that has been put forward by probably the foremost linguist of our time, Noam Chomsky, is that grammar operates without regard to other linguistic processes that may run in parallel, such as word selection, semantic structuring, phonetic articulation, etc. Grammar acts without concern to meaning.[3]

The autonomy of grammar illustrates a general trait of many cognitive processes called 'encapsulated' by Jerry Fodor (Fodor 1983). This feature is one of the prime tenets suggesting that the mind has a modular architecture, where processing components ('modules') operate exclusively on their own designated data base and according to their own 'grammar'. The module receives input from a limited range of sources, transforms it in a predetermined fashion and delivers its output to a central cognitive system that needs to collate it with outputs of other modules. This collating of information from different modules is the sense-giving action of the central cognitive system. Modularity of this kind ensures efficiency and speed, but it is *dumb* in the sense that it disregards other modules and conflict with them. As a result, the most indicative outcome of a modular process is an illusion or a paradox.

I claim here that truth axes behave like encapsulated processes: They automatically organize elements into a representation of reality, they derive meanings from this representation and construct compatible self-states. Like a module, a truth axis can give rise to representations that contradict the output of other truth axes, creating discord and tension within the psychic space in its entirety. I would like to take this analogy further, claiming that truth axes

3 In his first book 'Syntactic Structures' (Chomsky 1957), Chomsky presents a fairly radical position that resembles the view formulated by the Structuralists, according to which syntax is entirely autonomous of semantics. Though in his later writing (1965; 1975) the autonomy thesis is moderated, it is still easy to illustrate the dimensions in which, for Chomsky, syntax remains autonomous. Thus, for example, the ability of native speakers to automatically identify grammatically wrongly phrased sentences. They are unaware of the nature of mental grammar by means of which they construct and understand linguistic expressions, yet they are entirely in control of it at the level of implementation. When a native speaker rejects a sentence as 'ungrammatical' he views it as not belonging to his language even if he can't explain why it doesn't (Chomsky 1975, 93). The potency of automatically applied regularities is expressed in optical illusions in general and the Muller-Lyer illusion in particular. In this illusion a straight line with the fins of an arrow protruding outward appears to be longer than a line of the same length with the fins of the arrow pointing inward. Interestingly, these illusions are resistant to prior knowledge about them. Even after the perceiver has been presented with the facts and understands how the illusion 'works', he retains his original, and now evidently mistaken, sense. This resistibility is an illustration of the fact that the cognitive mechanism that creates the illusion is isolated from the systems of knowledge and memory and functions autonomously.

indeed carry a grammatical function. The grammatical function I refer to is not purely linguistic, but rather philosophic, as defined and elaborated by Wittgenstein.

The autonomy of grammar appears as a thesis in Wittgenstein across his philosophic thought, despite changes in his definitions of grammar across different periods. In the period of the Tractatus Logico-Philosopicus Wittgenstein grants grammar a sense-giving function that is utterly independent of reference. The structure of grammar here embodies the unity of recognizer and recognized, language and reality, and the logic that constitutes them both. Here, Wittgenstein's grammar is autonomous, precedes semantics and constrains meaning in different ways. It is a grammar that organizes signs into forms that contain their possible meanings. In this way, "the meaning of every linguistic sign is embedded in the grammar within which it is set" (Wittgenstein 1974:44).

In the 'Tractatus' Wittgenstein posits a single grammar that originates in the common structure of world and consciousness. This inevitable grammar determines the meaning of every sign. In 'Philosophical Investigations' Wittgenstein acknowledges a *plurality* of grammars, as he now understands grammar to be rooted in different forms of life, reflecting different social agreements. And yet, grammar maintains its function of constituting meaning and its priority over all semanticity. Each grammar, with its natural rules and concepts, produces a different 'sculpturing' and organization of facts, manufactures different meanings:

> Grammar is laid against reality like a ruler. ... [it] is not accountable to any reality. It is grammatical rules that determine meaning (constitute it) and so they themselves are not answerable to any meaning and to that extent are arbitrary...The rules of grammar are arbitrary in the same sense as the choice of a unit of measurement.
>
> WITTGENSTEIN 1974, PG: 184–5

We use the various language-games with their different grammars in an automatic and unconscious manner. We are not aware of the particular technique, "for it flows along underground, as it were, without our noticing it; and not until it openly contradicts our false imagination do we suddenly become aware of it" (Wittgenstein 1980, RPP: 77). This awareness may also be triggered by an encounter with a language different than our own (Wittgenstein 1981, Z: 413).

Across different languages and grammars, the same statement may receive different truth values: 'Agreement or disagreement with reality' would be something different in the different languages (Wittgenstein 1998, BBN: 81). This premise is echoed in Quine's translation manuals and conceptual schemes, as well as in Thomas Kuhn's symbolic paradigms (Kuhn 1996). We will always view reality from the perspective of a specific language and from the viewpoint its grammar dictates. However, there are different languages, different language-games, different grammars, through which we can view the world.[4] The grammar determines what makes sense 'within a given context' (Baker and Hacker 2005: 324), because context is also written into its rules of combination.

Inertia or respect for tradition may result in the fixation of a particular lexicon or grammar as formulated by a culture or a particular personal history. This can result in an entrenchment of a mental or emotional paradigm whose rigidity does not allow for the enrichment of experience and curbs the tendency to change it. On the other hand, when we realize the prominent role symbolic paradigms fill in our construction of reality, we become aware of the wide range of possibilities in defining the types of hierarchies and relations between words and things. These definitions make up the framework within which the subject conducts his life (Foucault 1994). The growing awareness of different grammars results in a significant epistemological shift toward the understanding that we can build more than one world by variable choices of lexicon or grammar.

Truth axes, as systems of organization in the psyche, function automatically and follow fixed rules of which we are unaware. *In that sense, truth rules work unconsciously as producers of meaning.* Grammar, with its formative rules, is part of our procedural unconscious. Its uncovering enables us to understand the mechanisms that create meaning and shape our world. Hence, the first task of an analyst is to identify the grammars of truth and the way they constitute the subject's experience of himself and his world. I will begin the next chapter with a phenomenological description of truth axes and their grammars.

---

4 This interpretation of Wittgensteinean grammar places him in a Kantian light, as he has indeed been positioned by several scholars. Finch claims that Wittgenstein is "the ultimate Kantian" (Finch 1977: 248), as does Pears (1970). Forster contends that: "Wittgenstein's position can quite properly be described as idealist, in a sense closely analogous to that in which Kant was" (Forster 2004: 17). For different views see for example Fogelin (1996), who thinks that Wittgenstein "has transgressed his self-imposed restrictions against substantive philosophical theorizing" (Fogelin 1996: 45) and Hilmy (1987) and Engelmann (2013).

CHAPTER 5

Theoretical and Practical Implications

In the previous chapters, I presented the rationale for accepting truth axes as organizing principles of the psyche. I introduced the complex structure of the truth axis, consisting of epistemic assumption, characteristic self-state, image of reality and experienced truth. I then described the needs and the developmental challenges associated with the constitution of truth axes. In this chapter, I shall describe some theoretical and practical implications of this conceptualization.

At the level of theory, I shall indicate how conceptualizing the psyche in terms of truth axes touches on two important issues in psychoanalysis: The first is the issue of the mind's topography, as expressed in the partitioning between the conscious and the unconscious. The second is the issue of defining the concept of self. After conceptualizing self and topography in terms of truth axes, I will outline the implications for psychoanalytic clinical practice.

But before engaging with these issues, I will present a phenomenological description of the truth axes as distinct experiential strata within the psyche that encompass the levels of sensation, encounter with the world and constitutive grammar. Throughout this description I will focus on a particular self-state associated with each axis, presenting a philosophic approach relevant to it that stands on the threshold of psychology and that has been developed in the context of and in relation to human needs. I then turn to psychoanalytic formulations and, at times, refer to relevant psychological research findings. This method of description has two goals: Firstly, to develop the idea that the different truth axes are psychic structures that act across mental levels, from the concrete to the abstract. Secondly, to present the self in an interdisciplinary manner, so as to investigate, validate and cross-validate its nature and mode of operation using different methodologies.

Expressions of Axial Self-States: Firstness, Secondness and Thirdness

In order to bring out the multi-layered nature of truth axes, I shall present them here across three levels of mental function: sensory experience (sensation), encounters with the world and grammar. I shall describe these three levels adopting Charles Pierce's (1894) categories of, respectively, Firstness, Secondness and Thirdness.

 | DOI 10.1163/9789004314993_007

Firstness – sensation: Firstness is a state of 'being' that exists in and of itself in a primal state, encountering nothing and serving no purpose. It exists as a feeling that permeates consciousness, a meditative state, neither unified nor segmented. Firstness is a quality and does not refer to anything beyond itself. It is the sensation of being immersed in one thing, mesmerized and aware of nothing else. Peirce describes a person staring at the color red, infused with its redness, not asking any questions about the color, not checking whether it is pleasant or not, but simply immersed in it. In Firstness there is no experiential element of external necessity, reason or need.

Firstness occurs in many experiential states but, for illustrative purposes, let me consider what Ogden (1989) referred to as the Autistic-Contiguous position. This is an early developmental phase of sensory and presymbolic experience, when the baby's prime contact with the object is that of feeling its skin against the body of the mother. Such tactile sensory experience consists primarily of textures and temperatures, but it allows the baby to give the mother a shape and a form, as well as perceive her rhythms and regularities. Winnicott describes a related experience, which he calls 'going-on-being', a state devoid of disturbance and demand for response, involving no directives, no defined movement or interest (Winnicott 1956). On this level of Firstness I will describe sensation and emotion characteristic of the axial selves.

Secondness – encounter with the world: Winnicott calls 'impingement' the external intrusions that violate the state of meditative quietude, such as a very loud noise, a sharp pain, etc. (Winnicott 1956, 1972). Impingement imposes upon the child a stimulus that is too powerful to be ignored and requires attention and response in order to return the psyche to quietude. This experience offers an example of what Peirce called Secondness, when an event of some magnitude and velocity acts upon consciousness. Whether positive or negative, this encounter always challenges the self into a state of responsiveness. As a result, the self 'splits' into internal and external, both of which are represented in the psyche.

Encounters of this sort form the basis for the paranoid-schizoid position as described by Melanie Klein and elaborated by Ogden. The self here experiences itself as an object to which 'things happen'. In the absence of an interpreting subject, the distinction between signifier and signified is blurred; perception and interpretation are one and the same and sensory experience remains mainly in the form of an effect and less in the form of significance. On this level of Secondness I will describe the typical ways in which the different axial selves encounter their world.

Thirdness – grammar: Thirdness is a category of mediating interpretation that consists of representations rather than of things. Norms, social structures and language are Thirdness phenomena, involving rules and regularity. In its active form, Thirdness transforms the concrete happenings of Secondness into thought and understanding, namely, phenomena that follow some general rules. These rules, by and large, combine elements and elemental sets into larger units of signification (or larger units of social order). It is this combinatory function that renders the notion of 'grammar' pertinent to analysis and interpretation.

I begin my description of truth-related selves with the Subjective-Existential axis, because its definition engages the whole range of conceptual building blocks that appear in the other axes as well. Moreover, the Subjective-Existential self is the most intuitive of selves: In fact, when people use 'self' without defining it – and often when they try to define it as well – they refer to the Subjective-Existential self. Finally, the Subjective-Existential self interacts powerfully with other axes and its description is conducive to the description of the others.

Subjective-Existential Selfhood: Kierkegaard, considered by many to be the father of Existentialist philosophy, described rational thinking as a good means to promote the natural sciences. But he did not believe that this mode of thought had much to contribute to coping with existential problems. Moreover, he saw that rationality offers itself at times as a convenient replacement for responsibility and choice. Existential rules, he argued, are different from rules of logic. They are not dictated by axioms or other sources transcendental to the subject, they do not necessitate coherence and they allow paradox in the process of creating meaning.

Grammar: The grammar that formulates authenticity is characterized by *contrast and paradox*, so authentic selfhood arises from within a *system of contradictions*. According to Heidegger and Sartre, one of the main contradictions of authenticity concerns freedom and subjugation. Heidegger, for example, thought that authentic existence and freedom can only be reached after confronting the inevitability of mortality, after gazing at one's own death. Only then can a person rise from his preoccupation with everyday distractions and gratifications and grant his life a form and a meaning (Heidegger 1996, 235\254). For Sartre, the concept of freedom is formed in light of the individual's acceptance of arbitrary and contingent meaninglessness. In other words – freedom may be formed when one acknowledges the fact that the values and principles we live by have no metaphysical or godly source, that there exists no source of signification that is external to the subject. Indeed, "Man is nothing else but that which he makes of himself" (Sartre, 1989).[1]

1 This idea is developed from its former articulation by Heidegger, who discussed nothingness and angst as experiences that return Dasein from its falleness. See Heidegger (1996, 315\343).

According to Sartre, freedom involves self-transcendence. To start with, one's self is never one with itself, never given in, or as, a complete presence. One is always able to assume a different self perspective and this inner distance or inner freedom serves Sartre for the definition of man: "Man is all the time outside of himself: it is in projecting and losing himself beyond himself that he makes man to exist; and, on the other hand, it is by pursuing transcendent aims that he himself is able to exist. Since man is thus self-surpassing…he is himself the heart and center of his transcendence" (Sartre 1989, see also Heidegger 1996, 45\49).

Freedom implies and defines the meaning of responsibility. Any deterministic claim regarding the self is, in Sartrean terms, a form of self-deception that denies the possibility of choice and of transcending one's self. However, just as transcendence may be denied, so may facticity, as happens in omnipotence or any other form of self-deception that implies that one can be everything.

The main determinant of existential grammar is paradox and the tension that it arouses. This paradox is expressed in Sartre's concepts of 'In-itself' and 'For-itself', which describe two distinct states of being that exclude each other and yet depend upon each other. The 'In-itself' is a state of being that reflects the givens of a man's existence. This is an inert solid state that any object may have. It simply 'is'. The 'For-itself' is a state that roughly represents subjectivity and the ability to reflect. It is defined "as being what it is not and not being what it is" (Sartre 1956, lxv). It is a dynamic state that acts upon the 'In-itself' in the form of negation or 'nihilation' and introduces its ability to transform within its own constraints. This is similar to the Heideggerian notions of 'facticity' and its 'transcendence' in their authentic mode of interplay. Facticity includes all characteristics, qualities and contingencies of a person that can be discovered by external investigation and it is often experienced as inevitability. Transcendence, on the other hand, is a first person positioning of the self in relation to the facticity in which it exists; It is the self's reference to the facts of its own existence and the ways they become meaningful. This unresolvable tension of opposites may collapse when a person deceives himself while identifying completely either with facticity or with transcendence.

Whereas Heidegger would place facticity in the past and transcendence in the future, for Sartre the dimension of time is more complicated than that. For him, "the past is not nothing; neither is it the present; but at its very source it is bound to a certain present and to a certain future, to both of which it belongs" (Sartre 1956, 100). Man lives under the inevitability into which he is born. However, he forms himself and his world by virtue of these circumstances. He gives them meaning by organizing a contingent and meaningless past into a structured and intentional present facing a potential state of affairs.

This organization is not predicated upon a 'simple' past in the way of factual eventuation, but rather makes the past answerable to a future that is unknown and as yet non-existent. The past is constituted as an 'In-itself' which the 'For-itself' now seeks to surpass in order to be what it seeks to be. Nihilation of past, present and future is effected by the ability to reorganize and transform: "It is this game of musical chairs at the heart of the For-itself which is Presence to being" (Sartre 1956, 142).

All in all, the grammar of authentic selfhood is formed by contradictions and paradoxes. In the transitions and simultaneous existence of the actual and the possible – between the manner in which a person defines his own existence and the manner in which he is defined by circumstance – man generates an experience of himself that is known to him, though difficult to pin down and articulate. This difficulty in articulation that always falls back into self-referencing is rooted in the dynamic nature of the Subjective-Existential self and in its sensitivity to imbalances and upsets that occur among its constitutive polarities and frequent transitions. This self is not necessarily coherent. It is formed in the light of others and not in compliance with them. Its focal point is the present that may continuously reiterate past and future. As such, factual elements are composed in varying relations with time. But with all of its doing and undoing of time, it is in the essence of the Subjective-Existential self that it longs to choose and assume responsibility for past choices.

The encounter with the world: The logic of paradox and contradiction is characteristic also of the Subjective-Existential self's encounter with the world. For Sartre, the encounter with the world is, in a large part, also the encounter with the other. When one looks at an other, one sees his factual appearance, his existence as an 'In-itself'. In the same manner, when an other gazes upon me, he sees me as an 'In-itself', relegates me to my being as an object, robbing me of my 'For-itself'. As Sartre puts it: "…it is the recognition of the fact that I am indeed that object which the other is looking at and judging. I can be ashamed only as my freedom escapes me in order to become a given object" (Sartre 1956, 261). On the other hand, *it is only by means of this other that I am given my experience of existing at all*:

> I am unable to know myself… I am absolutely nothing. There is nothing there but a pure nothingness encircling a certain objective ensemble… But all of a sudden I hear footsteps in the hall. Someone is looking at me. What does this mean?… It is this irruption of the self which has been most often described: *I see myself because somebody sees me….*
>
> IBID. 260, my italics

Herein again lies the paradox. The shame I experience when being objectified signifies my being something beyond an 'In-itself'. In a paradoxical fashion, what ensues from my having been objectified is my realization that neither I nor the other are objects (ibid. 262). We both have our 'For-itself' in a way that ensures our subjectivity and our freedom and implicates our grave responsibility to ourselves. Sartre (1989) links the good of the self and the good of others in a way that is stated simply and explicitly in 'Existentialism is a Humanism':

> "And when we say that man is responsible for himself, we do not mean that he is responsible only for his own individuality, but that he is responsible for all men... Nothing can be better for us unless it is better for all...". But then again, we fall into the heart of paradox, because it is I who is choosing for all: "Who, then, can prove that I am the proper person to impose, by my own choice, my conception of man upon mankind? I shall never find any proof whatever; there will be no sign to convince me of it... it is only I who chooses to say that it is good and not bad."
>
> SARTRE 1989, para:9

Like Heidegger, Sartre leaves this dialectical tension between self and other unresolved. The other enables my existence, but I must continuously wrest myself from his gaze and into my realm of freedom, spontaneity and responsibility. Here I am responsible for the other, as he is for me, though we may never see eye to eye as to the right way to realize this responsibility. This is the direct outcome of having no universal decree to guide us. In varying ways, we may continue to impinge upon each other, always trying to find our right distances and proximities in relating to others while not losing ourselves.

The encounter with the object contains its own tensions in existential experiencing. A characteristic of consciousness is its freedom from its object (Sartre 1956). Indeed, a defining structural characteristic of consciousness is its capacity to negate and it is this negation that ensures that consciousness can think of its object without getting lost in it. From Sartre's point of view, being conscious of something means being conscious of the fact that you are not identical to that thing. In that sense, consciousness is radically free in relation to everything external to it.

In his famous story 'Nausea', Sartre (1938/2007) brings forth his reflection on the structure of consciousness and displays what it means for consciousness to be faced with independent fact. As he sees it, this differentiation of the self from its surroundings provides insight into the ground of human freedom: Once the separation of subjectivity from its surroundings has been grasped clearly and distinctly, a *gap* is discovered within the self, an alienated part, and it is in this gap that our freedom resides. It is there that we realize, in our alienation from all that is given, that we are of a different order, because we can – by acts of consciousness – negate everything given.

Sensation: The acknowledgement of the basic state in which existence does not include meaning, inherent or a priori, is tantamount to the acknowledgement of nothingness, which is the bottom layer of human life. We enter here into another existential paradox that gives rise to the sensation of anxiety, anguish and alienation. Sartre explains that, as a conscious being, the 'For-Itself' recognizes what it is *not*: It is not a being-in-itself. "Nothingness is the putting into question of being by being – that is, precisely consciousness or For-self" (Sartre 1956, 79). Through the awareness of *what it is not*, the 'For-Itself' becomes what it *is*: A nothingness, wholly free in the world. Sartre summarizes this position by saying, "For consciousness there is no being except for this precise obligation to be a revealing intuition of something" (ibid. 618). Consciousness is Nothingness. Yet, as Nothingness it is also a revelation of being.

This recognition of nothingness gives rise to an incredible sense of hopelessness: One realizes that he is a nothingness, a lack. But once more a paradox is given even on the level of co-occurring sensations: "...it is in anguish that man gets the consciousness of his freedom, or if you prefer, anguish is the mode of being of freedom as consciousness of being; it is in anguish that freedom is, in its being, in question for itself". (ibid. 29). Anguish evolves into recognition: "This freedom...which manifests itself through anguish is characterized by a constantly renewed obligation to remake the Self which designates the free being" (ibid. 34–35). This *existential angst implies an exclusive first person experience that is not derived from the environment, but defined by its distinction from it.*

The first person moment and its distinction from everything external can also be found in William James's descriptions of the *core self*. Large parts of the structural characteristics of this self and its sensual experience coincide with the existential authentic self: It is a self of choice, spontaneity, singularity and agency. Whereas Sartre describes its experiential discovery by means of anguish, alienation and anxiety, James tries to capture the sensation of intimacy, identification and recognition one has when encountering the "...inner or subjective being, ...the most enduring and intimate part of the self, that which we most verily seem to be" (James 2013, 296). He notes how hard put one is to isolate and describe this evasive and almost undefinable element of the self in the stream of consciousness, but when it is present, its presence is recognized and intuitively known: "[It]...is felt by all men as a sort of innermost centre within the circle, of sanctuary within the citadel, constituted by the subjective life as a whole. ...when it is found, it is felt; just as the body is felt..." (ibid. 299).

This self is intuitively recognized and known, though difficult to articulate and define. It is innermost, well-guarded and not easily exposed. For James this self is closely linked to the experience of the body:

> ... This palpitating inward life is...that central nucleus which I just tried to describe... Whenever my introspective glance succeeds in turning round quickly enough to catch one of these manifestations of spontaneity in the act, all it can ever feel distinctly is some bodily process, for the most part taking place within the head... In a sense, then, it may be truly said that...the 'Self of selves', when carefully examined, is found to consist mainly of the collection of these peculiar motions in the head or between the head and throat. I do not for a moment say that this is all it consists of... But I feel quite sure that these cephalic motions are the portions of my innermost activity of which I am most distinctly aware.
>
> IBID. 301, 303

In psychoanalytic thinking, Laing and Winnicott both emphasize three aspects of the sensual characteristics of a true, subjective, inner self that echo James's characterization of the 'self of selves'. Firstly, it is anchored in the body, embodying its vitality, experiencing its innervations. Laing describes the sensation of a person who is in his own body as the sensation of being flesh and blood, having a sense of biological reality, solidity and anchorage (Laing 1960, 69). Winnicott also emphasizes the simple and basic experience of bodily existence: Heart beats, breathing, warmth, movement, etc. Being a living body suffices in order to feel the liveliness of a true self that is no more than an incorporation of the experiential elements of being alive (Winnicott 1960, 148–149).

The second point emphasized is of the true self as an initiator, agent, and source of action as opposed to it being reactive. For James this inner self is "what welcomes or rejects... It is the home of interest... It is the source of effort and attention, and the place from which appear to emanate the fiats of the will" (James 2013, 303). This same experience of initiative and spontaneity is given in Winnicott's conception of the spontaneous gesture that arises from within and is never responsive in its origin.

The third is the experience of sanctified privacy associated with this inner, true self of selves.[2] Winnicott posits that: "At the centre of every human lies a

---

2 Laing describes the fear of *engulfment* that arises when contact with the other threatens to negate the identity of the self and annul its autonomy (Laing 1960, 45–46). He also discusses

component that cannot be communicated, it is sacred and must be protected. It remains isolate, permanently unknown, in fact unfound" (Winnicott 1963, 187). Its violation and inappropriate exposure lead to an experience equivalent to "Rape, and being eaten by cannibals" and constitutes a sin against the self (ibid. 186). And yet, the fantasy of violation and engulfment is countered by "the fantasy of being found" and the catastrophe of remaining undiscovered (ibid. 178, 185). Winnicott describes this additional paradox in the following way: "it is joy to be hidden but disaster not to be found" (ibid. 185). It is "an inherent dilemma, which belongs to the co-existence of two trends, the urgent need to communicate and the still more urgent need not to be found" (ibid. 184).

In summary, the Subjective-Existential self's Firstness is characterized by primary sensations of bodily rhythm and vitality, privacy and sanctity of boundaries. Subjectivity and intuitive self-identification are uncovered and recovered in cycles of anguish, anxiety, and joyous vitality. Its Secondness comprises of inherent tension between the unique, spontaneous and choice making 'I' and its contingencies that form it and are transformed by it. Otherness, at times, may wholly compromise the 'I', which will recover itself through the inevitable experience of objectification and shame. Subjective-Existential Thirdness is characterized by containment of paradox and contrasts that remain unresolved. The orderliness of time is collapsed within this axis, the present moment serving as a vantage point for its reconstruction.

Subjective-Existential experiencing and selfhood are defined in relation to, and in the context of, other axes that are often experienced as contradicting or annulling their wholeness and boundaries. The Subjective-Existential self constantly negotiates facticity as it is given in correspondence to reality. It is often in relations of tension and contrast with Intersubjective truths that are experienced as imposing, trespassing and violating the authentic ones. Comprised of paradox, this selfhood may exist wholly in parallel to and in little interaction with rationality as given in the Coherent axis. It must avoid escaping into Ideal truths and understand that the ideals it requires must derive from itself.

Correspondent Selfhood: The Correspondent factual self exists in physical reality, as an element among elements, a fact among facts. It concentrates, first

---

the fear of *implosion* that derives from a radical form of trespassing, when a person experiences himself as an empty space that may be flooded, filled and abolished at any given moment. Lastly, there is the fear of *petrification*. Although interaction with the other has the potential of being vitalizing and enriching, one always fears it may be lethal and impoverishing. Thus, contact with the other may threaten the self's subjectivity and freedom (ibid. 48–49).

and foremost, on survival and is attuned to the experienced contingencies that affect it. At any given time, this self is equivalent to its observable manifestations and may be assessed and described according to distinct measures.

Grammar: The first structural principle of the Correspondent truth axis is the clear distinction between representations of the internal and external. The experiential-psychological platform of this axial self is rooted in the belief that reality is knowable, and that belief and fact may be easily compared. Externality is fully open to objective investigation by the Correspondent self, which is capable of being objective, impartial and interest-free. Space and time, as necessary constituents of objectivity, are also the general coordinates of the individual experiences that make up the Correspondent self.

The Correspondent self inquires and learns by what is given by the senses and may be clearly proven beyond reasonable doubt. It engages in data-based inference and acts as a neutral researcher who observes, raises questions, offers possible explanations or hypotheses, collects data in order to confirm or refute these hypotheses and finally comes to a general conclusion that serves as explanation and prediction.

The language of the Correspondent self is a propositional language, based on the logical structure of predicate calculus. Its formative structure is either definitional ('A house is a place to live in') or descriptive ('Cairo is the largest city in Egypt'). The grammatical structure of definitions (or axioms) and descriptive statements is identical, consisting of a verb phrase that predicates a noun phrase, but the former is always true, while the latter is either true or false. However, the rules of the Correspondent language are not only syntactic or semantic, they also concern contingencies, as implied in the notions of correlation and causality.

In its pure form, Correspondent language admits meaning only where reference and empirical observation exist. In fact, meaning is tantamount to a 'map' of reality in which a person – any person – can find his way. No preference is given to first person perspective over others, and significations of superstition, mysticism, magical thought and faith are not admitted as meaningful.

Encounter with the world: The Correspondent self is differentiated from the world around it and clearly acknowledges its 'otherness'. The world is given in dimensions of time, space, and events that occur outside of our control. This moves the self to such cognitive and behavioral actions as explanation, prediction and control. To this end, we aspire to make the reality around us more familiar, less alien. The more sense we can make of it, let alone predict what is to happen in it and even control it, the more we feel secure inside it. All other things being equal, our sense of knowing the world reduces our anxiety.

Reality often undermines man's ideals and wishes, as well as his needs for coherence and control. When the otherness of reality is perceived as dangerous and arouses fear, we often employ different forms of denial, non-perception, distortion, denial or, alternatively, react with preconditioned responses of fight or flight.

In psychiatry, many disorders are fashioned according to the accuracy in which reality is apprehended. Psychoanalysis, like philosophy, deals with the contingencies of reality as they confront the subject. Beginning with Freud (as described in Chapter 4), reality is recognized when it forces itself on the subject and it is rarely met willingly. Our first encounter with the otherness of reality is hostile, because otherness interferes with pleasure seeking and satisfaction. For this same reason, when man takes the otherness of reality at its stride, he is deemed mature, reflective, and wise.

Sensation: When faced with an aspect of reality that is not familiar to him, man first apprehends it as 'other' and experiences it as threat. As Dewey put it:

> Man finds himself living in an aleatory world; his existence involves, to put it baldly, a gamble. The world is a scene of risk; it is uncertain, unstable, uncannily unstable. Its dangers are irregular, inconstant... Although persistent, they are sporadic, episodic.
>
> DEWEY 1929, 41

On the other hand, the same sensations of foreignness, externality and unpredictability may, in a different temperament or at different times, produce excitement and a sense of vitality. James describes this in the following way: "That element in reality which every strong man of common-sense willingly feels there because it calls forth powers that he owns – the rough, harsh, sea-wave, north-wind element, the denier of persons, the democratizer". Men enjoying this experience of otherness are those who "... Sicken at a life wholly constituted of intimacy. There is an overpowering desire at moments to escape personality, to revel in the action of forces that have no respect for our ego, to let the tides flow, even though they flow over us" (James 2009, 90).

The five senses are dominantly positioned in this axis, as they are the Correspondent self's basic bearers of information. Sights, smells, sounds, textures and tastes are noticed, experienced and identified as they are, in a dimension that excludes their emotional experiencing. Before we like or dislike a sensation we sense it *impartially*, in a way devoid of all bias.

In conclusion, the Correspondent axis forms a factual reality comprised of sense data and the knowledge and truths inferred from it. Correspondent selfhood is especially responsive to these data and seeks to survive in the world by means of explanation, prediction and control. The Correspondent self is factual, practical and impartial as regards truth. It is realistic in the face of illusion and disillusioned in the face of concealment. It encounters a world that seems foreign and separate from itself, yet, endlessly attempts to know it. The otherness of the world may be perceived as exciting or frightening, in accordance with the temperament of the person experiencing it.

When looking at this axis in relation to the Subjective-Existential one, it appears at times as crushing facticity, while at others times it may appear as providing the circumstance upon which we may act. Tension may exist between the truths of this axis and other truths, originating in Ideal, Subjective-Existential, Coherent or Intersubjective axes. The latter is particularly pertinent in this respect, because Intersubjective truth may drive the subject to distort his perception of reality in order to better accommodate social demands. Another typical tension is the one existing between Correspondent and Ideal truths, when one is driven to do things that are not in accord with his values. Of course, when the individual lives under coercion or oppression, Correspondent truth may directly clash with Subjective-Existential truth and the subject may experience his life as divorced from anything he cares for.

Pragmatic Selfhood: The Pragmatic self relies on the Correspondent self in the sense of distinguishing between external and internal reality and apprehending reality as other from self. However, unlike the impartial realistic approach of the Correspondent self, the Pragmatic self is driven by particular and personal intentions and interests. It is not interested in the knowledge of the world per se, but rather in the ways this world may be negotiated in accordance with its own goals and motives. The Pragmatic self seeks not only to survive in reality, but to influence it too. It embodies personal intention and acts upon identified contingencies in a way that is calculated to result in desired outcomes.

Grammar: Like the Correspondent self, this self too creates its knowledge according to the information it gains from the senses, but it 'allows' itself to perform mental acts that are not acceptable by the Correspondent self. A Pragmatic self can be intuitive both when formulating its assumptions and when evaluating its actions and their results. It may believe and accept as true all information that promotes its internally generated experience of wellbeing. It ignores that which is not relevant to the particular problem and purpose at hand. In many cases, logical consistency is not considered to be binding.

The most fundamental link in the Pragmatic grammar is created by causality and the anticipation of future states, especially as they are effected by the subject's own actions. Here, the ultimate cause is the subject's intentions and the effects of the related actions on reality, both internal and external.

The 'shelf life' of Pragmatic truths is restricted to their service in specific contexts. The results are assessed in the present and reassessed again following action, in order to validate the truth value of the expectation. In this respect, Pragmatic logic is versatile and subject to few restrictions other than outcome.

Encounter with the world: The encounter with the world is central to the Pragmatic truth axis in the sense that truth values are always derived by collating intention with the concrete outcome of this intention. The intended outcome may occur in either external or internal reality. Consider, for example, the influence of religious belief on the self's experience of life as James describes it. This belief defines a domain in which the absolute distinction between internal and external – which is imperative for the Correspondent self – does not subsist. The Pragmatic self can 'split' in such a way that a segment of it acts as cause, while another segment is passive and serves as effect.

The Pragmatic self is expressed by means of its impact on the world. This has long been discussed in terms of, among others, determinism versus free will. In a deterministic world, the influence of the self's actions on itself and on the world are insignificant. By contrast, a world of free will is one in which the self and the world mutually constitute each other. It involves the self's experience of its own potential. James succinctly articulates this idea:

> The monstrously lopsided equation of the universe and its knower, which we postulate as the ideal of cognition, is perfectly paralleled by the no less lopsided equation of the universe and the doer. We demand in it a character for which our emotions and active propensities shall be a match.
>
> JAMES 2009, 84–85

Sensation: James describes the basic exciting experience of being able to impact reality:

> The great point is that the possibilities are really here... That is what gives the palpitating reality to our moral life and makes it tingle...with so strange and elaborate an excitement. This reality, this excitement, is what the determinisms, hard and soft alike, suppress by their denial that anything is decided here and now....
>
> JAMES 2009, 183

Only in an effectible world we may experience such emotions as fortitude, hope, rapture, admiration, earnestness, and the like; "That 'chance'...its presence is the vital air which lets the world live, the salt which keeps it sweet" (ibid. 179). In a deterministic world the subject will inevitably experience fear, disgust, despair or doubt, his mind left "prey to discontent and craving" (ibid.).

Empirical studies have dealt extensively with the effects of the experience of competence and incompetence on psychological well-being. The experience of the ability to influence the world, referred to as 'self-efficacy', appears as a special theme in social psychology (Bandura 1997; Seligman 1975). Both contend that we must maintain an experience of control regarding our environment, even if it is illusory, in order to be able to cope with hardship, stress and challenge. The experience of self-efficacy has been found to decrease stress and despair in the face of failure, and foster ambition and interest in the world (Bandura, 1982). Acquired helplessness has been identified as a detectable and repeatable phenomenon that can cause depression (Seligman, 1975). When aspirations are actualized, in effect or imagination, man experiences exuberance. The reverse emotion occurs as a result of infantile fixation on the experience of helplessness (Bibring 1953, 13). Various psychoanalytic writers have described the acquisition of experiences of competence, autonomy, mastery and control as key achievements in different stages of development (Erikson, 1968; Mahler 1974; 1975).

Pragmatic selfhood, predicated upon the will and motivation to impact the world in a way that aligns with its interests, does not always coexist peacefully with its Ideal or Coherent counterparts. It is also often in conflict with Intersubjective selfhood that prioritizes collective understandings, benefits and truths.

Intersubjective Selfhood: The Intersubjective as a whole may be seen as a collective kind of being, but the Intersubjective *self* is defined as a first person singular perspective. It is Intersubjective inasmuch as it always faces second and third persons, often in their plural forms of 'you' or 'them', but then it aspires to transform these impersonal entities into the first-person plural 'us'. Action, thought and emotion here are predicated on the connection between the subject and the people around him, especially those whom he considers to be significant and independent centers of agency and subjectivity. He shares with them certain common perceptions of reality and truth.

Grammar: The Intersubjective grammar has a number of rules which do not require coherence, correspondence with reality or authenticity. Firstly, there is no self without an other. Wherever self is, there other is too. In terms of existence, there is no priority: Self and other appear in one generative stroke. Secondly, the difference between self and other is a dimensionality difference. Specifically, the other lacks one dimension relative to self, the dimension of internality. Of course, the other is also a subject, he is also an intentional being, but his internality is not directly accessible by the self. This is part of his inherent 'otherness'. Thirdly, the *majority* (which is of significance to the individual) *rules.* Intersubjective truths may be achieved by open discussion, at times they are relayed by myth, at times we act upon them as Correspondent truths, unaware that they are imposed by norms or institutions that structure the consciousness of the majority we live with. In the course of human history, Intersubjective truths have served as a platform for folie a deaux, cults and even nations.

Intersubjective truths guide the motivations and actions of the Intersubjective self. Though bound to them, this self is often unaware of the ways in which its truths were formed. Social norms often disguise themselves, through their status of Intersubjective truths, as facts. This type of truth, which is often arbitrary with regard to the 'me', is the truth Heidegger refers to when discussing the logic of the 'they'. There is also a 'softer' version of Intersubjective truth which is often formed imperceptibly and collaboratively by the individual and the people around him as grounds for their common existence.

Encounter with the world: The 'world' in this truth axis consists of the people surrounding the subject, especially significant others. The subject's communication with this 'world' is what defines truth in this axis. Intersubjective selfhood bears close resemblance to the social self as described by James. It is a self that strives to be recognized and identifies itself with the recognition it achieves and with the great passionate desire to achieve it:

> A man's Social Self is the recognition which he gets from his mates. …we have an innate propensity to get ourselves noticed, and noticed favorably, by our kind. No more fiendish punishment could be devised…than that one should be turned loose in society and remain absolutely unnoticed by all the members thereof…a kind of rage and impotent despair would ere long well up in us, from which the cruelest bodily tortures would be a relief; for these would make us feel that, however bad might be our plight, we had not sunk to such a depth as to be unworthy of attention at all.
>
> JAMES 2013, 293

Fromm describes the extent to which man is dependent on this recognition and discusses the 'false consciousness' man is willing to develop while sacrificing and distorting his hidden fantasies and deep motivations in order to belong, be accepted and adjust to social norms (Fromm 1970). According to Fromm, the most outstanding discovery made by Freud was not the uncovering of man's drives, but his willingness to deny such a large portion of his inner existence in order to gain acceptance from the people around him (Fromm 1955, 77). When fearing rejection and exclusion, we tend to please, adapt, comply, act according to majority opinion even when it contradicts our discretion.

Daring to sound a minority opinion may often lead to being shunned from one's peer group (Schachter 1951) and the risk of ostracism keeps many desires in check.

Sensation: Man suffers mentally and physically when he lacks a sense of belonging (Baumeister and Leary 1995). The social pain caused by rejection simulates physical pain and moves in the same neurological nerve channels (MacDonald and Leary 2005; Eisenberger and Lieberman 2004; Panksepp 2003). The initial reaction to being ostracized or rejected is raw and irrational; it ignores information which could minimize the significance and relevance of the event by use of logic (Kipling 2007). This explains the divorce of the Intersubjective from the Correspondent and Coherent axes, as well as its encapsulated, automatic functioning. For most social animals, ostracism equals death (Gruter and Masters 1986) and, among humans, the reactions to it include alienation, depression, despair and a sense of worthlessness (Forgas and Williams 1998). Basic experiences of love – loving and being loved – are central to the development and maintenance of the self's vitality (Shaw 2003).

There are two main lines of psychoanalytic thought regarding contact with the other. They can loosely be referred to as the paradigm of drive and the paradigm of relation. The first perceives the primal self as solipsistic and the connection with the other as mediated by innate drives seeking satisfaction, while the second perceives the connection with the other as a primal drive in itself. Fairbairn was the first to articulate the need for the other as a basic drive. He transformed Freud's pleasure-oriented drive into an object-seeking one. Pleasure, according to this approach, is at most a means to the real end – the object (Fairbairn 1941). From Fairbairn's perspective, a newborn's innate orientation towards others is rooted in his adaptive biology (Fairbairn 1946, 140). This formulation places the Intersubjective truths at the same level of imperative as the Correspondent truths.

Sullivan too, and many intersubjective thinkers who followed in his footsteps, found man to be driven mainly by the search for contact with others, formed in a joint reality in which a child accepts social demands as imperative conditions. In later developments of the intersubjective theory, the psyche itself is perceived to evolve and be formed in intersubjective fields. Thus, it inevitably cooperates with others to form constructivist images of shared reality, common truths and identity.

The Intersubjective self is often in tension with Subjective-Existential selfhood, as clearly expressed in the Winnicottian terminology of 'true' and 'false' self. For the Intersubjective self, *basic* sensations lack the validity they enjoy in the Subjective-Existential realm, while special attention is given to sensations that are mediated by language and social convention (signs). In a like manner, the dimension of privacy is diminished because the self is publicly construed in the social and linguistic spheres. Intersubjective selfhood may compromise its perceptual apparatus in order to deny the perceptions of the Correspondent self. Often, the Intersubjective axis does not cohere with the subject's Ideal axis, creating a conflict between standards and principles on the one hand, and social pressures on the other hand. A whole range of experiments like, for example, by Milgram (1974) and Zimbardo (2007), attest to this kind of conflict.

Coherent Selfhood: The Coherent self is first and foremost a reflective one, observing its thoughts, emotions and actions and constructing narratives of itself and of its world. This process of reflection identifies the relationship among elements of experience and creates order and consistency among them. When there is lack of consistency between various beliefs and thoughts, restlessness and anxiety arise. The Coherent self seeks coherence not only within itself, but also in relation to the external world.

Grammar: The guiding principles of the Coherent grammar are consistency, uniformity and lack of contradiction between the system's sub-components. The Coherent self conducts itself according to the patterns of structuralism, which are not necessarily anchored in reality or in agreement with others. It exists as a text of sorts, producing meaning from the relations among its own components and creating narratives that address the first person in its singular and plural forms. The primary mode of Coherence is identity, namely, a sense of personal unity in face of the other and of one's self. Identity provides a sense of continuity, the ability to cross mental domains without causing an experience of rupture. Rationality is often adopted by this self as a pre-existing coherent system.

Encounter with the world: Man needs to create consistent narratives about the world. In the famous words of Einstein, god does not play dice with the universe. Sense data always lack order, and man needs to deliver the world from its chaos into consciously ordered systems. He creates narratives that connect between elements that seem fragmented and conflicting: "Gross experience is loaded with the tangled and complex; hence philosophy hurries away from it to search out something so simple that the mind can rest trustfully in it" (Dewey 1929, 26). As Dewey sees it, our magical safeguard against the uncertain character of the world is to deny the existence of chance, "to mumble universal and necessary law, the ubiquity of cause and effect, the uniformity of nature, universal progress, and the inherent rationality of the universe" (ibid. 44). From this perspective, divergent philosophies may be looked at as different ways of "supplying recipes for denying to the universe the character of contingency which it possesses so integrally... Quarrels among conflicting types of philosophy are thus family quarrels...concerned with imputing complete, finished and sure character to the world of real existence" (ibid. 47).

Thus, the challenge facing Coherent selfhood when encountering the world is the challenge of finding coherence. The price of coherence may be high in terms of Correspondence or Pragmatism: Reality or parts of it may be distorted by subordination to structured principles of uniformity and consistency. Nevertheless, the Coherent self is ready to pay this high price.

Sensation: The mental effort to achieve coherence always fails completeness. A remainder will inevitably exist outside of what has been ordered and will be experienced as "other and...un-included...something is always mere fact and givenness" (James 2009, 8). Successfully finding coherence in the sensual multiplicity brings along "a strong feeling of ease, peace, rest... The transition from a state of puzzle and perplexity to rational comprehension is full of lively relief and pleasure" (ibid. 63), "like the relief of the musician at resolving a confused mass of sound into melodic or harmonic order" (ibid. 65).

Many empirical studies have demonstrated that optimal human functioning requires a person to experience coherence between his various beliefs and between them and his actions and emotions. Stress is often experienced as a function of the extent to which events violate one's sense of coherence, the way one understands one's self and world and the congruence between them. A common psychological finding that supports poetic Jamesean intuitions is that cognitive dissonance is a psychic pain and drives man to abrogate the incongruence among his thoughts, beliefs, emotions and actions. The holistic assumption in this context holds that cognition and emotion are both significantly affected by the interactions between the different elements of psychic life (Wertheimer 1967; Festinger 1957). Mental processes stay in motion, stabilizing only when acquiring structural qualities like 'good form' (Heider 1960), 'optimal order' (Markus and Zajonc 1985), 'consonance' (Festinger 1957), or 'balance' (Rosenberg and Abelson 1960; Tannenbaum 1968). In these states of stability, all parts of a single unit are of the same dynamic nature, and elements of different nature are separated and distinguished from each other (Heider 1946).

Structural forces maintain the balanced structures, while states of instability drive the structure to continue searching for coherence and homeostasis (Heider 1958; Rosenberg 1968). In the face of dissonance, consistency and coherence are restored by replacing or omitting the elements that are incongruent with each other, either by adding congruent elements or by reducing the significance of the incongruent elements (Festinger 1957). This may result in distortion and denial. Empirical experiments show that the dynamic nature of cognitive consistency is bi-directional – data to conclusions and conclusions back to data (Simon and Holyoak 2002; Holyoak and Simon 1999).

In terms of truth axes, one of the Coherent self's main 'competitors' is the Correspondent self. The latter 'challenges' the ability of the former to integrate its propositions into a coherent system. The tendency for coherence drives man to not notice the elements that do not settle with the organizing paradigm of his world and diminish their significance. Thus, the fate of discordant elements and components is usually to be repressed, marginalized or denied. Similar fate applies to thoughts, perceptions or constructions that do not cohere with one's concept of one's self. The Coherent self also acts often in assessing the outputs of other components and influencing their acceptability for directing the subject's actions.

Ideal Selfhood: The Ideal self embodies the whole range of the subject's ideals, from the abstract and interpersonal to the concrete and actual. It exists in the subject's makeup as an imperative and a guide, supplying moral outlook and constraints and, at times, acting as barrier to free expression and development.

Grammar: The main determinant of the Ideal grammar is an ideal that can be represented in an object, a thought or a person. Truth values are derived by comparing the various elements against this ideal and checking for correspondence with it. This correspondence may exist irrespective of any other characteristic, because the Ideal grammar does not require realistic support, just as it does not require logical, causal or coherent relations. The Ideal truth of a person may take the shape of institutions, ceremonies and organizations inspired by the core elements of the ideal and built according to them. The ideal is absolute, whole and homogenous. Its language is binary by nature and it is typically dichotomous when referring to situations and aspirations, often dotted with superlatives.

The Ideal grammar aspires to overcome time. It provides consistent yet selective interpretations of the world and it strives for eternality (Dewey 1929, 27). The illusion of the eternal enforces the fallacy of selective emphasis: "The permanent enables us to rest, it gives peace; the variable, the changing, is a constant challenge...we can deal with the variable and precarious only by means of the stable and constant" (ibid.).

Encounter with the world: The ideal potentially forms common ground for the self and the world, overcoming the inherent alienation between them. In his essay on religious experience, James (2009) describes this subjective harmony and the unity that ideal divinity creates between man and his world. As James describes it, the atheist views the world in the third person, as a mere 'it'. Theism, on the other hand, turns the 'it' into a 'thou'. This covers the world with the mantle of the first person, thus making "it a part of me" (James 2009, 135). This merger brings about experiences of ecstasy: "consciousness of self-surrender, of absolute practical union between one's self and the divine object of one's contemplation" (ibid.).

In the psychoanalytic field, Kohut describes similarly the experience of merger and comfort with the early, idealized self objects. The impact of this experience sustains us throughout our life:

> However great our disappointment as we discover the weaknesses and limitations of the idealized selfobjects of our early life, their self-confidence as they carried us when we were babies, their security when they allowed us to merge our anxious selves with their tranquility – via their calm voices or via our closeness with their relaxed bodies as they held us – will be retained by us as the nucleus of the strength of our leading ideals and of the calmness we experience as we live our lives under the guidance of our inner goals.
>
> KOHUT AND ERNST 1978, 416

On the other hand, shame, disappointment and guilt are feelings that arise from the failure to live up to our ideals. When the pressure of the Ideal self becomes too intense, shame is experienced with every hint of failure, be it moral or defined according to external standards. (Kohut 1966, 253).

Both James and Kohut describe the driving force of ideals, as well as the serenity and sense of integrity they give rise to. James describes ideals in the context of religion but emphasizes that he is referring to the potential of any ideal to enhance well-being.[3] Kohut refers to the ideals embedded in the self as providing a healthy sense of direction and pleasure from being active and successful (Kohut 1966, 253).

Sensation: For James, the experience of the Ideal self includes integrity, dignity, serenity, simplicity, accuracy and validity, where self, world and ideal accord (James 2009, 188). In the absence of ideals, the self is vulnerable to experiences of vulgarity, restlessness, anxiety, pettiness and negativism: "The nobler thing *tastes* better" (ibid.), claims James, and so the self has "an innate preference of the more ideal attitude for its own pure sake" (ibid. 107).

Apparent tensions exist between the Ideal and the Correspondent selves. These reflect in the gap between what we hope to be – in thought, emotion and action – and what we actually are. Adhering to an Ideal truth may place one in conflict with Intersubjective truths as given in society. Yet, even in this situation, the Ideal self does not feel alone because it represents something larger

3 "The word 'God' has come to mean many things in the history of human thought, from Venus and Jupiter to the 'Idee' which figures in the pages of Hegel" (James 2009, 120–121).

than itself. Pragmatic and Ideal truths often battle in guiding plans and future actions.

Topography in Terms of Truth Axes

Truth axes may occupy different positions within the psyche, both as process and as product, and may acquire varyious degrees of consciousness. My discussion of truth axes and topography follows the logic of drive and repression, as well as the dynamics of a relationally formed unconscious of the type described by Harry Stuck Sullivan (1940; 1953) and Donnel Stern (1989; 1991; 2003). I will begin by differentiating these dynamics as they relate to both content and process.

The materials in the Freudian unconscious are conceived of as possessing identifiable and definable forms. For Freud, experiences may be forgotten, transformed, masked or disguised, distorted, blended with other experiences until undetectable, dissociated from other experiences, or simply denied. But in all cases and despite appearances, the distinct unconscious experience still exists "in the psyche" with "all of the essentials…preserved" (SE 23:260). Even when Freud spoke of *constructions* in analysis, and accepted that they might lack historical validity, he believed that they were based on a foundation of preserved material, which might reveal itself in the future.

By contrast, Harry Stack Sullivan (1940; 1953), followed by Donnel Stern, saw the unconscious as containing, at least to an extent, unformulated and undefined experience.[4] Sullivan viewed this absence of formulation as a mode of defense in the face of anxiety laden materials and situations. In Sullivan's description, the self is a system that includes all those experiences and ways of relating to others which have been found safe and secure. This self system rejects all experiences and modes of relating which are associated with anxiety. Mistrusting the unfamiliar, being afraid that it will threaten our security, we may not symbolize it, and its fully formulated meaning may never enter explicit awareness. One of the ways to avoid anxiety is simply not to formulate, not to know: "That is, one keeps certain material unformulated in order not to 'know' it" (Stern 1983, 74).

As a philosophical base for his description of the process that forms the unconscious, Stern refers to William James and Henri Bergson, both describing the emergence of thought from undifferentiated mental states. For James

4 "Much of that which is ordinarily said to be repressed is merely unformulated" (Sullivan 1940, 185).

especially, as formerly described, the content of consciousness is a small selection of clearly articulated thoughts, forged in a vast array of vague and unformed mental events. Language and focal attention formulate the formless and render it thinkable.

Stern also draws on cognitive psychological research in order to empirically support Sullivan's intuitions about the nature of the unconscious and its formation. Citing Neisser's work, Stern (1983) describes a two tiered process that explains the dividing line between unconsciousness and consciousness. The first stage in the evolution of consciousness is called 'pre-attentive processes'. Here, incoming information is broken up into large and vague chunks or blocks that are represented in iconic storage. Iconic storage is a short-term system: If items do not become the object of focal attention in the course of a few moments, they disappear from storage, which means they are no longer represented in psychic life at all. If, however, these elements become the object of focal attention, they are subject to further processing, which results in greater differentiation and detail. At this point, they enter consciousness and short-term memory and, depending on certain other factors, may enter long-term memory. In Neisser's model, the point at which material is either attended to and elaborated by the secondary process or allowed to decay is open to emotional influence. He calls this "*deliberately avoiding construction in certain areas*" (Neisser 1967, 303 In Stern 1983, 82). Stern states that, in this process, there are pre-existing biases that facilitate or inhibit construction in particular areas of experience (Stern 1983, 82–83).

According to this view, it is possible that experiences remain unformulated for various reasons. They might not have aroused the subject's attention, they may have been deemed irrelevant or of minor importance, or they may be experienced as conflictual and arousing anxiety. Stern (1983; 2003) argues that these unformulated experiences constitute a kind of relational unconscious in the sense that what is relegated to it has failed to be accepted as part of the subject's world and self-system.

In the terms of axes of truth, it may be assumed that, just as one's psyche may avoid formulating certain materials, *so it may fail to organize materials in a particular way*. Such failure may reflect the psyche's bias towards other kinds of organization. Similar processes were assumed by Loewald when he proposed that change in psychoanalysis may be the result of the *reorganization of experience*, and not of the uncovering of fully formed truth:

> Language, in its most specific function in analysis, as interpretation, is thus a creative act similar to that in poetry, where language is found for phenomena, contexts, experiences not previously known and speakable.

> New phenomena and new experiences are made available as a result of reorganization of material according to hitherto unknown principles, contexts, and connections.
>
> LOEWALD 1960, 25

Looked at in this way, the assumption that a structural organization of the various axes exists in every psyche may also have topographical implications. Continuing Sullivan and Stern's line of thought, one can assume that what is relegated to the unconscious is not necessarily or exclusively a *specific subject or emotion*, such as a death wish, a desire or repressed memory involving jealousy or incestuous desires. Rather, *it may be a particular orientation of the self towards himself or his world* as expressed in the axes of truth. Thus, because of an anticipated anxiety, a particular organization, including its accompanying self-state and image of reality (and its derivative memories, feelings, interpersonal positions, etc.), may be dissociated from consciousness. In other words, it is possible that certain axes of organization better realize innate tendencies – or are more acceptable in the subject's formative environment – and thus become the dominant organizational vehicle of the personality. At the same time, other axes develop to a lesser extent and remain unformulated, or may even be relegated to unconscious or dissociated positions.

My view of the dynamics of the unconscious also align with the Freudian tenet that inherent tensions always exist, to differing extents, between needs and their realization. Freud focused on two basic drives – the life and the death drives, and saw the Ego and the Superego as serving to manage these drives and their derivative needs in the face of reality and society. These higher agencies ensure the survival and the social adaptation of the individual. Freud's theory construed sex and aggression as the basic drives that give rise to illicit desires, which must be checked, dissociated and banned.

Over the years, the notion of 'basic drive' was debated and defined in different ways. What Freud posited as a drive toward pleasure was later presented as a drive toward the object. Kohut depicted how potent were the drives and needs associated with ideals, and how stunted a personality may be when this need was not provided for. To some extent, what I do here is redefine the status of a basic need in order to accommodate truth-seeking motives. These needs appear in various guises in theories about the subject and effectively define subjectivity.

All the needs that I specified, on the face of it, seem fairly legitimate in contemporary culture. That being said, it is not difficult to see how in relation to each and every one of the needs discussed, constraints are placed – either by the environment or by the conflicts that arise between needs. Indeed, that is fairly the nodal issue in this conceptualization: The psyche has complex needs. Their full satisfaction is never allowed and rarely possible. Moreover, their provision is not given, as Freud would have it, in an act of satisfaction, a discharge, a fulfillment of a wish. The provision of each need requires a total epistemic construction, comprising of an image of reality, an experienced truth and a self that constantly negotiate need in a joint dynamic.

What becomes unconscious is determined by the varying innate potency of the different needs in their interactions with a given environment. In relation to each need, we will find the familiar constellation of wish, censure, conflict and source of anxiety. Originating in these classically formulated dynamics, we will find repressed needs expressed by defense mechanisms, compromise-formations and various symptoms.

The Concept of Self in Psychoanalytic Thinking

In philosophy and psychoanalysis, the definition of self – one's nature as a person – is a complex, intricate, and subtle matter. In classic Greek philosophy, the self was considered a foundational element that captures the essence of being human and unifies consciousness over time. Plato, in many of his dialogues, identified the self with reason and intellect by virtue of its kindred connection to the Forms. Aristotle defined it by means of the *nous*, the divine faculty in man. He believed that by engaging in *theoria* – philosophizing – man actualizes his highest and most divine faculty, the one that most directly expresses man's very self. Despite their differences, Plato and Aristotle are classic thinkers in that they were both concerned with the essential, universal aspect of the soul, and focused less on the contingent, accidental and unique.

In modernity, uniqueness and subjectivity were placed center-stage. This began with Descartes, who traced all knowledge back to the self and its conscious states. The Cartesian self is more or less equated with subjective self-consciousness. Its conception as such led to the removal of self from the public sphere and its retreat into the private domain, where it is inherent, given-all-at-once and on its own. The postmodern approach reversed the view of self as private and solitary. Instead, it was tied up with language in a binding and permanent relation, thus placing the individual consciousness irrevocably in the public domain. Here, the self loses its delineation, existing within and reflecting the social whole. Consequently, the self also lost its singularity and became multiple and context specific.

The postmodern critique of the notion of self is not totally new. Hume, for example, argued that there exists a general human fallacy that causes us to attribute existence to anything we perceive, experience or think of: "Whatever we conceive, we conceive to be existent. Any idea we please to form is the idea of a being; and the idea of a being is any idea we please to form" (Hume 2012, part 1 Sec. vi). Hume noted another frequent error of perceptual reason that causes us to assume causality or unity for every set of phenomena that tend to appear in conjunction: "When any phaenomena are constantly and invariably conjoined together, they acquire such a connexion in the imagination, that it passes from one to the other, without any doubt or hesitation" (Hume 2012, part 3 Sec. 1). Our concept of the self is no exception and is a result of our natural habit of attributing unified existence to any collection of associated parts. This belief is natural, but there is no logical support for it. Wittgenstein (1999, cl.103–106) and proponents of the linguistic turn following him echoed Hume's opinion that the inference of the self is erroneous, arising from the ambiguities of language and supported by the modern-metaphysical tendency to believe that whatever receives a name must be an entity or a being.

When the self lost its essence, it also lost its unity (or the illusion of it). Postmodernism posited a fragmented self that had no essence and could be construed as comprised of images only (Allan 1997, 1). Devoid of its essential presence, the self was replaced by a fluid entity that Derrida called 'the free-play of difference' (1978). In the framework of this 'play', every object, including the 'object' of self, exists in the context of its opposite which, in turn, infiltrates the object and becomes part of its presumed existence. Pure, essential, foundational forms do not exist in postmodern philosophy. Contingencies are the only givens and isolated events attain form and meaning in a hermeneutic manner, in relation to some other events and by means of interpretation. In that sense, all objects are, first and foremost, signifiers. These signifiers maintain numerous, varied relations with their possible references, with that which, in the modern past, was considered to be their 'signified'.

The blurring of the orders of signifier and signified effectively removes the reality of the self as a frame of reference, leaving only possibilities, habitual ways of speaking and combinations of sameness and difference. In the condition of postmodernity, "the self is no longer [even] a meta-narrative, but one term among others for representing experience. Moreover, the self is polysemic, attached to and articulated by multiple systems of signs" (Gubrium and Holstein 1994, 685). Despite these formulations, the Cartesian conception of self remained dominant and culturally pervasive, backed by intuition and the privileging of individuality in liberal Western culture.

In psychoanalysis, as in philosophy, there is a lack of consensus about what the term 'self' means. Very roughly formulated, one can recognize in psychoanalytic thinking the same strains philosophy has struggled with, alternately focusing, on the one hand, on monadic, unitary and universal aspects of the mind and, on the other hand, on the intersubjective, multiple and unique ones. In tandem, the self is conceived of as discovered or as constituted, as given or as narrated, as private or as a misconception in the public sphere. One of the main controversies in this context concerns the issue of coherence and unity versus multiplicity and diversity.

In the field of psychological thinking, the idea that distinct organizations co-exist in the psyche is far from new and has, over time, been developed from different perspectives. 'Different kinds of organization' refers here to what Freud termed the 'Splitting of the ego', namely, the co-existence of two divergent tendencies within one subject.[5] Laplanche and Pontalis show that the term 'Spaltung', i.e., splitting, is very old and that it has been variously used throughout the nineteenth century in the fields of psychology and psychiatry. The term indicates the different ways in which man may be divided within himself, hosting opposing tendencies in his personality (Laplanche and Pontalis 1988, 427).

The idea that man is, in one respect or another, divided within himself may be found already in the divisions Plato and Aristotle made between the 'superior' and 'inferior' parts of the psyche. In modern psychological thinking, this idea was discussed by William James in his essay 'The Divided Self and the Process of its Unification' (James 2008). As James sees it, some persons are born with an inner constitution which is harmonious and well balanced from the outset. Their impulses are consistent with one another, their will follows without trouble the guidance of their intellect, their passions are not excessive, and their lives are not haunted by regrets. On the other hand, "Others are oppositely constituted; and are so in degrees which may vary from something so slight as to result in a merely odd or whimsical inconsistency, to a discordancy of which the consequences may be inconvenient in the extreme". James distinguishes here between the unified personality – all of whose values and emotions are congruent – and the 'divided' psyche, for whom "the world is a double-storied mystery" (James 2008, 163).

In the context of his times and of religious thinking, James sees the division of the self as keeping "...us from our real good" (ibid. 167), and the divided element is construed as an inherent defect. The different tendencies may be

5 In his study of fetishes, Freud writes: "...The two attitudes persist side by side throughout their lives without influencing each other. Here is what may rightly be called a splitting of the ego" (SE 23:204). Discussing the concept of splitting, Freud wonders whether the idea "Should be regarded as something long familiar and obvious or as something entirely new and puzzling" (SE 23:275).

deeply rooted so, in their struggle, the psyche becomes a "battle-ground for what he feels to be two deadly hostile selves…" (ibid. 171). According to James, psychic change may be either gradual or sudden, whereby a divided and unhappy self becomes unified.[6] Even when the change is seemingly sudden, it is an outcome of "…special cerebral functions unconsciously developing until they are ready to play a controlling part when they make irruption into the conscious life". This development for James is the outcome of a "subconscious incubation" of an "active subliminal self" (ibid. note 94). To understand what James meant, one has to understand his startlingly modern view of the psyche, which he describes in terms of a 'field': "a field of experience where there is not a single conception that can be sharply drawn. …the boundaries are always misty" (James 2008, 39). "This field of consciousness is a 'wave', impossible to outline with any definiteness" (ibid. 231).

James acknowledges the instability created by such a definition of psychic life. The soul he describes is manifold and dynamic, but he seeks within it unifying, focalizing tendencies and acknowledges the relief one finds in finding coherence and continuity.[7] The fields comprising the psyche are many, but the various systems are assumed to create contacts which mutually check or reinforce one another creating a "habitual center of energy" (James 2008, 196) that exists across this multiplicity.

In all areas of his theory, James deals with the tensions between multiplicity and change on the one hand, and points of stability and uniformity on the other hand. He recognizes the psyche's heterogeneity in the same way as he recognizes nature's infinite variety. However, where the psyche is concerned, he advocates the attainment of integrity so as to avoid troubling degrees of incompatibility and discord.

In classical psychoanalysis, conflict among discordant elements is viewed as a defining characteristic of the psyche. Yet, from Freud's topographic model, through Klein's depressive position and Kohut's nuclear self, health is grasped

6 For James, the term 'conversion' is here synonymous with psychic change. Despite the term's religious overtones, not all change is religious and sometimes the opposite: "…the new birth may be away from religion into incredulity; or it may be from moral scrupulosity into freedom and license; or it may be produced by the irruption into the individual's life of some new stimulus or passion… In all these instances, we have precisely the same psychological form of event, a firmness, stability, and equilibrium succeeding a period of storm and stress and inconsistency" (James 2008, 176).

7 "As our mental fields succeed one another, each has its center of interest…its limits are unassignable. Some fields are narrow fields and some are wide fields. Usually when we have a wide field we rejoice, for we then see masses of truth together, and often get glimpses of relations which we divine rather than see…" (James 2008, 231).

in terms of unity and integration. Only recently, contemporary thinking has begun to view positively the age-old idea of multiplicity as expressed in the concept of 'multiple selves' which gained momentum with the growing influence of postmodern ideas in psychoanalysis. In contemporary psychoanalytic thinking, the self as essence and foundation is by and large dismissed in favor of something fluid like an idea or a set of ideas, an experiential structure, an agency, one's unique life history and even an idea in someone else's mind (Mitchell 1991).

Following these conceptualizations and distancing himself from the classic psychoanalytic concept of a unitary and cohesive self, Stephen Mitchell writes: "We are all composites of overlapping, multiple organizations and perspectives, and our experience is smoothed out by an illusory sense of continuity" (Mitchell 1991, 127).[8] In his view, the manifold organization of self is constructed around different centers and object representations, derived from different relational contexts. Each organization embodies patterns of experience and of significant self-other configurations that create their own sense of self. These different organizations may be conflicting in nature, creating incompatible behavioral and emotional patterns. Different selves or self-states appear in an individual's consciousness, sometimes succeeding one another, sometimes existing alongside each other and at times also confronting one another. Thus, claims Mitchell, parallel perspectives and overlapping tapestries of meaning are formed, shaping psychic life in its entirety.

Bromberg presented a view of the normal mind as a multiplicity of self-states that, through the use of normal dissociation, allows a human being to engage the ever-shifting requirements of life's complexities with creativity and spontaneity. Bromberg's self is conceived of as a configuration of changing, dynamic, non-linear and non-sequential states of awareness, engaged in an "ongoing dialectic with the healthy illusion of a comprehensive self" (Bromberg 1998, 32). Aron states that: "as postmodern thought more and more locates the individual within a social, cultural, and linguistic context, it becomes increasingly difficult to view the self as separate and autonomous" (Aron 2003, 277). In Strenger's (2005) optimistic take on the issue, contingency is celebrated in an 'ethic of existential necessity', that is described as a project of "pluralism, contingency and reconfiguration of selves" (Apprey 2006, 904).

8 Mitchell presents his position as an extension of Sullivan's contention that the idea of a unified subjective self is illusory, indeed 'the very mother of illusions' in the service of allaying anxiety and distracting attention from ways in which one actually operates with others (Sullivan, 1938).

From this perspective, identity is no longer based on the agency of a central and omniscient ego, but rather arises from the constant and prolonged dialogue between aspects and qualities of the self that are attributed agent-like qualities, which may be called voices, sub-personalities, 'I-positions', personas or roles (Rowan 2010, 13). The extreme expression of this multiplicity is given in the definition of self as comprised from responses valid only within a specific set of circumstances. The components of this multiplicity are never regarded as entities resistant to change. Rather, each component is understood as a momentary position "that comes and goes" (Rowan 2010, 15). As Rowan articulates it: "The beauty of I-positions is that they are clearly postulated for the moment… There is no claim that they really exist…they are brought into being by the situation in which they appear. This is a brave new world, where we do not need anything other than the present moment" (ibid. 38). A representative of this perspective, who enhanced and developed it, is Hubert Hermans (2004) who coined the term "dialogical self". Hermans conceptualized the self in terms of a dynamic multiplicity of relatively autonomous I-positions in the landscape of the mind. The different parts of the self are involved in communicative interchange, each presenting a point of view, which may be in harmony or disharmony with other voices. There are voices that are more dominant than others and, in the final analysis, the significance of an event stems from the dialogue within the entire range of these voices.

In order to achieve an experience of unity and integration, the subject needs to develop self – reflexive points of view which take these differences into account and create narratives that explain them. Various names have been accorded to this self-observing function: Reflexive function (Fonagy and Target, 1996), metacognitive or meta-representative skills (Sperber 2000), meta-position (Hermans, 2003) and observing I (Leiman and Stiles, 2001). Rowan points out that what is consistent across these formulations is the refusal to grant these responses and functions concrete form or permanent status, as is the case in conceptualizations of ego states, sub-personalities, sub-selves and the like.

It is important to note that relational thinkers that have distanced themselves from essentialism and unity *do* acknowledge the self as a powerful intuitive concept which is essential for understanding the ongoing experience of unity and continuity (Stolorow and Lachmann 1980). Circumventing the need to assume its existence as a distinct entity, and yet preserving its experienced privileged status, they attempt to explain monadic states by emphasizing their experiential side. Becker and Shalgi, for example, offer the following formulation:

> The self experiences a monadic moment of being with and only with oneself. ... Monadic experiential moments such as these arise at critical crossroads of development as well as in the daily routine of life. ...moments of artistic creativity, eroticism, and daydreaming can all serve as monadic moments, potentially free of all context.
>
> BECKER AND SHALGI 2006, 162

In the span of time and the spirit of the eras, from William James to Stephen Mitchell, one can see the constant and the variable. The recognition of multiplicity of self appeared and reappeared throughout this time, but its nature changed from the essential to the experiential. In addition, the wish for an authoritative order has given way to the desire for democratic and productive dialogue. In other words, the 'social order of the multiple selves' has changed (Mendlovic 2009). Today, there are numerous supporters of the heterogeneous, pluralistic perspective on the self. Multiplicity is no longer regarded as esoteric, but rather as an indication of creativity and versatility.

This difference in valence is not only abstract, it influences values and ethics through definitions of pathology and health. Thus, classical psychoanalysis presented as a therapeutic objective the organization and maintenance of an integrated sense of self. Kohut, for example, sees as quite pathological the existence of subordinate selves, trapped in what he calls vertical and horizontal splits (Kohut 1972). The central thrust within mind is viewed as integrative, the continuous line of subjective experience forming the healthy core of the self. Analysts advocating multiple selves see this therapeutic stance in opposite terms, contending that it is restrictive and enhances dissociative and repressive tendencies. As Mitchell expressed it: "It is one of the great paradoxes of the analytic process that the more that the analysand can tolerate experiencing multiple versions of himself, the stronger, more resilient, and more durable he experiences himself to be" (Mitchell 1991, 140).

Several problems arise in the context of these conceptualizations. Firstly, as Mills sees it (Mills 2005, 2015), there is the problem of the postmodern denial of universals. Mills acknowledges that different experiences shape our individual epistemologies and, in turn, inform our personal identities and collective identifications. Therefore, we have different psychologies. But he contends that:

> ...this does not negate the notion of universals. Despite the fact that particular aspects of intra-psychic life may not be duplicated or identical to others' subjective experience...we are more fundamentally conjoined in essence than in phenomenology. This is one reason why we, as clinicians,

> fundamentally observe universal patterns emanating from within each individual psyche regardless of historicity, gender, culture, or race.
>
> MILLS 2015, 12–13

As examples of universals, Mills mentions defense mechanisms, endogenous drives, and the phenomena of transference and repetition.

Secondly, as regards psychoanalytic theorizing, Mills emphasizes the need for ontological and epistemological clarity regarding such a key concept as self. While poetically and intuitively understood by many clinicians, there is an urgent need to rigorously define and theoretically develop the notion of self. This is essential for psychoanalysis as a comprehensive theory of the human psyche.

Thirdly, and related to the former point, it is not clear how the idea of multiplicity – both in regard to truth and with regard to self – may lend itself to clear implementation in clinical technique. Again, in a discipline that aspires to theorize in the service of clinical practice, this is a major disadvantage.

The theoretical objective that these issues lead to, in my mind, is how to retain the particularity, openness and pluralism introduced by postmodern conceptions of self without losing Mills's common sense point about the value of general formulations? How can we define the unifying functions within multiplicity? And how do we manage to articulate our understandings in a coherent philosophic and metapsychologic framework? I address these issues and suggest an answer formulated in the terms of truth axes.

The Construal of Self in Terms of Truth Axes

The notion of self I pursue here takes its cue from existential and pragmatic philosophies, where the self is formed by the flux of experience, comprising images, thoughts, feelings and bodily sensations, as well as imprints of objects. The manner in which these elements are unified to form a self is theory dependent, effected by different principles, structures or interpersonal relations, in accordance with the particular perspective of the philosopher or the psychoanalyst.

I propose here the notion of truth axes as the organizing principles of the psyche that give the self its patterns of unity, continuity and coherence. This hypothesis is grounded in theoretical analysis that identifies truth as an overarching need, expressed across all dimensions of a subject's life – Subjective, Intersubjective, Pragmatic and Ideal, Correspondent and Coherent. However reality is construed, it organizes itself in relation to a truth natural to it.

These dimensions of the subject's life are determined and delineated by particular basic needs: The need to manage perceived factual reality and survive in it, the need to uphold guiding ideals, the need to maintain loyalty to one's authenticity, the need to construct a shared interpersonal reality, the need to lend continuity to perceptions of self and world, the need to promote goals. These needs inform the different dimensions of living, experienced by the subject as different images of reality. Each image conforms to the overarching need for truth, giving rise to its own natural version of it. The need is the 'engine' that creates a truth axis. It is the posited metaphysical element that sets the epistemic constructions in motion.

So, metaphysically motivated by basic needs, several epistemic perspectives are created, giving rise to different self-states. The various states of the self are not perceived here as sporadic, infinite or situational, which is the accepted position of many relational and postmodern writers (See Bromberg 2009; Mitchell 1991; Rowan 2010). Rather, the different self-states are understood as subject to general alignments that correspond to the different truth axes, beyond their rootedness in various relational contexts. This conceptualization acknowledges plurality and multiplicity on the one hand and, on the other hand, contends that the modes of organization that give rise to this multiplicity are universal and may be defined and described.

Following through this line of thought my argument leads to positing a multiplicity of selves. The question I now want to re-examine is whether an integrated self is at all possible and, if so, how is it formed? In order to tackle this issue I return to my epistemological analysis. For Kant, the movement between metaphysics and epistemology did not affect consciousness inasmuch as it remained universal, unitary and endowed with permanent constraints on the translation of noumena into phenomena. Aligning with one experiencing consciousness, we may posit one experiencing self. Yet, even in philosophy, we still encounter problems when we try to explain the ways in which consciousness becomes an individual, idiolectic self-consciousness. Stated differently, we encounter problems when we try to understand how the reflexive function of consciousness operates in relation to its experiencing function.

Why should this be a complicated matter? What is simpler then reflecting? This might be a point where philosophic thought caves into complexities unencountered in the experience of living. Philosophy must deal with the questions of how the splitting of consciousness is effected and how experiencing is distinguished from reflecting. But even if these issues are resolved – we still face the problem of infinite regress, for if there is reflection, why should there not be another reflection upon the first reflection, and so on?

Now, complicating matters even more, what happens when we posit multiple epistemologies within a single consciousness? And given that epistemic perspective gives rise to a particular reality, how do we manage to maintain a stable sense of reality in a mind of multiple realities? What modes of interaction do we posit between self-states that inhabit different images of reality? And finally, is there a coordinator for this complex traffic and if so, who is it?

I cannot here delve into the depth and complexity of these questions. Therefore, in addressing them, I will take the reflexive function for granted and deal with the multiplicity it needs to manage and coordinate.[9] Multiplicity is given in the form of several definable characteristic self-states and I assume their simultaneous existence in the psyche, albeit, in varying forms of dominance and different allocated positions inside and outside of consciousness. The self in its entirety is created by the experience arising from successive axially determined self-states and their composites of interrelations. I now pick up two elements from this definition: One that is more fluid and relates to 'succession' (of self-states) and the other with more of a fixed character, related to 'composition'.

The story of the self starts with the primordial, unintegrated states of the developing infant-toddler-child. In this post-natal period, according to most developmental psychoanalysts, the baby's experience is extremely fragmentary. This period is also when the various axial self-states have their beginning in a simple and uninhibited existence. Artless and unburdened by reflexive functions, they come into being in accord with basic psychic needs. Each state is happily oblivious of other self-states, as it is to conflict among them. Through interaction with the world, the different self-states begin to develop, both in themselves and in relation to other self-states. Some are facilitated by the environment and others are censored. Some may align in synergy while others relate as inherently conflicted.

Gradually, two constraints are imposed upon this fluid state. One is the inherent and overarching need for stability and coherence that motivates the formation of identity and self-knowledge. *This is the unifying principle that is secondarily imposed on the axes and coordinates among them.* Recall that each axis already expresses a similar unifying principle, which it imposes on the elements of raw experience. The second constraint is the incorporation of socialization as a stabilizing factor that is responsive to specific social context of development. These constraints act upon the axes in a way that gradually gives rise to a relatively stable configuration. This configuration, even if conflicted,

9 For a comprehensive discussion of the reflexive function of the self in philosophy and psychoanalysis see Gennaro (2012), Fonagy (1997) and Cavell (1985).

through its relative constancy, becomes familiar to the subject and creates his sense of self.

This self, like the mind as whole, is grasped by the subject as given. It is not homogenous or necessarily serene. It always contains elements from different axes, even some that may be experienced as foreign or hostile. But its stability allows it to forge into a comprehensive experience for the subject. This forms a Jamesian 'field', namely, a recognized habitual self.

The continuity of self-experience, then, is predicated upon axial configurations that have stabilized in certain patterns and that determine the personal, idiomatic discourse of the subject. In addition to the stability created by axial configurations is the possibility of change, reflected in 'successive' self-states. Succession creates *fluidity* in self-experience, which is expressed when different contexts trigger particular unexpected axial responses. This experience of 'unexpectedness' in mental life is created when a certain response originates in an axis dissociated from conscious experience.

The stable axial configurations serve as the epistemic horizon that structures our experience of self and world. Different life situations that trigger powerful responses may challenge the reigning configurations, leaving our experiences temporarily raw and incomprehensible. They are 'real' in the Lacanian sense. Such experiences constitute trauma inasmuch as they are unprocessed, isolated and threaten the psyche by their emotional power. When given in mild form, such experiences may mobilize the psyche, recruit unused resources and transform the reigning configurations.

The subject may, then, allow himself to 'drift' into unknown territory and 'lose' himself in experiences that are free of reflective constraints. When one 'loses' himself for long enough, he may restore a foreclosed grammar of experiencing and bring its transformative potential to bear upon his ongoing life. This grammar (informed by an organic somatic base, motivations, wishes and anxieties) might, through repeated activation and processing, come to be integrated and included in the accepted areas of self-experiencing.

The idea that the psyche contains points of stability, alongside fluid, transitory states of experiencing is not, of course, new in psychoanalytic thought. Bollas, for example, contends that all self-experiencing involves a division into a 'simple self' – immersed in desired or evoked events – and a 'complex', reflective self. The complex self knows itself and aligns with this knowledge, thus limiting its flexibility. The simple self does *not* know itself and is therefore open to novel experience. The complex self later takes up the integration of novel experiences by assimilating them into known patterns or creating\remembering unknown ones (Bollas 1992). Dana Amir discusses the interaction between the emergent and the continuous principles of the self, highlighting the function of each principle and the value of the interaction between them for mental health (Amir 2013).

Incorporating the idea of the familiar and the new, I assume a continuity of self (consciousness and experiencing) that evolved in relation to a relatively stable axial configuration. This self is not aware of the procedures that created it, but it *may* become familiar with the way it functions and thinks of itself and its world. Reflection of this self upon itself may reveal the grammar of its constitutive elements. But even when the self is constituted in axial poverty, incorporating few of the axes, unexpected experiencing that evolves outside the monitoring of the reflective function admits new elements into the self's scope of experience. *What I posit here is that novel forms of experience are neither endless nor mystic.* They may be known theoretically and the psyche may be predisposed to know them experientially. As I said earlier, these novel states might have already been experienced in their early infantile forms and may feel familiar when re-encountered.

Self-experiencing – including both reflection and encounters with the unknown – occurs in the spheres of the conscious and pre-conscious. Apart from this, we of course have the unconscious, which is construed here as a combination of classic and contemporary ideas. The classic unconscious comprises needs that are innate and that blindly seek provision and satisfaction. Any such need (like the one related to the sexual drive) may be censored by conscious activity, deemed unfit, unworthy or shameful. It will then function in the unconscious as needs do, pushing for expression and generating symptoms, tensions and dysfunctional behaviors. In the place of Freud's drives, I have posited several basic needs that, through their interactions with the environment or among themselves, may be censored and then repressed. Alongside the possible repression of needs, is the possibility that the object of repression is a *mode of organization*, a mode of interrelating between mental elements. Such repression necessarily denies the provision of an essential need and manifests as a lack in conscious experiencing, a blank or an empty register.

The *symptom*, offers the third channel by which the self may learn about itself. The first channel, reflection of the self upon its constituent elements, involves *conscious* action; the second channel involves unexpected experience. This 'unexpectedness' is mediated by dissociation, and *involves an interplay between the conscious and the pre-conscious*. The third channel – symptoms – involves deep unconscious layers. When analyzing symptoms, we actually deconstruct the (repressive) achievements of development. Reversing the chronological timeline, we may rediscover innate needs and primordial self-states that have been repressed, along with their modes of organization. These are the three channels by which the self may learn its axial grammars. Through them, it constitutes and understands its own subjectivity.

The Therapeutic Process and the Axes of Truth

In line with the conceptualization of the various axes of truth as organizing principles of the mind, the therapeutic process is conceptualized here as one which sets in motion a transitional passage between the different axes. In this construal of the psyche, the creation of dialogue among the different axes of truth, as they operate in the psyche of both analyst and analysand, becomes central to the therapeutic rational. Preclusion of any of the axes leads to its suppression, splitting and removal from the integrative experience of self.

Here, when the analyst explores his patient's experience of the world, he engages in a number of activities:

- He identifies the key axes along which the patient organizes his experiences. He examines whether they are organized by association to external reality, or according to an 'inner' compass; whether on the basis of ideals, or in an attempt to establish a shared reality with those around him and in response to their expectations, etc.
- As aforesaid, the emotional and cognitive organizations derived from each truth axis can be, to varying extents, adaptive or maladaptive. Thus, the Correspondent axis can be adaptively expressed as good reality testing or pathologically as, for example, an obsessive attachment to detail that prevents processes of signification. The Coherent axis may be expressed adaptively by a harmonious set of values and beliefs or pathologically by, for example, elaborate paranoid delusions. The Subjective-Existential axis may be expressed through ego-syntonic adherence to inner truths or, maladaptively, as experiences of alienation and fears of engulfment. The Intersubjective axis may be adaptively expressed through common enterprises, identification with institutions and norms, and productive partnership between the subject and others in the context of achievement and beliefs or, alternatively, may be pathologically expressed as a compulsive need to conform, driven by fear of rejection.
- The analyst identifies sources of tension and conflict which the patient brings with him to therapy. These tension-arousing conflicts can be conceptualized in terms of difficulty in experiential organization within one axis or, alternatively, in terms of difficulties in reconciling between axes and their derivatives. Still other difficulties may be borne of the suppression and exclusion of axes, which restrict the life experience of the patient. The analyst may also consider the consequences of collision between two organizing axes, for example, when a patient feels that some real life event (e.g., his promotion at work) is not compatible with a set of Coherent beliefs (e.g., that he is worthless). Such a collision may explain how a positive life event

may cause distress and crisis. In still another case, a patient may be guiding his life in accord with truths of the Intersubjective axis, but may feel wasted and lacking in vitality as a result of his conformity, restricting the expression of his Subjective-Existential axis. *On the whole, confinement within one axis tends to limit and restrict experience.* This principle inspires a general therapeutic guideline, whereby the analyst needs to hold in mind the various axes and make transitions among them in interpreting the patient's materials.

- One of the prime tasks of analysis is to investigate the developmental history of the various axes in order to learn the extent and the context of their evolution. The axes may have different landmarks in the patient's history, each defined by particular formative experiences such as fixations or traumata. Similarly, the temporal construction of the axes may follow different time lines. One axis may be fully developed by age four, for example, while another may have been arrested at childhood, its development maybe retriggered at a later time.
- In exploring the patient's developmental history, analysis strives to establish which life events, contexts, periods of life and significant others were influenced by which truth axis. A father figure may be strongly associated with the Ideal axis, formulating clear, distinctive truths that are experienced as the truths one must aspire to live by. Views of a similar kind may be governed by the Intersubjective axis because they are associated with the figure of a friend. They may then act as a basis for communication rather than as imperative guidelines. Different relationships associated with different axes may supply clues regarding their relative dominance in the patient's psyche, their interrelations and their experienced valence.
- Any formative life event may associate in a different manner with each of the axes. Here, analysis needs to examine the details of the experience in order to understand the event's repercussions in relation to each of the axes. Consider the experience of a child aged three temporarily losing sight of his parent during a walk along the promenade. Each axis might be differently shaped by such an experience. The image of a parent might have changed at that moment, turning an idealized version of an omnipotent parent into a fallible-Correspondent one, a parent capable of losing sight of his child. The feelings of abandonment and being lost as a Subjective-Existential experience might be balanced by an unusual excitement arising from this 'lostness'. At that moment, the child might discover a truth of himself that he has not been aware of and that might later guide his thought and action in the direction of the unknown. Perhaps the experience would have effected also a building of confidence on the Pragmatic axis, if the lost child was

able, at the time, to re-construe 'stranger' as a possible savior and had benefitted from his ability to enlist help. Now, some clinical questions may be formulated in terms of truth axes: If an event in the patient's consciousness remains connected to only one axis, is it because its trace in another axis has been suppressed, denied or disabled? In the course of their development, what axes drove the prime choices of the patient and what were the differential conflicts they gave rise to? Of course, other questions can be formulated in those terms.

- Another challenge facing the analyst involves the identification of the axes that structure the patient's transference. For example, when is the patient angry? Is it when his analyst is perceived as weak and ineffectual (pointing at Pragmatically related issues)? Or is he angry when his analyst was wrong about something and in that way injured his idealizing transferences? Is he angry when his therapist surprises him, testifying to his need for Coherence? What axes are projected upon the analyst or enacted in the transference? The positioning of analyst and analysand on differing axes of truth may explain what is experienced as an analytic impasse or an analytic resistance.
- The analyst needs to pay attention not only to the patient's attitude towards each of the axes of truth, but also to his own emotional responses and analytic insights. He should examine how axes are organized and the way in which they react to the patient's materials. The analyst should ask himself, for example, whether he tends to encourage authenticity and has a preference for it over other psychic languages. This would indicate a preference for the Subjective-Existential axis. Similarly, he may ask himself if he wishes to be in agreement with the patient and if he is sensitive to deviations from norms, revealing his own particular positioning vis a vis the Intersubjective axis and its derivative truths. On the Correspondent axis, the analyst may note what links the patient makes with external reality? Does he himself find these links important or detrimental to the patient's work? Then the analyst may consider to what extent he requires Coherence and how tolerant to paradox he is? Does he, for example, feel less comfortable with the contradictions inherent in the Subjective-Existential axis?

The analyst tries to examine the way his semi-conscious axial preferences contribute to the shaping of the transference. Can he, for example, work without idealization, does he seek intersubjective collaboration or signs of the patient's attachment to him? Is he often bothered by the relation of the patient's materials to reality as he perceives it and does he prefer interpretations that stress reality testing?

In other words, the analyst monitors the extent of empathy, identification or antipathy aroused in him by some materials related to one axis, in contrast to other materials, related to another and how this affects the level of interpretation and the the analytic relations.

- The ongoing analysis of the patient's behavior includes checking for the compatibility or its lack between the unconscious axis which happens to shape the transference and the conscious truth axis that shapes the contents of his discourse. It is crucial for analysis to be able to determine how the transitions between those axes are made possible and what the obstacles to such transitions are.

Another challenge involves the identification of axes as they manifest *simultaneously* on different levels of experiencing in conflicting ways. This may happen when sensation and grammar do not accord, when content and relation do not cohere. For example, an analysand might be relating an event impartially, 'objectively', with somatic reactions revealing suppressed Subjective-Existential meanings. Alternatively, an analysand may be manifestly planning pragmatically a particular action while experiencing, yet not articulating anxiety of censure. Again, he might be intersubjectively oriented in a project, yet seeking merger with a group in a way that is telling of needs along the Ideal axis.

- The analyst maintains awareness to the ways in which the forming of an object is related to the various self-states. This may occur even in relation to the subject's body. The Subjective-Existential self is bodily oriented and bodily aware. In different situations, it will seek to identify and register emotions by means of the body (e.g., feeling queasy, shaky, buoyant, tense, heavy, etc.). It has personal sensations and inclinations regarding its body, knowing well its pleasures, pains and appetites, and treating them with attention and respect. The Correspondent self sees the body as something to care for and is therefore mostly aware of signs that alert it to danger, such as pain or sickness, hunger or thirst. It knows the objective facts about itself, its height, weight and coloring. The fine-tuning of the Subjective-Existential self to the body lies outside of its scope and interest. The Pragmatic self experiences the body as a valuable self-serving mechanism that carries out will and motivation. For this self, the body may be a source of joy, living up to the demands put to it, carrying out intention with strength and vitality. Of course, the opposite may be true as well, when the body is experienced as disappointing and cumbersome (e.g., when failing in a race, experiencing a

> miscarriage, experiencing exhaustion, etc.). The Intersubjective self often views and experiences its body through the prism of society's norms and standards. This may imply bodily disciplines such as regarding odors and hygiene, whose violation may result in feelings of shame or pride. The Ideal self is often in difficult relations with its body image. It may align with a dieting body or a post-plastic-operation body or, at the extreme end, the ideal body of the anorectic patient. The Coherent self has clear ideas about its body's place in the larger scheme of life and, accordingly, may modulate the demands of the body. This involves the understanding of the body as it relates to other important elements in the subject's world: Love, health, success, etc. Clearly, many configurations may arise from the interrelations between the various images of the body as experienced by the different states of the self.

Different developmental histories determine different degrees of dominance for the various axes, as well as different relations among them, determining their nature as conscious or unconscious. A child growing in a very competitive environment, endlessly measuring competence, may learn to demand more of his body while acquiring secondary deafness to its sensations. An environment that focuses on social standing may strengthen the way the body is disciplined, in accordance with norms. Idealistic environments may teach a child to ignore Correspondent body signs, as in the renowned Sparta stories, where the true men persist in the face of immense bodily discomforts. Constant criticism and intrusiveness may create inflated Ideal body image, etc. Understanding these histories and the way they stunted or enhanced axial preferences becomes a prime objective in therapy.

The analytic space is often construed as a space which is formed between the analyst and the analysand through transference and counter transference, where meanings are created and played out. This space discursively links fantasy and reality, creating a 'poetic' situation with a multiplicity of figurative meanings, wherein the very possibility of meaningfulness arises. I suggest that this space may be constituted by the evolving shared ability of analyst and analysand not to gravitate toward and collapse into one particular axis of truth. Instead, they develop the ability to analyze the way in which movement between axes is enabled, whether it flows or rather is 'blocked'. These features of inter-axial movement are determined by the relative dominance of each axis in the psyche, especially as they appertain to the various wishes and anxieties associated with them.

The transition between the axes leads to the broadening of the space in which incompatibilities and contradictions may exist without there being a pressing need to square them in an arbitrary way. Thus, the analysand can better inquire into the range of meanings and truths by overcoming or circumventing the compulsion to determine particular meanings with which he identifies and which he may keep repeating. In this conceptualization, the capacity for figurative representation and for movement among possible representations on different axes forms a central therapeutic aim and offers the analyst some powerful guidelines. Axes of truth are not conceptualized as resting places, even if they may in fact fulfill such a function from time to time. Rather, the axes are viewed as having the potential to create continuous movement of images and meanings.

Through open dialogue among the axes, the multidimensionality of any statement is revealed, as are the related needs, anxieties and hopes. At its best, the dialogue between different languages of truth holds the potential of unravelling the dynamics of dissociation, denial or repressive authoritarianism. It sets in motion the encounter with and the recognition of the other. This 'other' holds views of the self that are different from the self's own constructions. The therapeutic objective is not necessarily to resolve conflicts, but rather to create the space in which they may be contained and processed so as to allow the experience of possibility and choice, in place of restriction and inevitability. This objective, as I will detail in some length in Chapter 7, is always examined against a particular patient's psychic resilience, expectations from analysis and innate tendencies.

In the following chapter, I present clinical cases and vignettes that illustrate how, methodically and theoretically, truth axes inform clinical work.

CHAPTER 6

Clinical Illustrations

In the present chapter, I use the model of truth axes in order to analyze the dynamics of impasse and therapeutic failure, as well as to suggest a methodology by which they can be addressed. An analysis that is going well is one in which, for better or worse, change is experienced. More often than not, a working analysis is one in which the analyst allows himself to be immersed in clinical detail, experiencing it without feeling the need for theoretical formulation. Yet, usually analysis will not proceed in its self-evident mode for too long. Soon it will meet obstacles that force the analyst to rearticulate and investigate his theoretical guidelines in order to persist and make progress. In that sense, analysis is an instance of human life where, most generally, according to Heidegger, we immerse ourselves with the world and only when impinged upon, only when something contradicts our unconscious and unformulated expectations, do we turn to deliberate thought. We then exit the zone of self-evidence that is given in our pre-reflective understanding of the world and seek to formulate an understanding of a different kind.

Most analysts have internalized various kinds of knowledge that have gradually come to shape their pre-reflective strata of clinical understanding. Most have a theoretical home base of sorts whose terms they employ when coming to formulate or explain their action to others or to themselves. This sort of intentional analysis is usually carried out in the context of therapeutic obstacles and impasses, when the analyst tries to theoretically understand the clinical situation in which he is immersed. He then articulates and examines the theoretical knowledge he otherwise employs unreflectively.

Analysts encounter various kinds of impasse in the course of their analytic career. This may concern a sense of failure or, especially, a sense that no progress is being made for a long stretch of time, despite working along well-trodden analytic routes. This kind of impasse may be experienced by the analyst as an 'existential crisis' and, in extreme cases, may cause the analyst to doubt his professional abilities in general:

> a psychoanalytic treatment can fail for many reasons, and the impasse is only one of them; but it is so singular that it merits preferential attention. Stealthy and silent, the difficulty of detecting and resolving it is intrinsic in its nature, as is studying it and reflecting on it. It is perhaps the worst risk in our hazardous occupation and the most certain threat to our

 | DOI 10.1163/9789004314993_008

> instrument of work. Just one of these cases is sufficient to shake our scientific ideology, because impasse is not simply an internal difficulty of the theory but a real anomaly, which brings into question the psychoanalytic paradigm and threatens with a crisis.
>
> ETCHEGOYEN 1991, 804

Impasse may be experienced as an existential crisis, but it may also serve as an opportunity for thought, innovation and creativity. An analysis in impasse drives the analyst to come to terms with the fact that there are obstacles that cannot be overcome by his habitual therapeutic attitude and technique. Rosenblum states that: "As a result [of impasse] we change our technique with different patients. Whatever the deviation each of us adopts, to the extent it deviates from what we consider our standard analytic technique, it reflects an internal decision that the patient needed something different in order to do the work of analysis" (Rosenblum 1994, 1259).

Chessik adds:

> This leads to an unresolved issue in the study of impasse. Many more traditional psychoanalysts claim that deviations in technique are often the *cause* of impasses in psychoanalysis, whereas a more adventurous group of psychoanalysts maintains that impasses can be avoided or resolved by the willingness on the part of the analyst to consider the point of view of other theories, and to provide interventions that are not called for by the particular theory to which the analyst usually is committed.
>
> CHESSIK 1996, 200

Thus, while some clinicians attribute impasse to inconsistency in technique or to a failure in its implementation, others argue that it is precisely the impasse that affords the opportunity to examine other theories different than the one held by the analyst and investigate their clinical implications. In any case, impasse is always a possibility, always holds a potential. A recent research investigated in some detail the way impasse experiences were construed by experienced clinicians to be essential for professional development (Moltu, Binder and Nielsen 2010).

In the present chapter I present the ways in which truth axes can help us understand the possibilities that impasse challenges us to unravel. In terms of truth axes, an impasse may develop in two general ways: First, when the contents or the grammar of a particular axis are excluded from the therapeutic engagement. Second, when analyst and analysand have incompatible truth profiles, namely, when their positioning and movement in relation to and across truth axes do not overlap.

As described in the previous chapter, every truth axis possesses unique features at the levels of sensation, grammar and encounter with the world (respectively, Firstness, Thirdness and Secondness). In the vignettes that I present here, I illustrate the workings of the truth axes across these three dimensions as they express themselves in conscious and unconscious behaviors of both analyst and analysand. I will analyze the clinical process in terms of truth axes and their different modes of expression and will indicate the clinical consequences of this analysis. Finally, I will show that suppression or exclusion of an axis of truth in one dimension does not prevent its expression in others. Thus, an axis might be prevented from manifesting in the content of the analytic discourse, but express itself in the grammar of analytic relations.

Case 1: An Ideal Execution of Love

I wish to analyze Irvin Yalom's story 'Love's Executioner' in order to illustrate the kind of insight that can be derived from identifying and mapping truth profiles in case-specific processes of therapy. In this case Yalom, with masterful narrative and clinical sensibility, shares with his readers a case of difficult impasse. With humor, authenticity and self-deprecation, Yalom describes impasse in a Socratic fashion: He offers the dialogue and the story, leading his reader to certain conclusions, but leaving her to digest and formulate them on her own. He does not do this work on her behalf. He does not spell out his own conclusions. I present here this case with a running commentary, using the conceptualization of truth axes. By doing so, I try to show how these concepts may help us employ the unique potential of impasse for clinical work.

In my analysis, I construe Yalom's engagement with the phenomenon of falling in love as a manifestation of Ideal-axis Secondness. Yalom presents himself as deeply suspicious of Ideal truths. He usually intervenes in order to diminish idealizations and insert Correspondent and intersubjective elements in their stead as leverage for the therapeutic effect. I hope to show that the truth axes model offers other strategies than those of Yalom's, which may explain and circumvent the difficulties that he encountered.

Yalom opens his story with a statement:

> I do not like to work with patients who are in love. Perhaps it is because of envy – I, too, crave enchantment. Perhaps it is because love and psychotherapy are fundamentally incompatible. The good therapist fights

> darkness and seeks illumination, while romantic love is sustained by mystery and crumbles upon inspection. I hate to be love's executioner.
>
> YALOM 1989, 15

This opening paragraph holds the crux of the story that is about to unfold. From the outset, Yalom openly states his firm therapeutic stance against illusion and idealization as expressed in the phenomenon of falling in love (to which I will refer here as '*in-lovedness*'). Simultaneously, he sorrowfully and resignedly admits his yearning for both idealization and in-lovedness, a yearning that has no place in his system of professional beliefs.

A semiotic analysis of this short passage unveils the structure of Yalom's world view, where two incompatible categories- falling in love and psychotherapy- are construed as antagonistic to one another. The semiotic relationship that expresses this antinomy is: Love ≠ Psychotherapy. This formula clearly shows the manner in which the Ideal grammar organizes categories into binary oppositions. In that sense, each category is absolute, homogeneous and closed. Its dictums are clearly defined and it is easy to determine what coheres with them and what does not.

Having described this dichotomy in the analytic space, Yalom presents the value of the opposing categories by means of the metaphor of light: *Love = enchantment = darkness* and *Psychotherapy = illumination*. Here, the psychotherapeutic process is on a par with light, illumination and enlightenment. Using this metaphor, Yalom 'mobilizes' an entire metaphysical attitude to support his stance. In their discussion of 'objective truth', Lakoff and Johnson (1999) illustrate how the age-old analogy between thought and sight presents truth as a kind of object which is there to be found and correctly apprehended, once the obstacles of darkness and ignorance are removed. One 'sees' what is 'really there'; in ignorance or bafflement, one is 'in the dark'. This widely used analogy was philosophically boosted by thinkers such as Plato, Aristotle and others, for whom truth concerns a reality that is completely separate from the thought processes that 'discover' it.

The analogy is so rooted in Western thinking that, even in psychotherapy, where the focus is on subjective experience, knowledge and enlightenment are equated to seeing clearly, in contrast to Yalom's patient Thelma, who is in a 'dark' state of being in love. The meaning of the case might have been construed differently had it been influenced by the less common metaphor – that of the blind prophet. Here, it is darkness that enables a clear and true sight, contrary to the more popular idiom.[1]

1 Of course, even in its inversed form, the metaphor of seeing preserves the separateness of truth from the (re)cognizing process.

Having determined the antonymous relation between 'in-lovedness' and psychotherapy, as well as their opposite valence, Yalom proceeds to give an account of Thelma's story. Thelma, aged 70, was a dancer in her youth. She arrives to therapy after a month long romance with her former therapist. Eight years elapsed between the ending of the affair and Thelma's approach to Yalom. Throughout these years, she underwent treatment with a number of therapists that failed to ease her misery. She desperately misses Matthew, the young therapist with whom she was romantically involved. A short time after their parting, Thelma attempted suicide and subsequently led a life entirely focused on the disappearance of her beloved object. She tried many times to contact Matthew; all her approaches went unanswered.

Yalom tried to diagnose Thelma's problem. He found it difficult to believe that love could dwell in an aged body such as Thelma's, thus defining another antonymous relation between old age and the state of in-lovedness. He concludes that Thelma wasn't 'suffering' from love, but rather from a rare 'variant' that she mistook for love, a state of 'obsessive love', fuelled by the emotional meagerness and dullness of her life and by the remembrance of what might have possibly have been her only contact with intimacy. The view of her condition as an obsession places Thelma neatly in the wider category of mental pathology.

Thelma rapidly and categorically objects to this classification. The term she chooses for her short romance illustrates the yawning gap between Yalom and her in understanding her experience with Matthew. Thelma stands her ground, saying to her therapist: "Those 27 days were a great gift… I don't want them treated as a disease" (Yalom 1989). By using medical jargon Yalom, in the Correspondent fashion of stating 'facts', attempts to distance Thelma's in-lovedness from the positive emotional world of giving, receiving and intimacy. When he does a similar thing again by using the concept of 'countertransference' to account for her feelings for Matthew, Thelma again protests: "Yes, countertransference… I'll be frank…that grates on me. It's as though I didn't matter, as though I were some innocent bystander in something he was playing out with his mother" (ibid. 38). Thelma here is standing her ground, defending her Subjective-Existential truth from the Correspondent construal Yalom imposes on her. As often happens along the Subjective-Existential axis, she 'reads' her response through a sensation that carries bodily connotations; the medical term he used was 'grating'[2] on her.

---

2 The synonyms given to grate are scrape, scratch, scuff clash. Thesaurus.com. *Roget's 21st Century Thesaurus, Third Edition.* Philip Lief Group 2009. http://www.thesaurus.com/browse/clash (accessed: August 17, 2015).

Yalom and Thelma are engaged in a grim duel to determine the axial construal of her experience. This manifests in the signifiers employed. Is her inlovedness a pathology that needs to be overcome? And how can such a signification cohere with Thelma's experience of it as a treasured gift? If a pathology, it merits the use of the verbs Yalom employs to disqualify her experience of love: 'Dislodge', 'eradicate' and 'extirpate'. These verbs are associated with violent distancing, destruction and war. Indeed, at least on the face of it, Yalom wears Thelma down into silent acceptance of his definition of the obsession as 'the enemy' (Yalom, 1989, 33). The argument between them is not about local signification, which words to use. Rather, it is about the adoption of a metaphor that will act as the dominant source of signification for the situation in its entirety. The semantic field in which the word 'obsession' belongs is the Correspondent, 'objective' medical field. The semantic field of the 'enemy' is the polarized one of good and evil, structured in line with Ideal axial Thirdness (grammar), the same axis that Yalom combats on the level of Secondness.

When he analyzes Thelma's obsession, Yalom introduces an additional dichotomy between a reality of full life and an empty fantasy: "…it bonded her to another – but not to a real person, to a fantasy" (Yalom 1989, 24); "for a love obsession drains life of its reality" (ibid. 31). Fantasy is not accepted as a part of reality. The two are in competition as opposite semantic fields. An additional antonym is created. The Subjective-Existential grammar would accommodate this paradox by intertwining reality and fantasy. But in the realm of Ideal or Correspondent grammars, the two are opposed and separated, on the grounds of either fact or value judgment.

Understandably, Yalom regards Matthew in an extremely negative way. As he sees it, Matthew is an abusing, unethical therapist who acts out his unresolved psychological issues at the expense of helpless patients. Thus, two polar versions of Matthew exist in the analytic space: Thelma's 'groundless' idealized one and Yalom's rendering of him as a miscreant. The gap is extreme, and Yalom puts it to Thelma cuttingly: "You've elevated him to a superhuman position. Yet he seems to be a particularly screwed-up person". This view is so entrenched that Yalom misses the elements that are incompatible with it. In his experience, male therapists who sexually 'assist' female patients usually do so when the patient is attractive and young. This clearly was not the case with Matthew and Thelma, but Ideal grammar doesn't contain grey areas and filters out particulars that don't fall in with its binary structures.

The Ideal axis grammar of polarities easily lends itself to structuring formations of superiority and inferiority, moral and otherwise. It is also well fitting to the distribution of power, ascribed one-sidedly to idealized figures and equipping them with their influence. Indeed, the issue of power constantly surfaces throughout the text: It shows in the power that Thelma bestows upon Matthew, as well as in the related lack of power experienced by Yalom. In struggling against the idealization of Mathew, Yalom is awed by Thelma's own power and aggressiveness.

Although totally discrediting the Ideal axis (as it manifests in the Secondness of in-lovedness), Yalom is trapped in its grammar, subjugating reality to binary and antithetical constructions. Sickness and health do not overlap, nor do fantasy and reality. This semiotic structure coheres with the rules according to which the paranoid-schizoid position operates, pitting good against evil, idealization against devaluation. No middle ground exists between the distinctly antagonistic and bounded spaces.

While Yalom is unaware of the Ideal, dichotomic grammar of his thought, he is painfully conscious of the interpersonal experience of merger, which is central to Ideal Secondness. Here, the solitary self ecstatically merges into an idealized 'us'. As Yalom puts it, "It's the common denominator of every form of bliss-romantic, sexual, political, religious, mystical" (ibid. 39). He experiences painfully the absence of this merger between Thelma and himself: "...we were not making contact. We might as well have been in separate rooms" (ibid. 25). Thelma interrupts him in mid-sentence and regards what he says as redundant (ibid. 26). He learns not to expect any personal satisfaction from his meetings with Thelma (ibid. 31), it hurts him that Thelma didn't address him by name (ibid. 41). All in all, he felt "confused and rejected" (ibid. 43).

While dismissing Thelma's idealization as pathology, Yalom tells us, honestly and transparently, with a touch of irony and self-deprecation, how he himself battles with the same longings, craving to idealize or to be idealized. He wishes to be the ideal therapist that will manage to cure Thelma ("...Twenty years of therapy? ...most of her therapists were young trainees. Surely *I* could offer her more") (ibid. 28); and he testifies in retrospect: "I was afflicted by what I now recognize as hubris – I believed I could help any patient, that no one was beyond my skills ...I think I had a premonition at the time that, before my work with Thelma was over, I would be called to account for hubris" (ibid. 29). As the contradictions unfold, we realize that Yalom attempts to substitute a symptom with what, in his perception of things, cannot be anything other than another symptom. In-lovedness is a secondary manifestation of the Ideal axis. Yalom yearns to replace it with Thelma's acceptance of an idealized version of himself in the transference relations.

Dwelling upon the nature of idealizations, Yalom recalls the experience of being the idealizing party, ruefully empathizing with Thelma. He recalls how he had at one time been obsessed by a beautiful woman with whom he had fallen badly in love. In her grip, he can think of nothing else and cannot enjoy a family holiday. A few days into that holiday, Yalom realizes that the rich reality of his life has been blotted out by his obsession. He fills with anxiety and longs to re-own the former wealth of his life, so he returns to therapy. Yalom relates: "A curious thing: my therapist eventually became a close friend and years later told me that, at the time he was treating me, he himself was obsessed with a lovely Italian woman whose attention was riveted to someone else. And so, from patient to therapist to patient goes La Ronde of obsessional love" (ibid. 32), giving rise to questions about boundaries, being in love and the yearning for merger with unattainable ideals.

Yalom's Ideal grammar is particularly notable against the background of a more moderately structured grammar which, perversely, first emerges in Thelma's expression of her yearning for Matthew. She doesn't crave an Ideally-structured timeless, perfect union but rather entertains modest hopes along the Correspondent and Intersubjective axes: "Most of the time, what's important is that he would wish me well" (ibid. 34); ... "I don't expect Matthew to love me again; I just want him to care about my being on this planet" (ibid. 27). What she craves here is recognition, not blissful merger. Yalom's binary grammar is again thrown into relief at the point in which he meets his imaginary adversary. As I describe below, Matthew appears on the scene in an intermixed complexity of strength and weakness, courage and fear, honesty and straightforward acceptance of responsibility for his past failings.

After months of therapy that afford no progress, Yalom decides on a confrontational approach. With Thelma's consent, he invites Matthew to a three-way meeting. He expects a young, unprincipled sociopath. Instead he encounters an artless man, who tells of a psychotic episode during which he had the affair with Thelma. In its wake, Matthew relates, he stopped working as a therapist and became an administrative manager of a Christian organization. In their shared hour, Matthew tells his story simply, expressing throughout his feelings of concern, fondness and compassion towards Thelma. He explains his reasons for severing all contact with her.

Matthew brings with him complexity and width of perspective, being very open, involved and ready to share. Yalom feels his head spinning and the reader shares his confusion as all his assumptions are refuted:

> Over the last several months, I had constructed a vision- or, rather, several alternative visions- of him: an irresponsible, sociopathic Matthew who exploited his patients; a callous and sexually confused Matthew who acted out his conflicts...; an errant, grandiose young therapist who mistook the love desired for the love required. Yet he was none of these. He was something else I had never anticipated. But what? I was not certain.
>
> IBID. 54

And now, the images floating through Yalom's mind are no longer uniform and coherent, no longer binarily structured. Rather, through the paradoxical Subjective-Existential grammar, a number of oxymorons come alive: "A well-intentioned victim? A wounded healer, a Christ figure who sacrificed his own integrity for Thelma?" (ibid. 54).

Yalom can no longer regard Matthew as simply an injurious individual. He now sees in him a person "after his own heart" (ibid.), a *working* patient who has recovered from his crisis by hard work, so as to be able, perhaps, to return to practicing as a therapist. In Yalom's mind, the question arises: "In this relationship, who had exploited whom?" (ibid. 54). Conceivably, the answer to this question would already be free of binary structure, would reach beyond 'abuser' and 'abused' and into complex life events, intricate significations and paradoxical patterns. The facts of the story hadn't changed. And yet, through Matthew's appearance on the scene as *subject* and through his complex portrayal of human life, love and suffering, different grammars emerge and with them new meanings.

When Matthew leaves, Thelma and Yalom quickly regress to their former grammar. Thelma returns to her tortured experience of Matthew as somebody who came to hate her, while Yalom falls back to treating her emotions as illusions and obsessions (ibid. 57). To make sure the 'job was finished', Yalom gives his construal of the situation a spatial dimension that totally undermines Thelma's understanding of what she had shared with Matthew: "He was in one place and you were in another...You cannot recreate a state of shared romantic love...because it was never there in the first place" (ibid. 58). Following this encounter, Thelma's condition deteriorated rapidly. She became depressed, apathetic and dull, felt there was nothing left for her to feel or live for, and that she was now simply waiting to die. She did nothing. She slept twelve hours a day. She describes her feelings: "it's like I've been in a magic show and now I've come outside- and it's very grey outside" (ibid. 60). Yalom realizes that having blown the illusion out of the water, he now has to be ready to deal with Thelma's despair. Despite her suffering, he perceives her anger and despair as affording excellent opportunity for productive work.

But Thelma does not work; she leaves therapy. She had lost all hope of a future and, along with it, the best days of her life. Thelma's husband, Harry, approaches Yalom with an unequivocal demand: "Give me back my wife Doctor, the old Thelma- just the way she used to be" (ibid. 64). As Yalom sees it Harry, like Thelma, "chose to embrace illusion" (ibid. 65) and he reflects angrily on the relief he would experience were he to be delivered from them both. And yet, at the same time, he feels awful and is filled with worry and self-recrimination, knowing he had botched the case beyond belief. He realizes that he "had stripped away defenses without building anything to replace them"(ibid. 65).

In the context of the binary grammar which resulted in the therapeutic impasse, it is interesting to note what Yalom chose *not* to share with Thelma. He did not tell her of the enjoyment he experienced during the 'role game' she had played with an imaginary Matthew. Neither did he tell her of the admiration and sympathy that Matthew aroused in him. Maybe if he told her, these feelings, by subverting the old binary view, could lay the ground for an intermediary space between polarities, a potential space for them share. However, Thelma and Yalom were caught up in a duel that was the direct outcome of their binary construction of reality.

This case illuminates the potency of grammar in the structuring of experience. Where content and grammar are incompatible, it seems that grammar gets the upper hand in determining the quality of relational spaces. At the level of content and narrative, Yalom is opposed to Thelma's idealization of Matthew. Yet, his thought and experience are structured wholly in Ideal grammar and do not allow him to develop a new ground, where Thelma could, perhaps, position herself when she eases the hold of the Ideal axis. Perversely, it was Matthew who brought *contents* characteristic of the Ideal axis in the form of temperate, paradoxical *grammar*. His presence immediately tilted the view, forming a new space for both Thelma and Yalom. Yet, this space dissolved as soon as Mathew left the scene.

A while after the termination of therapy, Yalom contacts Thelma. She doesn't wish to resume therapy, nor is she interested in coming for a monitoring session. But she sounds great. In passing, she tells Yalom that her meetings with Matthew make her very happy. Yalom is shaken: "What Matthew? How did that come about?" Thelma offhandedly relates that she and Matthew had agreed to meet for a chat every month or so. Bursting with curiosity, Yalom begins to question her. Thelma answers him in brief that all along she had explained that this was precisely what she needed. She also makes it clear that Yalom had lost his right to ask her personal questions.

Thelma agreed to participate in a follow-up research project conducted in the institute in which Yalom worked. Yalom read the account of Thelma's case, where she was diagnosed as no longer depressed. Her self-esteem was high and all indices of fear, hypochondria, obsessiveness, and psychosis were found to be low. The team conducting the research was unclear as to the nature of the therapy that had led to the impressive results, because the patient had been unwilling to discuss the therapy she underwent. From what they could gather, they assumed that Thelma's therapy was conducted according to a pragmatic orientation, aimed at easing symptoms, rather than achieving personality change by means of insight. Yalom concludes his story saying "Heady stuff! Somehow it afforded me little comfort".

Yalom's writing beautifully presents opposing trajectories that he transparently exhibits to his reader. He firmly upholds his truth while, simultaneously, undermining it. On a conscious level he completely endorses his therapeutic action of ousting a truth. Yet he shares with us, all the while, the way this same truth continues to haunt both him and the analytic dyad. Yalom illustrates the futility of his attachment to his truth, to the exclusion of other truths. In terms of my truth axes model, Yalom's conscious adherence to Correspondence and Intersubjectivity did not prevent the unconscious domination of the Ideal grammar in the therapeutic discourse, as he shares generously with his reader. His conscious rejection of Ideal Secondness, as expressed in Thelma's infatuation, co-existed with the illusory visions of love that continued haunting his mind and soul. The relentless conscious opposition to Ideal manifestations, alongside its grammatical dominance in structuring realities, drove the analysis into an impasse.

A self-psychologist might interpret this case as validating the healing force of idealized relations. This line of thought would hold the objection to interpersonal merging or to the blurring of boundaries as a theoretical and methodological mistake. A Freudian analyst may have sought here historical factors that caused Thelma to displace infantile oral needs and replace them with genital sexuality, creating a pathological vicious circle of repetition compulsion. Health here would have been restored when the working through of illicit desires would have been brought to consciousness and worked through, thus restoring reality testing. A Kleinian analyst would conceivably have focused on how aggression and jealousy got split off from the idealized 'good object', situating the drama in the phantasmatic realm. An intersubjective therapist might have focused on the difficulty Yalom and Thelma experience in establishing a shared reality, investigating their repetitive power struggles as reflecting the problematics of mutual recognition.

In the logic of truth axes, all of the above approaches prefer one axis over all others and might have fallen into an impasse due to narrowness. By distinction, my model stipulates a clear condition for successful therapy: The psyche's organic multilingualism must be acknowledged. Any therapist, regardless of what his orientation may be, would not have succeeded in his work with Thelma without acknowledging the experience of the Ideal axis. Only the conscious and legitimate incorporation of Thelma's idealizing needs into the analytic discourse could have created a secure base from which she could explore other languages, their foreignness and promise. These could bring into the light of reality a whole range of mental currents: foreclosed feelings, unfulfilled wishes, tremendous fears and unusual patterns of communication.

As mentioned in the previous section, in terms of truth axes, we would attribute the impasse in Thelma's analysis to the de-legitimation of Ideal constructions. De-legitimation, however, did not remove the Ideal grammar, but rather prevented the incorporation of other axial grammars. And yet, these found their complex and multiple expressions in the solution Thelma worked out with Matthew. In line with the paradoxical grammar of authenticity, Thelma did not ask which Matthew she meets every month: Is he her therapist? Her lover? Her friend? A unique configuration embodying all or neither of these possibilities? Following the sober tone of Correspondence, Thelma's expectations are realistic and she and Matthew met once a month for coffee. Thelma remained loyal to her Subjective-Existential truths and did not succumb to Yalom's charismatic and persistent advice to give up the gifts she had received from Matthew. Pragmatically, Thelma clearly found the cure for her malaise: Once a month she had coffee with a complex person with whom she had shared complex experiences.

Case 2: The Gap between Sense and Sensibility in the Text of Clinical Events

The following case is also taken from Yalom (1989), the case of Dave. I discuss it in order to illustrate a conflict between the Subjective-Existential and the Intersubjective axes of truth. As described in the previous chapter, Subjective-Existential Firstness is characterized by an experience of familiarity, vitality and spontaneity that are closely bound up with sensations of the body. Secondness holds inherent tensions between 'I' and the 'other' in the context of the experienced sanctity of bodily boundaries. Subjective-Existential Thirdness accommodates paradox and incompatibilities. The Intersubjective axis, on the other hand, constantly seeks to contain the 'I' inside the 'We'. Mutual recognition is sought in the encounter with the other and its grammar is comprised of common contract and consensus.

In discussing Yalom's case, I shall show how the analytic discourse, with its characteristic metaphors and connotations, expresses the Firstness of the Subjective-Existential axis, even while that same axis is rejected in the dimensions of Secondness and Thirdness. Intersubjective Secondness is defined as the therapeutic objective and the grammar it imposes on communication. The silenced Subjective-Existential continues to express itself in indirect semiotic ways such as tone, mood and rhythm. I will show again, like in Thelma's case, how the various axes of truth create different and contradictory significations. When these significations are not negotiated, analysis falls into impasse.

In the story 'Do Not Go Gentle', Yalom (1989) presents his patient Dave, aged 69 and married for the third time. At the beginning of Yalom's story, Dave terminates individual analysis and enters group therapy, again with Yalom as therapist. Dave's prime complaint concerns sexual performance, but on acquaintance with him, Yalom sees this difficulty as symptomatic of a larger intersubjective issue. Dave ceaselessly maneuvers in order to conceal something, and in this way infuriates those around him, particularly the women he is involved with. As part of his secretiveness, Dave asks Yalom to keep a suitcase of his, full of love letters from a former lover who had died thirty years earlier. Dave fears that in the eventuality of his own death, his wife would discover the letters and suffer unnecessary pain. Yalom is in two minds regarding Dave's request. He understands Dave's concerns, but he is apprehensive about being drawn into Dave's secretive patterns of behavior. He feels that this would maintain and validate these patterns. He therefore tells Dave that he will fulfill his request on condition that the pact between them will be fully disclosed to the group which Dave is due to join. An interesting deal is offered: Exposure in one place is agreed upon in exchange for the promise of secrecy in another. Pragmatic considerations are admitted into therapy. Dave declines and joins the therapy group without giving his letters to Yalom. This is his first act of opposition to considerations that are both Pragmatic and Intersubjective.

In the course of the group's work, Dave shares a dream and, in the ensuing discussion, the subject of his secret letters crops up. Dave invites Yalom to interpret his dream, and the latter responds that he cannot do so without revealing material from their personal meetings. Dave waives confidentiality and Yalom takes his consent to its limit. He tells of Dave's secret letters, and the group enters the formerly private areas of Dave's psyche. Like in Thelma's story, the outcome of the intervention speaks for itself: "The dream interpretative work was successful but the patient died" (Yalom 1989, 166). Dave leaves the group.

Here, Yalom starts reflecting on some difficult questions: Did the group expose too much? Try too quickly to "make a foolish old man wise"? (ibid.) Is it possible that despite the permission granted, Yalom betrayed Dave in discussing the letters? Had he clumsily fallen into a trap? In Yalom's view, Dave's termination of therapy was inevitable, though it might have been delayed. More than anything, Yalom feels sorry for Dave, "for his clinging to illusion…for his unwillingness to face the naked, harsh facts of life" (ibid.).

Here, like in Thelma's case, Yalom articulates his beliefs clearly: "yet I am not without faith, my Hail Mary being the Socratic incantation: The unexamined life is not worth living" (ibid. 154). Following is a statement that the reader may already be familiar with: "I war against magic" (ibid.). Thus, exposure and disclosure, alongside the repudiation of illusion, magic and secrecy in the name of intimacy and the ability to create it, become the pivotal issues in therapy. The ability to meet head on the 'naked, harsh facts of life' and to share them with others is highly prized and viewed as the positive outcome of a successful therapy.

But the question that arose in the previous story resurfaces: What in fact *are* the naked facts of life? When do we define something as pathological? Are we clear as to what standard we follow when doing so? May not an examined life worth living contain its secret, protected corners that have not been exposed to the light of shared investigation? Yalom poses these questions in all their complexity, for alongside his objection to furtiveness and secrecy he reveals that he too has a well-hidden, precious horde of yellowing letters which he hasn't looked at for years and yet cannot bring himself to destroy. When Dave terminates therapy, Yalom remains contemplating: What should *he* be doing with his own preciously concealed letters? Unresolved doubts, fears and anxieties regarding them surface. Yalom parts from Dave and his annoying furtiveness, but cannot elude the secretive patterns of his own behavior, the hidden parts of his psyche which cannot bear the light of intersubjective exposure.

Yalom advocates the Secondness of the Intersubjective axis, as expressed in open mutual contact with others, and of the Correspondent axis, as given in the encounter with 'naked facts', mercilessly empty of illusion and concealment. By contrast, Subjective paradoxical grammar is built upon the interplay of revelation and concealment, veiling and unveiling, which are perceived by Yalom as sabotaging healthy intersubjectivity. Both secrecy that protects authenticity and spontaneity are downplayed, but they express an undeniable and ineradicable aspect of human nature that Yalom is revealing to us with a masterful touch.

Yalom's Dave calls to mind Winnicott's (1963) formulation and characterization of the true self:

> I suggest that in health there is a core to the personality that corresponds to the true self …I suggest that this core never communicates with the world…and that the individual person knows that it must never be communicated with or be influenced by external reality.… Although healthy persons communicate and enjoy communicating, the other fact is equally true, that *each individual is an isolate, permanently non-communicating, permanently unknown, in fact unfound*.… incommunicado element, and this is sacred and most worthy of preservation. … Rape, and being eaten by cannibals, these are mere bagatelles as compared with the violation of the self's core, the alteration of the self's central elements by communication seeping through the defenses.
>
> WINNICOTT 1963, 186–7

In Dave's case (and to no lesser extent in his own) and despite lauding total openness, Yalom illustrates an inevitable Subjective–Existential fact of psychic life: Everyone experiences a dimension whose boundaries are sanctified. Everyone holds a secret that expresses the inherent paradoxical nature of authentic grammar; a grammar that reveals by concealing and conceals when exposed. Despite the belief in frank sincerity, intolerance of the concealed threatens to obstruct many channels of communication.

In Dave's story, as in Thelma's, the excluded axis – here the Subjective-Existential one, with its sanctified privacy- is explicitly downgraded, but reappears in the analytic discourse by linguistic means. Language guards what is ideologically ousted. The 'concealed case' of authentic subjectivity is placed, like Poe's purloined letter, in the public space of language. As I will show now, the language Yalom uses in describing his relations with Dave is highly evocative of physicality, brimming with somatic metaphors and associations, calling forth Subjective-Existential Firstness.

Yalom relates: "From the outset I had felt drawn to Dave" (Yalom 1989, 155), 'drawn', like, wanting to see from closer by, intrigued. Some charm has already been noted. Inquiring why Dave seeks therapy, Yalom addresses him with somatically-associated language. He does not ask, for example, 'what troubles you'? In a way that addresses thought, or alternately: 'How do you feel?' addressing emotion. Rather, he employs a metaphorical physiological terminology: "What ails?" Dave replies simply: "I can't get it up any more!" (ibid. 155). Astonished, Yalom looks at Dave: "his tall, lean, athletic body, his full head of glistening black hair...belying his sixty nine years" (ibid.). He immediately hopes that at Dave's age he will be sufficiently vital and alive to entertain such concerns.

Dave brings Yalom to engage with the body; its health, its decay, his hopes and his fears regarding it. He celebrates Dave's robust corporeality and desire, relays to the reader that both Dave and he are inclined "to sexualize much in our environment" (ibid. 155). But Yalom's sexualizing tendency is disciplined: "I contained it better than he, and had long since learnt to prevent it from dominating my life" (ibid.). He proceeds with differentiating himself from Dave, proclaiming his complete openness with his wife and some good friends. This is given in the text less than four paragraphs away from Yalom's admission of his own hidden letters. We receive here a short unwritten sermon: The body is admitted, sex and potency are admitted. But their unruliness and ruthlessness must be checked in at the door of intersubjective propriety. They are allowed as long as they do not disturb the balance and peace of the subject and his surroundings.

Yet, it seems that everything regarding Dave carries with it precisely this unrest. Yalom's portrayal of Dave's secretiveness is imbued with sensuality.

He describes Dave's long-past affair as: "Not delicious and clandestine but *deliciously clandestine*" (ibid. 153). Dave is "...aroused by, compelled by, secrecy, and often courted it at great personal expense" (ibid. 153). The relation between Yalom and Dave is described in terms of physical proximity (the emphases are mine): "I believe the *primary attraction* was to reminisce...My *connection* with him felt tentative. I always felt that *if I probed too far, ranged too close* to his anxiety, he would simply disappear...and I would never be able to *contact* him again'...a mistake would be fatal" (ibid. 156). "Asking me to keep the letters might thus be a way of perpetuating our *special and private relationship"* (ibid. 158). Dave's relations with the therapy group are also described in words laden with sexual connotation, where Dave is described as coy and flirtatious. When Dave's dream comes up in the group, Yalom describes his own corporeal reactivity: "I got greedy" (ibid. 163).

How does this language impact the reader? Over and again adjectives and verbs that Yalom employs connote eroticism. Many of them are bodily-based metaphors. There are two levels here, the explicit and the implicit. On the explicit level, when eroticism and the body are discussed as content, consciously and reflectively, they are acknowledged but regarded as naturally demanding sublimation and constraint. It is interesting to note what constraint is given here. Sexuality, falling in love, flirting, romance, all these are granted a position in life, as long as they do not impinge upon mature intersubjectivity, as long as they do not encourage furtiveness, as long as they are contained. Intimacy and sexualization are described by means of formulations such as: "What had prevented him from forming even one intimate, non-sexualized relationship with either man or woman" (ibid. 156). These formulations create a categorical separation between sexuality and intimacy; the former contaminates the latter. Only un-sexualized intimacy qualifies as 'real' intimacy.

On a different level, metaphorical language engages directly the dimension of sensation and circumvents the censoring of sexuality, appetite and desire in discourse. In the context of psychoanalysis, metaphor may be described as occupying an intermediate position between primary and secondary processes. While primary process is associated with chaos and secondary process with order or quiescence, the metaphoric process disorders and yet structures, thus optimizing creative risk taking (Borbely, 2008). Through this non-linear process, Yalom weaves the Subjective-Existential representation of the body into the reader's associations in an intermediary position between the sensed and the considered and presents him with an unarticulated paradox.

The manner in which metaphor introduces the body into discourse is untamed, because it circumvents conscious reasoning and social codes. But this untamed aspect remains, on the level of professed objectives and beliefs, ultimately delegitimized. In Yalom's description, freedom in bodily experience is only allowed through connotation. Yalom's singular reaction to Dave's person and presence is what accounts for his interest in Dave. But this reaction is not articulated and processed, and therefore remains 'hovering' as an encapsulated connotation, as a foreign unprocessed element. Yalom allows the creation of this authentic meeting between Dave and himself, but refuses to present it clearly as an acceptable experience. At the level of narrative, secrecy and sexualizing tendencies are criticized, but at the level of connotation they are treated with intricate combination of excitement, concealment and disclosure.

In Julia Kristeva's thought, images and corporeal metaphors of the sort employed by Yalom are part of the semiotic dimension of language, a dimension that introduces nuance and complexity into language, expressing the influence and impact of the drives (Kristeva 1980). Even when language establishes itself at the cost of repressing the drives, they return via the 'music' of speech and get reinforced by metaphors. The body is re-introduced into language and, with it, according to Kristeva, the maternal territory. Metaphors 'feminize' the 'name of the father', the 'law' to which Yalom adheres. It is this semiotic dimension that enables us to reach beyond the limitation of the unarticulated.

Yalom allows therapeutic discourse to express the level of Firstness of the Subjective-Existential axis, but he negates the legitimacy of other levels, unlike Winnicott, who taps into all levels, articulating bodily sensations, alongside grammatical rules (such as paradox) and the bafflement of encounter with the world (the incommunicado element). Winnicott expresses strongly the need to allow unveiled areas in the psyche, whereas Yalom de-legitimizes Dave's need for privacy, claiming that nothing can be gained by it. As Yalom describes it, privacy is intersubjectively constituted, almost fad-like. This stance undermines the Winnicottian emphasis on internality: "Long ago...therapy groups were reluctant to talk about sex. In the last two decades...money has become the private subject...but in Dave's group the burning secret was age" (Yalom 1989, 160). What is secret and private is not inherently given, but rather intersubjectively manipulated, changed and redefined, in line with times, fashion and need. The priority of Subjective-Existential privacy is undermined in its Intersubjective rendering as a 'fad'.

When the issue of Dave's old letters crops up in the group, Yalom again responds with verbs that carry heavy physical connotations. The word 'reveal' appears four times in Yalom's reflections (ibid. 64). Yalom states: "I knew it would be an error to force Dave into untimely revealing, or for me to reveal information...". The reader is struck here by the introduction of 'force', raising the suspicion that 'revealing' is not about information, but rather about Dave's very self. He is nakedly subjected to the group's scrutiny. A group member asks Dave: "how much extra would it cost to come out and say love letters?" (ibid. 163) The relations between Dave and the group are construed here in economic terms. Personal exposure, like a coin, is handed over to the merchant. The question articulated is: What is the going rate of Dave's privacy.

We see here the contrasting significations that the different axes give rise to. The event of self-disclosure signifies cooperation and proximity in the Intersubjective axis. Similarly, in the Pragmatic axis it is 'worthwhile', earning Dave 'points' and 'profits' in return for his self-exposure. By contrast, in the Existential axis, disclosure signifies disaster, the loss of selfhood. In this axis, friendship is measured by its ability to contain silence. These various significations imply different realities. The therapist, the group and the patient effectively dwell in parallel realities. The expression of these profound meanings by metaphors makes it difficult to openly examine them. They are posed as 'raw facts of life', rather than as human significations.

It is interesting to note that when Yalom checks with Dave how straightforward he's willing to be with the group, Dave replies with a bodily-removed intellectual metaphor: "Anything I've said to you is an open book" (ibid. 164). When Dave terminates his therapy, Yalom questions: "had we stripped away too much?" (ibid. 166), bringing on the connotation of forceful bodily exposure. Language now aligns with Dave's experience, drawing an analogy between the revealing of secrets and the 'stripping' of the body from its clothed protection. Without explicitly articulating it, the group, with Yalom's endorsement, has shamed Dave. Shame is often about having no clothes on (Kovecses 2008, 387).

If Yalom's main focus in 'Love's Executioner' was the Ideal axis, in 'Do Not Go Gentle' we find center-stage an implicit and elaborate analysis of bodily experience in the Subjective-Existential axis. This experience comes tied up with the sanctity of bodily and psychic privacy, as well as of interpersonal boundaries. Dave desperately avoids exposure in different ways. The sensibility he embodies is discussed on different levels, some explicit and some implicit, some literal and some metaphorical. Yalom uses metaphorical expressions that evoke the Subjective-Existential body in an erotic field. Language here reinforces the experience of the body as a locus of secrets, whose exposure implies danger and violation.

This case ends as did the one before it: Therapy succeeds, the patient exits. As in the Socratic dialogue, implications and conclusions are not spelled out in the text, but are rather derived and deduced from it. What is again brought forward strongly is the necessity of recognizing and identifying the various languages of truth and mapping out the complexity they inevitably give rise to. The body-near language Yalom uses to describe Dave and his contact with him loses its rich and tangible coloring when Yalom 'thinks' about Dave. It seems that, at a certain point, Yalom's sensations become resistant to mentalization, creating a gap between a Subjective-Existential dominated Firstness and a level of Thirdness that coheres with Intersubjective logic. This disconnection between Firstness and Thirdness translates eventually into Dave and Yalom's falling out. The therapeutic impasse is an inevitable outcome of the failure to create a space capable of containing the various axes, bringing to consciousness and accepting their various manifestations in the therapeutic discourse and the ensuing relations.

Case 3: Paradox

In the following lines I examine Winnicott's elegant and masterful therapeutic interventions in order to illustrate the therapeutic value of movement between axes of truth. In the case I follow here, Winnicott offers his patient a provocative interpretation that creates an extreme incongruence between Correspondent and Subjective-Existential axes. Winnicott's interpretation challenges Correspondent rules of identity and contradiction, thus destabilizing his patient's Coherent and Correspondent sensibilities. This analytic act engenders acute anxiety in the patient and brings him to the verge of insanity, an experience that is later processed in the transference relations. By introducing the Subjective-Existential grammar of paradox into the therapeutic discourse, Winnicott undoes the integrity of the patient's psychic organization in order to then proceed to reconstruct it. This dual process allows the patient to assimilate the polyphony of voices inside him, which he could not do before this incident. In what follows, I shall illustrate the way in which the terms of the truth axes may serve as conceptual and methodological means to formulate and understand clinical thought and technique. The case is directly quoted from 'Playing and Reality' (Winnicott 1971).

> I propose to start with a clinical example. This concerns the treatment of a man of middle age, a married man with a family, and successful in one of the professions. The analysis has proceeded along classical lines. This man has had a long analysis and I am not by any means his first psychotherapist. A great deal of work has been done by him and by each of us therapists and analysts in turn, and much change has been brought about in his personality. But there is still something he avers that makes it impossible for him to stop. He knows that what he came for he has not reached. If he cuts his losses the sacrifice is too great.

> In the present phase of this analysis something has been reached which is new for me. It has to do with the way I am dealing with the non-masculine element in his personality.
>
> On a Friday the patient came and reported much as usual. The thing that struck me on this Friday was that the patient was talking about penis envy. I use this term advisedly, and I must invite acceptance of the fact that this term was appropriate here in view of the material, and of its presentation. Obviously this term, penis envy, is not usually applied in the description of a man.
>
> The change that belongs to this particular phase is shown in the way I handled this. On this particular occasion I said to him: 'I am listening to a girl. I know perfectly well that you are a man but I am listening to a girl, and I am talking to a girl. I am telling this girl: "You are talking about penis envy"'
>
> I wish to emphasize that this has nothing to do with homosexuality.
>
> (It has been pointed out to me that my interpretation in each of its two parts could be thought of as related to playing, and as far as possible removed from authoritative interpretation that is next door to indoctrination.)
>
> It was clear to me, by the profound effect of this interpretation, that my remark was in some way apposite, and indeed I would not be reporting this incident in this context were it not for the fact that the work that started on this Friday did in fact break into a vicious circle. I had grown accustomed to a routine of good work, good interpretations, good immediate results, and then destruction and disillusionment that followed each time because of the patient's gradual recognition that something fundamental had remained unchanged; there was this unknown factor which had kept this man working at his own analysis for a quarter of a century. Would his work with me suffer the same fate as his work with the other therapist.
>
> WINNICOTT 1971, 72–73

Winnicott begins by describing therapeutic impasse. His patient has undergone years of therapy with numerous therapists and yet feels that he hasn't achieved relief or an experience of well-being. Winnicott realizes, in the face of this impasse, that he must search for something that is novel for the patient as well as for himself. He presents the patient with a startling interpretation that impacts the patient in a way that immediately reveals its validity: "On this occasion there was an immediate effect in the form of intellectual acceptance, and relief, and then there were more remote effects. After a pause the patient said: 'If I were to tell someone about this girl I would be called mad'". (ibid. 72).

Following the relief he experiences, the patient immediately addresses the contradiction that Winnicott's interpretation created. It is inconceivable that someone would identify a man as being a woman. If someone were to do so, it would probably indicate that they are insane. And indeed that would be the case, as far as the grammatical rules of Correspondence and Coherence are concerned.

The linguistic implications of this exchange may be described as follows: Winnicott's interpretation leads to a clear violation of the text's coherence. His interpretation violates a maxim of discourse, that of adherence to truth (Grice 1975). The statement 'you are a girl' is false. Indeed, it is meaningless in the context of literality. Therefore, the reader searches for a non-literal meaning that may render the text comprehensible.[3] One way of dealing with incompatibility of literal meaning is to substitute it with metaphorical meaning, to understand the statement to be a comparative pronouncement, such as a simile. Similes are rarely invalid as it is possible to find various ways in which similarity between two objects may be found.

The statement 'The patient is a girl' is a literally false one. The statement 'the patient is like a girl' could be a true one as in 'The patient is like a girl in that he is experiencing penis envy'. Another solution to the situation that arises from incompatibility of literal meanings involves a change in the categories used to construe a given situation. Thus, for example, it is possible to resolve the incomprehensibility of the statement 'the male patient is a girl' by understanding 'male' as belonging to the category of sex, and 'girl' as belonging to the category of gender, i.e., understanding the male patient to possess girl-like characteristics.

To wit, it is possible to arrange the text in a way that avoids dissonance or contradiction between its component parts. However, Winnicott abstains from any such explicit 'arrangement', leaving the grammatical violations of the Correspondent grammar to simmer. With one speech act, Winnicott effects two consequences. Firstly, he grants his patient the status of a 'girl', thus bringing him significant relief. Secondly and subversively, Winnicott challenges Correspondent logic. Which is to say: Not everything that is false according to Correspondent truth is false categorically and in all possible ways. In this way, Winnicott undermines the exclusive validity of this axis, a move that may have

3 Understanding non-literal significations, according to Glucksberg (2008), requires a number of distinct processing stages. The first involves reaching an understanding of the literal meaning of what has been said. In the second stage, that meaning is examined in its surrounding context. Thirdly, when the literal meaning cannot be assimilated into the context in a meaningful way, one seeks a non-literal meaning that may be compatible with it.

been bypassed with the aid of the explanations and formulations given above. But Winnicott leaves his subversive action un-remedied, thus creating space for the introduction of additional axial grammars into the analytic space. This deliberate undermining of Coherence and Correspondence expresses Winnicott's inclination to maintain, rather than resolve, tensions within the psyche, believing that the ability to contain them renders the psyche creative and resilient.

Having dealt with the subjects of sex and gender, Winnicott moves on to deal with the issue of insanity – sanity. Here too, he illustrates the ability of linguistic mechanisms to allow for paradox and contain it:

> The matter could have been left there, but I am glad, in view of subsequent events, that I went further. It was my next remark that surprised me, and it clinched the matter. I said: 'It was not that you told this to anyone; it is I who see the girl and hear a girl talking, when actually there is a man on my couch. The mad person is myself.'
>
> I did not have to elaborate this point because it went home. The patient said that he now felt sane in a mad environment. In other words he was now released from a dilemma. As he said, subsequently, 'I myself could never say (knowing myself to be a man) "I am a girl". I am not mad that way. But you said it, and you have spoken to both parts of me.'
>
> This madness which was mine enabled him to see himself as a girl from my position. He knows himself to be a man, and never doubts that he is a man. Is it obvious what was happening here? For my part, I have needed to live through a deep personal experience in order to arrive at the understanding I feel I now have reached.
>
> WINNICOTT 1971, 73

Clearly, Winnicott is in no hurry to part from the 'madness' that his patient introduced into the analytic discourse. On the contrary, he appropriates it. One can reasonably assume that Winnicott's patient, given the firm bond between him and his therapist, will not conclude that the latter is simply, literally mad. Rather, it would seem that Winnicott makes good use of the positive therapeutic alliance in demolishing yet another Correspondent truth, as given in the definition of insanity. When enabling madness and sanity to dwell together in his image, Winnicott models for the patient the way in which Correspondently or Intersubjectively-defined opposites, such as madness and sanity, may co-exist simultaneously in the psyche, as do the 'boy' and the 'girl'.

Winnicott's move is a structural–grammatical one, on the level of Thirdness: Opposites as known and defined according to the Correspondent or Coherent grammar are not mutually exclusive in Subjective-Existential grammar. The authoritarianism of the Correspondent axis has been undermined. Its grammatical rules are no longer all-pervasive in the psyche. The laws of identity and contradiction are not valid in all semantic and referential fields. Winnicott doesn't try to banish the Correspondent axis, only to bring it into dialogue with other axes. This is how we may understand also his subsequent interventions, when Winnicott turns to deal with interaction and mutual influences among the different axes:

> This complex state of affairs has a special reality for this man because he and I have been driven to the conclusion (though unable to prove it) that his mother (who is not alive now) saw a girl baby when she saw him as a baby before she came round to thinking of him as a boy. In other words this man had to fit into her idea that her baby would be and was a girl. (He was the second child, the first being a boy.) We have very good evidence from inside the analysis that in her early management of him the mother held him and dealt with him in all sorts of physical ways as if she failed to see him as a male. On the basis of this pattern he later arranged his defenses, but it was the mother's 'madness' that saw a girl where there was a boy, and this was brought right into the present by my having said 'It is I who am mad'. On this Friday he went away profoundly moved and feeling that this was the first significant shift in the analysis for a long time (although, as I have said, there had always been continuous progress in the sense of good work being done).
>
> IBID. 73

While Winnicott is a pioneer of paradoxical grammar, he seeks to go further, to find and explain the interplay between paradoxical and coherent grammars, in order to enable their coexistence in the psyche. After articulating his paradoxical intervention, Winnicott returns to Correspondent Secondness, looking for biographical events that had a role in creating his patient's conflicts. Investigating the past brings out clearly the way in which therapist and patient together deal with the tensions and incongruities of the different axes. The Correspondent axis holds certain historical events and the biological fact of the patient's male-ness; violating the Coherent rules of identity and contradiction and the empirical Correspondent truth that males are not female, the

Subjective-Existential axis allows the patient to exist as a girl. The Intersubjective axis is introduced with the entrance of the truth-norm of sanity into the analytic space, imbuing it with the axis's typical Firstness as expressed by fears of ostracism, derision and exclusion. Winnicott volunteers to hold on to this 'hot potato' of contradiction and paradox and later of madness, taking upon himself the risk of moving among truth axes, a move experienced here as bordering on madness and incurring potential public censure. Winnicott's introduction of these languages into the analytic space creates for his patient the possibility of being exposed to them, of learning to speak them, of using their possibilities to symbolize and reveal what has formerly been dissociated. This allows the containment of the incompatibilities that ensue from the interactions among the different axes.

This vignette is an elegant illustration of dialogue among truth axes, where the different terms of the model serve as a 'road map' for systematic articulation of clinical intuition and action. The identification of various grammars and the tensions that arise from their incongruences allow the re-introduction of a foreclosed language into the therapeutic discourse. The initial entering of foreign grammar into analytic and psychic space may trigger anxiety, unease and even fear of madness. These were modulated here by recourse to transference analysis. Winnicott is able to hang on to these tensions without explicit articulation but, for a clinician who is not such an intuitive genius, the axes of truth provide a conceptual framework that clarifies and formulates clinical events, as well as depicts the possibilities of therapeutic intervention in times of impasse.

Case 4: Endowing Empathy with Fresh Air

In his article 'Who Does Self-Psychology Cure', Bollas (1986) discusses Kohut's therapeutic approach. After outlining the rationale of his approach and its technical implementation, Bollas illustrates the rejuvenation that comes from introducing a novel grammar into a semantic space dominated by an existing grammar.

Bollas begins by discussing a fundamental tenet of Kohutian theory that is expressed in the concept of self-object, according to which various degrees of merger relations with significant others are maintained throughout one's life. In Kohut's view, these relations challenge the idea that separation-individuation is the goal or the defining moment in the subject's evolving identity. Promoting relations of merger in analysis determines much of the analyst's technique. Here, empathy acts as the nodal point of analysis. The analyst mirrors, contains and takes sole responsibility for narcissistic injuries and past empathic failures. He gently and painstakingly echoes the patient's emotion laden moments and offers to the patient his mature personality functions and subjugates his subjectivity to the nurturing of a vulnerable evolving subjectivity.

After presenting Kohut's approach, Bollas proceeds to discuss a number of Kohut's cited interventions that are inconsistent with it: "He tells a particularly hypomanic patient that he is an 'idiot', challenging him in a way that leads the patient to laugh and have a look at what he is doing". With a hint of biting humor, Bollas offers his critique of Kohutian selfobject relations, giving Kohut's own intervention as a compelling argument for the expression of the analyst's differentiated subjectivity as given in critical unempathic responses.

Kohut's understanding of analytic relations is compatible with the Secondness dimension of the Ideal axis. He encourages modes of relational merger that give rise to sensations of comfort and emotional resonance. However, Kohut's own quoted intervention undermines his proclaimed approach. By calling the patient 'an idiot', the analyst challenges him to adopt a position of self-scrutiny, inducing him to exchange the merged 'we' of the Ideal axis for the objectified 'I' of Correspondence. This Correspondent selfhood is objectified and the patient is encouraged to examine himself in a somewhat detached matter-of-fact manner. This speech act immediately effected a relational change and elicited a different self-state in the patient. In a similar manner and in the context of a different case,

> He [Kohut] openly acknowledges with a patient his pleasure in the patient's newly acquired abilities, indicating with one that he was 'glad' to see how the patient was doing. In effect, I think he believes that analysands develop not only through the content of interpretations, but also through the logic of the analyst's sensibility, namely, his particular range of skills in knowing the patient. Kohut's analysands, in their best moments, one is led to conclude, must have acquired a skill in bringing the best out of the other.
>
> BOLLAS 1986, 434

Bollas relates here to Kohut's analysands along the Pragmatic axis, humorously appreciating their ability to create the best parent that may be had for them.

This article may be seen as articulating Bollas' and Kohut's different approaches to therapy; alternatively, we can conceptualize the discussion it presents in terms of truth axes and the logic of the movement between their different grammars. Bollas' dispute with selfobject positioning need not amount to its absolute negation. Rather, Bollas may be understood as contending that a therapist should not restrict himself to one grammar. Such restriction is likely to stunt growth and constrict the range of expression allowed for various self-states. Kohutian transference relations are founded on the grammatical rules of the Ideal axis. An analyst is idealized, merger is allowed, promoted, and comfort is secured. The intervention quoted effects separation and reflectivity. Moreover, the analyst's subjectivity and personal tone are revealed, creating the beginnings of mutuality whose source resides in Intersubjective Secondness.

With the analyst's movement to another axis, we experience a flow of fresh air and the possibility of spontaneity and curiosity. These arise in the face of all that is 'not-me', all that is crude fact in the Correspondent reality. We may recall here the Jamesian description of

> that element in reality which every strong man of common-sense willingly feels because it calls forth powers that he owns- the rough, harsh, sea-wave, north-wind element, the denier of persons, the democratizer- [this element] is banished because it jars too much on the desire for communion. Now, it is the very enjoyment of this element that throws many men upon…a polemic reaction against the contrary extreme. They sicken at a life wholly constituted of intimacy. There is an overpowering desire at moments to escape personality, to revel in the action of forces that have no respect for our ego, to let the tides flow, even though they flow over us.
>
> JAMES 2009, 90

Bollas calls 'range of skills' what enables the analyst to 'know' his patient, which may be understood as the analyst's expertise in creating movement among epistemological perspectives. What Bollas calls the 'logic of the therapist's sensibility' is, in this context, the logic of transition between axial self-states; in the quoted case, the transition starts from Ideal Secondness to Correspondent Secondness and then to the margins of Intersubjective Secondness.

The first two examples I discussed illustrated the impact of excluding dimensions of one axis of truth or another. The third and fourth examples illustrated the ways in which master clinicians intuitively introduce novel grammars into an analytic space that is dominated by one axis. In both cases, the introduction effected was analyzed and described by means of truth axes, showing the way they may be employed in the articulation of both theoretical rationale and technique.

In the next two vignettes, drawn from the psychoanalytic literature, I will again analyze the therapeutic action in terms of movement among various axes of truth. In each case, I will re-formulate the writer's rationale for the presented intervention in terms of axes of truth. My aim in doing so is to show how the truth axes supply a potent and parsimonious means for explaining a wide range of phenomena, alongside their potential to create a semantic field in which the logic of various theoretical orientations may be included and addressed.

Case 5: Metaphor as a Coercive Agent of Coherence

The case cited in Symington's 'The Analyst's Act of Freedom as Agent of Therapeutic Change' (1983) illustrates wonderfully the differences between origin, validation and degree of dominance in the evolution of psychic truth. What is described in this case is the way a patient's Pragmatic truth undergoes two developments: Firstly, it receives intersubjective validation and thus achieves a secondary status of Intersubjective truth value. Secondly, in the Coherent self-state, it occupies a nodal position, dominating all other elements.

Symington's case also illustrates the complex situation in which Coherent grammar renders homogeneous whole areas of experiencing. Moreover, this process is guided by a truth that dwells in a different axis, here the Pragmatic one, but it moves on to receive Intersubjective validation. The therapeutic act is effected by the introduction of a different, Correspondent grammar, which deconstructs this complex configuration. Again, the therapeutic effect involves movement among the axes, triggered by the analyst's intervention.

> I was charging Miss M a little more than half of what my other patients were paying. She had been a clinic patient and I used to sigh to myself and say inwardly, 'Poor Miss M, £X is the most that I can charge her'. I did not in fact articulate it so clearly as that. In my mind it was like an acknowledged fact that everyone knows, like the unreliability of the English weather. It was part of the furniture of my mind and I had resigned myself to it in the same way as I reluctantly resign myself to the English weather. So the analysis went on and on with that assumption as its unquestioned concomitant until one day a startling thought occurred to me: 'Why can't Miss M pay the same as all my other patients?'
>
> Then I remembered the resentment she frequently expressed towards her boss who always called her 'Little Mary'. A certainty began to grow in me that I was the prisoner of an illusion about the patient's capacities. I had been lassoed into the patient's self-perception and I was just beginning to extricate myself from it. I then brought up the question of her fee and in the course of a discussion she said, 'If I had to pay more then I know I would'.

> She had now clearly told me that she had the capacity in her to pay more and that this could be mobilized if I changed my inner attitude towards her. A few sessions later I said to her, 'I have been thinking over our discussion about the fee. I charge most of my other patients £X and in our discussion I have not heard anything that makes me think that I should not charge you the same'.
>
> For two sessions she cried rather pitifully but then became resolved that she would meet the challenge. Soon she found a job that paid her one third more than her previous salary. In moving job she extricated herself from the patronizing tutelage of the boss who called her 'Little Mary'. She had been able to do this because she had first been freed from the patronizing attitude of her analyst. Shortly after this she finally gave the push to a parasitic boyfriend. Again I think she had been able to do this because she had been able to give the push to a parasitic analyst. These two events were soon followed by other favourable developments. I think the source of these beneficial changes was in that moment of inner freedom- when I had the unexpected thought: 'Why can't Miss M pay the same as my other patients?' I am calling this act of inner freedom the 'x-phenomenon'.
>
> SYMINGTON 1983, 283

Symington suggests the following explanation for the 'x-phenomenon':

> I think at one level the analyst and patient together make a single system…a corporate personality…the two are together part of an illusory system… As the analytical work proceeds the analyst slowly disengages himself from it… Psychoanalysis is a process which catalyzes the ego to ego contact: that area of the personality that is non-corporate, personal and individual… At the beginning of the analysis (and often for a long time)… analyst and patient are part of a system and are joined through the superego parts of their personalities. It is through the superegos that corporate personality is effected… Transference and countertransference are emotional expressions of this fusion…The analyst's inner act of freedom causes a therapeutic shift in the patient… It implies a form of communication between patient and analyst that is at the primary process level. It…works to free the two people from this corporateness.
>
> IBID. 290

Symington's discussion of the x-phenomenon touches upon the complexity and elusiveness of unconscious communication. He describes the way the analytic dyad creates a corporate system comprised of mostly unarticulated interpersonal and cultural meanings, within which their discourse evolves. Patient and analyst absorb meanings that are embedded in this system in an unconscious manner, mediated by superego elements communicated and enacted in the transference. The analyst is the first to perform an act of freedom that brings to consciousness the unarticulated truths on which this system is predicated. This immediately brings about the ability to question these truths, creating for the patient margins of freedom that have not been previously experienced.

What Symington describes here is a corporate personality that is intersubjectively predicated in two contexts: In the analytic dyad and in the social representation of each of the participants, as mediated by their superego function. As he sees it, the latter context is restrictive for the patient and analysis brings about a liberating movement. Symington is, of course, talking of the validation and the preservation of truth by intersubjective means. This is *always* the case regarding what is accepted as true by both participants in the analytic dyad (as in other contexts) and it is of course also true of all superego representations. But addressing in particular this case and the truth-value of 'little Mary', I believe we need to include considerations along Pragmatic and Coherent axes as well. We need to do this because often, *a symptom manifested on one axis does not originate there*. In order to understand the dynamics of a certain truth, these origins must be understood.

The first thing that needs to be recognized here is that the truth of 'little Mary' originated in the *Pragmatic* axis. She therefore inhabits a reality she cannot influence. This pragmatically-determined truth *then* received *intersubjective* validation by others and its scope of influence expanded as it became both a prime determinant of her *Coherent* identity and dictated a way of relating to her. What I wish to underline here as a guideline for clinical action is not given in Symington's vignette, namely, the need to closely investigate the axis-specific processes that created the nodal truth around which the symptom evolved in the course of the patient's history.

Investigating this history may explain two facets of the therapeutic effect: The first relates to reflecting upon actual experiences of incompetence. The second relates to the dominance that the Pragmatic axis occupies in Mary's psychic space. Investigating this fact may well uncover a whole scheme of signification in context: How was effectiveness perceived and valued in her environment? Who represented its demands and aspirations? Given the dominance of the Pragmatic axis, what was the value attributed to other axes? Such investigation could be a means for loosening the grip of one truth upon a patient's experience and of understanding why it was chosen as the central element in her coherent construal of herself.

As I explained previously, the guiding principle of Coherent grammar and selfhood is compatibility. Statements, beliefs, wishes and motivations must cohere in a comprehensive system. Paradox and discord must be resolved. This vignette gives us an opportunity to see metaphor as the linguistic means by which Coherent grammar is enacted.

Lakoff discusses the way in which an entire system of thought may be organized by a small number of metaphors (Lakoff 2008). This holds for world views as much as it does for a particular subject's perspective, including emotion, thought, communication and behavior. The image of Symington's patient is constructed around one central metaphor, that of a small child as given in 'Little Mary' or, rather, 'poor little Mary'. This metaphor of a small child automatically depicts Mary as vulnerable, fragile and in need of protection.

Mitchell (1998) analyzes the metaphor of the infant and its significance in shaping clinical work. He states that, when interpreting in the context of this metaphor, we may begin to think of certain wishes, fears and behaviors as if they were indeed fragments of infantile experience. In psychoanalytic thought, past and present merge, since the past is understood as reconstructing itself again and again in psychic reality. Therefore, from a psychodynamic point of view, the 'metaphored'-metamorphosed patient *is* an infant and we sometimes relate to him accordingly. Freud's infant is a conflicted troublemaker, demanding a firm hand and an abstinent manner, so that his prohibited desires may be brought to light, analyzed and eschewed. By contrast, the modern infant (Symington's) is seen as deserving of empathic understanding and requiring real experiences of nurturance in therapy in order to resume arrested development.

What is highlighted here is the importance of identifying the element that anchors coherent structures and narratives. This element may be a metaphor, a memory, or an event that serves the *structural function* of unifying a narrative. The element's specific *content* will reveal what other axes are implicated in the narrative. In this vignette, when the metaphor of the modern infant emerges, the therapist becomes aware of his overall pragmatic construction of the clinical situation, affecting both understanding and action in the analytic space.

Symington's moment of freedom involved a Correspondently determined thought that entered his mind: 'Why can't Miss M pay the same as all my other patients?' This thought was 'startling' for the analyst, not a part of the 'furniture of his mind'. This is mostly because the Correspondent axis was not the one structuring the reality of the analytic dyad. Despite that, being always active as an organizing principle of the mind, Correspondent axial construals continued to be generated in the analyst's mind, albeit subconsciously. When the thought offered itself, Symington immediately recognized it as true (along a different axis from the one he had followed before) and allowed it into the dyad, disordering its previously accepted truths.

What followed the interpretation may actually be understood as an enactment of a Pragmatically related drama. When the Correspondent axis enters the scene, Symington discovers a margin of freedom he had lacked before and presents an intuitive interpretation that is startling and 'ungrounded' in the context of its presentation. Now, this interpretation carries quite an impact. The patient is startled and then cries throughout the next sessions. Her response reflects transition, as given both in the challenge she has been faced with and the structural confusion she experiences. But what also exists in the session is the impact of the therapist's movement and intention. Effectively, the therapist models *effectiveness*. He is not afraid to *act*. This is often the case with interpretations but here, I believe, in the context of Mary's malaise, it carries great weight. This combined influence undermines the formerly entrenched Pragmatic truth and Mary experiences the new possibility of existing as an active agent in the world.

In contemporary psychoanalytic literature, moments of freedom are idealized as the unique intersubjective happenings that they indeed are. And yet, when intuition and interpersonal spaces do not succeed in working their magic, articulation of methodology may be helpful. In a sense, applying truth-axial terms may involve the introduction of prosaic, sober Correspondence into the realm of the poetics we all appreciate so deeply in our work. The next case offers a neat illustration of this.

Case 6: The Fall of Time and Sense in Love

The Ideal axis constitutes truth that is divorced of the senses. This truth does not require causal or logical justification, sensory or empirical validation. The ideal, like the truth it gives rise to, is eternal, and therefore the passing of time in ideally structured reality is unimportant. Correspondent truth, on the other hand, is anchored in the empirical and in the testimony of the senses, placing the present, past and future in ordered relations. Empirical realities are often construed and described in similar ways, thus providing a base for common observations and understandings which, in turn, may create intersubjective realities. In the following vignette I will show analytic work that bridges dissociated Ideal and Correspondent axes, in order to enable and mediate Intersubjective experiencing.

In his article 'Bold Analysis and Associative Dialogue', Hadar (1999) discusses psychoanalytic technique and the centrality of free association in the creation of therapeutic dialogue. Hadar marks free association not only as functioning in relation to unconscious material, but also as the watershed between cohesion and innovation in the evolution of analytic narrative. The benefit of relinquishing consistency and embracing subversive narratives lies in creating the possibility of richer and more adaptive constructions. That said, the therapist must be constantly attuned to maintaining the balance between cohesion and possibility, undoing narratives only inasmuch as the ensuing disorder does not threaten the patient's integrity. The therapist's interventions assimilate free associations within existing structures or, alternately, use them in undermining their existence.

In order to ensure the dismantling and enriching potential of discourse, Hadar suggests a therapeutic technique which does not rely exclusively on the patient. As Hadar points out, the patient is not always able to supply the free associations so crucial to analysis. Whether due to repression or resistance, psychic poverty, lack of skills or personal characteristics, the patient's ability to associate may be blocked in a way that calls for the analyst to set it in motion. When conditions demand it, Hadar advocates 'an associative dialogue' in which a therapist is called upon to share with a patient what goes through his mind in response to what the latter had said.

As an example of associative dialogue, Hadar offers the following vignette:

> To illustrate, a woman in her mid-30s once described to me a holiday she took with a new boyfriend at a hotel by the Dead Sea. She said the experience was wonderful, but she could not specify why, apart from alluding to a magical synchronization with her boyfriend. Their joint breakfasts best symbolized for her their idyllic togetherness. From previous occasions, I knew that the woman had a remarkable blindness to interpersonal dynamics when romantically aroused, which often later evoked in her a prickly kind of dismissive suspiciousness. I thought that her inability to attend to detail did her a poor service in the forging of a new relationship. I closed my eyes, imagined myself at the Dead Sea hotel, and prompted her by saying something like, "Getting up *late* for breakfast and making your way in the lift down to the restaurant, still a bit sleepy and not talking much. Just a short sentence about *how long it takes the lift to arrive* and an occasional look at him, accompanied by a smile." The woman said, "Actually, we did not use a lift because our room was at the same level as the restaurant." "Right," I said, "*And then* the smallish restaurant- quite surprising for a large hotel- with just a few *late* guests because most have already had their breakfast. Simple but neat tables, *many rearranged for lunch already*, no waiters and a deep silence". "That's a fairly accurate

> description," said the patient, who added with irony, "Were you there too?" I smiled and continued, "You sat down at the table and looked at the mountains on the other side of the sea, covered in a soft haze. He saw you looking and said, 'They look mysterious, don't they, in the haze?'" "You do seem to enjoy our holiday," the woman said, and I responded, "In fact, I am trying to do the work/suffering (*amal* in Hebrew) that it takes to preserve the pleasure". In the ensuing dialogue, the woman described her holiday in greater detail, which helped her (and me) to identify some of the sources of joy in her holiday.
>
> HADAR 1999, 115 emphases added

Hadar's patient is in love and expresses herself using classic Ideal content and grammar. Her 'wonderful' experience is whole in itself. It needs no description, no empirical anchoring. Merged with her boyfriend in "magical synchronization", she seems to hope a magic merger with Hadar will relay her experience to him. Sadly, her language, brimming with superlatives, blurred and amorphous, seems to leave her analyst cold. It seems that Hadar is struck by this lack of resonance, perhaps feeling something 'prickly and dismissive' himself. In analyzing this interaction, Hadar senses that his patient's inability 'to attend to detail' does her a poor service in the forging of relationships. Termed differently, Hadar senses that Ideal grammar in and of itself, cannot uphold experience, cannot suffice as a basis for communication or forging of meaningful relationships.

Closing his eyes, Hadar begins the labor of putting his patient in touch with additional grammars. Knowing his patient as lacking understanding of interpersonal dynamics, he offers her a Correspondent reality, supplying texture, time and color to the idyllic togetherness that might later elude her, leaving her empty and suspicious. Introducing a host of sensory details, he tries to establish a Correspondent reality as something she might hold on to and keep, as something she might share with others, perhaps also with her boyfriend, in pleasant reminiscing. He establishes points of reference, anchoring emotion and signification in sensed materiality.

Alongside the sensory facts he offers, Hadar introduces the dimension of time. The immaterial Ideal axis is oblivious of both Correspondent and Subjective time. As Hadar introduces Correspondence, he creates a matrix of time. In the few lines in which he imagines her vacation, time is referred to four times. The sensory reality of a surprisingly small restaurant in a big hotel, the visibility and the haze, the waiters getting ready for lunch, all are temporally strung together, granting the magical experience the solidity of the lived-in world.

Teaching his patient the grammar of Correspondence, Hadar is placing stepping stones that allow movement from the Ideal to the Intersubjective. Hadar invites the patient to discover the multiplicity and particularity of empirical reality. He tries to draw the music of the Ideal into sensed reality, showing the richness that may be achieved by their combination. He tries to convey, by means of what is happening in the 'here and now' of the session, how a sensed reality may be shared and communicated. The patient ironically asks if he had been to her hotel, but beyond the irony she seems to understand something: The details had indeed brought them together, perhaps helped her analyst share her experience, as if he too had been there.

In this example, as in the former ones, truth axes provide a methodological map of sorts, which enables to articulate and understand conscious and unconscious lines of communication in the analytic space. Hadar identifies Ideal axis functioning and the way it inhibits, indeed shuts down, Correspondent functioning. As often happens, when the magic, merger and bliss of love are activated, sense and time disappear. This fairly common phenomenon apparently acquired subversive proportions in Hadar's patient and impaired her ability to concretely anchor her emotional experiences. Hadar attempts to change the pattern of connectivity between the axes, freeing the temporal-sensory dimension of Correspondence from its inhibition in the context of the Ideal (falling in love). Dynamically viewed, we might explore what in the patient's early history had to be denied, perhaps even on perceptual levels, in order to maintain the continuity of positive feelings.[4]

---

4 The logic of truth axes dynamics may be expressed here in terms of neural activation. Thought and mental construals are physiologically subserved. Ideas and the concepts that make them up are physically 'computed' by brain structures. Reasoning is the activation of certain neuronal groups in the brain, given prior activation of other neuronal groups (Plaut 2002). The Neural Theory of Language (NTL- see Lakoff 2008) addresses the link between the psychic and the physiological, exploring thought processes by means of their bodily correlates. At birth, the brain consists of hundreds of specific regions that connect in particular ways to regions around them. Each neuron is linked to thousands of other neurons. By the age of five, more than half of these links disappear, those that have not been used. This is the vital formative process of the brain, that expresses what and how has been learned (Trevarthen 2001). The chains of communication between neurons gradually acquire fixed patterns of functioning. When a neuron is activated, it can activate or immobilize a neuron beside it. Such activation or inhibition expresses the relations between the semantic areas represented by these neurons (Plaut 2002). Lakoff describes different relations that may exist between various groups of neurons. A situation of mutual inhibition is one in which two groups of neurons are linked in a way that each delays the other's activation. In other words, when one group is activated, the second is inhibited. This, for example, is what happens when two incompatible ways of understanding a situation are equally accessible. Lakoff

In his article 'The Pursuit of the Particular', Levenson (1988) presents a view similar to Hadar's in that he places the deconstruction of the patient's discourse at the heart of the analytic work (italics in original text):

> ...however construed, for all of us the enrichment and deconstruction of the patient's story is our most powerful instrumentality. Even those analysts who pursue that Will o' the Wisp, the mutative interpretation, must begin with a free-associative deconstruction. It is not, *per se*, psychoanalysis, but it is the absolute precondition for psychoanalysis. To use an analogy, it is like the water that turns the millstone; to grind the grain...The Kabbalists say that the mystery of God lies in the particular. I am suggesting that the 'mystery' (the secret core) of psychoanalysis also lies in the pursuit of the particular, and the peculiar deconstructed mosaic of data (not a coherent narrative) which emerges, whether presented in the form of fantasy, free-association, or Sullivan's 'detailed inquiry' ...My therapeutic algorithm consists of a fixed and contained frame, *a deconstructive inquiry which potentiates defenses and leads to a much augmented version of the patient's operations in the relationship with the therapist.* ...To tolerate the fragmentation of meaning is to create new meaning. I am convinced, to pursue my analogy, that getting the wheels turning is ultimately far more important than what one grinds.
>
> LEVENSON 1988, 13–14

Levenson's metaphor of the millstone and the need to set it in motion brings forth what he sees as crucial elements of the psychoanalytic act. What was whole is 'grinded' into the particular; what is critical is the element that deconstructs and disrupts, that triggers movement, an element which gets the wheels

---

illustrates this state of affairs by reference to political ideology, where one world view (say Conservative) is incompatible with another world view (say Liberal), and therefore they are mutually inhibitory. However, examined in concrete terms, rather than ideologies, most people can imagine situations in which they would behave in accord with one world view and others in which they would behave in line with a different world view. True, each world view inhibits the other, but only when co-activated. When activated at different times, each can run its full course of activity. Lakoff termed these relations as 'The winner-takes-all circuit' (Lakoff 2008, 21). In the terms of NTL, truth axes are like world views, implemented by neural groups that are connected within and among themselves in fixed patterns. The relations between the various groups can be of the type described by Lakoff as mutual inhibition. Deconstruction and planned selective activating (as Hadar effects in his work) may alter the fixed neural connections, either within or among groups, allowing the occurrence of richer patterns of neural activation.

turning. Levenson, like Hadar, sees the potential source of this movement in the richness of detail, in the infinity of the particular. Another source of movement that taps directly into various reservoirs of particularity is unfailingly found by means of change of perspective. Movement among axes of truth brings about changes in perception, in self-states, in the realities inhabited. The transition among them *in itself*, prior to and regardless of what 'one grinds', brings about the possibility of airing fixated narratives.

The next two vignettes are brought from my clinic. The first deals with transition from the Intersubjective to the Pragmatic and Subjective-Existential axes. The second illustrates the way an object is represented differently across various axes of truth.

Case 7: Sadomasochistic Defenses against Agency and Choice

In the following case, I illustrate the way in which truth axes may interact so as to position one axis as a defense against another axis. Here I illustrate how an Intersubjective pattern dominates and conceals a Subjective-Existential conflict, forcing it to dissociate from both experience and analytic investigation.

Jill, mid-thirties, has been in therapy for four years. She is pleasant, good looking and has a good sense of humor. Born into a well to do family, her pleasantly experienced childhood was irreversibly shattered when her parents divorced. She was five at the time. Jill felt that the divorce had left her father lonely and miserable, her mother vital and empowered. Several years following the divorce Jill's mother remarried a man older then herself, powerfully rich, and described as intrusive, controlling and critical in his relations with Jill's mother and her three elder sisters. Jill relates that it took her mother two decades to gradually overcome her submissiveness and become stronger and more assertive in her relations with her stepfather. Jill, who describes an early princess-like childhood, with doting maids, cooks and her own large pink bedroom, was allotted chores and through high school strongly encouraged by her step father to work during holidays. At the time this was perceived by the sisters and their social milieu as arbitrary and unnecessary.

Growing up, Jill was popular and excelled in her law studies at a prestigious university. At that time, Jill experienced her first meaningful relationship with a man. She described her relations with him as calm, pleasant and companionable. Her sexual experience with him she described as unsatisfactory and overly polite, and when she left him she felt lacking in sexual experience and confidence. When her country of birth was thrown into civilian unrest, Jill was sent abroad and her adjustment was quick and smooth. Once again she was successful, socially and professionally.

At the time she sought therapy, Jill had been living with her boyfriend, Daniel, for several years. They first met when Daniel was employed and highly successful at a leading law firm. His efforts to create a private practice began well, but slowly faded into partial, and then total unemployment. Today he works at home; Jill is unclear about what he does. She is the home's breadwinner, responsible for paying the rent and the bills, looking after the house. For years Jill wants to marry and have children, but Daniel refuses on grounds that he doesn't feel 'happy' with Jill, that he finds her intellectually mediocre and inferior in comparison with him.

The first year of therapy revolved mostly around Jill's concern with getting married. She would speak of work, of home, family; everything seemed to be working fairly well in her life, apart from the static point in which her relations with her boyfriend seemed moored. She was talkative in sessions and yet they seemed to lack in content and emotional depth. Towards the end of the first year, almost every session witnessed a sharp transition. Jill would enter the room with her usual cheerful, warm attitude and talk easily and chattily of her day. Gradually she would slip into dejection, often crying and increasingly miserable as the session proceeded. When crying, she hardly spoke; I could make little of what was making her so miserable. The only thing she would relate and reiterate was her repetitive refrain about Daniel's unwillingness to marry.

Gradually overcoming her shame, Jill began to reveal the nature of her relationship with Daniel: an extremely troubled, abusive relationship, fraught with rage, frustration and humiliation. Daniel was obsessed with what he termed Jill's dysfunctional sexuality. He demanded that she indulge in a range of sexual acts and was constantly scornful and harshly critical of her 'performances'. Jill's therapy created tension between her and Daniel, and he tried in different ways to undermine it. He would not give her the car keys or threaten that if she were to leave the house she wouldn't be able to come back.

I felt very sympathetic towards Jill. I saw her as having been victimized twice: Once by her step-father and then by Daniel. Distanced and detached from her family abroad, hiding from her friends what she was going through at home, she seemed vulnerable, lonely and wronged. I was sole witness to her suffering and felt increasingly worried with the verbal and mental abuse she suffered daily. I appreciated her growing ability to reveal such difficulties and believed that her ability to communicate and share them would bring about the development of a witnessing function within herself. Once communicated and reflected upon, Jill would see the impossibility of subjecting herself to such abuse: She would express determination to leave Daniel or drastically change the patterns of relation with him. But months passed by and nothing changed. She arrived one session with a black eye. An argument had deteriorated to violence. She needed to see a nurse in the hospital's emergency. I was sure this would be a watershed; *now* she would get up and leave. She didn't. Eventually she began sharing her difficult situation with family and friends. That too made no difference. I sadly gave up the fantasy of one of her sisters flying in, taking Jill's hand, and walking her out of that house and into her own.

Over time, we began to investigate the way in which Jill's relationship with Daniel was a reenactment of her (and her mother's) relations with her stepfather. The two men were perceived as resembling one another in their arrogance, in their controlling behavior, in their blatantly censorious and intrusive relations with their partners. On the horizon of reenactment was the possibility that Jill, like her mother, would effect a change in her relations with Daniel. I hoped that linking past and present, articulating the origins of the pathological relations, would help Jill move on. That also was not to be. And I was bothered by something else as well; in the relations between Jill and myself I could detect nothing of the aggression, the scorn and censoriousness that characterized Jill's relations with Daniel and her stepfather.

I knew I was missing something and we were clearly making no progress. Jill was a seemingly exemplary patient, she never missed a session, never complained that therapy wasn't doing her any good. She seemed to expect so little, close to nothing from Daniel, from me. It seemed I was the only one distressed by her static situation. In supervision, I was advised to increase the frequency of our sessions from twice to three times a week. The rationale of this suggestion was that Jill may be clinging to her relationship with Daniel, because it was the only home she had.

Home, as a place and a time, began to be discussed. Jill would lose herself in memories of her early childhood home; she relived its destruction, describing feelings of impending disaster that would return and at times overpower her completely, as in the wake of the crisis that eventually brought about her emigration and the second disassembling of her family. She talked of a medical procedure that her mother had undergone when she was three. She was told of it only in retrospect, but recalls weeks of dark anxiety in the house. It became very obvious that Jill needed a home. And yet I found myself very reluctant to offer her one and add an additional weekly hour.

Over the subsequent weeks I began to understand what it was that I was shying away from: I was reluctant to commit myself. Jill was such a 'good' patient, in many ways. Intuitively I flinched from disturbing this balance. I understood I was on par with Jill's family. I was working with her, being with her, but at the same time keeping a safe distance from her. I wondered if I was reiterating a faulty, passive parental hold. Perhaps I (with Jill) was identifying with Daniel's pronouncement that this was the best that she could hope for. I was in some sort of a comfort zone. I was shying from making a choice.

The realization that I was avoiding commitment and choice, delivered me at once from Intersubjective to Existential considerations. I realized that Jill was doing much in *her* life in order to avoid commitment and choice. She chose to live with a severely controlling man, his egotism restricting her horizons. She chose to loosen hold of her bodily self and hand it over to Daniel's regimentation and derision. She refused to be in touch with any desire, to articulate anything that she wants, apart from marrying. She refused to *be*. Her dramatic and increasingly violent relationship with Daniel was a noisy camouflage of this tragic fact.

Somehow understanding this freed me into offering Jill another weekly hour. After a period of indecision regarding my offer, she became very ill and suffered a prolonged bout of abdomen pains, which failed to receive diagnosis and treatment. She became very depressed, regressed, repetitively preoccupied with the micromanagement of her physical symptoms. From within this misery, there was of course little question of choice. She began coming to therapy three times a week. We both had to attend to her body. She had come to the decision of adding a weekly hour not by means of reflective and deliberate choice, but rather by 'needing' it in a way that made it indispensable.

Jill encountered her body in a regressed and distressed mode and I tried to keep her company there. A whole line of aches, pains and allergies brought us in close contact with her body's surfaces. She emerged from her prolonged enigmatic illnesses with something new in her embodied experience of self, something detached from her former intersubjectively determined masochistic bodily image; she felt grateful for her newly discovered health. She could appreciate the whiteness of her skin when it reappeared from under angry rashes. I noticed immediately that she had agreed on some level to appropriate her body.

Whereas I had formerly understood and perceived Jill's life in intersubjective terms, I now felt that the transferential relations delivered me to the Existential truth: Jill was not up to taking responsibility for her life. She was almost comfortable handing her life over to others, Daniel or myself. With Daniel, she passively existed in any script he thought up. To me, she clearly conveyed in a variety of ways that she refuses to care for herself. In sexual relations she experienced ineptness and shame. All that she did so well in other areas of her life remained dissociated from any emotional relevance. The possibility of existing as an active and successful subject was wholly foreclosed.

Retelling myself the story of her life, I was now focused less on the abusive patterns and more on her pervasive passivity: Her home had been destroyed leaving her clueless and bewildered; her stepfather had 'trod all over her'; she was 'sent' to university and then abroad; She lived where Daniel wished, a busy urban environment in which she felt alienated. The fact that she had never formalized her status as citizen in the country took on new significance. Even when describing her career she would say how she was 'given' prizes and promotions, sounding mildly surprised, as if she had run into some good luck. The causes were always external to her. She herself was the effect. The Pragmatic axis was standing on its head.

Noting this, I introduced pragmatic considerations into our discourse. I began to mark Jill's power at home; her financial abilities, her unrecognized ability to maintain perfectly a demanding job and all household duties. I was surprised how unnoticed these facts had gone for so long. They were our "unexperienced known", allowing us not to digest and assimilate a major discordant fact: Jill was a grown-up. For her, this was an infuriating fact. She wanted the pink bedroom from which she had been torn.

When I first told her that she and Daniel aren't marrying because *she hasn't yet decided to marry him*, she reacted as though I were confused, or had somehow forgotten who did not want to marry whom. While she was suffering one of her frequent allergies, I suggested she see a nutritionist and have an allergy screening. She responded irritably, almost suspiciously. A few sessions later she told me that she felt I was no longer empathic with her troubles.

In a way she was right. I lost my empathy to her Intersubjective positioning as a victim. I lost my empathy to a self-state in which she was enclosed and that defined her as lacking potency and efficacy. I began to view her life from the Subjective-Existential perspective of her unwillingness to take responsibility for it, to articulate first person positioning in regard to her wishes and to the events of her life as she knew them. She was hiding in facticity, refusing any transcendence. When I disengaged from the Intersubjective and voiced the position that, regardless of what happens with Daniel, Jill must sort something out with herself, I was experienced as lacking in empathy, as suddenly foreign to Jill, as introducing a foreign element into the session. I believe that, in terms of grammar, I had indeed introduced foreignness. I had spoken a language Jill had long repressed, along with those parts of herself which it could express.

It seemed that something began to move. Jill begins dealing with the terrible loss involved in 'growing up'. She formulates in various ways her wish to have beside her a 'strong man-parent who knows everything', who can provide her with home and security; a man different from her weak, dull, biological father; a man who will never leave her or allow her home to (again) be destroyed. Painfully, she allows another known fact into the realm of experience: Daniel's impotence, his social detachment. She cries bitterly when she tells me of a dream in which her sister jumps off a high jagged rock. Daniel not only fails to catch her. He is crushed by her feather weight, perhaps by her own weight. For the first time she discovers she is angry with her mother for having brought her stepfather into the house and exposed her to his invasive behavior. But she is angrier still that everyone is so far away.

She begins to understand why she is so adamant about marrying Daniel. She can say that she knows that he will never leave her. It seems that, intuitively, she has hit upon the relational sado-masochistic truth: High dependencies forged in pain often replace trust and keep people put. Jill allows herself to admit an additional pragmatic truth: she might be keeping herself unattractive in order not to want or to expect too much. She is traumatized. She fears having anything, because having anything brings with it immediately the possibility of its loss. She can somehow see that she is perhaps navigating the seemingly inevitable life she is leading. She is sad, but at times grateful for these understandings. She is debating if to leave behind forever the pink rooms of her lost childhood.

In terms of truth axes, Jill's pathology was manifested in different ways across different axes. She entered therapy manifesting acute Intersubjective pathology, the origins of which could be found in her past experiences. These experiences defined for her the role of a person who was violated, abused, and victimized. She could inhabit this role indefinitely, in fairly ego-syntonic fashion. What surfaced in therapy was that this Intersubjective pattern, in its entirety, was part of a wider Subjective-Existential pathology, a manifestation of her relinquishment of responsibility, choice and control. Although the abusive relations easily fixated my attention and alarm, remaining in their context drew therapy into impasse. For it seemed that, as long as the therapeutic act focused on intersubjectivity, no progress was made.

The limited explanatory power of the Intersubjective axis revealed itself in what was played out within the transferential relations. Experiencing strongly Jill's passivity and reluctance to assume choice and responsibility through the transference-countertransference relations, I could begin thinking of the way Jill had divorced the possible Subjective-Existential reality she could create. Her stance was mirrored in my experience of being wholly responsible for her life, followed by my resistance to this responsibility. Jill's stoic attitude and my distress in the face of it posed questions that were better articulated and understood in terms of Subjective-Existential and Pragmatic axes, questions regarding a willingness to own a life.

Within the realities constituted by these axes, Jill's image deepened for me and became comprehensible. The drama she was caught up with was only seemingly Intersubjective. Having experienced repeated traumatic disruptions throughout her life (overwhelming facticity), Jill gave up on owning them, and with impressive tenacity refused responsibility within them (rejected transcendence). When choice and responsibility were addressed, when issues were formulated in terms of her own subjectivity (as opposed to relational terms) she was finally shaken from her stoic misery. When she was physically struck, she was indifferent. When she was addressed as an active, subjective agent, she was badly shaken.

When her body was drawn into therapy, it became a bit distanced from its Intersubjectively defined masochism and could be related to in terms of care. The deep regression she entered was a subjective happening, articulating her own resistance to anything that would foreclose the possibility of being a cared for child again. She refused to be the author of her life. Her potent, successful functioning in the world had to be dissociated from conscious experiencing, so as to ensure the impossibility of choice and responsibility. By redefining her bodily self and inverting her passivity, Existential and Pragmatic grammars were introduced into the analytic discourse. In terms of this new Existential language, Jill's troubles manifested in different forms and, more importantly, allowed dissociated self-states to accommodate these troubles.

Jill seems today to have a glimpse of the possibility of being effective in her life, a self-state that, for multiple reasons, had been dissociated from conscious experiencing. It had been crushed under harsh criticism; It had also been sustained as a continuous unarticulated protest: Jill refused to give up the possibility that someone would again take care of her as she had once felt taken care of.

Therapy is out of impasse, but in moving from her impassivity, Jill is frequently impatient and angry; she complains that before therapy she had a better understanding than she now has of what she wanted. She wants to know whether, in continuing therapy, she will find answers or go on losing those she already had. She questions my ability to help her wondering, often anxiously, if I can hold her weight, how far I will be willing to go with her. Her simultaneous disdain for, and identification with, her weak father began to be discussed. Her anxieties at times identify us all – herself, me and Daniel, with this impotent father. Pragmatic selfhood and reality haven't yet made her happy, but she has regained her mental motility.

Case 8: A Chain Worn Differently across Different Axes

Mark is a broker born into a wealthy family of industrialists. He is restless, frenetic and impressively bright. Though he is slightly short – a fact which pains him a great deal - he is popular, also among women. Mark admires his father, who set up an industrial empire, as well as his mother, who turned their house into one of the city's most prestigious social hubs. Regarded as a brilliant professional, he ended his years of internship in dispute after he had taken clients from his employers to set up an independent office of his own. His immense pride in his family was tangibly expressed by the chain around his neck. It had the family name engraved on a pendant, which the mother had ordered in gold for every member of the family.

Mark came for therapy troubled by difficulties in preparing application forms for a second degree abroad, as well as for his ambivalence about an intimate relationship. His feeling was that his girlfriend did not meet the 'aristocratic' standards set by his family and that he himself may not meet the standards set by Harvard and Yale, the schools to which he wanted to apply. After a few sessions he announced that 'therapy was not effective'. Despite this, he continued coming for therapeutic sessions and was fast in learning the therapeutic language. Therapy, however, like other areas of his life, was hampered by unease and restlessness.

In my experience, Mark always hastened to guess my view before I said anything; he spoke nine to the dozen and seemed always to be chasing after something beyond his reach. He was constantly expressing his disappointment in me and said that, in most occupations, the cost of services rendered was linked to output and results. Had I been an engineer, I would have been fired long ago. Feeling quite helpless and assuming my experience somehow reflected his own, I suggested that therapy failed to acquire a quality of significance as an expression of Mark's experience of *himself* as insignificant, in identification with how he was perceived by some members of his family. Mark rejected this interpretation contemptuously and impatiently.

At this stage, Mark did not experience himself as wanting or needing significant relationships. Intimacy was experienced as a 'drag' and he felt no need to be significant to others. Beyond appearing in the 'right' places, meeting up with friends seemed to him to be a waste of time and made him impatient. The interpersonal was for him mostly uninteresting when not defined as achievement. Mark had completely identified with the family ideal, for whom *success* as the one legitimate objective in a person's life. He was oblivious of any wish, thought or impulse that was incompatible with this ideal. He was, in that sense, like a devoutly religious person.

In the chasm between idealization and devaluation meanings, like his experience of self, crumbled and got annihilated. Mark's patterns of experience illustrated the way temporal structure was effectively destroyed within the Ideal axis; the present ceased to exist and the impression of the senses became negligible. As a by-product, particularities of communication also became unimportant. The binary nature and thin fabric of Mark's reality were understood as reflecting the dominance of the Ideal axis of truth, which had been disproportionately enhanced and cast the other axes into the shadow. Another active axis, though, was the Pragmatic one, representing the world as a means to an end, with Mark vigilantly aware of what he may 'use' in it, be it object, opportunity or person.

Mark rejected every interpretation that construed Subjective and Intersubjective meanings and truths. His feelings, as well as the feelings of others, held little interest for him. Although I realized that the therapeutic objective was extracting the foreclosed axes from the splitting and exclusion into which they had been thrust, it was clear I could do this only by making use of the grammars he understood and employed.

Mark always had the best of most things; the best cars, apartments, phones. He was obsessively preoccupied with technological gadgets, always needing the last, state-of-the-art model in every i-pad, laptop and cell-phone. His joy in a new acquisition would crumble in the course of a few days and the latest device would be thrown into a chest with other, older ones. This expensive preoccupation refused signification. When Mark replaced his cellular phone for the third time in the space of just a few months, he lost my phone number, like he did in the previous replacements. I commented that a device that was supposed to be used as a means of communication became meaningless when telephone numbers were lost each time the phone was replaced. My response on the Pragmatic axis stemmed from the lack of compatibility between the ordinary usefulness of the object (be it me or the phone) and its uselessness in Mark's usage.

His response surprised me, because we had never achieved any meaningful discussion of his obsession with novelties. He told me that he'd asked his mother a similar question. His mother was also in the habit of frequently changing cellular phones and every time she did so she would ask Mark to confirm his number. He said that this 'irritates' him and that he has no patience for her stupidity. I suggested that, in repeatedly forgetting his number, his mother was also 'dysfunctional', like a damaged device. I refrained from saying that Mark related to me like to a damaged device that wasn't providing him with the solutions; that he himself was damaged, like his mother, and that he related to me like she did to him. Remaining with Pragmatic considerations, he added that it was ridiculous that she so often upgraded her device. After all, unlike him, she didn't need to receive information across the globe in real time. He illuminated here how Pragmatic reasoning may be used as a defense in the face of the experience of indignity and insult that resulted from his mother's dysfunction.

And yet, a moment later he said something in embarrassment, breaking through the encapsulated Pragmatic preoccupation with gadgets. He said that, in fact, he too didn't really *need* such a state of the art device. He added in a mellow voice that he always wanted the best and, apparently, so did she. I noted the sadness of his tone, wondering what happened. He answered: "It's nothing, I've lost my focus". Outside of the Ideal and the Pragmatic, the multiplicity of information overwhelmed him. The loss of the binary map of his world, with its clear guidelines, was perhaps his first real experience of loss. The small step proved a large leverage for therapy.

On another occasion, Mark toyed with the arm rest of a disintegrating rattan chair in my clinic. He commented that the chair was old and ugly and asked if its tattered state bothered me. Instead of interpreting his response as devaluative, I replied that the chair, with its fibers coming apart, gave my fingers something to pull at. He smiled forlornly and said that I save myself great expenditures of energy by sticking with the chair and not replacing everything that is old. Having said that, he added that it looked awfully "shabby, really shabby…but solid. And quite comfortable. One can sit in such a chair". Then he told me that, before I had spoken of my fingers, he'd not noticed that his fingers were toying with the rattan fibers. Indeed, he added, he couldn't remember at all when he had last paid attention to his fingers. I commented something trivial about fingers being quite important in any task; one can't do a thing without them. He replied that, when executing tasks, the tasks are important, not the fingers themselves; that the task turned the fingers into nothing but equipment. It seemed that, at that moment, he first realized how significations may be crushed, when Pragmatic logic was sole ruler of reality. What made this moment yet more potent was its contact with a part of his body. Perhaps for the first time, this body, this vehicle of himself, was observed as existing in and for itself, absolved of serving a function.

The discussion about the chair was manifestly Ideal: the chair was old, ugly and tattered, was not smart or fashionable. On this level, the trajectory was one of idealization and devaluation, with its Intersubjective counterpart: I am nowhere close to Mark's flashy, smart existence. I chose to answer Mark in line with Pragmatic logic and subjective coloring: The chair gave my fingers something to toy with. From here Mark attached himself to the sensation of the fingers and, moreover, he grasped how 'being' may be subjugated to 'doing' in a restrictive way. There might be here a dawning of understanding as to how the Ideal and Pragmatically determined preoccupation with gadgets blinded him to sensation.

A few weeks later, Mark began to talk about minor episodes of impotence. He addressed these too in terms of failure and performance. His sex life, like so many other elements of his subjective individuality, were repressed or channeled into definitions of achievement. I was sadly aware how his girlfriend was not even mentioned in this context. It was all about him, how well he was doing, everything was described in terms of success or failure.

The Correspondent axis supplies us with an empirical sense of reality. It consists of the details of our daily lives; what we see, hear and feel. Our senses anchor us in present time and the facticity of the space around us. When we do not have a firm Correspondent reality, we travel in life with no compass. The present – in terms of the information it conveys and the presence it allows – is omitted from experience. Mark's reference to his fingers touched upon a new dimension of experiencing that could potentially enrich the reality of his life. I began asking him questions that were correspondently related, often perceived by him as trivial and irritating, but he agreed to answer them. I asked him about his home, his office, his daily life with his girlfriend – who made the coffee? Who tidied up the kitchen in the apartment they had moved into? How is housework done? How did they go about deciding what film to go to? How did he do the shopping? When and in what way did he feel that his office was clean or dirty etc. My questions comprised a Correspondent 'detailed inquiry' of sorts, aimed at hitting upon the source of the particular, hoping it would loosen up fixed realities and constructions that were empty of sensorial significance. Like in Hadar's case, the particularity of sensed reality held Intersubjective ramifications. Mark's associative web began to thicken, the new detailed reality formed new grounds for relationships. His girlfriend's small talk began to sound less jarring. He began to understand what people were saying to each other.

While working on his university applications, we came to see how the pursuit of the unattained, unrealized ideal- as personified in the family's definition of success- completely foreclosed the contact with Mark's feelings and the concreteness of thought. The ideal of studies abroad began to translate into a potential present reality, which he gradually became aware of. He told me that he'd always felt that speaking English was like holding pebbles in his mouth. He repeatedly talked about how, during winters, he suffered from the cold. His language reflected his newly discovered sensed self and, with it, re-linked his ideal and sensed states of self. Sensation was leading him to experience 'spontaneous movements' from within and created a clearer difference between what came from within and what came from without.

He re-assessed his plans along the Pragmatic axis. What would he gain from studying abroad? And why was it previously clear to him that he had no option other than to do that? Was this truth, a truth that was valid for his two elder brothers, valid also for him? Dialogic space began to be created between the axes, the Correspondent and Subjective-Existential axes adding dimensions to a reality formerly construed solely by Ideal and Pragmatic considerations. Correspondent grammar substantiated the present and enabled Mark to approach Subjective truths through his body.

For the first time Mark mentioned his grandfather, a simple and sad man of limited means, who had been distanced from the family by his mother. The grandfather was a collector of coins and stamps, and Mark began to take an interest in them. Hearing his grandfather's story, he began to create a concept of the past. Paying his grandfather a rare visit, he heard of his longing for his late wife, a grandmother Mark never knew. She had been a housewife, far from beautiful, judging by the pictures he had seen. His grandfather told many stories of her, small unimportant, sometimes funny, events they had shared. Mark was amazed at his grandfather's enduring, yet soft and loving, grief. He couldn't at first understand why his grandfather hadn't remarried, how he could bear the lack.

At that time, Mark began to feel phases of disinterest in his work, bouts of depression. He said he couldn't imagine himself grieving that way over anyone. His own inability to experience loss was felt now as a deprivation, a lack. His brother told him that it seemed that therapy wasn't helping him, that he wasn't looking well and advised him to see a renowned therapist who often appeared on the media. Though I didn't appear in his Google search as impressive enough, Mark decided to continue his therapy with me, saying that it was "no easy task for us to have learned to tolerate one another". Trying to preserve the coherence in his life, he told me that he is confident that one day I will also succeed, receive recognition.

I didn't interpret this statement. I left it hanging as testimony to his attachment to the Ideal axis. He so much wanted to idealize. I had no intention of removing this axis from his world. When Mark located my success in the future but could now accept me as I was in the present, he was already expressing the mitigation of the tyranny that the Ideal axis formerly imposed. No longer always present, we left the Ideal to linger as a future image, acting as directive and motivation.

I refrained also from interpreting Mark's shame at the way his mother had distanced her own father from the family. He was aware of this, but avoided relating to or criticizing it. Apparently, the mother had imposed a policy of erasing the past, of avoiding pain and grief, of denying poverty and need and replacing them with omnipotent illusions of abundance. Her inability to cope with the loss of her mother and with her father's withdrawal into himself after his wife's death, had led her to 'flee' into the future. There she could forget her humble past, forget all she lacked in the present. She froze herself and her family into sterile perfection, devoid of pain. By discussing Mark's mother, we rehabilitated time and the past added a whole new dimension to his present malaise. His mother was suppressive of the Subjective, Correspondent, and Intersubjective axes of truth. As a way of protecting a subjectively injured mother, Mark and his brothers adopted the language she could bear.

At around this time, Mark started paying attention to the chain around his neck. The chain, which for many years he had worn with pride, became heavy around his neck. He started to conceal it under his shirt and discovered, to his surprise, that he worried that 'bad' things might happen to him were he to remove it. The fear was testimony to the magical quality that the image of his family was imbued with. The Ideal seems often to converge upon the magical. He jokingly referred to the chain as a 'collar' and once said more seriously that he felt like Frodo Baggins of 'Lord of the Rings', who had to destroy the all-powerful ring he carried on a chain around his neck. One could see how the chain had moved from its existence as an object of permanent significance into an intermediate space within which Mark was able to notice and analyze its different aspects, as well as play with its meanings. In time to come, the chain was torn. Mark was staggered. The reality of the chain, its crude empirical existence, was a complete surprise to him. I said that it was hard to imagine that his parents, his family, also had Correspondent aspects, factual qualities that may be disappointing, frightening and even shocking, because of the vulnerability they implied. On the other hand, these same aspects carried with them a sense of relief, inasmuch as they made it possible to see that the familial decrees were not absolute. When he set off on a challenging voyage to Africa, Mark had to decide whether or not to take the chain with him. Many thoughts arose in his mind about the benefit and the burden that the chain/family held for him. When he decided not to take it with him and gave it to his mother for safekeeping, he saw the hurt in her eyes. She suddenly seemed to him short, like himself.

I was now able to articulate with him the Intersubjective contracts that were required in order to sustain the family myth; the vulnerability discovered with the collapse of that myth; the fear of being left alone and isolated, of having to exist in proportion to his real size, unmerged with the sustaining-but-depleting power of his family. When the chain or, as Mark said, 'only just a chain!' was handed over to his mother, Mark saw the smallness of his mother and his rush of feelings began to constitute Intersubjectivity in his experience.

CHAPTER 7

Translation, Dialectics, Dialogue

In the previous chapters I have discussed the way in which each axis, in its entirety, functions according to fixed grammatical rules and, in that sense, is structured like a language. This chapter draws upon the metaphor of language and develops it in order to examine the different ways in which truth axes may interrelate. My analysis is based on three modes of interrelation between (psychic) languages or elements therein: Translation, dialectic and dialogue.

First, I present the definitions of each of these processes as formulated in philosophic or semiotic thought. Second, I review briefly the ways these concepts are employed, elaborated and implemented in psychoanalytic thought. I show how the different modes of interrelation give rise to three distinct understandings of the psychoanalytic endeavor. Each depicts differently the boundaries between languages and speakers; each locates differently the source of meaning in discourse and each defines differently the objectives of the analytic process. Third, I will show how the different modes of interrelation manifest in the model of truth axes. Finally, I discuss again the concept of self, showing how the three modes elaborate our understanding of the constitution of self, its dynamics and its functioning.

Translation

Defining Translation: In translation, one system of signs which functions according to a given code is replaced by a different system of signs that follows a different code. Translation may be intralingual, when a given message is rendered differently in words of the same language. Interlingual translation involves transferring a message given in one language ('source language') into a different linguistic code ('target language'). Inter-semiotic translation involves the reformulation of a message given in a certain semiotic code- road signs, for example- into another system that may be utterly different from the first- like natural language, for example (Jakobson 1992).

In its traditional sense, translation does not create or discover new associations between elements and does not introduce new meanings. Rather, it takes a set of meanings that are encoded in a source language and maps them onto an identical (or rather, homeomorphic) set of meanings encoded in a target language. Yet, objective obstacles in the process of translation are recognized,

 | DOI 10.1163/9789004314993_009

which render impossible the production of a perfect translation, namely, one that is completely equivalent to the source text. There are inherent differences between languages.[1] Not all that may be thought and articulated in one language may be safely transferred into a different language, consisting of different concepts and categories (Schulte and Biguenet 1992, 7). In philosophic and semiotic thought, this issue is tied up with the question of universality versus singularity in linguistic representation.[2]

Broadly put, universality posits a unity across languages, notwithstanding their phenomenological multiplicity. This unity may be attributable to different factors: Common, innate syntactic structures that are determinants of every language (Chomsky 1975); the reliance of all languages on a universal language of truth (Benjamin 2002); common categories of meaning that are very general and create a shared core across languages (Weigand 2007) and, lastly, a commonly perceived reality that is represented in different ways across languages, but serves as a common reference.

By contrast, the singular or monadic conception of language sees signification as prior to any thought or reality and, in this way, conceives of every language as creating its own ontology. Each language, by means of its semantic and syntactic categories, structures thought and reality in different ways. Signification is determined by the structure of a particular language and therefore cannot be carried over in an equivalent manner into a different language. An extreme version of this conception holds that even perceptual mechanisms are mediated by linguistic concepts and therefore speakers of different languages actually *see* and *sense* different realities (Boas 1964; Sapir 1964).

In the monadic conception, losses and distortions in translation are inevitable. But even the universal approach, where common structures across languages are posited, must give account of the way we bridge the gaps between the parameters that remain free across languages. It too acknowledges that different structure, contents and ways of expression that are particular and contextual cannot be simply and wholly conveyed in the transition between languages.

Since language is a carrier and an embodiment of a culture, it also incorporates a particular ideology that it reflects and expresses (Bassnett 2004; Venuti

1 Jakobson points out how difficult it is to achieve complete equivalence even in intralingual translation, as we have to make use of combination of code units to interpret meaning and as even synonyms cannot guarantee full equivalence.

2 See Steiner (1975) for a comprehensive historical review of the universal-monadic controversy.

1992).[3] In that sense, speaking a language- be it theoretic, artistic or psychic- is effectively an implementation of its values in a total and unconscious manner. A simple example of this may be seen in the manner in which different languages incorporate gender differences. While some encode gender at the grammatical level, where each noun is gendered, whether living or non-living, other languages only encode gender at the semantic level, where it represents real differences. Clearly, a whole attitude to gender comes here with the code itself, prior to any subjective experience.

This aspect of language defines translation as a political and ideological action (Spivak 1993). Translation becomes an arena of negotiations between cultures, placing side by side whole systems of connotations and implications that are typical of the source and the target cultures (Toury 1978). The translator crosses these constraints between and within the source and target cultures, opening a wide door for significations that are novel with regard to the source (Venuti 2008).

The second factor that undermines equivalence and fidelity in translation involves the translator himself. Even when striving, meaning-wise, for transparency or for idealized passivity with regard to the original text and the source-language (the stand advocated by mainstream translation theory, see Robinson 1991, 110; Venuti 1992, 4) the translator is always implicated in his translations. He makes various crucial decisions and these are influenced by his personal preferences. Apart from that, not all translators withhold their subjectivities. Some explicitly and consciously instill their translations with their own personal preferences; others do so without being aware of it.

For years, a 'good' translation was considered one that reduced to a minimum any trace of the translator, i.e., produced a text that does not appear to be a translation.[4] But this translation, Venuti argues, is one that does not allow the

3 Ideology here refers to a body of ideas and doctrines that reflect a given group's needs and aspirations and serves as its ideational platform for structuring a social or political system. As a concept, ideology refers to all processes, signs, symbols and values associated with this platform. Some view Ideology as a necessary medium through which subjects relate to their social system. Others see ideology as a means for mobilizing political power. For a detailed in depth discussion of ideology, see Eagleton 1991.

4 In terms of the translator's role, the good translation was traditionally considered to be one that makes the target- reader comfortable in reading the text. This implies the tempering of foreign influences that originate in the culture or grammar of the source language or of the translator. In his lecture 'On the different Methods of Translating', Schleiermacher (Schleiermacher 1813\1992) identified two options that stand before the translator – 'domestication' (drawing the author towards the reader) and 'foreignizing' (drawing the reader towards the author). Diverging from tradition, he showed clear preference for the latter and spoke against the

identification of the multiple determinants that affected it and, indeed, hides them. When the veil of transparency is lifted, the translator is immediately revealed in two aspects of his unconscious motive: The personal and the social-ideological aspects that inevitably leave their mark on the translated text. Becoming assimilated in the text, they are then mistakenly attributed to the original text.

The translator's biases and choices produce a significant impact. He often imposes upon his translation political and social hierarchies that structure the target language, and indeed may even use the translation as a means of undermining them (Venuti 2008, 34). These influences are accepted as inevitable, but Venuti stresses the importance of their not remaining *invisible* or unconsciously effected. Rather, the politically and socially minded translator will appraise these effects and the way they affect his translations.

Douglas Robinson, like Venuti, contends that the translator's presence must be clearly and distinctly defined, and in a bold move suggests him as the co-author of the original text (Robinson 1991, 110). This approach gives rise to a host of ethical questions: Who is the author of the translated text? To whom does it belong? Who is entitled to introduce change in it? If the translator introduces pre-meditated changes, does he state them explicitly or does he insert them in a way that will make them attributable to the original author? And when introducing changes, does the translator see himself as an instrument of the original author's intention or as a conveyor of a different agenda? Does he have ideological identifications that cohere with those of the original author? And what should be done, asks Robinson, when the translator finds himself to be a better writer than the original author? What is added and what is lost in translation? I will proceed now to review the use of the concept of translation and these associated conundrums as they manifest in psychoanalytic discourse.

Translation and Psychoanalysis: Freud often used the metaphor of translation in order to explain the essential transition that is effected by psychoanalysis – from unconscious to conscious, from the language of drive, wish and desire to the language of words and facts[5] (SE 23:96). On the intra-psychic level, the

---

automatic standardization created by the domestication method. For Schleiermacher, the translator is not a mere conduit for foreign works. Rather, he is a cultural ambassador educating his readership in foreign customs, expression, thought and sensibility. In this way the translator combats xenophobia and enriches his own culture and language, integrating foreign influence and nuance within it.

5 It should be noted that, according to Freud, translation processes also occur between nonverbal languages that are different from each other. Dream work is defined as translation of a

transition is usually made by verbally articulating materials such as visual images, emotions and phantasies. The conversion of these phenomena into words is the means by which they are made conscious (SE 14:165). Accordingly, the role of the analyst is defined as translating the patient's unconscious processes into conscious ones (SE 14:166; SE 15:435; SE 23:159; SE 23:286). The analyst translates dreams (SE 9:60; SE 9:110) into rational processes (SE 22:220), transforms its manifest content into an articulated wish (SE 15:129).

As Freud saw it, symptomatic, primary process languages – hysterical, phobic or obsessive – conceal an existing architecture which may be revealed and converted into secondary processes. His model clearly distinguishes both the drive-laden, symptomatic language from the verbal one, and the subjectivity of the author\analysand from that of the translator\analyst. The analyst\translator is expected to understand the meaning of the original patient\author, have perfect knowledge of both source and target languages, and be able to clarify obscurities in the symptom\text. This knowledge is the source of his authority. He is cautious not to contaminate the original subject matter with his own subjectivity and, as a translator, seeks fidelity and equivalence of meaning. The translation as a therapeutic act reconstructs and reorganizes the psychic material and structure of the patient.

In a letter to Fliess, Freud describes translation as a constructive activity in mental life, and describes the psyche as constituted by successive registrations of the psychical achievement of successive epochs of life. Freud posited that psychic structure is achieved by a process of stratification, whereby "memory is present not once but several times over...laid down in various species of indications" (SE 1:232). "At the frontier between two...epochs, a translation of the

script or language into a different language (SE 15:172), while the manifest content of dreams is mostly a translation of latent thoughts into visual formats (SE 18:242; SE 20:43–44). Dream work does not maintain the distinctions of the original text when translated to another language (SE 15:171–172), and its manifest content is a tainted translation, abridged and incomprehensible (SE 20:43). This content may then be re-translated into a conscious and understandable language. Visual screen memories are another example of the translation of memory traces into visual images (SE 3:321). Nonverbal translations are also characteristic of hysteria, in which attacks are described as "nothing else but phantasies translated into the motor sphere, projected on to motility and portrayed in pantomime". (SE 9:229). Translations in hysteria can be mediated by symbolic processes that explain the form of the symptom. Thus, the neurological symptom that appeared on Elizabeth Von R's face was semantically interpreted by Freud as connected to her experience of her husband's comment as a slap in the face. The hysterical patient who becomes obsessive is a "bilingual document" (SE 12:319). In this manner, dreams and hysterical phobias were understood by Freud as translations of ideas into different languages of psychic reactions (SE 4:259).

psychical material must take place... Every later transcript inhibits its predecessor and drains off the excitatory process from it" (ibid. 235).

Repression, or a 'failure of translation', is effectively a disruption in the successive translations of psychic materials into mature forms, leaving the untranslated material in primitive, anachronistic language, different from the one employed in the more developed areas of the psyche. Psychopathology is construed here as a disruption in processes of translation: "I explain the peculiarities of the psychoneuroses by supposing that this translation has not taken place in the case of some of the material... Thus an anachronism persists: In a particular province fueros are still in force, we are in the presence of survivals" (ibid. 234).

Thinkers after Freud maintained that translation serves as a 'truly theoretical nodal word', a 'unified field concept' that illuminates elements and angles of psychoanalysis (Mahony 1980; Bass 1985; Priel 2003). The model of translation in psychoanalytic process implies a few presuppositions: Firstly, it assumes that the text that the analyst encounters- in the form of transference relations, dreams and symptoms- has a fixed, particular meaning that may be translated into the language of secondary processes. Secondly, the symptom-encoded source text is understood to have a single identified author – the analysand. The Freudian subject, bodily-based, is essentially distinct and differentiated from other subjectivities. The translator must withhold his subjectivity in order not to mar the original meanings of the author\patient as encoded in symptomatic language. Although it may be impossible to achieve complete equivalence and fidelity in translation, it remains the analyst's\translator's commitment to aspire to do so. Thirdly, translation assumes a conversion, a substitution of the old by the new. One language is effectively displaced by a different one. Fourthly, the new is considered the 'better', the healthier of the two languages. The translation from the primary to the secondary representation enhances reality testing, as it distinguishes the real from the illusory, the true from the distorted and the traumatic events from their symptomatic conversion.

Healthy development is predicated on the ability of the evolving principle of reality to dominate the logic of primary process. The analyst's role consists of joining forces with this principle and channeling the energy of the drives into accepted sublimated modes. This is the accepted definition of Freud's statement 'where id was- ego shall be' (SE 22:80). This therapeutic agenda is formulated, in line with the conception of development, as a linear chronological evolution, from the illusory and primitive to the mature and realistic.

Despite his careful and methodical approach, Freud recognized the fact that the message as encoded in the source (primary process) could not be truly equivalent to the target languages of psychoanalysis (secondary process). Therefore, the analyst's translation of the analysand's discourse must inevitably hold within it a *difference*.[6] Freud emphasized the inherent difference between the modes of conscious and unconscious processes, where one was never a mere reflection or copy of the other.

An additional complexity in translation has to do with the analyst/translator's subjectivity. On the face of it, Freud's analyst/translator is naïve, transparent, a tabula rasa. He converts a primary, primitive, drive laden language into a mature one and, beyond that, his presence is not supposed to be felt. He should aspire to have "undergone a psychoanalytic purification and have become aware of those complexes which would be apt to interfere with his grasp of what the patient tells him" (SE 12:115–116). And yet, Freud assumed, there would be resistances at work in the analyst's mind that might disturb the analyst's ability to grasp the true meaning of his patient's discourse.

I will now explain what is lost (and gained) in translation by recourse to the inherent difference between languages and its convergence upon the translator's subjectivity.

What is Lost in Translation? In 'Three Essays on Sexuality' Freud describes maternal care as inevitably involving sexual excitation (SE 7:223), but he does not discuss its repercussions in the child. In his 1949 essay 'The Confusion of Tongues', Ferenczi addresses the vicissitudes of these early sexual messages and excitations as they exist in the dyadic space of the mother and the child. The child, states Ferenczi, understands only the language of tenderness and when he meets passionate love, "the consequence must needs be that of confusion of tongues, which is emphasized in the title of this address" (Ferenczi 1949, 228). What cannot be understood and translated into the child's psychic language is dissociated and split off from it. Many such events will bring about multiple splitting, with each split-off part 'speaking' a different language and giving rise to fragmentary discontinuities.

Laplanche, like Ferenczi, addresses the sexual messages the child encounters, but whereas Ferenczi sees these encounters as *possibly* occurring, Laplanche sees them as inevitable. In this context, Laplanche formulates the

6 Even in Freud's metaphor of transmission he does not describe transparent, direct processes of transferal. Rather, he describes a process involving deconstruction and reconstruction: "[the analyst] must adjust himself to the patient as a telephone receiver is adjusted to the transmitting microphone. Just as the receiver converts back into sound waves the electric oscillations in the telephone line… , so the doctor's unconscious is able to form the derivatives of the unconscious which are communicated to him, to reconstruct that unconscious, which has determined the patient's free associations" (SE 12:115–116). We find here the idea that the basic transformation of codes is never a simple transferal of meaning.

concept of 'primal seduction', which becomes nodal in his understanding of psychic structure and functioning. For Laplanche, primal seduction is an inevitable part of the basic movement of parental care. It consists of the adult proffering to a child "verbal, nonverbal and even behavioral signifiers that are pregnant with unconscious sexual significations" (Laplanche 1987, 126). The messages that the adult delivers to the child carry an element of disturbance or noise because of the essential asymmetry between the adult and the child. The adult has a developed unconsciousness and sexuality, and therefore his messages to the child, from a psychoanalytic perspective, are compensatory configurations of his inhibited phantasies and sexual excitations. The child translates this sort of a message to the best of his ability, but there will always be an untranslated 'remainder' that renders the message enigmatic, and interferes with the ordinary, regulatory and digestive processes of the psyche.

Laplanche differentiates between two forms of incorporative processes, which he terms 'implantation' and 'intromission':

> While implantation allows the individual to take things up actively, at once translating and repressing, the process of intromission is one which blocks and short-circuits the differentiation of the agencies in the process of their formation and puts into the interior an element resistant to all metabolisation.
>
> LAPLANCHE 1990, 136

It is this violent intromission of adult signifiers that paralyzes the ordinary processes of primal translation-repression by the infant. The result is a residue in the psyche of something that cannot be translated and processed in the ordinary manner. These are 'unsignifying signifiers', which have lost their semiotic function and have acquired an object-like character. For Laplanche, this is the origin of the total exciting drive that endlessly attacks the body's homeostasis in its demand for release. What is lost in translation becomes a drive that seeks expression, seeks future additional possibility of translation and assimilation.

The Analyst's Subjectivity- Personal and Ideological Bias in Translation: A neat illustration of the translator's subjectivity is given in Freud's essay on de Vinci. Bass (1985) described how an unconscious mistake in translation heavily affected Freud's theorizing when writing of de Vinci. In this essay, Freud accepts the translation of the Italian word 'nibio' – meaning 'kite', into the German word 'geier' – meaning 'vulture'. Freud provides a psychoanalytic interpretation of de Vinci's assumed homosexuality based on the presence of the assumed vulture in his childhood memory\phantasy. The vulture is a bird perceived as both male and female, suggesting the shift in de Vinci's desire from the maternal breast to the penis. The mistake, Bass claims, originated in Freud's unconscious wish to validate his ideas of a primitive maternal phallus and archaic pictography in dreams and phantasies (Bass 1985, 136).

Another example of a translator's bias, according to Arrojo (2007), appears in Laplanche's new French translation of Freud, where traces are seen of Laplanche's unresolved oedipal issues with his mentor, Lacan. Arrojo points out that this translation changes many of the expressions upon which Lacan formulates his theories. In that sense, Laplanche's oedipal rivalry with Lacan appears in a camouflaged way in his translation of Freud and biases his choice of terms (Arrojo 2007, 174).

The bias of the analyst's subjectivity in his capacity as translator of the patient's primary processes has been extensively discussed in classical psychoanalysis in terms of counter-transference that, ideally, must be abdicated. In contemporary psychoanalytic thought, this aspired abdication has been recognized as impossible to achieve and the analyst's counter-transferential response has been investigated in the various ways in which it influences metapsychological formulation and clinical technique.[7]

Irwin Hoffman was one of the first to openly acknowledge the inevitable involvement of the analyst's subjectivity in his work, arguing that only by following such acknowledgement may the analyst's influence be assessed, understood and actively modulated. Hoffman argues that while analysts, by and large, recognize the fact that they are not neutral and that objectivity is impossible, they paradoxically maintain the belief that a neutral stance actually exists and should be attained. It is this aspiration that Hoffman finds both hypocritical and evasive of responsibility. As he puts it, the analyst's hands are not clean. They will never be clean.

Moreover:

> The fact is that analysts cultivate 'unobjectionable positive transference', which may include a certain degree of idealization. The resulting special power that the analyst has gives him or her a fighting chance against the destructive influences of the patient's past, but there is also reason for the participants to be concerned about the danger of the patient's compliance with what the empowered analyst seems to want.
>
> HOFFMAN 2009, 619

---

7 The move of the analyst from this 'transparent' Freudian position to an actively subjective one is discussed in detail in Govrin's (2004) book.

The point here for Hoffman is that we must give account of how we influence our patients and accept responsibility for it. The analyst must engage in a self-inquiry that examines cultural, moral, characterological, and counter-transferential influences, of which he or she may not be conscious (ibid. 619–620).

Hoffman takes an additional significant step in investigating the analyst's unconscious influence when he illustrates the way psychoanalytic theories and perspectives effectively actualize ideological positions and ethical values, *without this being evident at the time of their clinical implementation.* Addressing this point, Hoffman discusses, for example, "the ideology of psychic determinism" (Hoffman 2009, 828). In its classic Freudian construal, "the patient's freedom was precluded by the combination of forces acting on his ego" (ibid.). This constriction of freedom applies to the therapist as well as to the patient: "the analyst's freedom was also virtually eliminated by the requirement that he or she follow whatever scientific method was necessary to explore and discover the truth about the patient's unconscious uninfluenced by the analyst" (ibid.).

The issues of determinism and free will are a philosophic matter but they translate, as Hoffman illuminates, into the ethical. This is not problematic in itself; it only becomes so when this translation is effected unawares, assimilated into theories whose manifest contents are totally removed from this subject matter and thus conceal it. Clinicians often tend to adopt theories whose basic tenets suit in various ways their personal tendencies, their values and their ethics. Theory and the values it incorporates presume an unarticulated 'horizon' of preexistent meanings. These are actualized and implemented clinically in ways that influence the patient, without this action being deliberated, reflected upon and accounted for by the analyst.

What we end up with, as Hoffman states and I elaborate, is a whole chain of influences on clinical action: Personal, theoretical, ethical and ideological. Whether we intend it or not we produce and implement values. Or as Hanly puts it: "psychoanalytic work does in fact alter the values of our patients" (Hanly 1993, 8). Attitudes regarding counter-transferential reactions are also ideologically determined and are heavily value-laden. Kohut, for example, valued dependency. In his view autonomy may well be an expression of denial and avoidance. Freud, Kernberg and Mahler, of course, advocate the opposite. For them, individuality and autonomy are viewed as positive objectives; from yet another angle, they may be viewed as serving capitalist culture that requires well-functioning self-sufficient individuals. Freud advocated and valued objectivity. Winnicott gave dreaminess its positive standing. Relationists believe in mutuality. Others see their practice of self-disclosure as an exhibitionistic tendency.

From the moment an analyst makes his theoretical choice and joins institutions that house like-minded professionals, a theoretical guideline becomes an imperative. The clinical implementation of theory becomes an imposition of ethics that is not clearly accounted for and, indeed, is often obfuscated by theoretical rationale. A similar awareness of values implicitly embedded in theory was proposed by feminist critiques of Freudian psychoanalysis (Chodorow 1980; Gilligan 1982; 1986).

Hanly (1993) analyzes the danger of psychoanalysis ossifying into ideological truth, despite the challenge it had originally posed to various ideological, religious and philosophic beliefs about human nature. This danger of ideological deterioration exists and originates, as Hanly sees it, in the process of training analysis. In a didactic analysis, a candidate enters into regressive transferential relations with his analyst, which may "facilitate reality testing and ego maturation everywhere else, [but] compromise the analysand's ability to be objective about his analyst and perpetuates a regressed dependency on him" (Hanly 1993, 4). It may also bring about idolatry of persons and ideas that may cause them to be perceived as an infallible "system of absolute truth" (ibid. 5). In this way theory, ideology included, is incorporated in an uncritical manner.

This intertwining of ideology and theory is not particular to classic theory, but rather applies across all psychoanalytic stances. Maxson (1992), for example, discusses the way relational thinking has changed attitudes regarding autonomy. She cites Stolorow and Atwood, who find autonomy to be grounded in "an isolated mind perspective…that conflicts with the contemporary psychoanalytic goals of mutual recognition and attachment" (ibid. 59). Hoffman (1983; 1991) argues that psychoanalysis has, to its detriment, relied on an outdated 'asocial' conception of the patient as a person in isolation. This sort of criticism, claims Maxson, undermines the idea that autonomy is a basic human need that promotes personal strength and self-sufficiency in favor of a differently defined social matrix (Maxson 2009).

What I stress here is the connection between theoretical assumptions and ideology. In their clinical implementation, different theories prioritize certain values and actualize particular ethical stands. Every psychoanalytic theory incorporates basic assumptions about the nature of man and his ties with the surrounding environment. These assumptions imply therapeutic objectives that are also value laden. Especially, mental 'health' is defined according to values and so does the stated objective of analysis. These values offer professionals an anchorage of certainty, but risk imposing upon analysis some rigid forms of truth and ideology. Translation, a replacement of one language with another, is effectively the replacement of certain values by others.

Translation and Truth Axes: As I described in the previous sections, the psyche is predisposed to create six basic organizations, six grammatical patterns. Throughout her development, the child constructs different axes and languages that are driven by her innate basic needs. But this development is always situated in a particular environment in which certain languages are more frequently and comfortably used than others. This may encourage the development of certain grammars and inhibit others, thus rendering the child fluent in some languages, while mute and tentative in others.

Borrowing terms from Laplanche and Ferenczi, I claim that, when one encounters (internally or externally) a message that is formulated in an unknown or unemployed language, it creates 'untranslated' enclaves in the psyche. As I see it, this unknown language is not necessarily sexually predicated. It may be any language that expresses any organic need and that is given to the child by an adult in a form which he cannot digest. When a message is represented in an unknown language, it remains enigmatic and causes disequilibrium, usually manifesting in indigestible excitation. Of course, all six language types are organic to the psyche but, if they remain undeveloped at the time in which they touch upon consciousness, they cause the same effect of indigestible excitation. The languages that the child can neither speak nor comprehend become untranslatable, foreign fixtures in his psyche, creating complexes that are retained in unprocessed form. They will constantly seek release, constantly seek possibilities of re-translation and assimilation.

Freud and Laplanche posited that these enclaves will be processed by transforming their primitive language into one more developed. My claim here picks up the dynamics described, but implements them in a multilingual environment that does *not* posit diachronic development among languages and does not believe that materials of one language may be translated into a different language. *Rather it argues for their inherent difference and untranslatability into one uniform language. Therefore, what these enclaves demand is not translation but expression.* What has been repressed demands possibility of expression and legitimation of positioning in psychic space.

A child growing in a multilingual environment will have a better chance to learn how to employ and comprehend various grammars. A child growing in an environment which has accorded dominance to one language at the expense of others will necessarily form these enclaves of unexpressed registers. Although particular situations may require dominant involvement of one grammar, this always remains a local condition. The general case remains that all axes have organic and necessary functions in the psyche.

Introduced here is a trade-off. A particular language may be appointed singular status and dominance as a means of managing particular life conditions. It might prove efficient and optimal in the situation employed. Permanently employed to the exclusion of other axes, this situation will limit the subject's scope of signification in general and the analytic space in particular. Translation in the sense of conversion, substitution and displacement is an act that restricts the ability to perceive, understand and interpret certain human dimensions and to experience their associated fears and hopes. On the other hand it affords the clarity and comprehensibility the use of one language (in place of many) may grant. In all cases, it is a value-laden act that prioritizes one (ideological) language over another, situating the translator as a mediator between them. As such, it must be identified, reflected upon and articulated.

The model of translation, implemented as environmental imperative or therapeutic act, will always involve loss, repression and subjugation of the omitted or substituted languages. Since each axis of truth originates in a basic innate need, the order of priority among them is necessarily a secondary imposition. The prime task of therapy is to balance out for such secondary impositions when they give rise to distress.

The Freudian analyst aspires to be a 'transparent' translator, unencumbered by bias, tendency and values. Over the years it has been largely accepted in psychoanalytic (and semiotic) theorizing that such transparency does not and cannot exist. Translators and analysts must be aware that they always exert an influence – personal and ideological. Indeed, a choice of psychoanalytic theory is already, in many ways, a value-laden choice, expressing ideals of 'healthy' subjectivity that are placed as objectives to be attained.

An analyst making a choice of theoretical orientation should be able to understand the truths implied within it and the effect of their adoption on other grammars and truths. Goldberg (1984) illustrated how concepts employed by different psychoanalytic theories (part-object, self-object and transitional object) are not interchangeable though they may all refer to the same early object of attachment. Their mutual untranslatability is rooted in the different systems to which they belong, systems that hold different assumptions on the nature of the subject and his development.

The concept of truth axis is one which tries to contain the epistemological and ideological aspect of language by means of admitting and advocating its plurality in the psyche. It acknowledges the human demand for direction, goal and certainty. But simultaneously, it creates the possibility of dynamic movement among certainties, without allowing any given grammar or truth to dominate our life and thought, either as analysts or as analysands.

Dialectics

Defining Dialectics: The philosophical dialectic method as originally articulated in Ancient Greece is rooted in the recognition of man's ability to think, obtain knowledge and reflect. As a method of argument and investigation, dialectics examined basic assumptions and revealed logical contradictions within and among them. The metaphysical assumption underlying this form of dialectic is that objective truth may be obtained by a pure rational process. This process reveals mistaken and inaccurate, subjective assumptions and, by being critical about its own method, promotes true and correct knowledge of reality.

Modern dialectics, by contrast, dismisses the classic dichotomy between objective thinking and subjective perception of reality. Modern philosophers, led by Kant and later Hegel, collapsed the division of objective and subjective, consciousness and the world of 'things', conceptual process and history. Hegelian consciousness was no longer perceived as separate from the world and in dualistic relations with it. Rather, it was understood to be formed, negated and preserved by its empirical 'other'. This form of dialectic no longer seeks to replace the mistaken with the correct, but takes an existential leap which places the objective and the subjective in dialectical relations of recognition and definition, deeming irrelevant the search for a one dimensional 'objective' reality.

The transition from classical to modern dialectics leads to a new perspective on matter, its boundaries and its potential transfigurations. While the old philosophic system perceives homeostasis and differentiation as universal goals, the new approach claims the opposite: Matter is always in motion and transformation is the formative principle of the universe. Unlike in the Aristotelian logic, even opposites are not perceived as permanently and statically distinct. Every process involves the collision of opposites, as well as their mutual integration, negation and confirmation, culminating in the forming of a merged entity (synthesis) which will, in turn, undergo the same process anew, with its own phenomenal contradictions. Development is understood as driven by the force of these contrasting opposites, where evolution constantly aims higher with every synthesis it creates. Finally, in Hegelian logic, quantity transforms into quality, like when rising temperatures transform water into steam and falling temperatures turn it into ice. The main impact here is that gradual changes over time have some critical points at which the object changes its nature and becomes quite different from what it has been beforehand.

A third version of dialectic is presented here, that effects a subtle shift in the meaning of the Hegelian synthesis. It preserves the Hegelian idea of interacting differences that incessantly change, but assumes also that something of their original condition at starting point remains unchanged. Moreover, the synthetic product of dialectic is formed by means of *supplement and complementarity rather than by fusion and merger*. This mode of dialectic was articulated in the context of translation.

Goethe is often perceived as the original formulator of this dialectic when stating that in translation: "the foreign and the native, the unknown approximation and the known, keep moving toward each other" (Goethe in Robinson 1991, 88). The principle here is that the negations – the foreign and the domestic – keep converging upon each other.

Goethe undermined the possibility of clear differentiation between languages and Derrida (1992) continued this project by undermining the distinction between original and translation. The difference between the two may seem obvious, both technically and temporally, but Derrida problematizes it by arguing that not all translations and not all originals have the same status. Every text has a close predecessor, rendering it a translation and, by induction, a multiple translation. It is never possible to pin down and define an 'original author' just as it is impossible to define or identify a 'signified' pure of signifiers. There is no primal word, not even a proper word, that is in itself pure, whole and sufficient unto itself: "For, in the very tongue of the original narrative there is a translation, a sort of transfer, that gives immediately (by some confusion) the semantic equivalent of the proper name, which by itself, as a pure proper name it would not have" (Derrida 1992, 224). Every word, every *name*, says Derrida, begs translation. Even "God weeps over his name…he pleads for a translator" (ibid. 227).

These ideas are both elaborated and stated plainly in Borges's thought of dialectic translation, which is based on two assumptions: The first is that an 'original' text does not exist. The second is that the reader of a text is always an active elaborator of its untranslatable meaning. A text, according to Borges, cannot be completely original because it acts as a translation of the author's thought, a translation that always also distorts the originary thoughts to the extent of rendering it impossible to reconstruct. But even if we were to reconstruct the original thought, we may never be able to clearly separate it from the tradition in which it brewed. In that sense, every text is a second order translation, a translation of a translation. The inevitable transformations introduced by the translator are perceived as enhancing and enriching the work, complementing and supplementing it (Borges 1999).

Dialectics in Psychoanalytic Theory: In 1941 Karen Horney left the orthodox, Freudian psychoanalytic school together with a number of other analysts. Horney questioned the basic assumption of the traditional approach, namely, that man is a biological being driven by sex, greed, and cruelty (Horney 1946, 66). This description, for Horney, suits the neurotic, whereas a healthy man is capable of being enriched by his biological potential and free of it to the extent that enables him to change, adapt and rise above it.

The psychoanalytic community rejected Horney not only because of the content of her ideas, but mostly because of her modes of reasoning. Horney argued for the existence of *dialectic relation* between the individual and his surroundings, and saw this dialectic as entailing a potential for growth and change. Debating Horney's innovative approach, Ludwig Jekels contended that, because it implies the possibility of unlimited development, dialectic denies the basic tenets of psychoanalysis that define the limitations of man and humanity (Jekels 1941, 242). Illustrating further the incompatibility of dialectics and basic psychoanalytic concepts he summarizes: "No, honestly, there is no bridge from psychoanalysis to dialectic".[8]

Over the years, modern psychoanalytic thinking has increasingly been influenced by the Hegelian dialectic. This line of thinking questioned classical distinctions between mental categories and agencies and re-formulated ideas about the processes of identity formation and its change in psychoanalytic treatment. A prime example of this inclination can be seen in Ogden's work. In two articles published in 1992, Ogden attempts to demonstrate that the modern dialectic approach is *not* new to psychoanalytic thinking, but is rather a basic and essential component of it, indeed, implicit in Freud's line of thought. Ogden accepts Freud's formulation of a diachronic developmental approach – from the unconscious to the conscious, from primary to secondary thought processes. But he is of the opinion that, at the same time, Freud constantly struggled with the limitations of linear thinking and positivistic conceptualizations of causality. This linearity of thought, claims Ogden, obscures the

---

8 Jekels begins his argument thus: "In order to avoid misunderstanding I wish to emphasize, that I do not desire to make a polemic against Dr Horney's New Ways in Psycho-Analysis the main subject of this lecture. This polemic should rather be a transition to a much more important topic, namely the discussion of the relationship between psychoanalysis and dialectic" (Jekels 1941, 228). Exemplifying the impossibility of dialectic in psychoanalysis, he discusses the concept of the Freudian unconscious: "This contrast opens a gulf between the two doctrines [psychoanalysis and dialectic] on account of the following difference. "Dialectic implies that every state of a phenomenon conceals in itself its strictly contradictory tendency: its negation. Now listen to Freud's conception of the unconscious: "The unconscious consists of representations of instincts which are impulses of desires. These impulses of instincts are coordinated, they do not contradict each other". Further: "There are no negations in this system". Summarizing, Freud calls the lack of contradiction "the chief characteristic of the unconscious". (ibid. 251).

radical nature of the psychoanalytic project. It undermines the idea that the experiencing subject can be understood only as a product of an ongoing process in which he constitutes and transcends himself in the dialectic of conscious and unconscious processes, unity and separateness, interiority and exteriority (Ogden 1992b, 613). The processes are "always generating mutual influence, so that each pole is not only dependent on its opposite for its meaning, but is actually imbued with qualities that are more prominently defining of the opposite" (Hoffman 2001, 480; Ogden 1994, 14).

In the past decades, many traditional psychoanalytic concepts have been reexamined and rephrased in terms of modern dialectics, especially in Relational and intersubjective psychoanalytic literature. Becker and Shalgi (2006) review how processes of signification and change are defined, for example in terms of dialectics occurring between ritual and spontaneity (Hoffman 1999), meaning and death (Becker 1973), old and new (Greenberg 1999), and repetition and transformation (Lachmann 2001). Issues focusing on the tension between the self and object relation have been expressed in the dialectics of mutuality and autonomy (Aron 1996; Mitchell 1997), recognition and destruction (Benjamin 1992), self-expression and self-subordination and presence and absence (Peltz 1998).

These opposites depict contrasting ways of being defined as part of a mutual, fruitful existence. Their interaction may be understood by referencing the Kleinian positions: the positions are different; movement is effected between them: this movement gives rise to certain compositions that would not have existed without it. And yet the basic positions as defined do not change. This is one mode of dialectic that exists on a conceptual level, and it must be differentiated from a dialectic that exists on an epistemological level.

To construe and illustrate the difference between these two levels in which we can follow the workings of dialectics, I will draw on Mills's (2005) helpful differentiation between two forms of intersubjectivity in the analytic literature: A developmental view and a systems view. Benjamin may represent the first form, presenting as developmental achievements the recognition of the subjectivity of the other and the ability for mutual recognition. Both are borne of the dialectics between recognition and destruction. As I understand it, both her account of mature intersubjectivity and her differentiation between object and subject relatedness is comfortably situated in critical realism, with its demarcation of the internal from the external. This is different from the work of Hoffman (1991) and Mitchell (1991), for example, who posit dialectics as having a transcendental, *constitutive* function in regard to subjectivity. This is because subjectivity is always both situated in, and determined by, an intersubjective matrix, from which it is inseparable in any form. In the following comments I discuss a few intersubjective thinkers who situate dialectic on the second level described here.

The Status of the Subject in the Dialectic Process: If we follow the dialectic logic through, the self in its entirety ceases to be a distinct entity and becomes a process of transformation that repeatedly defines the other and is, in turn, defined by the other in ongoing interactions. In this perspective, the subject of analysis forms and reforms in an intersubjective space by a process of mutual and creative negation, preservation and recreation (Ogden 1992b, 619). Subjectivity and intersubjectivity are thus inextricably bound together.

The constitutive nature of the dialectic process in analysis appears powerfully in Ogden's notion of the 'analytic third' where, through the interplay of subjectivities, an additional intentionality arises and takes part in analysis. In an article entitled *The Analytic Third*, Ogden (1994) makes a transition from a two-person to a three-person psychology, with the analytic third perceived as "an entity that subjugates the subjectivities of both analyst and analysand and that seems to take on a life of its own". Regarding this entity, Ogden explicitly contends that:

> The task is not to tease apart the elements constituting the relationship in an effort to determine which qualities belong to whom; rather, from the point of view of the interdependence of subject and object, the analytic task involves an attempt to describe the specific nature of the experience of the unconscious interplay of individual subjectivity and intersubjectivity.
>
> OGDEN 2004, 168

Ogden's dialectics has aroused broad sympathetic applause, alongside severe criticism. Hanly (2004) accepts that empathic identification is crucial in allowing the analyst to experience and imagine the inner world of the analysand. Nevertheless, he doubts the need for a third entity in order to achieve or describe this experience. Integration and loss of boundaries are part of the revival of early experiences, but they don't necessarily

> warrant the inference of a third entity that exists independently of the different transferential, countertransferential, and reality-bound relations formed by one member of the analytic dyad with the other…a third participant…a co-created subjectivity of some sort, with some kind of life of its own.
>
> HANLY 2004, 286

Mills (2005) doubts that an entity such as Ogden's 'third' may possess any of the defining features of subjectivity, namely, agency, autonomy, freedom and so forth.[9] He questions the definition both of the concept of the 'third' and the concept of the 'shared intersubjective field', on which the former is based (see also Goldberg 1998[10]).

Positing a shared subjectivity in the analytic process undermines the patient-subject as an autonomous agency (see also my discussion of this matter in Chapter 3). Accordingly, concepts associated with it lose their transparency. Introspection becomes a process that is in essence dialogic; free association becomes a co-constructed process; differentiation becomes an illusion.

The Analytic Act in the Psychoanalytic Dialectic: In a dialectic understanding of development and the therapeutic encounter, the distinction between realistic and subjective, self and other, is no longer possible. Development occurs in a psychological field established by the different subjectivities of child and environment, of patient and therapist. In that sense, there is a mutual process in play, a process in which the representations of all participants in the interaction are established and reestablished, mediated by processes of assimilation and accommodation. This understanding reformulates the meaning of psychoanalytic interpretation.[11]

Originally understood as effecting the transition of *pre-existent meanings* from unconscious, drive-laden expression to consciously articulated verbal

---

9 "How can a system acquire an agency of its own? How can the interpersonal field become its own autonomous agent? What happens to the agency of the individual subjects that constitute the system? How can a 'third' agency materialize and have determinate choice and action over the separately existing human beings that constitute the field to begin with? What becomes of individual freedom, independence, and personal identity with competing needs, intentions, wishes, and agendas that define individuality if the 'system' regulates individual thought, affect, and behavior? What happens to the system if one participant decides to no longer participate? Does the system die, is it suspended, does it reconstitute later? What becomes of the system if one participant exerts more will or power over that of the other subject? Is not the system merely a temporal play of events rather than an entity? And if these experiences were possible, it would render the system impotent, acausal, and nonregulatory, which directly opposes the relational view that the intersubjective field, dyadic system, relational matrix, or analytic third has causal influence and supremacy over the individual autonomy of its constituents" (Mills 2005, 161).

10 "So, too, does the idea of a shared intersubjective field leave one puzzled as to what composes the field, how one utilizes this shared entity, and just what happens to it when the individual subjectivities go their own way" (Goldberg 1998, 223).

11 An excellent discussion of the many modes of interpretation is given in Aguillaume (2007). I focus here only on the difference between discovering meaning and co-creating it.

expression, interpretation here becomes a joint event, predicated on emotional interaction in the here-and-now analytic experience. The psychic history of the analytic subject is no longer the object revealed by interpretation; rather, it is created in the intersubjective motion of transference-countertransference relations as they are understood by analyst and analysand. Here, the idea of insight separate from the relationship, within which knowledge of self and other is constructed, is rejected. This is a formulation that takes the logic of dialectic to the extreme. Many reservations regarding it are expressed by relational writers (see Orange 1992; Benjamin 1997), but the theoretical coherence of the intersubjective epistemological logic defines it as an issue to be considered.

The course and objectives of analytic work construed by the logic of the third form of dialectic formerly described is illuminated in Priel's construal of interpretation as un-mimetic, intersubjective translation. Priel presents analysis as creating a unique dialect, a co-production of analyst and analysand that potentially supplements, rather than restores, an original, unconscious meaning. Here, the analyst's task is to elaborate and enhance the patient's processes of signification.

Priel makes use of Borges's theory of artistic translation as a paradigm which brings forth the quality of *difference* as represented in various languages; this quality enables different subjective experiences which, in themselves, are essential conditions for intersubjectivity. In this construal, the therapist simultaneously preserves and transforms the language of the patient in relation to both the therapeutic context and his own subjectivity: "The analyst thus uses a blended voice that speaks in part the voice of the patient's projected internal objects (or selves), and in part the analyst's own subjectivity" (Priel 2003, 139).

In the dialectic described by Priel, we see both the element of difference and the element of composition. Elements exist in themselves, but do not suffice in themselves. They beg their own enhancement by supplement, complementarity and elaboration. This can be done only by an otherness that recognizes their singularity and transcends it by virtue of its difference. Though both elements join in new creation, they cannot be described as given in a state of fusion.

To summarize, in psychoanalytic literature the dialectic logic has been presented as an alternative to the logic of translation. It does not assume linear conversion of one language to another, but the merging of their characteristics and their articulation in more developed forms. Here, the message and its potential meanings are formulated as part of the joint journey of author and translator, analyst and analysand. The analyst is no longer 'transparent'; he is subjectively involved and a co-creator of meaning. The differentiation of subjectivities is neither assumed nor aspired to. Selfhood, in this logic, is conceived of as an intersubjective process that challenges the monadic notion of man and the concepts associated with it, like boundaries, autonomy, authenticity, etc. In line with dialectic logic, there is no hard core definition of the analytic objective, rather an interest in finding the inner and outer conditions that best enable the subject to develop himself in an intersubjective, significant environment.

Dialectics and Truth Axes: The truth axes model is not dialectic by nature. It is based on the claim that six distinct modes of organization function in the psyche, driven by and satisfying different emotional needs. These axes do not converge synthetically; they are not necessarily congruent in the meanings they generate and indeed may give rise to conflicting perceptions, meanings and interpretations. The needs that motivate the constitution of each axis, together with the developmental struggles that establish them, are posited as continuously relevant throughout the life span of the subject in their *differential* sources, expressions and objectives. Every axis, by means of a distinct grammar, gives rise to singular construals. All construals are of equal value and validity in the subject's psyche.

Even at times when axial *products* of perception and interpretation merge or create configurations of compromise, *the processes of their creation and maintenance remain distinct*. Each axis encompasses in a singular way what other axes cannot. Though the axes do not strive towards unification and their modes of processing are always distinct, their products may interrelate in a manner of translational dialectics (the third form of dialectic formerly described). They do *not* merge, but they complement and supplement each other in expressing needs and providing for them in ways that one single axis cannot give rise to.

The needs driving the axes are driving the axes are posited to be universal, as are the organizational patterns that they generate. But the products of the axial processes, as expressed in content and configuration, *are always uniquely individual*, with different developmental histories determining the relative dominance and experienced legitimacy of each axis. Although the development of all axes begins in an environment that deeply affects their forms and expressions, they all gradually differentiate from this environment and acquire their autonomous mode of functioning. Thus they define *a differentiated subject*. This differentiation is assumed also in analytic relations. The analyst is required to recognize his particular configuration of axes in ways that will insure that it is neither mistaken as common ground between him and his analysand, nor is it imposed upon the latter.

Although dialectic logic does not determine the relationships *among* the axes and is not assumed to exist between subjects in *general*, it is an active component in some of the axes. For example, Subjective-Existential grammar is dialectic inasmuch as it is created through paradox and the negotiation for relative weight among polarized elements. And yet, these elements interact *but do not merge*. In the Intersubjective axis, on the other hand, dialectics carries a constitutive function, with self and other being in relations of mutual determination. This defines an area of self-experience in which boundaries are permeable and dependence on language and culture is significant.

The desired therapeutic dynamics in the context of truth axes is not dialectic, it does not aspire to unify negations, but rather to identify and preserve the distinctiveness of the different languages. Analysis should best aspire to familiarize the subject with all truth languages in their *particularities*. This may reduce the foreignness of some of the languages and, with it, reduce the anxiety that arises from unfamiliar, excluded languages. It may also enlarge the scope of signification, experience and articulation, creating multidimensionality, instead of unifying and blurring singularities.

Dialogue

Defining Dialogue: Martin Buber and Mikhail Bakhtin have made the notion and process of dialogue a cornerstone of their theories. In examining the manner in which dialogue operates among truth axes, I rely heavily on their ideas, so I start by briefly reviewing their work and I then apply their definitions in the context of truth axes.

For Buber, dialogue is far more than a conversation or the kind of understanding that may be reached by means of a conversation. Rather, it is the essence of human existence. Man in himself is nothing but an abstraction; he comes into being only in the sphere of a living relation to another man.[12] Buber uses three terms by which he depicts an array of constructs and processes. These are the 'I', the 'Thou' and the 'it'. Roughly defined, the 'I' is identified as self-experience, while 'Thou' refers to a subjective and dynamic agency other than self; 'it' is something static that allows categorization and may be known to self. For Buber, the "primary words are not isolated words, but combined words…the one primary word is the combination 'I-Thou', the other primary word is the combination 'I-it'" (Buber 1950, 1). This is because the 'I' is always given in a relation and defined by it, a relation either with an 'it' or a 'thou'. These two relations represent the basic twofold situation of human life. 'I-Thou'

12 "Relation provides man's becoming" (Buber 1999, 9); "Human life and humanity come into being in genuine meetings" (ibid.14).

indicates a relation of subject to subject, a relation of reciprocity involving an encounter, while 'I-It' indicates a relation of a person to a thing, of subject to object, involving some form of utilization, domination or control, even if it is only objective knowing.

Buber's formulation of selfhood calls to mind Winnicott's description of the evolution of the child-subject from the mother-child matrix. For Buber, the 'I' exists from the beginning only in an 'I-Thou' relation and only emerges as a separate entity through a long developmental process that is culture-specific. The primary field of subjectification is therefore an 'I-Thou' field. The subject evolves from within it and gradually becomes aware of himself.[13] Having achieved self-awareness, he enters the relation 'I-it' and, through this, creates his ordered, categorized world, wherein dwell memory, stability and coherence. In the 'I-it' relation, one man does not see or meet another man, he meets only what he knows of him. In the 'I-it', discourse with the other is monologic in the sense that it contains only one speaker.

Leaving the coherent positioning of 'I-it' and re-entering the realm of 'I-Thou' requires directness and wholeness, will, grace and mutuality, a focusing of the mind: "The primary word I-Thou can be spoken only with the whole being" (Buber 1950, 2). Only when man is willing to loosen his hold on the coherent world of his knowledge, may he be able to truly turn to another man and reconstitute himself. Because only in the realm of I-thou can a subject be realized, only there he is supplied with the existential and ontological reality "in which the self comes into being and through which it fulfills and authenticates itself" (Friedman 2002, xv).

In its pure form, the 'I-Thou' relation is fluid and transitory, an experience of being that cannot be cognized. Therefore, every Thou "by its nature, is fated to become a thing, or continually to re-enter into the condition of things" (Buber, 1950, 16). This does not reflect a failure; rather, it is "part of the basic truth of the human world, that only It can be arranged in order. Only when things, from being our Thou, become our It, can they be coordinated. The Thou knows no system of co-ordination" (Buber 1950, 30). Man cannot persevere in the 'I-Thou' relationship, but only within it may meaning be created. 'Therefore, the 'I-Thou' and 'I-It' are attitudes that stand in fruitful and necessary alternation with each other. So long as this alternation continues, man's existence is authentic.

Otherness, particularity, uniqueness – these are the prerequisites of dialogue. Dialogue does not involve merger and loss of boundaries: "Rather, and preeminently, we have the Thou in opposition because we truly have the other who thinks other things in another way" (Buber 2002, 32). The 'I-Thou'

---

13 "I become through my relation to the Thou; as I become I say Thou" (Buber 1950, 10).

relationship teaches us to meet others and to hold our ground when we meet them.[14] This means that experiencing the other side or, as Buber later calls it, 'imagining the real', goes hand in hand with remaining on one's own side. "Certainly, in order to be able to go out to the other you must have the starting place, you must have been, you must be, with yourself" (ibid. 24).

By contrast to Buber, who emphasizes the actuality of dialogue between two subjects, Mikhail Bakhtin discusses dialogue as, among others, a textual entity or an internal, intrapsychic process. Like Buber, Bakhtin does not see dialogue as striving toward agreement or consensus. Rather, he defines it as a vital ontological component of human existence and strongly opposes it to dialectics, in which the two contrasting aspects of the dialogue – the thesis and the antithesis – eventually converge in the creation of a third entity. A dialectic approach, according to Bakhtin, is not dialogic. It is monologism disguised as dialogism.

In Bakhtin's dialogical world, contrasts and contradictions are not resolved. This is illustrated beautifully in his following description of Dostoyevsky:

> Where others saw a single thought, he was able to find and feel out two thoughts, a bifurcation; where others saw a single quality; he discovered... the presence of a second and contradictory quality. Everything that seemed simple became, in his world, complex and multi-structured. In every voice he could hear two contending voices, ... But none of these contradictions and bifurcations ever became dialectical, they were never set in motion along a temporal path or in an evolving sequence: they were, rather, spread out in one plane, as standing alongside or opposite one another, as consonant but not merging or as hopelessly contradictory, as an eternal harmony of unmerged voices or as their unceasing and irreconcilable quarrel.
>
> BAKHTIN 2003, 91

14 In a true dialogic meeting, man both becomes and transcends himself. Within it, each subject makes his dialogic partner 'present' through an imaginary process: "the realization of the principle in the sphere between men reaches its height in an event which may be called 'making present'...it rests on a capacity possessed to some extent by everyone, which may be described as 'imagining the real': ...I imagine to myself what another man is at this very moment wishing, feeling, perceiving, thinking, and not as a detached content but in his very reality, that is, as a living process in this man" (Buber 1999, 14). For Buber, the significance of this process is not only psychological, but also ontological: "'becoming a self with me'...is ontologically complete only when the other knows that he is made present by me and when this knowledge induces the process of his inmost self-becoming. For the inmost growth of the self is not accomplished...in man's relation to himself, but in the relation between one and the other...in the mutuality of the making present" (ibid. 16).

In the Bakhtin/Dostoyevsky universe, even agreement is dialogic by nature: It does not create a unity of the different voices and does not lead to an ultimate truth as it does in a monologic world.

Like Buber, Bakhtin sees subjectivity as evolving and gradually distinguishing itself from others: "Consciousness awakens to independent ideological life precisely in a world of alien discourses surrounding it, and from which it cannot initially separate itself" (Bakhtin 2003, 79). The discourse one is born into is authoritarian, governed by paternal discourses, be they religious, political or moral. Bakhtin calls the word of the father 'epic' (Bakhtin 2003, 78); it is one dimensional and has one general meaning (Bakhtin 2003, 182–3).

Self-awareness is achieved when the authoritarian social voice is internalized and refined, acquiring a delicate tone of irony or parody. In this way, consciousness begins to transform the 'sacred' word into a relative word, one that appears alongside others, articulated in other voices, possibly in opposition to them. The process of internalization loosens the chains that bind authoritarian ideology to inner speech. Inner discourse, which was at first a mere introjection of the discourse of the other, begins to rebel against the self-evident categories of this otherness.

Development, both general and ideological, is expressed in the powerful inner struggle among different perspectives, values and types of discourse. Bakhtin resembles object-relation thinkers when saying that: "Certain kinds of internally persuasive discourse can be fundamentally and organically fused with the image of a speaking person" (Bakhtin 2003, 79). This 'image of a person' creates the autonomous subjectivity of the subject through the various dialogic processes that unveil and extend it, as well as converse with it and struggle against it. The unique voice of subjectivity is born from within the other's discourse.[15]

Not only subjectivity, but also the meaning of a word is created in the space between self and other. Language for Bakhtin is not comprised of lexically defined words, but of words that carry meaning only within the context of an utterance. Reminiscent of Davidson's passing theories, only particular social interaction can determine which of a word's various meanings and connotations become influential at any given moment.[16]

---

15 Bakhtin precedes Lacan in predicating subjectivity on the discourse of the other and the evolving relations with it. Without the discourse of the other as a point of departure, both individual consciousness and meaning are impossible (Bakhtin 2003, 52).

16 By emphasizing that signification occurs in the creative zone that lies between the self and the other, Bakhtin criticizes the Sausserian abstract structural definition of language (Bakhtin 2003). Buber, like Bakhtin, argues that speakers cannot agree beforehand what

Dialogic understanding is not only active; it also carries a quality of challenge and defiance. Every act of understanding gives rise, at some point, to a new utterance that opposes the first. From Bakhtin's perspective, the relation between understanding and opposition parallels the relation between one line of dialogue and the next. As opposed to the sacred and authoritarian word, which hinders and petrifies thought, stands the productive force of the argument and the generative dynamics of opposition: "In the act of understanding, a struggle occurs that results in mutual change and enrichment" (Bakhtin 2003, 17).

In Bakhtin's opinion, the interaction between different contradicting voices is a required condition for creativity. Passive and receptive understanding of the word contributes nothing to it. Discourse, creativity and subjectivity are mutually created by means of a struggle between two contravening forces that together establish the energetic principle of (linguistic) life. The centripetal force in language aims to center and unify meanings. This force ensures the common grounds of understanding needed for social life. Every dominant social group\inner voice harnesses this force in order to impose its truth upon an existing discourse. In opposition to this centralizing process stands a centrifugal force, the force of heteroglossia, which de-constructs and stratifies discourse into a multitude of perspectives.

Heteroglossia, for Bakhtin, means recognizing the ideology-saturated quality of language. As he sees it, various types of discourse represent specific systems or ideologies. The many social languages that take part in heteroglossia at any given moment of history are all,

> ...specific points of view on the world, forms for conceptualizing the world in words, specific world views, each characterized by its own objects, meanings and values. As such, they all may be juxtaposed to one another, mutually supplement one another, contradict one another and be interrelated dialogically. As such, they encounter one another and coexist in the consciousness of real people.
>
> BAKHTIN 2003,115

words mean and there will always be differences in the significations they understand a particular word to have. Though, on the face of it, this may seem an obstruction in the process of communication, Buber sees it as an opportunity for the evolution and enrichment of meaning: "The word that is spoken is found rather in the oscillating sphere between the persons, the sphere that I call the 'between' and that we can never allow to be contained without a remainder in the two participants" (Buber 1965, 112). Thus, every dialogic participant is a thinker, a creator of meaning, and the dialogue empowers its participants.

Freedom depends on dialogism and heteroglossia. Any uniform discourse that constitutes a truth becomes relative by means of its dialogic connection to a different social discourse that embodies a different perspective. This dialogic relation brings about the "destruction of any absolute bonding of ideological meaning to language" (Bakhtin 1982, 369). Recognizing this is nothing less than "a radical revolution in the destinies of human discourse: The fundamental liberation of cultural-semantic and emotional intentions from the hegemony of a single language…as an absolute form of thought" (Bakhtin 1982, 367). What is generally true for human discourse is also true for a particular consciousness. This is the most powerful and positive concept that emerges from the dialogic perspective on the human mind: Heteroglossia creates conditions of freedom for consciousness.[17]

Like Buber, Bakhtin emphasizes the element of differentiated subjectivity in dialogue. Dialogic orientation concerns openness and seriousness regarding the other, an effort to understand and empathize with him and yet, recognize him as a different perspective from that of one's self. In this way, and in this way only, can discourse remain independent and unique subjectivity may come into being. The participants in a dialogic process are two distinct individuals. Each is in possession of a circumscribed subjectivity; an 'I' that has developed and defined itself in the context of an ongoing dialogue with an external other. While this dialogue is a scene of differentiation, it simultaneously allows each participant to perceive the other's perspective, sense his selfhood within himself and strive to comprehend and experience it. The other's experience of uniqueness hones one's own experience of uniqueness. Polyphony exists both in one's surroundings and in one's self.

Meaning in the dialogue is perceived as an ongoing, evolving process. Each participant brings into it his language and idiolects, references and connotations, and these begin to interrelate in processes of symbolization that create novel constructions of meaning in the shared space of the dialogue. The dialogue is carried on simultaneously between self and other and between the many voices, past and present, of the self. For Bakhtin, we are forever within an idio-somatic, heteroglotic dialogue, both within ourselves and among others. In this dialogue singularity is both revealed and transformed. It is transformed not through the merging with otherness, but rather through proximity to otherness: "A language is revealed in all its distinctiveness only when it is

17 When researching Dostoyevsky's work, Bakhtin analyzed its multiplicity of voices and termed it 'polyphony'. Later in his work, when he coined the term Heteroglossia, he used it to refer to the multiplicity of languages in social systems. This reflects a change in focus and not in essence, as Bakhtin sees all social discourse as having a subject, a speaker.

brought into relationship with other languages, ... Against the dialogizing background of other languages...each language begins to sound differently than it would have sounded 'on its own', as it were (without relating to others). Individual languages, their roles and their...meaning are fully disclosed only within the totality of an era's heteroglossia" (Bakhtin 1982, 412–3).

Dialogism in Psychoanalytic Thought: Dialogic logic may connect to psychoanalysis on several dimensions like the analytic relations, the analytic objectives and the understanding of signification and subjectivity in the patient's mind.

In therapeutic relations, the purity of the 'I-Thou' as expressed in transparency and mutuality is, by definition, impossible. Yet, for Buber (1999), this relation remains the focus, foundation and goal of any therapy. Healing takes place in the intermediate space between analyst and analysand, man and man, man and community. Ventimiglia (2008) sees elements of the 'I-Thou' relationship in relationally-oriented psychoanalysis, especially its emphasis on reciprocity and its recognition of the patient's need for an authentic encounter.

Ventimiglia believes that *now moments* (Stern et al. 1998) effect existential healing through encounter rather than through insight and analysis (Ventimiglia 2001). A now moment is one in which a unique and vital encounter takes place between analyst and analysand. This encounter demands from the analyst a response that is specific and personal, one that cannot be formulated in advance or by means of accepted guidelines of technique (Stern 1998, 2007). In dialogical models, like in Bion's famous dictum and in Buber's optimal positioning regarding the other, the good analyst frees himself as far as possible from preconceptions and reified categories.

Priel (1999) emphasizes the manner in which dialogue informs psychoanalytic discourse with its singular emphasis on simultaneously occurring voices within and among participants. Drawing an analogy between true and false selves and discourse that is correspondently polyphonic or epic, Priel sees psychoanalytic discourse as aspiring to deconstruct the epos into polyphony. In the epic genre, facts are absolute, there is one accepted version of the story and the epic hero is always identical to himself. The perspective of the story is coherent and one-dimensional. By contrast, the polyphonic novella brings forth contemporariness and is open-ended. The present becomes the center of temporal human orientation and the world is in an unfinished, changing, evolving process. Objects exist in a state of emergence and the hero of the novella is in a process of realizing an unclearly defined potential. While the epos is based on consensual and accepted knowledge, the polyphonic novella questions truth and knowledge. From a dialogic perspective, the deconstruction of epos in analysis involves the engagement of the inner discourses and dialogues of both analyst and analysand. In that sense, the fantasies and associations of the therapist serve as an active and responsive context from which the negating word develops and meets the discourses of the patient.

The dialogic model in psychoanalysis has clear and describable characteristics. Firstly, we have two (or more) distinct subjectivities. Secondly, there are identifiable languages acting as the media of the dialogue. Thirdly, we have the tacit assumption that the interaction between subjectivities and languages creates a space of signification, where conflict and opposition are played out and contained. The objective here is to set discourse free from restrictive authoritarianism and enable creativity in its stead.

Dialogue and Truth Axes: Bakhtinian and Buberian dialogue aspires to an open-ended process of signification as the subject's discourse is constructed, deconstructed and reconstructed, interacting with other discourses and languages, both internal and external to him. In contradistinction to this dynamic signification stands Bakhtin's epic discourse and Buber's monologic 'I-it' relation. The former regards the relation between man and the multilinguistic world in which he lives, when only one language rules; the latter between man and the other, when one subjectivity trespasses upon another. Monologic or epic construal of the world leads to experiential constriction and dissociation of self-states. The logic of dialogue manifests clearly in an analysis that assimilates the theory of truth axes in the *distinctiveness of both subjectivity and languages.*

Distinctiveness of Subjectivity- A dialogue is conducted when subjects are able to retain their subjectivity and transcend it. Otherness is a prerequisite of dialogue. An analytic encounter that is predicated upon dialogic logic assumes two distinct subjectivities. A subject here is understood as existing in a given state of affairs: His personal and historical life circumstances, his unique familial and general culture, his bodily conditions and his affect formations. His processes of signification are in constant interaction with this state of affairs: One construes, contemplates and acts in ways that reconstruct and reshape the lived-in world. Each subject has specific characteristic configurations according to which he symbolizes his world. These configurations are always uniquely individual, with different developmental histories determining the relative dominance and experienced legitimacy of each axis. *Each subjectivity has its unique and particular structure, its singular history and history of singular construals.*

Distinctiveness of Language – The dialogic model bases itself on the simultaneity of multilinguisity. It does not assume linear development, conversion between languages over time, or unification of their characteristics. Indeed, dialogue involves the *refinement of a particular way of being.* A dialogue between different languages is not aimed at blurring their identity, but rather at honing the statements that may be thought and articulated only by means of a singular lexicon and grammar. True dialogue has the potential to reveal all dimensions of an event- the demands, fears and hopes associated with it- in a way that can unravel the dynamics of repression, denial or conversion.

This dialogue primarily involves getting to know the Other – both internal and external – the other that is excluded from personal identifications and, at times, embodies their negation and threatens their integrity. The model of truth axes attempts to objectify the languages of the psyche. It seeks to characterize the unique mix of vocabulary, grammar, sensation and interpersonal encounter which create the unique episteme of every axis. These are drawn out from specific contents and phenomenological expressions in the analytic space. Bringing the episteme to the forefront allows identifying, analyzing and defining its formative principles. Each language directs our gaze differently, creates selective, distinct and unique patterns of attention and leads to different construals of life, of adversity, of development and of potential healing processes. The scene we see at any given point in time is but a 'slice' of the existential array of all languages.

What is expressed here abstractly may be described experientially. Every state of affairs that is subjectively experienced serves as input to all truth axes and the significations that they give rise to. *Therefore, what happens to us happens several times*, in overlap or in succession. It happens once as a subjective event, then as an intersubjective one, a pragmatic event and so on. Accordingly, the subject is aware of himself in different ways, certain self-states are more accessible to his experience, others evasive or completely foreclosed. Often this is experienced by the subject as conflict and discord, giving rise to tensions and anxiety.

Conflict – Conflict is inherent in dialogic logic. Understanding implies opposition, opposition testifies to understanding. The process of granting meaning inevitably involves controversy and active resistance. This conflict occurs between particular voices, as they are situated within the psyche, or between subjectivities. Intra-psychic conflict is inherent in the truth axes model, because the needs that create the axes, and the related processes, often do not cohere. Axis-specific images of reality do not overlap and the emergent self-states often give rise to different emotions and motivations.

The theme of need-related conflict is well elaborated in psychoanalytic theory. Freud spoke of conflict between wish, reality and social prohibitions in a way that is suggestive of the inherent conflict between, respectively, the Subjective-Existential, Correspondent, and Intersubjective truth axes. Winnicott saw the Subjective-Existential and Intersubjective truth axes as expressing the ongoing interaction and the defensive interrelations of the true and false selves in their oscillation as conflicted self-states. Kohut held the drama of idealization and narcissistic vulnerability as central to psychic structuring and in conflict with Intersubjective and Correspondent constraints. Benjamin focused on the struggle to acknowledge the other and accept the inherent need for recognition that lies at the heart of subjectivity.

The terms and logic of truth axes enable the various dramas and conflicts to be drawn into one field of reference and be analyzed in their various interrelations. The aim of therapy is not to resolve conflict, but to establish a space in which it can be contained and allow processing and articulation of the multiple facets of every experience. While meanings may clash and negate each other, they are also the source of the word's richness. This polyphony lies at the heart of every word, object or event and promises to free the mind from epic monologic states and reinstate a dynamic space of signification.

Therapeutic Objective -The subject's experience of self and world arises from the complex and unique relationship among the truth axes, according to their different degrees of salience and their different layouts in the conscious and unconscious spheres. An experience of well-being is predicated on the ability to allow the expression of needs and pursue their realization as they arise from different modes of organizational psychic functioning. In the logic of truth axes, the ability to contain and express more languages (aspiring to all languages) acts as a therapeutic objective. This requires well defined boundaries for each self and the ability to recognize their attitudes to the various axes.

As a corollary, the analyst can facilitate the economy of multiple selves to the extent that he is able to evaluate the workings of the different truth languages within himself, as well as in relation to the analysand. In other words, the optimal positioning of the analyst should allow him to reflect upon attitudes regarding truth axes- both his own and his analysand's. Their subjectivities interact and impact upon each other, but they remain fairly distinct and do not merge.

The therapeutic process begins with the identification and diagnosis of monologic and epic states. Diagnosis here means identifying the possibility of a truth language that, explicitly or implicitly, dominates, neutralizes or excludes other languages, thus creating authoritarian discourse. The origins and repercussions of this dominance are explored. Following such inquiry, the patient may still prefer one language over another and tend to rely on its accessibility and facility at capturing his states of mind. Yet, there is already a difference wrought. This difference lies in the realization that the language employed is neither absolute nor epic; rather, it is recognized as locally beneficent, effective in one specific situation. Even when not realized, the possibilities of choice among various languages already exist, and in their existence alter the prior state of self-experiencing.

The general theoretic rationale of truth axes posits that distress and tension arise when the psyche compulsively translates experience into one linguistic pattern which does not allow for all dimensions of experiencing demanded by the psyche's inherent needs. Epic discourse constantly forms pockets of repressed remainders which, in turn, bring about foreclosures, splits and dissociations. In the general case, analysis aspires to create a space that allows for transition among languages, aspires to re-ignite the process of dialogue, both internally and intersubjectively.

And yet, as stated before in the context of translation, we always face a trade-off between clarity and comprehensibility on the one side, and on the other – the admittance of complexity and multidimensionality that the satisfaction of our psychic needs demands but that may overwhelm us. We are forever moving between these poles, as context and psychic resilience allow. *The possibility of dialogue among psychic languages is not posed here as an ideal, but rather as a model that accommodates what our psyche both demands and rejects, both creates and shies away from.*

It seems that the precarious balance of this tension is achieved in the psyche by the creation of multiple axes, with each axis centralizing around its gravitational truth. Assuming this multiplicity and developing its implications- both theoretical and practical- may allow us to hold the tensions between inherently determined plurality and the likewise inherent demand for stability and anchorage. It may also allow us to achieve good theoretical understanding and rigorous formulation without ossifying them into static certainties.

The Analytic Stance- As analysts, we strive to see the subject who seeks our help and offer him what he needs in order to promote his well-being. In the context of my theoretic model (as in many others), we don't know in advance the problems or their solutions. Although I highlight here the potentialities of dialogue and dialogic methodology, we only know a situation when it presents itself to us. Psychic organizations are built in different ways; some express many axes, and some express few. A particular psychic structure may admit very few axes into consciousness and yet prove stable and well-functioning, allowing the experience of well-being. Analysts are usually proficient in investigating ill feelings, but they do not know in advance what leads to distress or what may grant its relief. We must be able to offer dialogue and yet, we do not impose it.

The analyst in this theoretic model acts as an epistemological expert. Traditionally, the therapist based his authority on a truth which he knew, mastered and employed. His authority was undermined in the postmodern era by the relinquishing of a single truth. In my model, I ascribe the analyst's authority to his epistemic expertise, his ability to know the epistemic layout of the psyche, recognize the particular configurations in it and make democratic and pluralistic use of a variety of languages. The analyst identifies the different appearances of each epistemic language on the levels of sensation, grammar and encounter with the world. He thinks by means of languages, knows them and consciously objectifies them. This expertise comprises his professional authority. As part of his expertise, he must be able to diagnose his own and his patient's attitude to every one of these languages. He aspires to learn all the truth languages irrespective of his feelings, preferences and identifications. The analyst is also required to admit into the analytic space languages that he finds unappealing. He must recognize the standing and relevance of any language in the entirety of psychic economy and structure. If he recognizes his internal objections as a hindrance, the analyst may need to investigate them in self-analysis, so as to render them accessible both for himself and for his patient.

Can all of these demands be truly met? The expectation to identify languages and diagnose the subject's attitude towards them is implicit in the general analytic imperative: 'Know thyself'. Processes of self-analysis are standard and accepted both in training and in the daily work of every therapist. The analyst is not expected to be neutral in his relation to the different languages, to equally identify with them or to be devoid of natural preferences and tendencies. His challenge consists in being aware of these tendencies. He is required to acknowledge the existence of all of these psychic languages in himself and do so in a manner that allows him to employ any language when needed by the patient.

For understanding the analytic stance I advocate here, it is pertinent to remember that, beyond preferences and identifications, all truth axes express basic needs and are determined by them. Therefore, they all simultaneously exist in the psyche, even when not accessible to conscious experiencing or when experienced as averse. When initiating a dialogue of truth languages, we draw these automatic need-driven processes into consciousness, delineating the ways meanings are determined and identifying the psychic balances of wish and anxiety on which they are predicated. We acknowledge that our practice is value-laden in that it often prioritizes psychic needs. We take ethical responsibility for our action.

At times, therapists encounter patients they feel they shy away from treating. Some feel this way about sex offenders or criminals in general, others experience this with individuals who hold political views that are radically different from their own. There are therapists who know that, because of their personal life circumstances, they cannot treat patients facing grief, addiction etc. Therapists often intuitively know what types of patients and problems should be referred to which of their colleagues. In an unformulated manner, as we know our circumstances so we know our languages as well as those of our colleagues. In extreme situations, there are languages we cannot speak or languages that should not be spoken. There are patients and problems that we cannot treat, while some of our colleagues can do so.

Nonetheless, in ordinary situations, we can develop considerable linguistic agility; we can learn languages throughout our lives. We have the resources and the power to acquire new languages and learn how to speak them. The analyst's attitude may, at times, echo the writer's relation to language. In the words of Bakhtin:

> Thus a prose writer can distance himself from the language of his own work, while at the same time distancing himself, in varying degrees, from the different layers and aspects of the work. He can make use of language without wholly giving himself up to it, he may treat it as semi-alien or completely alien to himself, while compelling language ultimately to serve all his own intentions. The author does not speak in a given language (from which he distances himself to a greater or lesser degree), but he speaks, as it were, through language, a language that has somehow more or less materialized, become objectivized...
>
> BAKHTIN 1981, 116

The Self Revisited

Let me turn now a final glance to the concept of self and its definition. To briefly reiterate, the notion of self I develop here assumes a base of unprocessed experiences, comprising images, thoughts, feelings and bodily sensations, as well as imprints of objects. I posit truth axes as the organizing principles of this flux of experience. The self gradually evolves from this organization, acquiring progressively its unity, continuity and coherence.

This positioning of truth as an organizing principle of the psyche is grounded in a theoretical analysis that repeatedly identifies truth as an overarching need that is expressed across all dimensions of a subject's life: Subjective, Intersubjective, Pragmatic and Ideal, Correspondent and Coherent. These dimensions are experienced as different realities, each reality organizing itself in relation to a truth that is natural to it. Finally, experientially, truth and self are intimately related. The seeking of the one involves the finding of the other. Intuiting the one implies the knowledge of the other.

The truth axes that structure the psyche define its epistemic multiplicity. Possible realities emerge in relation to each axis and selves emerge as subjective counterparts of these realities. The *self in its entirety is viewed as the experience arising from successive axially determined self-states and their composite interrelations*. Self-experiencing contains a static and a fluid element. The static is a relatively stable configuration of axes that was determined by a particular developmental history. The self may reflect on this configuration at its leisure, pondering the grammars of its constitutive parts. The fluid element is comprised of experiences that surprise, intrigue or challenge the subject, experiences that activate an axis that is ordinarily dissociated from conscious experiencing. The self develops in and through those channels that allow it to become acquainted with the axial grammars that have undergone various processes of suppression.

Whereas the processes of axial construction and symptom formation occur *unconsciously*, these processes of reflection and self-learning (that occur in the context of surprising experiences that are determined by dissociated axes) are conscious and pre-conscious. These are the processes that, in contemporary psychoanalytic formulations, constitute the prime arena of both subjective experiencing and clinical psychoanalysis, often under the heading of 'transitional space'.

Winnicott situated the transitional space between inner and outer realities, where a natural habitat may allow subjectivity to develop and negotiate its existential conditions (Winnicott 1951). Ogden elaborated on Winnicott and thought that the potential space arises from the dialectic tension between the poles of reality and fantasy. He construed pathology as the collapse of the dialectic tension into one of its constituent poles (Ogden 1993). However, the logic of truth axes casts doubt upon the role that is assigned by Winnicott and Ogden to the external-internal divide. Truth splits across essential dimensions that cannot be grasped in this logic. Instead, I posit that transitional and potential spaces are created among any (or all) of the axes of truth and their experiential and hermeneutic expressions. The dynamics to which the axes are subject – translation, dialectic and dialogue – determine the characteristics and qualities of the potential space they create.

In the transitional space, self-experiencing is continuous and may oscillate between the known and the novel. The versatility and resilience of the space and the experience of self within it are shaped by the characteristic patterns of relations among the different axes. A space governed by translational processes may be clear in its formulations, but will contain pockets of dissociated experience: that which has failed to be stated or has been suppressed. This will result in the restriction of experience and the domination of authoritarian patterns, in a way that may give rise to persecutory anxiety.

Hegelian dialectic allows into the realm of self-experiencing constructions in which axial products cohere. This creates a flattening effect upon experience, due to evasion of conflict and particularity. Dialectics might also generate a histrionic, blurred redolence to inhibited thought processes, because unchecked they may evolve uncoordinated and disparate, challenging possibilities of synthesis. Translational dialectic, as defined formerly, substitutes merger with supplement and complementarity. As such, its products are biased towards compromise formations. Such formations may be complex and heterogeneous, but are vulnerable, as they heavily rely on the balance that the gestalt is predicated upon. Direct conflict or incoherence will seriously threaten it.

The psychic space created by dialogue among axes probably allows maximum plurality in self-experiencing. In its ability to uphold difference, contain conflict and enhance the unique and the singular, it loses some serenity, coherence and predictability, but gains in versatility, tolerance, vitality and depth. As self-experiencing, this space incorporates the encounter with otherness as value and objective.

When patients seek analysis, they arrive with stable axial configurations and accepted modes of interrelations between them, be they translation, dialectic or dialogue. It is always a challenge to understand the origin of a patient's distress, because only then may it be properly addressed. Indeed, it may very well be that a patient lives well in axial poverty and in modes of translation, his distress arising from some aspect that doesn't demand the deconstruction of his basic psychic organization. We always consider how much deconstruction a self-organization can tolerate without being endangered by decompensation.

The point I make here is that *we do not impose the model of dialogue on any one but ourselves as analysts*. This dictum is the only position that allows us to recognize and grant legitimacy to any and every axial language in which the subject is anchored. This position also allows us to monitor the influence we exert on our patients. In that sense, my definition of a dialogic-analytic self expresses both an ethical stand and its methodological implementation, based on self-inquiry.

Conclusion

I have written this book about truth. It seems that I have done all that can be done to undermine my object. I have fragmented it from unity into multiplicity; I have transformed it from point to process and damaged its static forms; I have converted it from fact to psychic principle, tying it up irrevocably with the subject and his psychological makeup. And yet, I have subjugated the subject to its unshakeable experiential force, accepted truth as the imperative that rules all processes of emotion and thought.

Of course, I have not managed this feat on my own. An incredibly small part of it involves novel formulation on my part. Rather, what I have done was to gather several perspectives that deal with the concepts of truth and self – psychoanalytic, philosophic and semiotic – into a dialogic space and allowed them to interact, to reveal their multiple interrelations. These interrelations gave rise to meanings and significations that I tried to order and to articulate.

Stated in a most concise and general way, what my inquiry here has brought forth is that subjectivity is predicated upon epistemic multiplicity. The world is what we make of it. We live and move in realities we create. But this is not nearly as nihilistic and fragmentary as it might sound. Our construals of realities are several, but finite. Their composition follows general patterns of unchanging rules. They are generated by several basic needs. Each one gravitates around its point of truth. In many ways we retain our commonality as Human Subject. Within the bounds of this commonality, the psyche is infinitely creative in its ability for combination on the levels of perception, emotion and symbolic expression, thus accommodating our endless singularities as particular subjects.

What is clearly seen here is the complementary action of centripetal and centrifugal forces. On one hand, every subject is constrained by his psyche's basic needs and the overarching imperative for stability and structure. These constraints are the unifying force within and across subjects, the centripetal force. On the other hand, creativity and the endless idiosyncrasy of life as it interacts with emotion, express the centrifugal force in its endless deconstruction and reconstruction of configurations and meanings. These forces mold us as subjects, jointly determine across times and contexts how far we may roam from our known truths in search of the novel.

Introducing the concept of truth axes, I have tried to outline and describe throughout the book their characteristics and manifestations. At all times, I have emphasized the singularity of each axis, its unique ability to contain, construe and express an aspect of experiencing that cannot be contained or

 | DOI 10.1163/9789004314993_010

expressed by any other axis. I have stressed that these axes are not in competition with each other. Rather, they are complementary, arising from different needs and expressing their associated dreads and desires. Axial terms capture the complexity of human experience as we encounter it in our clinical work. We often see our patients battling among their conflicting truths, baffled by the different ways in which they experience one single event. Our work often consists of creating a space that may contain these various versions of world, self and experience, acknowledging and recognizing their validity, though they often do not cohere.

Highlighting this clear differentiation among axes, I have posited each axis to be an encapsulated register, operating automatically and efficiently on its given data base, ordering reality in a way that is not accessible to reflective knowledge. Whereas the intermediate stages of processing within an axis are opaque, its outputs are phenomenologically salient. The subsequent process that consciousness employs in ordering the multiplicity of axial products is effectively the process of acquiring an identity, developing a self.

I have used several terms to express the multidimensionality of the axes, at times describing them as experiential strata, at times as epistemic perspectives or languages. What is preserved across these terms is the generative position they ascribe to the *relations among elements*. What differentiates the axes is the way they select, prioritize and combine elements. The combinatory ordering of elements is what gives rise to meaning and signification in such diverse systems as perception, emotion, thought and language.

In drawing the analogy between language and axis, I have brought forward and emphasized the bond between structure and signification, order and meaning. The idea that a subject is predicated upon the language he speaks in the sense of not being able to think beyond his language's scope of signification is a veteran one, and has been expressed in many elegant ways. When we learn new languages, changes inevitably occur in our perception and thought: "In learning a foreign language one must map out several new spheres [...] that did not exist before...relationships unknown until then are discovered. [...] Polyglotism increases the flexibility of thinking since, through the learning of many languages, the concept increasingly separates itself from the word" (Schopenhauer 1992, 33).

In 'gathering' the different truth languages into the clinical analytic space, we separate the concept of truth from the word and the world, creating spaces of signification. We discover relationships among elements, and thus we move beyond content and narratives and into grammars. We deconstruct, we search for basic configurations that have caused a personality to suffer distress. We take ordered processes and throw them into disarray. We undo developmental achievements and reverse the influences of time in order to reconstruct the psychic space in a way that allows the patient not to suffer what he had suffered before; in a way that allows him to be freer, more alive and stronger in the pursuit of his goals.

Structuring the analytic discourse, we find again the centrifugal and centripetal forces, constructing and deconstructing form and content, balancing islands in the flux of consciousness. This versatility of reconfiguration hinges upon an egalitarian ethics: We do not posit a diachronic development that is known in advance. We aspire not to ascribe a-priori values to axes. We try to create a space of experiencing in which the wishes borne of one axis are not annulled due to prohibitions dictated by another.

Analyst and analysand form a field which aspires to hospitability through experiential breadth, verbal approximations and countless misinterpretations and mistranslations. A word always gives rise to another word that opposes it in the sense of positioning as a question what was given as a statement. When hospitability overcomes xenophobia, these differences may be reflected upon. They may be seen to arise from various needs and wishes, associated with particular anxieties and longings, expressing the gaps between different forms of logic and structure. In the dialogic-analytic space, these significations may be traced back historically, be associated with significant needs and others and be processed in the various patterns of transference and counter-transference.

Bakhtin, whose work was instrumental in grasping the mind's multiplicity of voices, dwells on the effects of bringing differences in touch with each other. He says:

> After all, it is possible to also objectivize one's own particular language, its internal form, the peculiarities of its world view, its specific linguistic habitus, only in the light of another language belonging to someone else. Only polyglossia fully frees consciousness from the tyranny of its own language and its own myth of language.
>
> BAKHTIN 1986

Bakhtin's words touch upon another point I wish to stress in my conclusion and that is the crucial role that analysis ascribes to 'self' facing the 'other'. Crudely put, what is my 'own', what is familiar to me, is my self and my truth. What is foreign to me is always grasped as my other. Subjectivity is always tied up with centralizing the self, and the other is always *somebody's* other, never an other in itself. It is an other that *becomes* other due to my having had to centralize myself. In that sense, self and other are also products of the tension between the need to centralize and stabilize, as against the drive to deconstruct, de-stratify and bring into disarray. When we focus on one truth, one language or one register, 'others', in their foreignness, come alive around the centralized 'me'. Easing the hold on truth modifies the experience of the 'other' and places him anew in the realm of what may become 'mine'.

The balance between me and the other has been discussed throughout the book in three contexts: Languages of truth, psychoanalytic theories and psychoanalysis in its relation with its neighboring disciplines. What I have tried to show in this method is that each psychoanalytic theory focused on one or two truths or epistemologies and created a deep analysis of their evolution, from the level of need to the level of health, pathology and therapeutic objectives. From the book's vantage point, the different psychoanalytic theories are not seen as competing, but as creating a theoretic arc that parallels the epistemic multiplicity of the mind.

In the same vein, attitudes among psychoanalysts regarding interdisciplinary discourse vary. Some appreciate its benefits, understanding that psychoanalysis, as a relatively young science, may have much to gain from centuries of reflection upon subjectivity. Others appreciate philosophy's contribution to psychoanalysis in grounding and granting rationale to paradigms of analytic thought and action. Still others employ philosophic concepts (such as epistemology) when trying to lend coherence to psychoanalytic formulations. But I think that many psychoanalysts are indifferent to philosophy, as they may be to semiotics, critical theory and other neighboring disciplines.

In this book, I have tried to familiarize my reader with some concepts of philosophy and semiotics, alongside and by interaction with psychoanalytic concepts. I believe that, here too, we may benefit from the engagement between centripetal and centrifugal dynamisms, allowing them to create a multidisciplinary dialogue and to newly define what is 'ours' and what isn't. This may allow us all, analysts and analysands alike, larger spaces for thought and signification.

As aforesaid, a space – psychic, theoretic, linguistic or social – that is predicated on dialogue is a resilient one. It tolerates and contains an inherent element of conflict. It preserves heterogeneity in the face of a constant need for certainty, for stability, for truth. It is always an aspiration, an asymptotic goal. There are always unifying forces working against it. For here in ending, we meet our point of departure: The subject needs his truth. In constituting what he knows of it, he constitutes himself. In many ways his truth is synonymous to his identity and serenity.

And yet it seems the subject does not want his truth *only*. He wants much more. He is curious and eager; he seeks the novel and the unknown. He is a hopeless explorer. And so he tries to live among the centrifugal and centripetal forces he harbors. He unifies and deconstructs what he knows of himself and his world. He tries to break out of what he formerly grasped as his knowable limits. As Wittgenstein would have it: "The limits of my language mean the limits of my world" (Wittgenstein 2010, 5.6), and my world demands its limits in order to exist as such. Moreover, "the feeling of the world as a bounded whole is the mystical" (ibid. 6.45). When all languages abound, our heads may indeed spin, we may lose the familiar which we recognize as our self and we may touch upon the mystic.

Psychoanalysis, in this sense, is a transitional way station of deconstruction. It may bridge the points marked here as the certain and the mystic, the epic and the dialogic. If it can afford awareness of multiplicity, legitimize it and create dialogue, it achieves a grand objective. In the best of scenarios, it is incorporated by the subject as a space within himself.

The subject's ability to disarray, to venture into the unknown, is predicated on the quality of the primary holding he received. The capacity to devolve into creative fragmentation hinges on basic trust that this fragmentation will coalesce; it hinges on the belief that the distress caused is temporary, that the depth and complexity realized in psychic space will promote better living. Analysis may offer another chance for experiencing a primary kind of holding and, through this, afford a unique journey away and towards truth.

Bibliography

Aguillaume, Romulo (2007). "Interpretation and Method". *Int. Forum Psychoanal.*, 16:240–246.

Allan, Kenneth (1997). "The Postmodern Self: A Theoretical Consideration". *Quarterly J. Ideology,* 20 (1&2):3–24.

Amir, Dana (2013). *On the Lyricism of the Mind.* Tel-Aviv: Magnes (Hebrew).

Appelbaum, Jerome (2011). "Should Psychoanalysis become a Science?" *American J. Psychoanal.,* 71:1–15.

Apprey, Maurice (2006). "The Designed Self: Psychoanalysis and Contemporary Identities by Carlo Strenger". *Int. J. Psycho-Anal.*, 87:900–904.

Aquinas, Thomas (1948). *Summa Theologiae.* Translated by The Fathers of the English Dominican Province Benzinger Bros., New York, NY. Accessed 23.7.2015. Source: http://www.sacred-texts.com/chr/aquinas/summa/sum019.htm.

Aristotle. (1930). *Categories.* Translated by Edghill, E.M. Accessed 23.7.2015. Source: http://classics.mit.edu/Aristotle/categories.mb.txt.

Aristotle (2015) *Metaphysics, 4:1.* Translated by W.D Ross. Accessed 23.7. 2015. Source: http://classics.mit.edu/Aristotle/metaphysics.4.iv.html.

Arlow, Jacob A. (1996). "The Concept of Psychic Reality – How Useful?" *Int. J. Psycho-Anal.*, 77:659–666.

Aron, Lewis (1996). *A Meeting of the Minds: Mutuality in Psychoanalysis.* New York: Analytic Press.

——— (2003). "Clinical Outbursts and Theoretical Breakthroughs". *Psychoanal. Dial.,* 13:273–287.

Arrojo, Rosemary (2007). "Translation as an Object of Reflection in Psychoanalysis". In Kittel, H., Armin, Paul F., Greiner, N., Hermans, T. and Koller, W. eds. *Übersetzung Translation Traduction: An International Encyclopedia of Translation Studies.*

Austin, John L. (1973). *How to do Things with Words.* Second Edition. Cambridge: Harvard University Press.

Baker, Gordon P. (1998). "The Private Language Argument". *Language & Communication,* 18:325–56

Baker, Gordon and Hacker, Peter M.S. (2005). *Wittgenstein: Understanding and Meaning, Volume 1 of An Analytical Commentary on the Philosophical Investigations Part I: Essays.* Second, extensively revised edition, Oxford: Blackwell.

Bakhtin, Mikhail M. (1982). *The Dialogic Imagination: Four Essays.* Translated by Emerson, C. and Holquist, M. eds. Austin: University of Texas Press.

——— (2003). In Morris, Pam ed. (2003). *The Bakhtin Reader: Selected Writings of Bakhtin, Medvedev and Voloshinov.* London: Arnold.

Balsam, Rosemary H. (2000). "The Power of Feelings: Personal Meaning in Psychoanalysis, Gender, and Culture". *Psychoanal. Q.*, 69:816–820

——— (2008). "The Essence of Hans Loewald". *J. Amer. Psychoanal. Assn.*, 56:1117–1128.

Bambach, Charles (2003). *Heidegger's Roots: Nietzsche, National Socialism and the Greeks.* Ithaca: Cornell University Press.

Bandura, Albert (1982). "Self Efficacy Mechanism in Human Agency". *American Psychologist,* 37 (2):122–147.

——— (1997). *Self Efficacy: The Exercise of Control.* New York: W.H. Freeman.

Barthes, Roland (2001). *Mythologies.* Translated by A. Lavers. New York: Hill and Wang.

Bass, Alan (1985). "On the History of a Mistranslation and the Psychoanalytic Movement". In Graham, J.F. ed. *Difference in Translation.* Ithaca and London: Cornell UP.

Bassnett, Susan (2004). *Translation Studies.* London: Routledge.

Baumeister, Roy. and Leary, Mark R. (1995). "The Need to Belong: Desire for Interpersonal Attachments as a Fundamental Human Motivation". *Psycholog. Bull.,* 117:497–529.

Becker, Mitchel and Shalgi, Boaz (2006). "The Dialectic between Self-determination and Intersubjectivity in Creating the Experience of Self". *Psycho. Study. of the Child,* 61:155–169.

Bell, David (2009). "Is Truth an Illusion? Psychoanalysis and Postmodernism". *Int. J. Psychoanal.*, 90:331–345.

Benjamin, Jessica (1990). "An Outline of Intersubjectivity: The Development of Recognition". *Psychoanal. Psychol.*, 7S:33–46.

——— (1991). "Commentary on Irwin Z. Hoffman's Discussion: Toward a Social-Constructivist View of the Psychoanalytic Situation". *Psychoanal. Dial.,* 1:525–533.

——— (1992). "Recognition and Destruction: An Outline of Intersubjectivity". In: Skolnick, N. and Warshaw, S. eds. *Relational Perspectives in Psychoanalysis.* Hillsdale, NJ: The Analytic Press, pp. 43–60.

——— (1994a). "What Angel Would Hear Me? The Erotics of Transference". *Psychoanal. Inq.*, 14:535–557.

——— (1994b). "Commentary on Papers by Tansey, Davies, and Hirsch". *Psychoanal. Dial.*, 4:193–201.

——— (1995). *Like Subjects, Love Objects: Essays on Recognition and Sexual Differences.* New Haven: Yale University Press.

——— (1997). "Psychoanalysis as a Vocation". *Psychoanal. Dial.*, 7:781–802.

——— (2000). "Intersubjective Distinctions: Subjects and Persons, Recognitions and Breakdowns: Commentary on Paper by Gerhardt, Sweetnam, and Borton". *Psychoanal. Dial.*, 10:43–55.

Benjamin, Walter (1992). "The Task of the Translator". In Schulte, Rainer and Biguenet, John eds. (1992). *Theories of Translation: An Anthology of Essays from Dryden to Derrida.* University of Chicago Press.

Berkeley, George (1871/2002). "Principles of Human Knowledge". In *The Works of George Berkeley*. Oxford: Clarendon Press. Accessed 23.8.2015. Source: https://books.google.co.il/books?id=_mpbAAAAQAAJ&printsec=frontcover&dq=The+works+of+George+Berkeley&hl=iw&sa=X&ved.

Bibring, Edward (1953). "The Mechanism of Depression". In Greenacre, P. ed. *Affective Disorders; Psychoanalytic Contributions to Their Study*. New York: International Universities Press, pp. 13–48.

Bion, Wilfred R. (1954). "Notes on the Theory of Schizophrenia". *Int. J. Psycho-Anal.*, 35:113–118.

——— (1959). "Attacks on Linking". *Int. J. Psycho-Anal.*, 40:308–315.

——— (1962a). *Learning from Experience*. London: Heinemann.

——— (1962b). "The Psycho-analytic Study of Thinking". *Int. J. Psycho-Anal.*, 43:306–310.

——— (1965). *Transformations*. London: Tavistock.

——— (1970). *Attention and Interpretation: A Scientific Approach to Insight in Psycho-analysis and Groups*. London: Tavistock.

Blackburn, Simon and Simmons, Keith eds. (1999). *Truth*. Oxford: Oxford University Press.

Blum, Harold P. (1981). "Some Current and Recurrent Problems of Psychoanalytic Technique". *J. Amer. Psychoanal. Assn.*, 29:47–68.

Boas, Franz (1964). "On Grammatical Categories". In Hymes, D. ed. *Language in Culture and Society*. New York: Harper and Row, pp. 121–123.

Bollas, Christopher (1986). "Who Does Self Psychology Cure?". *Psychoanal. Inq.*, 6:429–435.

——— (1992). *Being a Character*. New York: Hill and Wang.

Borbely, Antal F. (1998). "Metaphor and Psychoanalysis". In Gibbs, R.W. ed. *The Cambridge Handbook of Metaphor and Thought* (2008). Santa Cruz: University of California Press.

Borges, Jorge L. (1932/1999). "The Homeric Versions". In Weinberger, E. ed. *Selected Non-fiction*. Translated by Allen, E. et al. New York: Penguin Books, pp. 69–74.

Bourdieu, Pierre (1985). "The Social Space and the Genesis of Groups". *Theory and Society*, 14:6, pp. 723–744.

Bouchard, Marc-Andre (1995). "The Specificity of Hermeneutics in Psychoanalysis: Leaps on the Path from Construction to Recollection". *Int. J. Psycho-Anal.*, 76:533–546.

Bromberg, Philip M. (1995). "Resistance, Object-Usage, and Human Relatedness". *Contemp. Psychoanal.*, 31:173–191.

——— (1998). *Standing in the Spaces: Essays in Clinical Process, Trauma and Dissociation*. London: The Analytic Press.

——— (2009). "Truth, Human Relatedness, and the Analytic Process: An Interpersonal/ Relational Perspective". *Int. J. Psycho-Anal.*, 90:347–361.

Brottman, Mikita (2009). "Psychoanalysis and Magic: Then and Now". *Am. Imago,* 66:471–489.

Brunner, Jose (2007). "The Naked Mother or, Why Freud Did Not Write about Railway Accidents". *History and Psychoanalysis,* 9: 71–82.

Buber, Martin (1950). *I and Thou.* Translated by Smith, R.G. Edinburgh: T&T Clark. Accessed 23.7.2015, source : https://archive.org/stream/IAndThou_572/BuberMartin-i-and-thou_djvu.txt.

——— (1965) *The Knowledge of Man. A Philosophy of the Interhuman.* New York: Harper and Row.

——— (1999). *Martin Buber on Psychology and Psychotherapy: Essays, Letters and Dialogues.* ed. Agassi, Judith B. Syracuse: Syracuse U.P.

——— (1947/2002). *Between Man and Man.* Translated by Smith, R.G. London and New York: Routledge.

Buford, Thomas O. ed. (1970). *Essays on Other Minds.* Chicago: University of Illinois Press.

Burgess, Alexis G. and Burgess, John P. eds. (2011). *Truth.* Princeton: Princeton University Press.

Cannon Dale (1996). "An Existential Theory of Truth". *The Personalist Forum,* 12(2):135–46.

Carveth, Donald L. (1984). "The Analyst's Metaphors: A Deconstructionist Perspective". *Psychoanal. Contemp. Thought,* 7:491–560.

Cavell, M. (1983). *The Psychoanalytic Mind: From Freud to Philosophy.* Cambridge: Harvard University Press.

——— (1985). "The Self and Some Related Issues". *Psychoanal. Contemp. Thought,* 8:3–27.

——— (1998). "Triangulation, One's Own Mind and Objectivity". *Int. J. Psycho-Anal.,* 79:449–467.

Chessik, Richard D. (1996). "Impasse and Failure in Psychoanalytic Treatment". *J. Amer. Acad. Psychoanal.,* 24:193–216.

——— (2003). "Psychoanalytic Peregrination V: The Zollikon Lectures". *J. Amer. Acad. Psychoanal.,* 31:343–348.

Chesterton, Gilbert K. (1908/2005). *The Suicide of Thought in Orthodoxy.* Project Gutenberg eBook. Accessed 20.7.2015. Source: http://www.gutenberg.org/cache/epub/130/pg130.html.

Chodorow, Nancy (1980). "Gender, Relation and Difference in Psychoanalytic Perspective". In Eisenstein and Gardine eds. *The Future of Difference.* Boston: G.K. Hall.

Chomsky, Noam (1957). *Syntactic Structures.* London: Mouton.

——— (1965). *Aspects of the Theory of Syntax.* Cambridge: M.I.T. Press.

——— (1975). "Questions of Form and Interpretation". *Linguistic Analysis,* 1:75–109.

Collins, Sara (2011). "On Authenticity: The Question of Truth in Construction and Autobiography". *Int. J. Psycho-Anal.*, 92:1391–1409.

Davidson, Donald (1969). "True to the Facts". In Horwich, P. ed. (1994). *Theories of Truth*. Cambridge: Cambridge University Press.

——— (1986). "A Nice Derangement of Epitaphs". In Ernest, L. ed. *Truth and Interpretation: Perspectives on the Philosophy of Donald Davidson*. Oxford: Blackwell, pp. 433–446.

——— (1996). "The Folly of Trying to Define Truth". *The journal of Philosophy*, 93(6):263–278.

——— (1997). "Truth Rehabilitated". In Brandom, R. ed. (2000). *Rorty and His Critics*. Oxford: Blackwell.

——— (2001). *Subjective, Intersubjective, Objective*. Oxford: Clarendon Press.

Derrida, Jacques (1976). *Of Grammatology*. Translated by Spivak, G.C. Baltimore: Johns Hopkins University Press.

——— (1978a). "Violence and Metaphysics". In *Writing and Difference*. Translated by Bass A: London. Routledge & Kegan Paul.

——— (1978b). *Writing and Difference*. Translated by Bass A. London: Routledge & Kegan Paul.

——— (1981). "Plato's Pharmacy". In *Dissemination*. Translated with an Introduction and Additional Notes, by Johnson, B. London: The Athlone Press, pp. 61–173.

——— (1992). From "Des Tours de Babel". In Schulte, Rainer and Biguenet, John eds. (1992). *Theories of Translation: An Anthology of Essays from Dryden to Derrida*. Chicago: University of Chicago Press.

De Saussure, Ferdinand (1986). *Course in General Linguistics*. Translated by Harris, R. Chicago and La Salle. Illinois: Open Court.

Dewey, John (1929). *Experience and Nature*. Accessed 21.8.2015, source: https://archive.org/stream/experienceandnat029343mbp/experienceandnat029343mbp_djvu.txt.

——— (1960). *The Quest for Certainty*. Capricorn Books. Accessed 21.8.2015, source: https://www.marxists.org/reference/subject/philosophy/works/us/dewey.htm.

Eagleton, Terry (1991) *Ideology: An Introduction*. London: Verso.

Eigen, Michael (1981). "The Area of Faith in Winnicott, Lacan and Bion". *Int. J. Psycho-Anal.*, 62:413–433.

Eisenberger, Naomi I. and Lieberman, Matthew D. (2004). "Why Rejection Hurts: A Common Neural Alarm System for Physical and Social Pain". *Trends in Cognitive Science*, 8:294–300.

Eissler, Kurt R. (1964). "Mankind at Its Best". *J. Amer. Psychoanal. Assn.*, 12:187–222.

——— (1971). *Talent and Genius*. New York: Quadrangle.

Elleray, Rebecca (2007). "Kierkegaard, Socrates and Existential Individuality". *Richmond Journal of Philosophy*, 16:1–12.

Engelmann, Mauro L. (2013). *Wittgenstein's Philosophical Development: Phenomenology, Grammar, Method and the Anthropological View*. New York: Palgrave Macmillan.

Erikson, Erik (1963). *Child and Society*. New York: Norton.

——— (1968). "Life cycle". In *International Encyclopedia of the Social Sciences*. New York: Crowell Collier and Macmillan, pp. 286–292.

Etchegoyen, Horacio R. (1991). *The Fundamentals of Psychoanalytic Technique*. Translated by Pitchon, P. London: Karnac.

Fairbairn, William R.D. (1941). "A Revised Psychopathology of the Psychoses and the Psychoneuroses". In Fairbairn, William R.D. (1952). *An Object Relation Theory of the Personality*. New York: Basic Books.

——— (1946). "Object–Relationships and Dynamic Structure". In Fairbairn, William R.D. (1952). *An Object Relation Theory of the Personality*. New York: Basic Books.

——— (1952). *An Object Relations Theory of Personality*. New York: Basic Books.

Ferenczi, Sándor (1949). "Confusion of the Tongues between the Adults and the Child – The Language of Tenderness and of Passion". *Int. J. Psycho-Anal.*, 30:225–230.

Festinger, Leon (1957). *A Theory of Cognitive Dissonance*. Evanston: Row Peterson.

Finch, Henry Le Roy (1977). *Wittgenstein – The Later Philosophy: An Exposition of the 'Philosophical Investigations'*. Atlantic Highland: Humanities.

Fiumara, Gemma Corradi (1992). *The Symbolic Function*. Oxford: Blackwell.

Fodor, Jerry (1975). *The Language of Thought*. New York: Crowell Press.

——— (1983). *The Modularity of Mind*. Cambridge, MA: MIT Press.

Fogelin, Robert J. (1996). "Wittgenstein's Critique of Philosophy". In Sluga, H. and Stern, D. eds. *The Cambridge Companion to Wittgenstein*. Cambridge: Cambridge University Press.

Fonagy, Ivan (2001). *Languages within language: An Evolutive Approach*. Amsterdam: John Benjamins.

Fonagy, Peter and Target, Mary (1996). "Playing with Reality: I. Theory of Mind and the Normal Development of Psychic Reality". *Int. J. Psycho-Anal.*, 77:217–223.

——— (1997). "Attachment and Reflective Function: Their Role in Self-organization". *Development and Psychopathology*, 9:679–700.

——— (2007). "The Rooting of the Mind in the Body: New Links between Attachment Theory and Psychoanalytic Thought". *J. Amer. Psychoanal. Assn.*, 55:411–456.

Forgas, Joseph P. and Williams, Kip D. eds. (1998). *Social Influence: Direct and Indirect Processes*. New York: Psychology Press.

Forster, Michael N. (2004). *Wittgenstein on the Arbitrariness of Grammar*. Princeton: Princeton University Press.

Fosshage, James L. (2011). "The Use and Impact of the Analyst's Subjectivity with Empathic and other Listening/Experiencing Perspectives". *Psychoanal. Q.*, 80:139–160.

Foucault, Michel (1994). *The Order of Things*. New York: Random House.

Frege, Gottlob (1892/1952). "On Sense and Reference". In Geach, P. and Max Black eds. *Translations from the Philosophical Writings of Gottlob Frege*. Translated by Black, M. Oxford: Blackwell, pp. 56–78.

Freud, Sigmund (1886–92). *Extracts from the Fliess Letters*. SE 1, 175–279.
——— (1886–1895). *Project for a Scientific Psychology*. SE 1, 283–399.
——— (1891/1953). *On Aphasia*. trans. Stengel, E. New York: International Universities Press.
——— (1893). *On The Psychical Mechanism of Hysterical Phenomena*. SE 2, 1–19.
——— (1893–5). *The Psychotherapy of Hysteria from Studies on Hysteria*. SE 2, 253–307.
——— (1899). *Screen memories*. SE 3, 301–323.
——— (1900). *The Interpretation of Dreams*. SE 4, 96–310.
——— (1900-1). *The Interpretation of Dreams*. SE 5, 339–623.
——— (1905a). *Fragment of an Analysis of a Case of Hysteria*. SE 7, 7–112.
——— (1905b). *Jokes and Their Relation to the Unconscious*. SE 8, 9–181.
——— (1905c). *Three Essays on the Theory of Sexuality*. SE 7, 125–244.
——— (1906). *Psycho-analysis and the Establishment of the Facts in Legal Proceedings*. SE 9, 103–114.
——— (1907). *Delusions and Dreams in Jensen's Gradiva*. SE 9, 7–95.
——— (1909). *Some General Remarks on Hysterical Attacks*. SE 9, 227–235.
——— (1911). *Formulations on the Two Principles of Mental Functioning*. SE 12, 213–227.
——— (1912). *Recommendations to Physicians Practicing Psycho-analysis*. SE 12, 109–121.
——— (1913). *The Disposition to Obsessional Neurosis: A Contribution to the Problem of Choice of Neurosis*. SE 12, 313–326.
——— (1914). *On Narcissism*. SE 14, 67–103.
——— (1915a). *The Unconscious*. SE 14, 164–204.
——— (1915b). *Instincts and Their Vicissitudes*. SE 14, 117–140.
——— (1917). *Mourning and Melancholia*. SE 14, 237–259.
——— (1916–1917). *Introductory Lectures on Psycho-analysis*. SE 15, 83–228.
——— (1921). *Group Psychology and the Analysis of the Ego*. SE 18, 69–143.
——— (1923a). *The Ego and the Id*. SE 19, 3–48.
——— (1923b). *Two Encyclopaedia Articles*. SE 18, 235–259.
——— (1925/6). *An Autobiographical Study*. SE 20, 6–71.
——— (1930). Civilization and Its Discontents. SE 21, 64–148.
——— (1932). *My Contact with Josef Popper-Lynkeus*. SE 22, 219–224.
——— (1933a). *New Introductory Lectures on Psychoanalysis*. SE 22, 3–158.
——— (1933b). *The Question of a Weltanschauung*. SE 22, 158–184.
——— (1937). *Constructions in Analysis*. SE 23, 255–271.
——— (1938a). *Splitting of the Ego in the Process of Defence*. SE 23, 271–279.
——— (1938b). *Moses, His People and Monotheistic Religions*. SE 23, 54–103.
——— (1938–1940). *An Outline of Psychoanalysis*. SE. 23, 141–291.
——— (1940). *Some Elementary Lessons in Psycho-analysis*. SE 23, 281–286.

——— (1953–1974). SE – *The Standard Edition of the Complete Psychological Works of Sigmund Freud.* In Strachey, J. ed. and trans. London: Hogarth Press (in text reference: SE).

Friedman, Maurice (2002). "Introduction". In Buber, Martin (1947/2002) ed. *Between Man and Man.* Translated by Smith, G.R. London and New York: Routledge.

Friedman, Lawrence (1999). "Why is Reality a Troubling Concept?" *J. Amer. Psychoanal. Assn.,* 47:401–425.

Fromm, Eric (1947). *Man for Himself: An Inquiry into the Psychology of Ethics.* Greenwich, Conn: Fawcett.

——— (1955). *The Sane Society.* Greenwich, Conn: Fawcett.

——— (1968). *The Revolution of Hope.* New York: Harper and Row.

——— (1970). *The Crisis of Psychoanalysis.* Greenwich, Conn: Fawcett.

Fultner, Barbara (2003). "Introduction". In Habermas, J. ed. *Truth and Justification.* Translated by Fultner, Barbara. Cambridge, Mass: MIT Press.

Gadamer, Hans Georg (1976). *Philosophical Hermeneutics*, Translated by and ed. David E. Linge, D,E. Berkeley: University of California Press.

——— (2004). *Truth and Method,* second revised edition. Revised and translated by Weinsheimer, J. and. Marshall, D. New York: Continuum.

Gedo, John E. (1997). "Reflections on Metapsychology, Theoretical Coherence, Hermeneutics, and Biology". *J. Amer. Psychoanal. Assn.,* 45:779–806.

Gennaro, Rocco (2012). *The Consciousness Paradox.* Cambridge, MA: MIT Press.

Gill, Merton M. (1994). "Conflict and Deficit. Review Essay on Conflict and Compromise: Therapeutic Implications". *Psychoanal. Q.*, 63:756–778.

Gilligan, Carol (1982). *In a Different Voice: Psychological Theory and Women's Development.* Cambridge, Mass: Harvard University Press.

——— (1986). "Remapping the Moral Domain: New Images of the Self in Relationship". In Heller, T. Sosana, M. and Wellberry, D. eds. *Reconstructing Individualism.* Stanford: Stanford University press.

Glasersfeld, Ernst von (1984). "An Introduction to Radical Constructivism". In Watzlawick, P. ed. *The invented reality.* New York: Norton, pp. 17–40.

Glucksberg, Sam (2008) "How Metaphors Create Categories – Quickly". In Gibbs, R.W. ed. *The Cambridge Handbook of Metaphor and Thought.* Santa Cruz: University of California Press.

Goldberg, Arnold (1984). "Translation between Psychoanalytic Theories". *Annual of Psychoanalysis,* 12:121–135.

——— (1998). "Deconstructing the Dialectic". *Int. J. Psycho-Anal.,* 79:215–226.

Gordon, Hayim (2001). *The Heidegger-Buber Controversy: The Status of the I-Thou.* Westport Conn.: Greenwood Press.

Govrin, Aner (2004). *Between Abstinence and Seduction: The Analysis of American Psychoanalysis.* Tel Aviv, Israel: Dvir (Hebrew).

Greenberg, Jay and Mitchell, Stephen (1983). *Object Relations in Psychoanalytic Theory*. Cambridge, MA: Harvard University Press.

Grice, Paul H. (1975). "Logic and Conversation". In *Syntax and Semantics 3: Speech Arts*, pp. 41–58.

Gruter, Margaret and Masters, Roger D. (1986). "Ostracism as a Social and Biological Phenomenon: An Introduction". *Ethology and Sociobiology*, 7:149–158.

Gubrium, Jaber F. and Holstein, James A. (1994). "Grounding the Postmodern Self". *The Sociological Quarterly*, 35(4):685–703.

Haar, Michel (1996). *Nietzsche and Metaphysics*. Translated by Gendre, M. Albany: State University of New York Press.

Habermas, Jürgen (2003). *Truth and Justification*. Translated by Fultner, B. ed. Cambridge, MA: MIT Press.

Hadar, Uri (1999). "Bold Analysis and Associative Dialogue". *Psychoanal. Dial.*, 9:109–127.

——— (2001). *Analytic Psychotherapy as a Communicational Process*. Tel Aviv, Israel: Dvir (Hebrew).

Hanly, Charles (1990). "The Concept of Truth in Psychoanalysis". In Hanly, C. ed. *The Problem of Truth in Applied Psychoanalysis*, pp. 1–24. New York: Guilford.

——— (1993). "Ideology and Psychoanalysis". *Canadian Journal of Psychoanalysis*, 1:1–17.

——— (1995). "On Facts and Ideas in Psychoanalysis". *Int. J. Psycho-Anal.*, 76:901–908.

——— (1999). "Subjectivity and Objectivity in Psychoanalysis". *J. Amer. Psychoanal. Assn.*, 47:427–444.

——— (2001). "Critical Realism: Distinguishing the Psychological Subjectivity of the Analyst from Epistemological Subjectivism". *J. Amer. Psychoanal. Assn.*, 49:515–532.

——— (2004). "The Third". *Psychoanal. Q.*, 73:267–290.

——— (2009). "On Truth and Clinical Psychoanalysis". *Int. J. Psycho-Anal.*, 90: 363–373.

Hegel, Georg W.F. (1953). *Reason in History, A General Introduction to the Philosophy of History*. Translated by Hartman, R.S. New Jersey: A Liberal Arts Press Book, Prentice Hall.

——— (1807/1977). "Independence and Dependence of Self-consciousness". In *Phenomenology of Spirit*, translated by Miller, A.V. Oxford: Oxford University Press.

——— (2005). *Preface to the Phenomenology of Spirit*. Translation and Running Commentary by Yovel, Y. New Jersey: Princeton University Press.

Heidegger, Martin (1981). "Nur noch ein Gott kann uns retten". Der Spiegel 30 (Mai, 1976):193–219. Translated by Richardson, W. as "Only a God Can Save Us". In Sheehan, T. ed. *Heidegger: The Man and the Thinker*, pp. 45–67.

——— (1992a). *Parmenides*. Translated by Schuwe, A. and Rojcewicz, R. Bloomington: Indiana University Press.

——— (1992b). *Metaphysical Foundations of Logic*. Translated by Heim, M. Bloomington: Indiana University Press.

——— (1996). *Being and Time*. Translated by Stambough, J. Albany: State University of New-York Press.

——— (1947/1993) "Letter on Humanism". In Translated by Capuzzi, A. and Krell, D.F. eds. *Basic Writings*. New York: Harper Collins.

Heider, Fritz (1946). "Attitudes and Cognitive Organization". *J. of Psychology*, 21:107–111.

——— (1958). *The Psychology of Interpersonal Relations*. New York: Wiley.

——— (1960). "The Gestalt Theory of Motivation". In Jones, M.R. ed. *Nebraska Symposium on Motivation*, Vol. 8. Lincoln: University of Nebraska Press, pp. 45–172.

Heimann, Paula (1952). Preliminary Notes on Some Defence Mechanisms in Paranoid States. *Int. J. Psycho-Anal.*, 33:208–213.

Hempel, Carl G. (1935/1994). "On the Logical Positivists' Theory of Truth". In Horwich, P. ed. *Theories of Truth*. Cambridge: Cambridge University Press.

Hermans, Hubert J.M. (2003). "The Construction and Reconstruction of a Dialogical Self". *Journal of Constructivist Psychology*, 16(2):89–130.

——— (2004). "The Dialogical Self: Between Exchange and Power". In Angus, L. and McLeod, J. eds. *The Handbook of Narrative and Psychotherapy: Practice, theory and research*. London: Sage.

Herrick, Judson C. (1956). *Evolution of Human Nature*. Austin: University of Texas Press.

Hetherington, Stephen (2012). "Epistemology's Past Here and Now". In Hetherington, S. ed. *Epistemology: The Key Thinkers*. New York: Continuum International Publishing Group.

Hilmy, Stephen S. (1987). *The Later Wittgenstein: The Emergence of a New Philosophical Method*. Oxford: Blackwell.

Hoffman, Irwin Z. (1983). "The patient as Interpreter of the Analyst's Experience". *Contemp. Psychoanal.* 19:389–422.

——— (1991). "Discussion: Toward a Social-Constructivist View of the Psychoanalytic Situation". *Psychoanal. Dial.*, 1:74–105.

——— (1998). *Ritual and Spontaneity in the Psychoanalytic Process*. Hillsdale, NJ: The Analytical Press.

——— (1999). "Response to Reviews by J. Benjamin, L. Sass, and L. Friedman of Ritual and Spontaneity in the Psychoanalytic Process". *J. Amer. Psychoanal. Assn.*, 47:907–919.

——— (2001). "Reply to Reviews by Slavin, Stein, and Stern". *Psychoanal. Dial.*, 11:469–497.

——— (2009). "Therapeutic Passion in the Countertransference". *Psychoanal. Dial.*, 19:617–637.

Holyoak, Keith J. and Simon, Dan (1999). "Bidirectional Reasoning in Decision Making by Constraint Satisfaction". *J. Exp. Psychol.*, 128:3–31.

Horney, Karen (1946). "The Future of Psychoanalysis". *Am. J. Psychoanal.*, 6:66–67.

Horwich, Paul (1990). *Truth*. Oxford: Blackwell.

——— (1994). *Theories of Truth*. Brookfield VM: Dartmouth.

Hume, David (1738/2012). *A Treatise of Human Nature*. Project Gutenberg EBook. Accessed 30.8.15. Source: https://www.gutenberg.org/files/4705/4705-h/4705-h.htm.

Husserl, Edmund (1983). *Ideas Pertaining to a Pure Phenomenology and to a Phenomenological Philosophy*. Translated by Kersten, F. The Hague: Martinus Nijhoff.

——— (1999). *Cartesian Meditations*. Translated by Cairns, D. Dordrecht/Boston|London: Kluwer Academic Publishers.

Jackendoff, Ray (1992). *Semantic Structures*. Cambridge, MA: MIT Press.

Jakobson, Roman (1960). "Linguistics and Poetics". In Sebeok, T. ed. *Style in Language*, Cambridge, MA: M.I.T. Press, pp. 350–377.

——— (1992). "On Linguistic Aspects of Translation". In Schulte, R. and Biguenet, J. eds. *Theories of Translation: An Anthology of Essays from Dryden to Derrida*. Chicago: University of Chicago Press.

James, William (1907/2004). *Pragmatism: A New Name for Some Old Ways of Thinking*. Project Gutenberg EBook. Accessed 5.8.2015. Source: http://www.gutenberg.org/catalog/world/readfile?fk_files=3440524.

——— (1902/2008). "The Divided Self and the Process of Its Unification". In *Varieties of Religious Experience*. Project Gutenberg EBook. Accessed 5.8.2015. Source: http://www.gutenberg.org/catalog/world/readfile?fk_files=3043757.

——— (1897/2009). *The Will to Believe*. Project Gutenberg EBook. Accessed 5.8.2015. Source: http://www.gutenberg.org/files/26659/26659-h/26659-h.htm.

——— (1912/2010). *Essays in Radical Empiricism*. Project Gutenberg EBook. Accessed 5.8.2015. Source: http://www.gutenberg.org/files/32547/32547-h/32547-h.htm.

——— (1890/2013). *The Principles of Psychology*. eBooks@Adelaide. Accessed 5.8.2015. Source: http://ebooks.adelaide.edu.au/j/james/william/principles/.

Jekels, Ludwig (1941). "Psycho-Analysis and Dialectic". *Psychoanal. Rev.*, 28:228–253.

Johnson, Barbara (1981). "Translator's Introduction". In Jacques Derrida ed. *Dissemination*. London: Athlone, pp. vii–xxxiii.

Jung, Carl G. (1927/1970). "The Structure of the Psyche". In Adler, G. and Hull, R.F.C. eds. and trans. *The Collected Works of C.G. Jung*. Vol. 8. Princeton: Princeton University Press.

——— (1936/1969). "The Archetypes and the Collective Unconscious". In Adler, G. and Hull, R.F.C. eds. and trans. *The Collected Works of C.G. Jung*. Vol. 9. Princeton: Princeton University Press.

Kant, Immanuel (1781/2013). "On External Objects". In *The Critique of Pure Reason.* Translated by J.M.D. Meiklejohn. Project Gutenberg EBook. Accessed 30.8.2015. Source: http://www.gutenberg.org/files/4280/4280-h/4280-h.htm.

Kierkegaard, Soren (1985). *Philosophical Fragments*. Translated by Hong, H. and Hong, E. eds. Princeton, NJ: Princeton University Press.

——— (1989). *The Concept of Irony with Continual Reference to Socrates.* Translated by Hong, H. and Hong, E. eds. Princeton, NJ: Princeton University Press.

Klein, Melanie (1964). *Contributions to Psychoanalysis.* 1921–1945. New York: Mcgraw-Hill.

——— (1930). "The Importance of Symbol Formation in the Development of the Ego". In Klein, M. ed. (1964). *Contributions to Psychoanalysis, 1921–1945.* New York: Mcgraw-Hill.

——— (1932). "The Psychoanalysis of Children". In Klein, M. ed. (1964). *Contributions to Psychoanalysis, 1921–1945.* New York: Mcgraw-Hill.

Kohut, Heinz (1966). "Forms and Transformations of Narcissism". *J. Amer. Psychoanal. Assn.*, 14:243–272.

——— (1959). "Introspection, Empathy, and Psychoanalysis". *J. Amer. Psychoanal. Assn.*, 7:459–483.

——— (1971). *The Analysis of the Self.* New York: International Universities Press.

——— (1972). "Thoughts on Narcissism and Narcissistic Rage". *Psychoanal. St. Child.*, 27:360–400.

——— (1977). *The Restoration of the Self.* New York: International Universities Press.

——— (1982). "Introspection, Empathy, and the Semicircle of Mental Health". *Int. J. Psychoanal.*, 63:395–408.

——— (1984). *How Does Analysis Cure?* In Goldberg, A. and Stepansky, P. eds. Chicago: University of Chicago Press.

——— (1985). *Self psychology and the Humanities: Reflections on a New Psychoanalytic Approach.* Strozier, C. ed. New-York: Norton.

Kohut, Heinz and Wolf, Ernest (1978). "The Disorders of the Self and Their Treatment: An Outline". *Int. J. Psycho-Anal.*, 59:413–425.

Kovecses, Zoltan (2008). "Metaphor and Emotion". In Gibbs, R.W. ed. *The Cambridge Handbook of Metaphor and Thought.* University of California, Santa Cruz.

Kripke, Saul (1982). *Wittgenstein on Rules and Private Language.* Oxford: Blackwell.

Kristeva, Julia (1980). *Desire in Language: A Semiotic Approach to Literature and Art.* New York: Columbia University Press.

Kuhn, Thomas (1962/1996). *The Structure of Scientific Revolutions.* Chicago: University of Chicago Press.

Künne, Wolfgang (2003). *Conceptions of Truth.* Oxford: Clarendon

Lacan, Jacques (1977). *Ecrits, A Selection.* New York: Norton.

Lachmann, Frank M. (2001). "Dialectics Forever". *Psychoanal. Dial.*, 11:213–219.

Laing, Ronald D. (1960). *The Divided Self.* London: Tavistock.

Lakoff, George (2008). "The Neural Theory of Metaphor". In Gibbs, R.W. ed. *The Cambridge Handbook of Metaphor and Thought.* University of California, Santa Cruz.

Lakoff George and Johnson, Mark (1999). *Philosophy in the Flesh: The Embodied Mind and its Challenge to Western Thought.* New York: Basic Books.

Laplanche, Jean (1984). "The Drive and Its Source-Object: Its Fate in the Transference". In Fletcher, J. ed. *Essays on Otherness.* London: Routledge.

——— (1987). *New Foundations for Psychoanalysis.* Translated by Macey, D. Oxford: Basil Blackwell.

——— (1990). "Implantation, Intromission". In Fletcher, J. ed. *Essays on Otherness.* London: Routledge.

——— (2008). "Narrativity and Hermeneutics: Some Propositions". *Psychoanal Q.,* 77:1016–1018.

Laplanche, Jean and Pontalis, Jean-Bertrand (1988). *The Language of Psychoanalysis.* London: Karnac.

Leiman, Mikael and Stiles, William (2001). "Dialogical Sequence Analysis and the Zone of Proximal Development as Conceptual Enhancements to the Assimilation Model". *Psychotherapy Research,* 11:311–330.

Levenson, Edgar A. (1988). "The Pursuit of the Particular – On Psychoanalytic Inquiry". *Contemp. Psychoanal.,* 24:1–16.

Levinas, Emmanuel (1969). *Totality and Infinity: An Essay on Exteriority.* Translated by Lingis, A. Pittsburgh: Duquesne University Press.

——— (1981). *Otherwise than Being or Beyond Essence.* Translated by Lingis, A. Boston: Martinus Nijhoff.

——— (1985). *Ethics and Infinity: Conversations with Phillipe Nem.* Translated by, Cohen R. Pittsburgh: Duquesne University Press.

Loewald, Hans W. (1960). "On the Therapeutic Action of Psycho-analysis". *Int. J. Psycho-Anal.,* 41:16–33.

Loewenstein, Rudolph M. (1956). "Some Remarks on the Role of Speech in Psychoanalytic Technique". *Int. J. Psychoanal.,* 37:460–467.

Lund, Julie (2002). "Resolving the Inconsistencies in Aquinas's Truth Theory". *Aporia.* Accessed 11.8.2015. Source: http://aporia.byu.edu/pdfs/lund-resolving_the_inconsistencies_in_aquinass_truth_theory.pdf.

Lynch, Michael P. (2001). *The Nature of Truth: Classic and Contemporary Perspectives.* Cambridge, MA: The MIT Press.

MacDonald, Geoff and Leary, Mark (2005). "Why Does Social Exclusion Hurt? The Relationship between Social and Physical Pain". *Psycholog. Bulletin,* 131:202–233.

Mahler, Margaret (1974). "Symbiosis and Individuation: The Psychological Birth of the Human Infant". In *The Selected Papers of Margaret S. Mahler*, vol. 2. New York: Jason Aronson.

——— (1975). "On the Current Status of the Infantile Neurosis". In *The Selected Papers of Margaret S. Mahler*, vol. 2. New York: Jason Aronson.

Mahony, Patrick (1980). "Toward the Understanding of Translation in Psychoanalysis". *J. Amer. Acad. Psychoanal.*, 28:461–475.

Markus, Hazel and Zajonc, Robert B. (1985). "The Cognitive Perspective in Social Psychology". In Lindzey, G. and Aronson, E. eds. *Handbook of social psychology*. New York: Random House, pp. 137–230.

Masson, Jeffrey M. (1984). *The Assault on Truth*. New York: Pocket Books.

Maxson, Leslie (2009). "The Dialectic in Autonomy and Recognition: A View into the Analytic Dyad". *Int. J. Psycho-Anal. Self Psychology*, 4:59–79.

Mendlovic, Shlomo (2009). *The Social Order of the Multiple Self-s: Psychoanalysis after Post-modernism*. Tel-Aviv: Resling (Hebrew).

Merleau-Ponty, Maurice (1958). "The Body as Expression and Speech". In *Phenomenology of Perception*. Translated by Smith, C. New York: Routledge.

Milgram, Stanley (1974). *Obedience to Authority: An Experimental View*. New York: Harper Collins.

Miller, Patricia C. (1994). *Dreams in Late Antiquity: Studies in the Imagination of a Culture*. Princeton, NJ: Princeton University Press.

Mills, Jon (2005). "A Critique of Relational Psychoanalysis". *Psychoanal. Psychol.*, 22:155–188.

——— (2011). "Deconstructing Hermes: A Critique of the Hermeneutic Turn in Psychoanalysis". *Am. J. Psychoanal.*, 71:238–245.

——— (2015). A Critique of the Postmodern Turn in Relational Psychoanalysis. Keynote Speaker at the Conference "Relational Psychoanalysis and Its Critics" held at the IARPP and Bar-Ilan's Multi disciplinary Studies Unit, in February 2015. Accessed 11.8.2015. Source: https://www.youtube.com/watch?v=JfYcI_sCOZM.

Mitchell, Stephen A. (1991). "Contemporary Perspectives on Self: Toward an Integration". *Psychoanal. Dial.*, 1:121–147.

——— (1997). *Influence and Autonomy in Psychoanalysis*. New Jersey: The Analytic Press.

——— (1998). *Relational Concepts in Psychoanalysis*. Cambridge, MA: Harvard University Press.

Moltu, Christian, Binder, Per-Einar and Nielsen, Geir Høstmark (2010). "Commitment under Pressure: Experienced Therapists' Inner Work during Difficult Therapeutic Impasses". *Self and Identity*, 9:241–256.

Moore, George E. (1901/1993). "Truth and Falsity". In Baldwin, T. ed. *Selected Writings*. New York: Routledge, pp. 20–22.

Morris, Pam ed. (2003). *The Bakhtin Reader: Selected Writings of Bakhtin, Medvedev and Voloshinov*. London: Arnold.

Mulhall, Stephen (2007). "Wittgenstein's Private Language: Grammar, Nonsense and Imagination". In *Philosophical Investigations, §§ 243–315*. Oxford: Clarendon Press.
Nagel, Thomas (1986). *The View from Nowhere*. Oxford: Oxford University Press.
Nietzsche, Friedrich (1873/1976). "On Truth and Lie in an Extra-Moral Sense". In *The Portable Nietzsche*. Translated and ed. Kaufmann, W. New York: Viking Penguin.
——— (1882/1974). *The Gay Science: With a Prelude in Rhymes and an Appendix of Songs* (1974). Translated with commentary, Kaufmann, W. New York: Vintage Books.
——— (1886/2009). *Beyond Good and Evil*. Translated by Zimmern, H. Project Gutenberg EBook. Accessed 5.6.2015. Source: http://www.gutenberg.org/files/4363/4363-h/4363-h.htm.
——— (1888/1968). *The Will to Power*. Translated with commentary, Kaufmann, W. New York: Vintage Books.
Nunberg, Herman (1955). *Principles of Psychoanalysis*, New-York: International University Press.
Ogden, Thomas (1989). "On the Concept of an Autistic-Contiguous Position". *Int. J. Psycho-Anal.*, 70:127–40.
——— (1992a). "The Dialectically Constituted/Decentred Subject of Psychoanalysis I. The Freudian subject". *Int. J. Psycho-Anal.*, 73:517–526.
——— (1992b). "The Dialectically Constituted/Decentred Subject of Psychoanalysis II. The Contributions of Klein and Winnicott". *Int. J. Psycho-Anal.*, 73:613–626.
——— (1993). *The Matrix of the Mind*. Northvale, NJ: Aronson.
——— (1994a). "The Analytic Third: Working with Intersubjective Clinical Facts". *Int. J. Psycho-Anal.*, 75:3–19.
——— (1994b). *Subject of Analysis*. Northvale, NJ: Aronson.
——— (1997). "Some Thoughts on the Use of Language in Psychoanalysis". *Psychoanal. Dial.*, 7:1–21.
——— (2004). "The Analytic Third: Implications for Psychoanalytic Theory and Technique". *Psychoanal. Q.*, 73:167–195.
Orange, Donna (1992). "Perspectival Realism and Social Constructivism: Commentary on Irwin Hoffman's 'Discussion: Toward a Social-Constructivist View of the Psychoanalytic Situation'". *Psychoanal. Dial.*, 2:561–565.
——— (1995). *Emotional Understanding: Studies in Psychoanalytic Epistemology*. London: The Guilford Press.
——— (2001). "From Cartesian Minds to Experiential Worlds in Psychoanalysis". *Psychoanal. Psychol.*, 18:287–302.
——— (2003). "Antidotes and Alternatives: Perspectival Realism and the New Reductionisms". *Psychoanal. Psychol.*, 20:472–486.
Orange, Donna, Atwood, George E. and Stolorow, Robert D. (1997). *Working Intersubjectively: Contextualism in Psychoanalytic Practice*. Hillsdale, NJ: Analytic Press.

Orange, D.M., Stolorow, Robert D and Atwood, George E. (1998). "Hermeneutics, Intersubjectivity Theory, and Psychoanalysis". *J. Amer. Psychoanal. Assn.*, 46:568–571.

Panksepp, Jaak (2003). "Feeling the Pain of Social Loss". *Science*, 302:237–239.

Pears, David (1970). *Ludwig Wittgenstein*. New York: Viking Press.

Peirce, Charles Sanders (1877). *The Fixation of Belief*. Accessed 25.7.2015. Source: http://www.bocc.ubi.pt/pag/peirce-charles-fixation-belief.pdf.

——— (1878). "How to Make Our Ideas Clear". *Popular Science Monthly*, 12:286–302. Source: http://www.peirce.org/writings/p119.html.

——— (1894). *What is a Sign?* Accessed 25.7.2015. Source: http://www.iupui.edu/%7Epeirce/web/ep/ep2/ep2book/ch02/ep2ch2.htm.accessed.

——— (1958). *Collected Papers of Charles Sanders Peirce*. Hartshorne, C., Weiss, P. and Burkes, A. eds. Cambridge, MA: Harvard University Press.

Peltz, Rachael (1998). "The Dialectic of Presence and Absence: Impasses and the Retrieval of Meaning States". *Psychoanal. Dial.*, 8:385–409.

Pepitone, Albert (1966). "Some Conceptual and Empirical Problems of Consistency Models". In Feldman, S. ed. *Cognitive consistency: Motivational Antecedents and Behavior Consequents*. New York: Academic Press, pp. 257–297.

Pinker, Steven (1989). *Learnability and Cognition: The Acquisition of Argument Structure*. Cambridge, MA: MIT Press.

Pimentel, Dror (2009). *The Dream of Purity: Heidegger with Derrida*. Jerusalem: Magness Press (Hebrew).

Plato (2000). *Republic*. Translated by Jowett, B. Accessed 23.7. 2015. Source: http://classics.mit.edu/Plato/theatu.html. The Internet Classics Archive by Daniel C. Stevenson, Web Atomics.

Plaut, David C. (2002). "Graded Modality-Specific Specialization in Semantics: A Computational Account of Optic Aphasia". *Cognitive Neuropsychology*, 19:603–639.

Popper, Karl R. (1959). *The Logic of Scientific Discovery*. London: Routledge & Kegan Paul.

——— (1969). *Conjectures and refutations*. London: Routledge &Kegan Paul.

Priel, Beatrice (1999). "Bakhtin and Winnicott". *Psychoanal. Dial.*, 9:487–503.

——— (2003). "Psychoanalytic Interpretations". *Int. J. Psycho-Anal.*, 84:131–142.

Quine, Willard V. (1960). *Word and Object*. Cambridge, MA: MIT Press.

——— (1995). "Reactions". In Leonardi, P. and Santambrogio, M. eds. *On Quine: New Essays*. Cambridge: Cambridge University Press.

——— (1996). "Progress on Two Fronts". *J. of Philosophy*, 93(4):159–163.

Ramsey, Frank P. (1927). "Facts and Propositions". *Proceedings of the Aristotelian Society*, 7:153–170.

Renik, Owen (1998). "The Analyst's Subjectivity and the Analyst's Objectivity". *Int. J. Psycho-Anal.*, 79:487–497.

Ricoeur, P. (1970). *Freud and Philosophy: An Essay on Interpretation.* New Haven, CT: Yale University Press.

Robinson, Douglas (1991). *The Translator's Turn.* Baltimore, MD: Johns Hopkins University Press.

Rorty, Richard (1989a). *Contingency, Irony, and Solidarity.* Cambridge: Cambridge University Press.

——— (1998b). *Truth and Progress.* Cambridge: Cambridge University Press.

Rosegrant, John (2010). "Three Psychoanalytic Realities". *Psychoanal. Psychol.,* 27:492–512.

Rosenberg, Milton J. (1968). "Hedonism, Inauthenticity, and Other Goads towards Expansion of a Consistency Theory". In Abelson, R.P., Aronson, E. McGuire, W.J., Newcomb, T.M., Rosenberg, M.J. and Tannenbaum, R.H. eds. *Theories of Cognitive Consistency: A Sourcebook.* Chicago, IL: Rand McNally, pp. 73–111.

Rosenberg, Milton J. and Abelson, Robert P. (1960). "An Analysis of Cognitive Balancing". In Rosenberg, M.J. Hovland, C.I. McGuire, W.J., Abelson, R.P. and Brehm, J.W. eds. *Attitude organization and change: An analysis of consistency among attitude components.* New Haven, CT: Yale University Press, pp. 112–163.

Rosenblum, Stephen and Chused, Judith (1994). "Analyzing the 'Unanalyzable' Patient: Implications for Technique". *J. Amer. Psychoanal. Assn.,* 42:1251–1259.

Rowan, John (2010). *Personification: Using the Dialogical Self in Psychotherapy and Counselling.* London: Routledge.

Russell, Bertrand (1906/1994). "On the Nature of Truth and Falsehood". In Horwich, P. ed. (1994). *Theories of Truth.* Cambridge: Cambridge University Press.

Sartre, Jean-Paul (1956). *Being and Nothingness.* Translated by Barnes, H. New York: Philosophical Library.

——— (1946/1989). "Existentialism is a Humanism". In Translated by Philip, M., Kaufman, W. ed. *Existentialism from Dostoyevsky to Sartre.* Meridian Publishing Company. Accessed 23.8.2015. Source: https://www.marxists.org/reference/archive/sartre/works/exist/sartre.htm.

——— (2007). *Nausea.* Translated by Lloyd, A. New York: New Directions Publishing.

Sapir, Edward (1964). "Conceptual Categories in Primitive Languages". In Hymes, D. ed. *Language in Culture and Society.* New York: Harper and Row, p. 128.

Schachter, Stanley (1951). "Deviation, Rejection, and Communication". *J. Abnormal Social Psychology,* 46:190–207.

Schermer, Victor (2011). "Interpreting Psychoanalytic Interpretation: A Fourfold Perspective". *Psychoanal. Rev.,* 98:817–842.

Schafer, Roy (1980). "Narration in the Psychoanalytic Dialogue". *Critical Inquiry,* 7:29–53.

——— (1983). "Essays on the Construction of the Psychoanalytic Narrative: Listening, Intervention, and Interpretation". *Psychoanal. Contemp. Thought,* 6:403–404.

——— (1992). *Retelling a Life: Narration and Dialogue in Psychoanalysis*. New York: Basic Books.

——— (1995). "In the Wake of Heinz Hartmann". *Int. J. Psycho-Anal.*, 76:223–235.

——— (1996). "Authority, Evidence, and Knowledge in the Psychoanalytic Relationship". *Psychoanal. Q.*, 65:236–253.

Schleiermacher, Friedrich (1813/1992). "On the Different Methods of Translating". In Schulte, R. and Biguenet, J. eds. *Theories of Translation*. Chicago: University of Chicago Press.

Schopenhauer, Arthur (1800/1992). "On Language and Words". In Schulte, R. and Biguenet, J. eds. *Theories of Translation*. Chicago: University of Chicago Press.

Schulte, Rainer and Biguenet, John eds. (1992). *Theories of Translation: An Anthology of Essays from Dryden to Derrida*. Chicago: University of Chicago Press.

Segal, Hannah (2006). "Reflections on Truth, Tradition, and the Psychoanalytic Tradition of Truth". *Am. Imago*, 63:283–292.

Seligman, Martin (1975). *Helplessness: On Depression, Development, and Death*. San Francisco: Freeman and Co.

Seligman, Stephen (2003). "The Developmental Perspective in Relational Psychoanalysis". *Contemp. Psychoanal.*, 39:477–508.

Shaw, Daniel (2003). "On the Therapeutic Action of Analytic Love". *Contemp. Psychoanal.*, 39:251–278.

Simons, Peter (1987). *Parts: A Study in Ontology*. Oxford: Clarendon Press.

Simon, Dan and Holyoak, Keith J. (2002). "Structural Dynamics of Cognition: From Consistency Theories to Constraint Satisfaction". *Personality and Social Psychology Review*, 6:283–294.

Solomon, Sheldon, Greenberg, Jeff and Pyszczynski, Tom (1992). "A Terror Management Theory of Self Esteem and its Role in Social Behavior". In Zanna, M. ed. *Advances in Experimental Social Psychology*. New York: Academic Press, pp. 93–159.

Spence, Donald P. (1982). *Narrative Truth and Historical Truth: Meaning and Interpretation in Psychoanalysis*. New York: Norton and Co.

——— (1983). "Narrative Persuasion". *Psychoanal. Contemp. Thought*, 6:457–481.

Sperber, Dan ed. (2000). *Metarepresentation*. Oxford: Oxford University Press.

Spinoza, Baruch (1989). *Ethics*. Translated by Boyle, A. Introduction and Notes by G.H.R. Parkinson. London: Everyman Classics.

Spivak, Gayatri Chakravorty (1993). "The Politics of Translation". In Spivak, G.C. ed. *Outside in the Teaching Machine*. New York: Routledge, pp. 179–200.

Steiner, George (1975). *After Babel: Aspects of language and Translation*. Oxford: Oxford University Press.

Stern, Donnel B. (1983). "Unformulated Experience – From Familiar Chaos to Creative Disorder". *Contemp. Psychoanal.*, 19:71–99.

——— (1989). "The Analyst's Unformulated Experience of the Patient". *Contemp. Psychoanal.*, 25:1–33.

——— (1991). "A philosophy for the Embedded Analyst: Gadamer's Hermeneutics and the Social Paradigm of Psychoanalysis". *Contemp. Psychoanal.*, 27:51–80.

——— (2003). *Unformulated Experience – From Dissociation to Imagination in Psychoanalysis*. Hillsdale, NJ: The Analytic Press.

Stern, Daniel (2007). "A Felicitous Meeting of Attachment and Relational Psychotherapy". *Relat. Psychoanal. J.*, 1:1–7.

Stern, Daniel, Sander, Louis, Nahum, Jerry, Harrison, Alexandra, Lyons-Ruth, Karlen, Morgan, Alec and Bruschweiler Nadia, Tronick, Edward (1998). "Non-Interpretive Mechanisms in Psychoanalytic Therapy". *Int. J. Psycho-Anal.*, 79:903–921.

Stern, David G. (2011). "Private Language". In Kuusela, O. and McGinn, M. eds. *The Oxford Handbook of Wittgenstein*. Oxford: Oxford University Press, pp. 333–50.

Stolorow, Robert and Lachmann, Frank M. (1980). *Psychoanalysis of Developmental Arrests. Theory and Treatment*. New York: International Universities Press.

Stolorow, Robert, Brandchaft, Bernard and Atwood, George (1987). *Psychoanalytic Treatment: An Intersubjective Approach*. Hillsdale, NJ: The Analytic Press.

Stolorow, Robert D. (1986). "Critical Reflections on the Theory of Self Psychology: An Inside View". *Psychoanal. Inq.*, 6:387-402T

Stolorow, Robert and Atwood, George (1992). *Contexts of Being*. Hillsdale, NJ: The Analytic Press.

Stolorow, Robert D. and Atwood, G.E. (1997). "Deconstructing the Myth of the Neutral Analyst: An Alternative from Intersubjective Systems Theory". *Psychoanal. Q.*, 66:431–449.

Stolorow, Robert, Orange, Donna and Atwood, George (2001). "World Horizons". *Contemp. Psychoanal.*, 37:43–61.

Stolorow, Robert D., Orange, Donna and Atwood, George (2001a). "Cartesian and Post-Cartesian Trends in Relational Psychoanalysis". *Psychoanal. Psychol.*, 18:468–484.

Storey, David E. (2015). *Naturalizing Heidegger, His Confrontation with Nietzsche, His Contributions to Environmental Philosophy*. Albany: State University of New York Press.

Strawson, Galen (2013). "Nietzsche's Metaphysics". In Dries, M. and. Kail, P. eds. *Nietzsche on Mind and Nature*. Oxford: Oxford University Press.

Strawson, Peter F. (1950). "Truth". *Proceedings of the Aristotelian Society*. 24:129–156.

Strenger, Carlo (2005). *The Designed Self: Psychoanalysis and Contemporary Identities*. Hillsdale, NJ: The Analytic Press.

Sullivan, Harry S. (1940). *Conceptions of Modern Psychiatry*. New York: Norton.

——— (1953). *The Interpersonal Theory of Psychiatry*. New York: Norton.

Summers, Frank (2008). "Theoretical Insularity and the Crisis of Psychoanalysis". *J. of Psychoanal. Psychology.*, 25:413–424.

Symington, Neville (1983). "The Analyst's Act of Freedom as Agent of Therapeutic Change". *Int. R. Psycho-Anal.*, 10:283–291.

Tannenbaum, Percy H. (1968). "The Congruity Principle: Retrospective Reflections and Recent Research". In Abelson, R.P. Aronson, E. McGuire, W.J. Newcomb, T.M. Rosenberg, M.J. and Tannenbaum, R.H. eds. *Theories of Cognitive Consistency: A Sourcebook*. Chicago: Rand McNally, pp. 52–72.

Tarski, Alfred (1944/1994). "The Semantic Conception of Truth". In Horwich, P. ed. *Theories of Truth*. Cambridge: Cambridge University Press.

Teicholz, Judith (2000). "The Analyst's Empathy, Subjectivity and Authenticity: Affect as the Common Denominator. How Responsive Should We Be?". In Goldberg, A. ed. *Progress in Self Psychology*. Mahwah, NJ: Analytic Press. 16:33–53.

Toury, Gideon (1978). "The Nature and Role of Norms". In Holmes, J. Lambert, J. and van den Broeck, R. eds. *Literature and Translation*. Leruven: Acco, pp. 83–99.

Trevarthen, Colwyn (2001). "The Neurobiology of Early Communication: Intersubjective Regulations in Human Brain Development". In Kalverboer, A.F. and Gramsbergen, A. eds. *Handbook on Brain and Behavior in Human Development*. Dordrecht, The Netherlands: Kluwer, pp. 841–882.

Van Bark, Bella S. (1955). *Am. J. Psychoanal.*, 15:4–7.

Venuti, Lawrence ed. (1992). *Rethinking Translation – Discourse, Subjectivity, Ideology*. New York: Routledge.

Venuti, Lawrence (2008). *The Translator's Invisibility: A History of Translation*. New York: Routledge.

Ventimiglia, Gary (2008). "Martin Buber, God, and Psychoanalysis". *Psychoanal. Inq.*, 28:612–621.

Vygotsky, Lev (1934/1997). *Thought and Language*. Kozulin, A. ed. Cambridge, MA: MIT Press.

Weigand, Edda (2007). "The Sociobiology of Language". In Grein, M. and Gutenberg, J. eds. *Dialogue and Culture*. Universität, Mainz, E. Amsterdam: John Benjamins.

Wertheimer, Max (1967). "The General Theoretical Situation". In Elli, W.D. ed. *A Source Book of Gestalt Theory*. New York: Humanities Press, pp. 12–16.

White, R.S. (2011). "Bion and Mysticism: The Western Tradition". *Am. Imago,* 68:213–240.

Williams, Kipling D. (2007). "Ostracism: The Kiss of Social Death". *Social and Personality Psychology Compass* 1(1): 236–247.

Winnicott, Donald W. (1949). "Mind and Its Relation to the Psyche-Soma". In Winnicott, D. ed. (1975). *Through Pediatrics to Psychoanalysis*. London: Hogarth Press, pp. 245–255.

——— (1951). "Transitional Objects and Transitional Phenomena". In Winnicott, D. ed. (1975). *Through Pediatrics to Psychoanalysis*. London: The Hogarth Press, pp. 229–243.

——— (1956). "Primary Maternal Preoccupation". In Winnicott, D. ed. (1975). *Through Pediatrics to Psychoanalysis.* London: The Hogarth Press, pp. 306–316.

——— (1958a). "Child Analysis in the Latency Period". In Winnicott, D.W. ed. (1965). *The Maturational Processes and the Facilitating Environment: Studies in the Theory of Emotional Development.* London: The Hogarth Press, pp. 115–124.

——— (1958b). "The Capacity to be Alone". In Winnicott, D.W. ed. (1965). *The Maturational Processes and the Facilitating Environment: Studies in the Theory of Emotional Development.* London: The Hogarth Press, pp. 29–37.

——— (1960). "Ego Distortion in Terms of True and False Self". In Winnicott, D.W. ed. (1965). *The Maturational Processes and the Facilitating Environment: Studies in the Theory of Emotional Development.* London: The Hogarth Press, pp. 140–153.

——— (1963a). "Communicating and Not Communicating Leading to a Study of Certain Opposites". In Winnicott, D.W. ed. (1965). *The Maturational Processes and the Facilitating Environment: Studies in the Theory of Emotional Development.* London: The Hogarth Press, pp. 179–193.

——— (1963b). "Dependence in Infant Care, in Child Care, and in the Psycho-Analytic Setting". *Int. J. Psycho-Anal.,* 44:339–344.

——— (1965). *The Maturational Processes and the Facilitating Environment: Studies in the Theory of Emotional Development.* London: The Hogarth Press.

——— (1968a). "Playing: Its Theoretical Status in the Clinical Situation". *Int. J. Psychoanal.,* 49:591–598.

——— (1968b). "Communication between Infant and Mother, and Mother and Infant, Compared and Contrasted". In Winnicott, C. Shepherd, R. and Davis, M. eds. (1987). *Babies and Their Mothers.* Reading, MA: Addison-Wesley (Original work published 1968), pp. 89–103.

——— (1969/1971). "The Use of an Object and Relating through Identifications". In Winnicott, D.W. ed. (1971). *Playing and Reality.* London: Tavistock. pp. 86–94.

——— (1971). *Playing and Reality.* London: Tavistock.

——— (1972). "Mother's Madness Appearing in the Clinical Material as an Egoalien Factor". In Giovacchini, P.L. ed. *Tactics and Techniques in Psychoanalytic Therapy.* London: Hogarth Press.

——— (1975). *Through Pediatrics to Psychoanalysis.* London: Hogarth Press.

——— (1989). "The Fate of the Transitional Object". In Winnicott, C., Shepherd, R. and Davis, M. eds. *Psycho-analytic Explorations.* Cambridge, MA: Harvard University Press, pp. 53–58.

Wittgenstein, Ludwig (1974). *Philosophical Grammar.* Translated by Kenny, A. Rush Rhees ed. Oxford: Basil Blackwell (in text reference – PG).

——— (1977). *On Certainty.* Translated by Anscombe, G.E.M. and Paul, D. Anscombe, G.E.M. and von Wright, G.H. eds. Oxford: Blackwell.

——— (1980). *Remarks on the Philosophy of Psychology.* Translated by Anscombe, G.E.M. Anscombe, G. and von Wright, G.H. eds. Oxford: Basil Blackwell (in text reference – RPP).

——— (1981). *Zettel.* Translated by Anscombe, G.E.M., Anscombe, G. and von Wright, G.H. eds. Oxford: Basil Blackwell (in text reference – Z).

——— (1998). *Notebooks.* Translated by Anscombe, G.E.M., Anscombe, G. and von Wright, G.H. eds. Oxford: Basil Blackwell (in text reference – BBN).

——— (1999). *Philosophical Investigations.* Translated by Anscombe, G.E.M. Oxford: Basil Blackwell.

——— (2010). *Tractatus Logico-Philosophicus.* Translated by Ogden, C.K. London: Kegan Paul, Trench, Trubner and co. Accessed 26.8.2015. Source: https://www.gutenberg.org/files/5740/5740-pdf.pdf.

Yalom, Irvin D. (1989). *Love's Executioner and Other Tales of Psychotherapy*. London: Karnac.

Yovel, Yirmiyahu (2005). "Commentary". In Hegel, Georg W.F. ed. *Preface to the Phenomenology of Spirit.* Princeton, NJ: Princeton University Press.

Young, Robert M. (1994). *Mental Space*, Process Press. Ch. 8. Accessed 25.7.15. Source: http://human-nature.com/mental/chap8.html.

Zahavi, Dan (2003). "Husserl's Intersubjective Transformation of Transcendental Philosophy". In Welton, D. ed. *The New Husserl: A Critical Reader.* Bloomington, IN: Indiana University Press.

——— (2005). *Subjectivity and Selfhood: Investigating the First-Person Perspective.* Cambridge, MA: MIT Press.

Zepf, Siegfried, Hartmann, Sebastian and Zepf, Florian (2007). "Constructivism in Psychoanalysis". *Canadian J. Psychoanal.*, 15:3–21.

Zimbardo, P.G. (2007). *The Lucifer Effect: Understanding How Good People Turn Evil.* New York: Random House.

Index

Locators in *italic* followed by *d* refer to Diagrams. Thus, *66d1* refers to Diagram 1 on page 66. Locators followed by n or nn refer to footnotes. Thus, 54n9 refers to footnote 9 on page 54; 82nn4–5 refers to footnotes 4 and 5 on page 82.